Populist radical right parties in Europe

As Europe enters a significant pha̱   ̱ntegration of East and West, it faces an increasing problem with the rise of far-right political parties. Cas Mudde offers the first comprehensive and truly pan-European study of populist radical right parties in Europe. He focuses on the parties themselves, discussing them both as dependent and independent variables. Based upon a wealth of primary and secondary literature, this book offers critical and original insights into three major aspects of European populist radical right parties: concepts and classifications; themes and issues; and explanations for electoral failures and successes. It concludes with a discussion of the impact of radical right parties on European democracies, and vice versa, and offers suggestions for future research.

CAS MUDDE is Senior Lecturer in the Department of Political Science at the University of Antwerp. He is the author of *The Ideology of the Extreme Right* (2000) and the editor of *Racist Extremism in Central and Eastern Europe* (2005).

Populist radical right parties in Europe

Cas Mudde

University of Antwerp

CAMBRIDGE
UNIVERSITY PRESS

CAMBRIDGE UNIVERSITY PRESS
Cambridge, New York, Melbourne, Madrid, Cape Town, Singapore, São Paulo

Cambridge University Press
The Edinburgh Building, Cambridge CB2 8RU, UK

Published in the United States of America by Cambridge University Press, New York

www.cambridge.org
Information on this title: www.cambridge.org/9780521616324

First published 2007

Printed in the United Kingdom at the University Press, Cambridge

A catalogue record for this publication is available from the British Library

Library of Congress Cataloguing in Publication data
Mudde, Cas.
Populist radical right parties in Europe / Cas Mudde.
    p.   cm.
Includes bibliographical references and index.
ISBN-13: 978-0-521-85081-0 (hardback)
ISBN-10: 0-521-85081-9 (hardback)
ISBN-13: 978-0-521-61632-4 (paperback)
ISBN-10: 0-521-61632-8 (paperback)
1. Political parties – Europe.   2. Conservatism – Europe.   3. Populism – Europe.
4. Right and Left (Political science)   5. Europe – Politics and government – 1945 –
I. Title.
JN50.M84   2007
324.2'13094 – dc22   2006101016

ISBN 978-0-521-85081-0 hardback
ISBN 978-0-521-61632-4 paperback

For Jan, Sarah and Sivan

"I hate white people."
"Why?"
"They're mean."
"Did white people ever bother you?"
"Hell, naw! I wouldn't let 'em," she said belligerently.
"Then why do you hate 'em?"
"'Cause they're *different* from me. I don't like 'em even to look
at me. They make me self-conscious, that's why. Ain't that enough."
"If you say so, baby."
(Richard Wright, *The Outsider*. New York: Harper & Brothers, 1953, 48)

"The enemy is the gramophone mind, whether or not one agrees with
the record that is being played at the moment."
(George Orwell, "Telling people what they don't want to hear:
the original preface to Animal Farm", *Dissent* (Winter 1996): 59–64 [63])

Contents

Tables

Acknowledgments

> At times our own light goes out and is rekindled by a spark from another person. Each of us has cause to think with deep gratitude of those who have lighted the flame within us.
>
> (Albert Schweitzer)

Writing a book with such a broad geographical scope one always has to rely upon the insights from many other scholars. As the literature on populist radical right parties is highly limited in terms of cases and topics studied, e.g. an enormous predominance of studies on France and Germany, I depended for much information upon the personal insights from many of my colleagues of the ECPR Standing Group on Extremism & Democracy. Several of these national experts were willing to fill in my short questionnaire on particular populist radical right parties (see appendix B), the data of which have proved essential for many chapters of this book. Other friends and colleagues helped me with obtaining specific data and translating some primary sources. My special thanks go to Daniele Albertazzi, Florian Bieber, Michaela Grün, Tim Haughton, J. W. Justice, Ioannis Kolovos, Natalya Krasnoboka, Borbala Kriza, Nicole Lindstrom, Miroslav Mareš, Oscar Mazzoleni, Juan Anton Mellón, Daniel Milo, Niall O Dochartaigh, Michael Rossi, Marek Rybář, Maria Spirova, Peter Učeň, and Eric Weaver. They are proof that even in this competitive period of "publish or perish" academic cooperation is still possible. I hope to return the favor in the future.

I also sent out a slightly revised questionnaire to some fifteen populist radical right parties, mostly smaller organizations from Eastern Europe. While some email addresses bounced, most parties must have received the questionnaire. Unfortunately, only two responded. The Irish Immigration Control Platform (ICP) wrote a short email back, of which the key message was: "Since we are not a party and are strictly single issue I do not see how we can fall within your remit." Despite the reference to Sartori's minimal definition of political parties in my answer, I did not hear from them again. The only party to send back a completely filled out questionnaire was the French Front national, ironically the best-studied of all parties. I want to thank Patrick Gaillard, from the communications directorate of the FN, for taking the time to respond to my query.

Over the period of writing this book, I presented various earlier draft versions of chapters to audiences around the globe. It would go too far to mention all of them, so I will provide just a short overview: conferences, such as the tenth annual conference of the Association for the Study of Nationalities (ASN) in New York and the Politicologenetmaal in Antwerp; specialized workshops at the Department of Government of the Ben-Gurion University of the Negev in Beer-Sheva and at the European Center of the Australian National University in Canberra; and lectures at Sciences-Po in Paris, the University of Texas at Dallas, and the Contemporary Europe Research Centre of the University of Melbourne. I want to thank everyone who attended these meetings for their curiosity and valuable feedback.

Several colleagues have commented on earlier drafts of one or more of the chapters. I feel privileged to have received so much interest in my work from people who are tremendously busy with putting out so many important studies on the same topic themselves. Special thanks go to David Art, Hans-Georg Betz, Alexandre Dézé, Dani Filc, Susanne Frölich-Steffen, Nonna Mayer, Lars Rensmann, Damir Skenderovic, Joop Van Holsteyn, and Lien Warmenbol. Their comments have often been confronting, but they were always constructive and useful.

Leading the life of an academic "Gypsy" does involve many a lonely moment, but I feel blessed to have some true friends among my colleagues. Petr Kopecký, Luke March, Ami Pedahzur, and Joop Van Holsteyn all share an interest in "my" topic, but work (mainly) on other topics. This notwithstanding, all have in their own way contributed more to this book than they will ever know. I hope I will be able to repay them for many more years to come.

Much of the secondary literature was collected during my (too) short stints as visiting scholar at various institutions. In the summer of 2001 I fought off the many lures of beach life in California to make full use of the extensive facilities of the University of California, Santa Barbara (UCSB). I want to thank Peter H. Merkl for helping me set up this visit and the Department of Political Science for hosting me. In April 2005 I stayed for three weeks at the Center for European Studies of New York University (NYU). I owe Leah Ramirez and Martin Schain eternal gratitude for enabling me to experience the wonderful world of the Elmer Holmes Bobst Library. Housed at the buzzing Washington Square in The Village, the Bobst Library is an intellectual oasis for scholars and students alike; not just for its fantastic collection, but even more importantly for its accessibility. It serves as an enlightening example for all university libraries.

Similarly, working a few weeks in the highly personal and surveyable library of my old institution, the Central European University in Budapest, in the summer of 2005, was a treat. I thank Zsolt Enyedi, Éva Lafferthon, and Krisztina Zsukotynszky for helping me arrange this trip, and my many old colleagues and students for our trips along memory lane.

More new, but definitely as exciting, is my current experience as Fulbright EU Scholar-in-Residence at the Center for Comparative European Studies of Rutgers, the State University of New Jersey, in New Brunswick. Here, Jan Kubik, Susanna Trish, and Audrey Boyd have helped me adjust in an extremely short period, so that I could still meet my deadline, despite the rather hectic move from Belgium to the US. Special thanks go to my new personal editor, Amy Linch, who unselfishly put her PhD on hold to edit my manuscript. Amy introduced words I had never encountered before and forced me to clarify many of my assumptions and thoughts. Without her, this book would truly not be the same.

Working at a small university in Europe, which the University of Antwerp undoubtedly is, has many advantages, often outweighing the disadvantages. However, when writing a book such as this, extensive library facilities are essential. The trips to other universities were vital for getting access to all the articles and books I had seen referred to in other works, yet did not have access to in Antwerp. I can only hope to have more opportunities to visit them in the future. Whether this will be the case depends to a large extent on the generosity of academic funding bodies, to which I already owe a great gratitude.

During my time at the Department of Politics of the University of Edinburgh (2000–2002), my research was supported by the British Academy and the Carnegie Trust for the Universities of Scotland. Since I moved to the Department of Political Science at the University of Antwerp in the summer of 2002, a grant from the Flemish *Fonds voor Wetenschappelijk Onderzoek* (Fund for Scientific Research, FWO) has enabled me to go to New York. Finally, the Fulbright Fellowship has enabled me to work during the last stage of the book in the US, shielded from the daily administrative and teaching duties of my home university.

Special thanks go to my many former colleagues and students from all over the globe. While working on this book, I have taught courses on "Extreme right parties in Europe" in many different countries and at various universities. Without both the encouragement of my colleagues and the criticism of my students I would have neither embarked upon writing this book, nor finished it. More importantly, my students have often forced me to reconsider the few certainties I thought we held in the field.

Finally, my deep gratitude goes to my first group of (former) PhD students at the University of Antwerp: Sarah De Lange, Sivan Hirsch-Hoefler, and Dr. Jan Jagers. They have given me the energy and intellectual stimulation to bite through the (many) moments of despair and self-doubt. All three have very different backgrounds and personalities, but share the wonderful combination of intellectual curiosity and personal warmth. I dedicate this book to them.

Abbreviations

AN	National Alliance
ANL	Anti-Nazi League
ANO	Alliance for a New Citizen
AP	Swiss Car Party
AS	Social Alternative
ASN	Association for the Study of Nationalities
AUNS	Action Society for an Independent and Neutral Switzerland
AWS	Solidarity Electoral Action
BBB	Bulgarian Business Bloc
BNP	British National Party
BNRP	Bulgarian National Radical Party
BZÖ	Alliance for Austria's Future
CAP	Common Agricultural Policy (EU)
CD	Centre Democrats
CDU	Christian Democratic Union
CEEC	Central Eastern European country
CP'86	Centre Party '86
CSU	Christian Social Union
DFP	Danish People's Party
DLVH	German League for People and Homeland
DN	National Democracy
DPNI	Russian Movement against Illegal Immigration
DUP	Democratic Unionist Party
DVU	German People's Union
EC	European Communities
ECPR	European Consortium for Political Research
EK	National Party (Greece)
EM	Hellenic Front
ENU	European National Union
EPEN	National Political Union
EPP	European People's Party

ERSP	Estonian National Independence Party
EU	European Union
EUMC	European Monitoring Centre on Racism and Xenophobia
F	Freedomites
FA	Freedomite Academy
FI	Go Italy
FIDESz-MPS	Alliance of Young Democrats–Hungarian Civic Movement
FN	National Front (France)
FNb	National Front (Belgian)
FNB	New Front of Belgium
FNJ	Youth National Front
FP	Freedom Party
FPd	Progress Party (Denmark)
FPÖ	Austrian Freedom Party
FPS	Freedom Party of Switzerland
FRP	Progress Party (Norway)
FWO	Fund for Scientific Research
HB	People Unity
HDZ	Croatian Democratic Movement
HF	Hellenic Front
HOS	Croatian Defence Force
HSP	Croatian Party of Rights
HSP-1861	Croatian Party of Rights–1861
HZDS	Movement for a Democratic Slovakia
ICP	Immigration Control Platform
IKL	Patriotic National Alliance
IRA	Irish Republican Army
KE	Greek Hellenism Party
KSČM	Community Party of Bohemia and Moravia
LAOS	Popular Orthodox Rally
LDPR	Liberal Democratic Party of Russia
LN	Northern League
LNNK	Latvian National Independence Movement
LPF	Lijst Pim Fortuyn
LPR	League of Polish Families
MDF	Hungarian Democratic Forum
MEP	Member of European Parliament
MHP	Nationalist Action Party
MIÉP	Hungarian Justice and Life Party
MNR	National Republican Movement

MS-FT	Social Movement–Tricolor Flame
MSI	Italian Social Movement
NBP	National Bolshevik Party
ND	New Democracy
NDP	National Democratic Party
NF	National Front (Britain)
NOP	National Rebirth of Poland
NPD	National Democratic Party of Germany
NS	National Party (Czech Republic)
NSA	National Union Attack
NWO	New World Order
ODS	Civic Democratic Party
ONP	One Nation Party
PASOK	Panhellenic Socialist Movement
PiS	Law and Justice Party
PRM	Greater Romania Party
PRO	Constitutional Offensive Party
PSM	Socialist Labor Party
PSNS	Real Slovak National Party
PUNR	Party of Romanian National Unity
RBF	Republican League of Women
REP	The Republicans
RMS	Republicans of Miroslav Sládek
RNE	Russian National Unity
SD	Sweden Democrats
SF	We Ourselves
SNP	Scottish National Party
SNS	Slovak National Party and Slovene National Party
SP	Socialist Party
SPÖ	Serbian Renewal Movement
SPR-RSČ	Association for the Republic–Republican Party of Czechoslovakia
SPS	Socialist Party of Serbia
SRS	Serbian Radical Party
SSP	Scottish Socialist Party
SVP	Swiss People's Party
TB	Fatherland and Freedom
TDI	Technical Group for Non-Attached Members – Mixed Group
UCSB	University of California, Santa Barbara
UDMR	Democratic Alliance of Hungarians in Romania
UEN	Union for Europe of Nations

UKIP	UK Independence Party
UNA-UNSO	Ukrainian National Assembly–Ukrainian People's Self-Defense
UPR	Union for Real Politics
VB	Flemish Block/Flemish Interest
VU	People's Union
VVD	People's Party for Freedom and Democracy
WASPs	White Anglo-Saxon Protestants

Introduction

But the extremists of the movements of the Right do deserve a measure of dispassionate attention, not because of services they have rendered America but because they have reflected tensions endemic in the entire population and in the very structure of American life.

(Bennett 1990: 6)

The observation that European politics is dominated by political parties which are older than most of their electorates still holds true for much of Western Europe. And even if party systems seem to be more in flux in the twenty-first century, not only in the Eastern part of the continent, they are still largely controlled by members of the traditional party families, notably the conservatives and Christian democrats, socialists and social democrats, and liberals. In fact, only two new party families have been able to establish themselves in a multitude of European countries since the Second World War: the Greens (or New Politics) and the populist radical right. And only the latter has been able to gain results in both parts of Europe.

Seen in this light, it does not seem strange to have yet another book on this topic. After all, the populist radical right is the only successful new party family in Europe. Moreover, given the unprecedented horrors of the Second World War, and the more recent nativist wars in the Balkans, the destructive threats to liberal democracy of the populist radical right seem reason enough for the extensive study of the phenomenon. Not surprising then, that the populist radical right is one of the few academic topics that one can study without having to defend the relevance of one's choice.

But one can go even further. I often start my presentations, academic or otherwise, by pointing out that "the extreme right" is actually not "blowing for a general attack on the parliaments" of Europe (Fromm & Kernbach 1994: 9). In fact, it is still a relatively marginal electoral force in the vast majority of European countries. Still, none in the audience sees this as a good reason for me to either leave or question my almost ten-year career in this subfield of political science. In fact, most often the reaction is one of utter disbelief or annoyance: "why are you playing down the dangers of the extreme right?"

Also within the large and ever growing scholarly community "researchers recognize that the renaissance of right-wing extremism has become a more or less Europe wide phenomenon" (Rensmann 2003: 95). This general consensus notwithstanding, the empirical facts cannot be ignored. Leaving aside definitional issues for the moment, "it seems that support for far-right parties expanded measurably in the 1980s, but in more recent years it has tended towards slower growth, again with a handful of exceptions" (Wilcox et al. 2003a: 129). And even with the "measurable expansion" in the 1980s and the "slower growth" in the 1990s, the average percentage of voters for "far right" parties in four-teen Western European countries was only 6.5 percent in the 1980s and just 8.3 percent in the 1990s (Wilcox et al. 2003a: 128). The situation in postcommunist Eastern Europe is quite similar, despite the often alarmist accounts of the 1990s.

Obviously, there are important exceptions. For example, in countries such as Belgium (Flanders) and Serbia, populist radical right parties belong to the electorally strongest political actors, while in others like Austria and Slovakia they are or have been part of the national government. Moreover, politics is about more than mere electoral facts; it is also about perceptions. In this respect, populist radical right parties are certainly politically relevant, if only because they are perceived as such by large parts of both the elites and the masses. And, particularly in multi-party systems, small parties can weigh (heavily) on national policies and social values, even if in (semi-)permanent opposition.

Despite its relatively limited electoral and political significance within European politics, particularly if compared to the established party families, no party family has been studied as intensely as the populist radical right. Whereas the (edited) books on party families like the Christian democrats or liberals can be counted on the fingers of one or two hands, those on the populist radical right (irrespective of the term used) might already outnumber the combined total of books on all other party families together. Moreover, whereas other fields of political science are increasingly dominated by Anglo-Saxon publications, the study of populist radical right parties is truly international, with a roughly equal number of French and English book publications and a predominance of German studies (e.g. De Lange & Mudde 2005). While it might be overly critical to state that "[s]erious comparative scholarship on the radical right is still in its infancy" (Minkenberg 2000: 170), there are many aspects of the populist radical right party family that still need study or further clarification.

The vast majority of research on populist radical right parties has focused exclusively on (some) countries in Western Europe. This is particularly the case with the few comparative single-authored monographs (e.g. Carter 2005; Givens 2005; Kitschelt & McGann 1995; Betz 1994), but also with the bulk of edited volumes (e.g. Blaise & Moreau 2004; Perrineau 2001; Pfahl-Traughber 1994) and journal articles (e.g. Van der Brug *et al.* 2005; Ignazi 1992). Some of these studies have also included non-European "Western" countries, most notably from the Anglo-Saxon world (e.g. Decker 2004; Betz & Immerfall 1998; Minkenberg 1998). In sharp contrast, only a little work has been done on Eastern Europe (e.g. Mudde 2005a; Ramet 1999a), let alone on non-Western countries outside of Europe (e.g. India; see Rösel 2003; Andersen 1998).

As a consequence, there is "a lack of a comparative pan-European perspective" in the field (Anastasakis 2000: 6). It is virtually only in edited volumes that in addition to a majority of West European countries at least some East European cases are also included; although in most cases these studies do not entail a systematic comparative framework or conclusion (e.g. Werz 2003a; Hainsworth 2000a; Cheles *et al.* 1995). It is the explicit aim of this book to provide such a pan-European perspective, even though this does not necessarily limit the findings to the European context; i.e. most conclusions are considered to be valid for the populist radical right *tout court*, irrespective of geographical context, at least till this has been disproved by systematic empirical study.

Obviously, one can question why a pan-European perspective should be pursued, given the inevitable problems involved (e.g. different recent history, even more language problems, lack of data). First and foremost, a pan-European perspective dramatically increases the number of cases, most notably of (relatively) successful populist radical right parties. While the populist radical right is "stronger than ever" (Merkl 2003a), at least in the postwar period, there are still only a few cases of successful parties, both in electoral and political terms. Second, much of the so-called East will or has become part of the so-called West through membership in the European Union, and it is to be assumed that the (alleged) differences that might warrant distinct study at this moment will soon be irrelevant, given the homogenizing effects of EU membership.

While a pan-European perspective might be preferable for the above stated reasons, some important queries remain. Much literature on Eastern Europe argues that the region is fundamentally different from "the West," including Western Europe, and should therefore not be studied with similar concepts and theories. However, I concur with those who have argued and proven, both on theoretical and empirical ground, that although differences do exist, also within the two regions, so-called

"Western" concepts and theories go a long way in explaining developments in postcommunist countries (e.g. Clark 2002; Schmitter & Karl 1994).

Recent comparative literature on party politics in postcommunist Europe has emphasized the large similarities with the West, pointing to an increasing convergence of the former East and West (e.g. Bohrer II *et al.* 2000; Lewis 2000). There is no reason to assume that this would be significantly different for populist radical right parties. So, this book rejects neither *a priori* the received wisdom that the populist radical right in Eastern Europe differs fundamentally from its comrades in the Western part of the continent (e.g. Thieme 2005; Merkl 2003b; Butterwege 2002; Minkenberg 2002b), nor the possibility that these differences are relatively irrelevant for many specific research questions (e.g. Blokker 2005; Rensmann 2003; Weichsel 2002). Most importantly, there are clearly political parties on both sides of the former Iron Curtain that share a similar ideological core, which we refer to here as populist radical right, justifying their inclusion in one study. Whether this is the only thing they share, or whether they are also in other respects fairly similar, is to be proven in empirical analysis rather than by provisional observation.

In addition to a pan-European perspective, this study will also take a party-centric approach. Already in 1968, well before the (latest) ascendancy of rational choice theories, Giovanni Sartori criticized the "sociology of politics" for its "objectivist bias" – dealing almost exclusively with "the consumer" (i.e. the voter) and ignoring "the producer" (i.e. the party).

Now the greater the range of politics, the smaller the role of 'objective factors'. All our *objective certainties* are increasingly exposed to, and conditioned by, *political uncertainty*. If so, it is an extraordinary paradox that the social sciences should be ever more prompted to explain politics by going *beyond* politics. (Sartori 1990 [1968]: 181–2)

Three decades later, Alan Ware notes the continuing predominance of the "sociological approach" in the study of political parties: "In this approach political institutions are mere intermediaries, and in seeking causal explanations of politics it passes quickly over them and concentrates on the ultimate determinants – the patterns of social conflict in that country" (Ware 1996: 9).

Economic and sociological determinisms also dominate the field of populist radical right studies. Virtually all explanations of the phenomenon treat the populist radical right as a passive consequence of macro-level socioeconomic developments. Not surprising then that little research is done on (the role of) the parties themselves. And although eminent party scholars have argued that "the centrality of ideology in party politics is undeniable" (Ware 1996: 17), still relatively little attention is being paid to party ideology in studies of political parties in general, and populist radical right parties in particular.

In short, this book aims to make a threefold contribution to the literature. First, by providing a state-of-the art discussion of the key literature on several aspects of the study of the populist radical right it endeavors to present an *overview* of the key writings in the field. Second, by critically assessing the various claims made in the literature, it offers significant *revisions* of some of the commonly held misperceptions about the populist radical right party family. Third, and most important, by taking a pan-European and party-driven perspective it offers important *innovations* with regard to various aspects of the populist radical right (i.e. concepts, issues and explanations). As Lars Rensmann has argued:

The analysis of Eastern European post-Communist nationalism is particularly interesting in light of advanced theories on the extreme right that are predominantly based on the specific empirical conditions in Western postindustrial societies – conditions that only partly apply to Eastern Europe. (2003: 118)

Obviously, this is not the ultimate study of the European populist radical right. For instance, it focuses almost exclusively on political parties, leaving aside highly important developments within nonparty organizations and subcultures (e.g. Mudde 2005a; Minkenberg 2003). It also poses at least as many questions as it answers. Most importantly, it is based partially on secondary sources and therefore suffers from some of the same weaknesses as the rest of the literature; i.e. a predominance of certain parties (notably the FN) and a lack of reliable information (in whatever language) on several others. Consequently, most conclusions offered in this study are to be seen, first and foremost, as hypotheses to be tested in further, more systematic and comprehensive studies.

Othon Anastasakis has identified three major shortcomings in the study of the populist radical right in general: "a lack of a commonly accepted definition, a confusing terminology and a difficulty in the categorization of the variety of cases" (2000: 5). Similarly, Peter H. Merkl has postulated that "experienced analysts still disagree on categorization, labels and boundaries between its different manifestations" (2003a: 4). The two chapters of the first part of the book will address these shortcomings by presenting an overview of the state of affairs in the field and by providing a comprehensive framework for analysis.

The first chapter of this book addresses the first two points, though without any illusion or even desire to overcome the lack of consensus. Differences of opinion on which term to use and how to define the core characteristics of this phenomenon are in themselves not a big problem. Rather, the lack of clear definitions and the interchangeable use of different terms for identical phenomena undermine the ability to compare insights between studies and thereby further the general knowledge on the topic. The first chapter is therefore meant to be, first and foremost, *my* interpretation of how best to define and term the phenomenon at hand. Even when colleagues disagree with my definition or term (or with both), the discussion nevertheless enables them to assess the strengths and weaknesses of the further discussions in this book.

Chapter 2 deals with one of the least developed features of the study of the populist radical right: the categorization of the parties. The main aim of the chapter is to introduce a method for doing this as accurately as possible. While the method proposed is more difficult and intensive than the few alternatives used so far, i.e. expert studies and the party manifesto project, it is more accurate and less susceptible to "common wisdom" (which is often not much more than prejudice). The chapter discusses many individual parties from both the East and the West, in particular certain borderline cases, but some remain to be determined by colleagues with (much) more intimate knowledge of those parties. The final list of populist radical right parties, presented in appendix A, is therefore mostly a suggestion – although some core members of the party family will be identified unequivocally.

The second part of the book takes up a variety of issues in relation to populist radical right parties; some central to the field, others until now fairly marginal. The chapters are scheduled in such a way that we move from the micro- to the macro-level in terms of ideological constructs, addressing respectively, enemies, women, economy, democracy, Europe, and globalization. The prime focus in all chapters is on the ideological position(s) of the populist radical right, although other aspects of the different relationships will also be addressed.

Chapter 3 deals with a central issue of the populist radical right, i.e. its enemies. Rather than losing ourselves in a plethora of idiosyncratic enemy descriptions, the chapter presents an overview of more general enemy images (argumentations) on the basis of a two-by-two typology. In addition, we look in more detail at the role that three traditional enemies play in the contemporary populist radical right parties: the Jew, the Muslim, and the Rom ("Gypsy"). These enemy images provide not only a better insight into what and whom the parties are against, but also into what they support, and how they see themselves and their own nation.

The relationship between populist radical right parties and women has received only passing attention in most major works on the topic. With the exception of some feminist authors, most scholars in the field merely note the significant underrepresentation of women in the electorates and memberships of these parties. What virtually all studies have in common, however, is that this lack of attraction of populist radical right parties for women is explained by the alleged particularly sexist nature of these parties. Chapter 4 presents extensive new empirical data to qualify the underrepresentation of women within the electorates and parties of the populist radical right. In line with these new findings, the sexism thesis is largely rejected and an original alternative explanation is suggested.

The next chapter addresses one of the most important misunderstandings about the populist radical right, i.e. the predominance of neoliberal economics. As a consequence of the huge influence of two of the seminal books in the field (i.e. Kitschelt & McGann 1995; Betz 1994), many scholars have come to emphasize the importance of neoliberal economics in the ideology and to the electorate of populist radical right parties. Chapter 5 will revise this view on two counts: the content of the socioeconomic program and its importance to the populist radical right.

A special place in the debate about the populist radical right is reserved for its relationship to democracy in general, and liberal democracy in particular. Many authors have discussed the alleged tension and even opposition between the two, but most accounts are highly abstract, referring more to general principles rather than concrete proposals. Chapter 6 analyzes the key characteristics of populist radical right democracy and compares them to the fundamentals of liberal democracy. On the basis of this comparison, a theoretical threat assessment is presented.

European cooperation is a highly topical issue in comparative politics in general, and in relation to the populist radical right in particular. Rejection and even sepsis of European integration is increasingly seen as a key feature of populist radical right parties; indeed, some parties seem to be classified as members of the party family purely on the basis of their anti-EU attitude (e.g. ODS, UKIP). Chapter 7 provides a short historical overview of the positions of different populist radical right parties towards European integration in general, and the EC and EU in particular. It further discusses the various European utopias that exist within the party family and the attempts at European cooperation between populist radical right parties.

The last chapter of part two deals with opposition to globalization, which has become a hot topic in politics and political science in recent years. Various accounts on the so-called antiglobalization movement have been published, mostly by their activists or sympathizers, but few touch upon the views of the populist radical right on this topic. Chapter 8 presents the main arguments of the party family on the different processes of globalization. It shows that the populist radical right considers globalization to be a multifaceted enemy, though few of the parties devote much attention to it (yet).

The third and last part of the book addresses what constitutes probably the most difficult aspect of the study of contemporary populist radical right parties, explaining their electoral failures and successes. It argues that the major assumptions underlying most research in the field are seriously flawed and have led to a predominance of macro- and micro-level studies of the demand-side. Instead, an argument for a major change in perspective towards meso-level studies of the supply-side, most notably of the populist radical right parties themselves, and a differentiation of theoretical models for the phases of electoral breakthrough and persistence is put forward.

The final chapters of the book present and integrate the main conclusions and suggestions for further studies along the same lines. In addition, they assess the relationship between populist radical right parties and European democracies: addressing both the impact *of* the populist radical right parties on the European democracies and of these democracies *on* these parties. The concluding chapter ends with a reminder of the key message of the whole book: populist radical right parties themselves should be put at the center of future research on their electoral and political failures and successes.

Part I

Concepts

1 Constructing a conceptual framework

> The belittlement of definitions is wrong on three counts. First, since definitions declare the intended meaning of words, they ensure that we do not misunderstand each other. Second, words are also, in our research, our data containers. Therefore, if our data containers are loosely defined our facts will be misgathered. Third, to define is first of all to assign limits, to delimit.
>
> (Sartori 2004: 786)

1.1 Introduction

Several recent studies on the topic of our concern have started by paraphrasing the famous opening sentence of Karl Marx's *Communist Manifesto*: "A specter is haunting Europe, it's the specter of . . . ," followed by the author's term of preference (e.g. Jungwirth 2002b; Papadopoulos 2000). The author will then simply assume that the preferred term accurately labels the "specter," that the term itself has a singular and comprehensible meaning, and that readers are in agreement with the categorization of the various manifestations of that "specter."

In fact, during the last few decades commentators worldwide have concurred in their assessment of the similarities and dangers of European political parties as seemingly diverse as Jean-Marie Le Pen's Front national (National Front, FN), Pia Kjærsgaard's Danske Folkeparti (Danish People's Party, DFP), or Vladimir Zhirinovsky's Liberal'no-demokraticheskoi partii Rossii (Liberal Democratic Party of Russia, LDPR). But seldom did they manage to agree on terminology. Both in the media and in the scholarly community an unprecedented plethora of different terms has been put forward since the early 1980s.

Without claiming to be exhaustive, titles of (comparative) books and articles in various languages on the topic include terms like *extreme right* (e.g. Schain *et al.* 2002a; Perrineau 2001; Hainsworth 2000a; Ignazi 1994; Pfahl-Traughber 1993; Stouthuysen 1993), *far right* (e.g. Jungerstam-Mulders 2003; Roxburgh 2002; Marcus 2000; Cheles *et al.* 1995), *radical right* (e.g. Ramet 1999a; Minkenberg 1998; Kitschelt &

McGann 1995; Merkl & Weinberg 1993), *right* (e.g. Betz & Immerfall 1998; Hockenos 1993), *radical right-wing populism* (e.g. Zaslove 2004a; Betz 1994), *right-wing populism* (e.g. Eismann 2002; Decker 2000; Pfahl-Traughber 1994), *national populism* (e.g. Backes 1991; Taguieff 1984), *new populism* (e.g. Lloyd 2003; Taggart 1995), *neopopulism* (Betz & Immerfall 1998), *exclusionary populism* (e.g. Betz 2001), *xenophobic populism* (e.g. DeAngelis 2003), *populist nationalism* (e.g. Blokker 2005), *ethno-nationalism* (e.g. Rydgren 2004a), *anti-immigrant* (e.g. Gibson 2002; Fennema 1997), *nativism* (e.g. Fetzer 2000), *racism* (e.g. MacMaster 2001; Husbands 1988; Elbers & Fennema 1993), *racist extremism* (e.g. Mudde 2005a), *fascism* (e.g. Ford 1992; Laqueur 1996), *neofascism* (e.g. Fenner & Weitz 2004; Karapin 1998; Cheles *et al.* 1991), *postfascism* (e.g. Mellón 2002), *reactionary tribalism* (e.g. Antonio 2000), *integralism* (e.g. Holmes 2000), and *antipartyism* (e.g. Bélanger 2004).

This terminological chaos is not the result of fundamental differences of opinion over the correct definition; rather, it is largely the consequence of a lack of clear definitions. Few authors define their topic by offering a clear and unambiguous definition and showing that the parties in question also meet this definition (see Kolovos 2003; Mudde 1995b). Instead, they often do not provide a definition at all, and use different (undefined) terminology interchangeably. In fact, it is not exceptional to see one author use three or more different terms to describe the same party or group of parties in one article, if not on a single page.

In recent years, a number of scholars have started to devote more serious attention to the question of terminology. Rather than simply choose one term to describe the phenomenon they are studying, or wield several that capture the phenomenon more fully but with a significant sacrifice in precision, they provide an elaborate discussion of the pros and cons of different terms before presenting the one they prefer (e.g. Betz & Johnson 2004; Backes 2003a; Ignazi 2003). Some authors also point to the existence of different subgroups within the larger political family of "the extreme right" (see also Carter 2005; Camus 2003; Kitschelt & McGann 1995). This positive development notwithstanding, the increased academic attention devoted to definitions and terminology has not brought us any closer to a consensus. While some single-case studies might not need more than a specific working definition to get started, studies that are comparative either in place or time, particularly of the scope applied here, require clear definitions that can travel beyond a specific locale or temporal context.

Therefore, the first matters of concern in this book are definition and terminology. These tasks are not as straightforward as it might seem, which partially explains their neglect in the literature. The complexity of rectifying our terms will become clear through the following discussion.

1.2   How to start? The challenge of circularity

In defining what is still most often called the "extreme right" party family, one is faced with the problem of circularity: we have to decide on the basis of which *post facto* criteria we should use to define the various parties, while we need *a priori* criteria to select the parties that we want to define. In other words, whether we select as representatives of the party family in question the Dutch Lijst Pim Fortuyn (List Pim Fortuyn, LPF) and the Norwegian Fremmskrittpartiet (Progress Party, FRP) or the Italian Movimento Sociale–Fiamma Tricolore (Social Movement–Tricolor Flame, MS-FT) and the German Nationaldemokratische Partei Deutschlands (National Democratic Party of Germany, NPD) will have a profound effect on the ideological core that we will find, and thus on the terminology we will employ.

One solution to the problem of circularity is to adopt the Wittgensteinian concept of "family resemblance" (cf. Collier & Mahon 1993); i.e. none of the parties are exactly the same, but each family member will have some features in common with all other members. Schematically, one could picture this as a collection of concentric circles, but one in which no section is part of all circles. In other words, no ideological feature is shared by all parties.

While the Wittgensteinian concept of family resemblance might afford great flexibility, it will render theoretizing with respect to the success and failure of this group of parties extremely difficult, if not impossible. For instance, the sharp increase in immigration might explain the success of parties that share an anti-immigrant or xenophobic streak, but how does it relate to the one or more family members who do not share that particular ideological feature?

A second approach is based on Max Weber's famous ideal typical model; i.e. the family is defined on the basis of an "ideal type," which no family member resembles fully, but all will look like in one way or another (e.g. Kitschelt & McGann 1995). The problem is fairly similar to the one described above. First of all, it is unclear how much resemblance is required to be included in the family, an ambiguity compounded by the overlap between ideal types. Second, when it is unclear which parties share which features of the ideal type, theoretizing for the whole party family becomes problematic.

A third method is quite similar to that of the ideal type, but defines the whole family on the basis of an existing party, a kind of *primus inter pares* or prototype – one party that exemplifies the whole family. The problem, obviously, is how (i.e. on the basis of which criteria) to select the *pater familias*? For example, Piero Ignazi (1992) argues that the Italian Movimento Sociale Italiano (Italian Social Movement, MSI) has functioned as the defining party for the whole party family, while others see the French FN in this role (e.g. Rydgren 2005b; Backes 1996; Kitschelt & McGann 1995).[1] None of the authors provides empirical evidence for his or her claim, however.[2] In other words, one has first to define the core (ideology) of the FN and then find out whether this core is shared by the other family members. If this is the case, one can try to define the whole party family on the basis of that core (ideology) of the FN.

The last two approaches are related and can be seen as opposite strategies. They are similar in the fact that they do not share the weaknesses of the earlier three approaches. Most importantly, they work with classical rather than radial categories (e.g. Mahoney 2004; Collier & Mahon 1993), which is far less problematic in terms of theorizing on the basis of the concept. Consequently, the conceptualization used in this study will be based upon these two approaches.

The fourth approach is to define the group on the basis of the "lowest common denominator," i.e. on the basis of the (few) features that *all* individual members have in common. This would lead to a so-called "minimum definition" (cf. Eatwell 1996), which delineates the bare core of the ideologies of the individual parties, but at the same time the full core of the whole party family. Obviously, this is the most difficult approach, because ideally one would need to study the ideologies of *all* (alleged) members of the party family. Alternatively, one could use a "most dissimilar system design" (Przeworksi & Teune 1970), i.e. look for similarities among a selection of party family members from backgrounds as dissimilar as possible.[3]

The fifth, and last, approach is the direct opposite of the previous one in that it looks for the "greatest common denominator" and employs a "most similar system design" (Przeworksi & Teune 1970), i.e. similarities among a selection of party family members from backgrounds as similar as possible. The aim is to find a "maximum definition," i.e. the greatest

---

[1] In later publications Ignazi has qualified his earlier statement, arguing that the MSI is the defining party of the subgroup of "traditional" extreme right parties and the FN "the prototype of postindustrial extreme right parties" (1997: 57).

[2] The only partial attempt has come from Jens Rydgren (2005b), who has argued that the FN has provided the "extreme right" in Western Europe with a "new master frame" to overcome their previous phase of marginalization as a consequence of the legacy of the Second World War.

[3] Implicitly, this was done in a recent study analyzing parties from Belgium, Italy, New Zealand, and Switzerland (Betz & Johnson 2004).

possible number of similarities within (part of) the family (see Mudde 2000a).

In the following sections I will develop both a minimum and a maximum definition for the party family under study.[4] Obviously, the two cannot be used interchangeably; the choice between a minimum and a maximum definition has severe consequences for the inclusion and exclusion of individual parties. Consequently, the two have to be seen as different if overlapping party families, with the "maximum" group being a subgroup of the "minimum" group.

1.3   The minimal definition

The construction of a minimum definition depends to a large extent on how broadly applicable, or in other words how "minimum," the definition needs to be. Should it be able to accommodate all political parties that have *at some time* been linked to this party family, including the Slovak Hnutie za demokratickě Slovensko (Movement for a Democratic Slovakia, HZDS) or the Portuguese Partido do Centro Democrático Social (Social Democratic Center Party)? Or should the definition be more exclusive, yet still able to include all those parties that are *generally* considered to be part of the group, such as the French FN and the Hungarian Magyar Igazság és Élet Pártja (Hungarian Justice and Life Party, MIÉP)? It makes sense to base the minimum definition on the second approach. In other words, the aim of the minimum definition is to describe the core features of the ideologies of all parties that are generally included in the party family.

In his influential work on political ideologies, Michael Freeden (1996) has argued that every ideology has core and peripheral concepts. Following up on this insight, Terence Ball has elaborated:

A *core* concept is one that is both central to, and constitutive of, a particular ideology and therefore of the ideological community to which it gives inspiration and identity. For example, the concept of 'class' (and of course 'class struggle') is a key or core concept in Marxism, as 'gender' is in feminism, and 'liberty' (or 'individual liberty') is in liberalism, and so on through the list of leading ideologies. (1999: 391–2)

Core concepts can also be seen as "individually shaped coathangers on which additional concepts may be draped" (Freeden 1997: 5).

---

[4] This is not the same as the recently developed "min-max strategy" (Gerring & Barresi 2003), which develops minimum and maximum definitions for the same term, whereas here different terms are used for the two definitions, to prevent conceptual stretching.

If one looks at the primary literature of the various political parties generally associated with this party family, as well as the various studies of their ideologies, the core concept is undoubtedly the "nation." This concept also certainly functions as a "coathanger" for most other ideological features. Consequently, the minimum definition of the party family should be based on the key concept, the nation. The first ideological feature to address, then, is nationalism.

1.3.1   Nationalism

Hundreds of books and articles have been written about the concept of nationalism. While there is some truth in the critique that the contemporary studies are more numerous but less innovative than the earlier literature, particularly compared to the classics of the pre-1960s (e.g. Deutsch 1953; Kohn 1944; Hayes 1931), many important contributions have been made since the earlier "Golden Age" of nationalism studies. Most notably, under the influence of grand scholars like Ernest Gellner (1983) and Eric Hobsbawm (1990), nationalism was redefined as a political doctrine rather than an attitude.

It is also in this tradition that nationalism will be defined here, that is, as a political doctrine that strives for the congruence of the cultural and the political unit, i.e. the nation and the state, respectively. In other words, the core goal of the nationalist is to achieve a monocultural state. As Koen Koch (1991) has elaborated, a key process for achieving this is internal homogenization, which ensures that the state includes only people from one's "own" nation. Internal homogenization can be achieved by (a combination of) various strategies, including separatism, assimilation, expulsion, and ultimately genocide.

Koch also distinguishes the process of external exclusiveness, which aims to bring all members of the nation within the territory of the state. In a moderate form, this can be achieved by population transfer, i.e. by moving extraterritorial nationals (back) inside of the state boundaries. A more radical interpretation considers a certain territory as belonging to the nation, whether inhabited by nationals or not, and wants to enforce external exclusiveness by means of territorial expansion (irredentism). While irredentism might be supported at the theoretical level, it is not considered a primary and realistic goal by all contemporary nationalists (see also 6.2.1).

To use the term "nationalism" in a nonqualified way is virtually meaningless these days. Conceptual stretching has made nationalism an almost omnipresent concept with a plethora of subtypes. Indeed, some authors even talk of "nationalist multiculturalism" (Nimni 1999) or "multicultural nationalism" (Maddens & Vanden Berghe 2003). Among the most widely used distinctions is that between *ethnic* (alternatively: "cultural" or "racial") nationalism, on the one hand, and *state* (alternatively: "civic," "territorial," or "political") nationalism, on the other (e.g. Greenfeld 2001; Spencer & Wolman 1998).[5]

While nationalism may not be universal (Gellner 1997), it has been the founding ideology of the global division of territory into (so-called) nation-states since the late eighteenth century. Indeed, state nationalism is so pervasive in the founding ideologies of many countries (e.g. France) and even supranational organizations (e.g. the United Nations) that it fails to distinguish clearly between different party families (cf. Billig 1995).[6] That said, limiting the maximum definition to just ethnic nationalism might overcome the problematic delineation of boundaries, but only at the cost of creating new problems of exclusiveness.

As Andreas Wimmer (2002) has shown convincingly in a recent comparative study, nationalism always includes political/civic and cultural/ethnic aspects. In other words, in practice nationalism always includes a combination of (elements of) ethnic and state nationalism. We will therefore interpret nationalism in a holistic way in this study, i.e. including both civic and ethnic elements. Within this interpretation the combination of nationalism with internal homogenization and external exclusiveness also makes far more sense. Moreover, if the distinction between state and ethnic nationalism is exchanged for a definition of nationalism that includes elements of both, but does not require either one in full, the classification of several political parties will no longer prove so problematic.

While this (re-)definition of nationalism will solve many problems involved in distinguishing the parties we are interested in here from other parties, it might still be too broad. Most notably, it will not be able to make a distinction between "moderate" nationalists, notably so-called liberal nationalists,[7] and the "radical" nationalists with whom we are concerned. In this respect, the term nativism provides the answer.

---

[5] Obviously, there are other distinctions as well, such as that between "Risorgimento" and "integral" nationalism (e.g. Alter 1989), but they are less dominant in the nationalism literature and, more importantly, in the discussions about the parties that concern us here.

[6] One could argue that other party families, ranging from secular conservatives to social democrats, also subscribe to basic state nationalist ideological tenets.

[7] I have serious reservations regarding the term liberal nationalism, which seems a *contradictio in terminis* as liberalism is essentially an individualist ideology, yet nationalism is fundamentally collectivist. However, I feel unqualified to argue this position convincingly, and do not believe it is vital for the primary arguments advanced here. Consequently, in this study liberal nationalism will simply be accepted as a legitimate subtype of nationalism (on liberal nationalism, see most notably Tamir 1983; for an empirical critique, see Abizadeh 2004).

1.3.2   Nativism

The term nativism is mainly current in the American literature, and has so far been applied only scantily in studies on the European party family in question (see Betz 2003a; Veughelers & Chiarini 2002; Fetzer 2000). The concept of nativism is used in various academic disciplines, including anthropology, education, history, linguistics, philosophy, and psychology, though not always in an identical manner.

In anthropology, nativism has been applied to social movements that proclaim "the return to power of the natives of a colonized area and the resurgence of native culture, along with the decline of the colonizers. The term has also been used to refer to a widespread attitude in a society of a rejection of alien persons or culture" (www.encyclopedia.com). While anthropologists reserve nativism for nonindustrial cultures (e.g. Wallace 1969), historians have applied the term also to Western contexts (most notably US American). Some have employed it in a manner consistent with its use in anthropology; contemporary European authors use the term "anti-immigrant" (e.g. Gibson 2002; Fennema 1997) to describe "anti-alien" movements (e.g. Bennett 1990).

In *Strangers in the Land*, the famous study of American nativism (1860–1925), John Higham rejects "reducing nativism to little more than a general ethnocentric habit of mind" (1955: 3). Instead, he argues that nativism is "a certain kind of nationalism," leading him to the following conclusion:

Nativism, therefore, should be defined as intense opposition to an internal minority on the ground of its foreign (i.e., 'un-American') connections. Specific nativistic antagonisms may, and do, vary widely in response to the changing character of minority irritants and the shifting conditions of the day; but through each separate hostility runs the connecting, energizing force of modern nationalism. While drawing on much broader cultural antipathies and ethnocentric judgments, nativism translates them into a zeal to destroy the enemies of a distinctively American way of life. (Higham 1955: 4)

According to Walter Benn Michaels, "as nationalism turns into nativism . . . it becomes also a kind of pluralism. From the standpoint of the 'native,' this must involve the repudiation of any attempt to blur differences" (1995: 69). Moreover, he argues, "[i]n pluralism one prefers one's own race not because it is superior but because it is one's own" (Michaels 1995: 67). In other words, "the essence of nativism is its preference for the native exclusively on the grounds of its being native" (Michaels 1995: 14). This interpretation of pluralism (at least within nativism) is remarkably similar to the "ethnopluralist" argument of Alain De Benoist and the *nouvelle droite*, i.e. nations/cultures are "equal but different" (e.g. De Benoist 1985; cf. Betz 2003a).

If the anthropological and the historical definitions are combined, and stripped of their particular spatial and temporal features (cf. Friedman 1967), a generic definition can be constructed, which closely resembles the combination of xenophobia and nationalism. In this interpretation, nativism is defined here as *an ideology, which holds that states should be inhabited exclusively by members of the native group ("the nation") and that nonnative elements (persons and ideas) are fundamentally threatening to the homogenous nation-state.* The basis for defining (non) "nativeness" can be diverse, e.g. ethnic, racial or religious, but will always have a cultural component (cf. Bennett 1990; Friedman 1967; Higham 1955).

Obviously, the determination of native(ness) is subjective, i.e. "imagined," like that of the nation (Anderson 1983). Hence, it will often be contested. For example, both WASPs (White Anglo-Saxon Protestants) and various "Indian" tribes claim to be the true "native Americans," the latter having currently won the symbolic yet important battle over the right to bear the name. Similarly, both Arab Palestinians and Jewish Israelis claim to be the true native people of the territory of the current state of Israel.

In this interpretation, the term nativism clearly constitutes the core of the ideology of the larger party family. Moreover, as a minimum definition, it is far more suitable than alternative terms like nationalist, antiimmigrant, or racist. In comparison to the broad term nationalism, nativism has the advantage of excluding liberal forms of nationalism. Furthermore, while nativism could include racist arguments, it can also be nonracist (including and excluding on the basis of culture or even religion). And, finally, while acknowledging the tremendous importance of xenophobia and opposition to immigration to the parties in question (e.g. Betz 1994; Von Beyme 1988), nativism does not reduce the parties to mere single-issue parties, such as the term antiimmigrant does (see Mudde 1999).

This is particularly important if the concept is to "travel" to the Eastern part of the European continent. In postcommunist Europe mass immigration has so far remained a fairly marginal concern, yet xenophobia and nationalism have played an important role in various parts of the region. The term nativism, as defined above, is able to accommodate the xenophobic nationalist reactions to (so-called) indigenous minorities from parts of the majority populations (e.g. "Estonian Estonians" versus "Russian Estonians" or "Slavic Slovaks" versus "Hungarian Slovaks"); as well as those from minority members to either the majority population or other minorities (e.g. "Hungarian Slovaks" against "Slavic Slovaks" or against "Gypsies").

Though the term nativism is a more accurate and inclusive alternative to the terms most commonly employed in the literature, it is not entirely free from liability. Most notably, the term's currency has largely been limited to the English language, specifically the American and Australian literature. Indeed, it has no equivalents in other major languages. However, this is not a compelling reason to reject the term.

1.4   A maximum definition

In an earlier work, I employed a similar system design to conduct qualitative content analysis of the internally and externally oriented party literature of five parties in three countries: the Vlaams Blok (Flemish Block, VB) in the Dutch-speaking part of Belgium (i.e. Flanders); the Deutsche Volksunion (German People's Union, DVU) and Die Republikaner (The Republicans, REP) in Germany; and the Centrumdemocraten (Center Democrats, CD) and the Centrumpartij '86 (Center Party '86, CP'86) in the Netherlands (Mudde 2000a).

The three countries clearly differ in many respects, but within even the limited larger context of Western Europe they constitute a fairly homogeneous group. They are all highly developed welfare states, which share, admittedly in different ways, a "Germanic" culture. Furthermore, they are each home to a variety of parties alleged to share an ideological core, generally identified as "extreme right," that differ, *inter alia*, in terms of the extremity of those ideological features (for a full clarification of the selection criteria, see Mudde 2000a: 17–18).

The study established the key ideological features of the individual parties (see table 1.1) as well as the four core ideological features that the five parties have in common (i.e. nationalism, xenophobia, welfare chauvinism, and law and order). In an effort to find a suitable designation for this ideological combination, I came to the following unsatisfying conclusion:

It seems therefore most useful to stick with the term 'extreme right'. Though the ideological core falls only just within the definition of right-wing extremism, and the term provides some semantical confusion, alternative labels do not justify the rejection of what is still the most generally used term to describe this particular party family. (Mudde 2000a: 180)

Since then, inspired by the skepticism of my students and the critical and encouraging critiques from various colleagues, I have come to the conclusion that my earlier findings have to be revised on at least two accounts.

First, some definitions of the concepts used in the original study turned out to be either inaccurate or too confusing. As argued above, the rigid distinction between state and ethnic nationalism has both empirical and theoretical problems (cf. Rensmann 2003: 108–11). Additionally, the

Table 1.1 *Summary table of ideological features per party** (C = core; p = present, not core; i = indication, not explicit)

FEATURE	REP	DVU	VB	CD	CP'86
NATIONALISM	C	C	C	C	C
Internal homogenization	C	C	C	C	C
External exclusiveness	i	i	C		C
Ethnic nationalism	i	i	C		C
State nationalism				C	
EXCLUSIONISM					
Ethnopluralism		i	C		C
Anti-Semitism	p	C			C
XENOPHOBIA	C	C	C	C	C
STRONG STATE					
Law and order	C	C	C	C	C
Militarism		i			
WELFARE CHAUVINISM	C	C	C	C	C
TRADITIONAL ETHICS	C	p	C	p	p
REVISIONISM	C	C	C		i

Note: * I have left out idiosyncratic core features, like chauvinism (DVU) and ecologism (CP'86).
Source: Mudde (2000a: 170)

conceptualization of the strong state as an ideological feature is complicated by its traditional association with militarism. While militarism has become relatively obsolete, updating the concept by eliminating it leaves only the very general feature of law and order, which, though relevant, does not capture the essence of the parties' emphasis on hierarchical authority. Finally, populism was defined as a political style, in line with much of the literature within the field of extreme right parties at that time (see Mudde 2000a: 13). Since the study was based on the central concept of the party family, defined exclusively through the criterion of ideology (see Mudde 2000a: 2–5; also Mair & Mudde 1998), populism was disregarded in the content analysis. In retrospect this was an unfortunate decision, based largely on my too limited knowledge of the broader literature of populism at the time.

The third and last problem with the earlier approach deals with the (lack of) internal hierarchy of the ideological features. All four features of the maximal definition were taken to be of equal importance. However, if the ideological core is also analyzed using the "causal chain approach" (Mudde 2000a: 23–4), it becomes clear that welfare chauvinism is less important than the other ideological features. In fact, economics is a topic of secondary importance to these parties (see chapter 5), and welfare chauvinism can be understood as a nativist vision of the economy.

In light of these revisions, the maximum definition should be revised into a combination of three core ideological features: nativism, authoritarianism, and populism. Before continuing with the quest for the correct term to label this combination, a short discussion of the three features of the revised ideological core is necessary.

The key ideological feature of the parties in question is *nativism*, as defined above, i.e. as an ideology, which holds that states should be inhabited exclusively by members of the native group ("the nation") and that nonnative elements (persons and ideas) are fundamentally threatening to the homogenous nation-state.[8] The nativist dimension includes a combination of nationalism and xenophobia, two of the key features from the earlier study.

The second feature, authoritarianism, is defined very differently in various fields of study. In research on democracy and democratization the term "authoritarian" refers to nondemocratic regimes, often distinguished from the even more restrictive totalitarian regimes (e.g. Linz 1993). However, in this study authoritarianism is defined in line with the dominant tradition in social psychology and the Frankfurter Schule. The concept is informed by the operationalization of "The Authoritarian Personality" of Theodor Adorno and his collaborators, who interpret authoritarianism loosely as "a general disposition to glorify, to be subservient to and remain uncritical toward authoritative figures of the ingroup and to take an attitude of punishing outgroup figures in the name of some moral authority" (Adorno *et al.* 1969: 228).

Whereas Adorno and his colleagues conflate authoritarianism with various other attitudes and ideological features, including anti-Semitism and ethnocentrism (e.g. Kirscht & Dillehay 1967; Christie & Jahoda 1954), Bob Altemeyer has disentangled the various elements and bases his definition of "right-wing authoritarianism" on a combination of three features of the famous F-scale: authoritarian submission, authoritarian aggression, and conventionalism (1981: 147–8). According to him

The right-wing authoritarian believes authorities should be trusted to a relatively great extent, and that they are owed obedience and respect . . . Criticism of authority is viewed as divisive and destructive, motivated by sinister goals and a desire to cause trouble. (1981: 151)

Right-wing authoritarians are predisposed to control the behavior of others through punishment. (1981: 153)

---

[8] The ideological predominance of nativism can also be found among the parties' members (e.g. Klandermans & Mayer 2005) and voters (e.g. Lubbers 2001).

Altemeyer speaks of "right-wing" authoritarianism because his operationalization refers to "established" authorities (1981: 152). There is no reason to limit the concept of authoritarianism in this way, however, particularly if it is defined in an ideological rather than an attitudinal sense. Thus, authoritarianism is defined here as the belief in a strictly ordered society, in which infringements of authority are to be punished severely. In this interpretation, authoritarianism includes law and order and "punitive conventional moralism" (Smith 1967: vi). It does not necessarily mean an antidemocratic attitude, but neither does it preclude one. In addition, the authoritarian's submission to authority, established or not, is "not absolute, automatic, nor blind" (Altemeyer 1981: 152). In other words, while authoritarians will be more inclined to accept (established) authority than nonauthoritarians, they can and will rebel under certain circumstances.

The third and final core feature is *populism*, which is here defined as an ideological feature, and not merely as a political style. Accordingly, populism is understood as a thin-centered ideology that considers society to be ultimately separated into two homogeneous and antagonistic groups, "the pure people" versus "the corrupt elite," and which argues that politics should be an expression of the *volonté générale* (general will) of the people (Mudde 2004: 543; also Jagers 2006). Populist ideology reveres the "common sense" of the people, or of "the heartland" (Taggart 2000). In the populist democracy, nothing is more important than the "general will" of the people, not even human rights or constitutional guarantees (see, in more detail, chapter 6).

1.5   Towards a conceptual framework

Having satisfied the quest for definitions, it is now time to find the best term to describe the maximum definition. Given the terminological confusion within the field, this is not an easy task. There is no consensus to follow, let alone a conceptual framework that relates the different terms to each other. To help find an answer to the question of terminology, I have constructed a ladder of abstraction (Sartori 1970) of the "family" of nativist ideologies on the basis of a large variety of international secondary sources. Obviously, this conceptual framework is based more on *my interpretation* of the literature than on the exact definitions of individual authors.

The basis of the conceptual framework is the ideological feature of the minimum definition, i.e. nativism. We hope to find the best-suited term by ascending the ladder, i.e. moving step by step upwards from nativism to, ultimately, the extreme right – which is defined here as a combination of nativism, authoritarianism, and antidemocracy (see table 1.2).

Table 1.2 *Ladder of abstraction of nativist ideologies*

Ideology	Key additional feature
Extreme right	
	Anti-democracy
Radical right	
	Authoritarianism
Nativism	
	Xenophobia
Nationalism	

This conceptual framework, however, is limited by its inability to accommodate populism. While some authors have included populism as part of their definitions of subsets of the extreme right, notably fascism and National Socialism (e.g. Griffin 1991; Linz 1976), they tended to interpret populism more loosely than it is construed in this study; i.e. identifying it in the basis of the party's support (i.e. cross-class) and organizational structure (i.e. direct leader–masses link and mass mobilization). If populism were to be included at a lower level of the ladder, e.g. between nativism and radical right, this would mean that the radical right (and all types above it) cannot be elitist, as this is the antithesis of populism (Mudde 2004). This contrasts with much of the literature, which stresses the centrality of elitism in many nativist ideologies, including fascism and National Socialism (cf. Gregor 2000; Payne 1995; De Felice 1977).

In light of this conceptual framework then, the maximum definition best fits the term radical right, albeit a specific subtype, i.e. a populist version of the radical right. Most logically, this leads to the adoption of the term "radical right populism" or "populist radical right." However, before settling the question of terminology we first have to solve two potential problems regarding both terms: clarity and semantics.

The term "radical" in contemporary usage is often associated with "the right" but it originated at the other end of the political spectrum. Traditionally, the term radical was used for the supporters of the French Revolution, i.e. the "left" (Schwartz 1993; also Ignazi 2003), and, particularly within the Latin languages, it is still used with respect to left-wing groups, such as the French Parti radical de gauche (Radical Left Party) and the Dutch Politieke Partij Radikalen (Political Party Radicals), or by progressive liberal groups, such as the French Parti radical (Radical Party) and the Partido radicale italiano (Italian Radical Party).[9]

---

[9] Simon Hix and Christopher Lord distinguish between two main streams within the liberal political family, of which the "*Radical Liberals* emphasize social and political freedoms" (1997: 32).

Hans-Georg Betz and Carol Johnson have argued that "[r]adical right-wing parties are [thus] radical both with respect to the language they employ in confronting their political opponents and the political project they promote and defend" (2004: 312). This comes close to Ignazi's (2003) recognition of the "antisystem" dimension of these groups, a key criterion in his definition of the *extreme* right. The problem with both definitions is that they are (too) relativist. What is considered to be "radical" depends to a large extent on the political culture of the country: the same language or project can be deemed radical in one country, yet mainstream or moderate in another. And what is antisystem obviously depends on, well, the system.

Therefore, in this study radical is defined as opposition to some key features of liberal democracy, most notably political pluralism and the constitutional protection of minorities (Mudde 2006a, 2005c). Obviously, this definition renders the term most useful within a liberal democratic context; but it does not preclude its use in other political systems. However, since the term "radical" does refer to many different ideologies and movements it requires additional designation to indicate the direction of radicalization.

The concept of the "right" (or "right-wing") is hardly less problematic. Within political philosophy, "'[t]he Right' in its most general sense denotes a philosophy that was hostile to the politics of modernity, with its ideas of emancipation and rationality" (Schwarzmantel 1998: 112; also Eatwell 1989). Some authors also define the contemporary radical right in terms of a radical opposition to (post)modernization (e.g. Minkenberg 1998). However, opposition to modernity does not feature (prominently) in the ideologies of many of the contemporary parties. In fact, as various scholars have argued, the quintessential extreme right, i.e. Italian Fascism and German National Socialism, was not unequivocally antimodern either (e.g. Sternhell 1996; Griffin 1991; Gregor 1974). Rather, one could argue that the radical right strives for an "alternative modernity" (Griffin 1999a: 301).

Within most empirical political scientific studies, the right is defined first and foremost on the basis of the socioeconomic dimension. Here, the right believes in the self-regulating power of the market and thus favors a government *laissez faire* attitude towards it, while the left distrusts the market and wants the state to play an important role within the economy (e.g. Schwartz 1993). There are two reasons why this definition of the right does not make much sense here. First, economics is not a core feature of the party family's ideology. Second, many of the parties in question are not right-wing in this sense, as they support a (chauvinist) welfare state and protectionist policies (see further in chapter 5).

Norberto Bobbio (1994) provides an alternative distinction between left and right based on the key feature of (the propensity to) egalitarianism that better illuminates the difference between the parties in question and the traditional right. Following Bobbio, the key distinction in this study will be based on the attitude toward (in)equality: the left considers the key inequalities between people artificial and wants to overcome them by active state involvement, whereas the right believes the main inequalities between people to be natural and outside the purview of the state.[10] As Gill Seidel argues, "right-wing discourse is a discourse of order grounded in nature" (1988b: 11).

Thus, while concepts that include confusing and contested terms such as radical and right are not ideal, they can be used if clear definitions are provided. Here, the term *radical* is defined as opposition to fundamental values of liberal democracy, while *right* is defined as the belief in a natural order with inequalities. Consequently, the combination of ideological features of the maximum definition can best be labeled as either populist radical right or radical right populism. The choice is not completely arbitrary, however.

The reason the term *populist radical right* is preferred here over radical right populism is not the all-too-common urge to be original, given that the former term is quite rare (e.g. Filc & Lebel 2005) compared to the relatively common latter term (e.g. Evans 2005; Rydgren 2005a; Betz 1994). Rather, the prime rationale is of a semantic nature. In "radical right populism" the primary term is populism, while "radical right" functions merely to describe the ideological emphasis of this specific form of populism. Populist radical right, on the other hand, refers to a populist form of the radical right. Given that nativism, not populism, is the ultimate core feature of the ideology of this party family, radical right should be the primary term in the concept. Henceforth, this study will focus on populist radical right parties, i.e. political parties with a core ideology that is a combination of nativism, authoritarianism, and populism.

1.6   Delineating the borders

If the concept of the populist radical right is to be of any use in the study of party families, it must be able to delineate a unique family of political parties. In other words, while these parties should share the core of ideological features defined above, members from other party families

---

[10] This is more a personal interpretation and summary than a literal quotation of Bobbio's arguments, who defines the two more strictly and relatively, i.e. on the basis of their relative propensity towards egalitarianism.

should not. This does not seem to present a problem for the larger party families of the center-right (i.e. Christian democrats and liberals) and the left (i.e. communists, Greens, social democrats). But in the case of some other (smaller) party families, particularly among the right, certain ideological features will overlap. Consequently, it is important to clearly delineate the borders between the populist radical right and other party families.

1.6.1   Conservatives

Although the conservatives belong to one of the oldest party families in Europe, their character and distinctiveness is much in dispute. Whereas most scholars include a separate conservative family in their list of party families (e.g. Gallagher *et al.* 2005; Lane & Ersson 1999; Von Beyme 1985), some group them together with other parties. Indeed, most scholarly contributions on conservative parties are published in edited volumes that also include Christian democratic parties (e.g. Delwit 2003; Layton-Henry 1982a; Veen 1983); though some feature "moderate" (Morgan & Silvestri 1982) or "center-right" parties (e.g. Wilson 1998).

The term conservative is a notoriously difficult concept to define. It has both an absolute and a relative meaning, which are often conflated. In its relative meaning, conservative denotes an attitude to *conserve* the status quo, in contrast to the progressive favoring of change, and reactionary preference for a return to the past. Obviously, relativist concepts are highly problematic in comparative studies, whether they are spatial or temporal. What is conservative in one country or at one time, could be progressive or reactionary in another country or at another time. Consequently, an absolute definition is preferable.

In its absolute meaning, conservative refers to a certain ideology, although its specific character is again highly contested. In the literature on political parties, rather than political philosophy, conservatism is most often defined on the basis of the following features: authoritarianism, traditionalism, religiosity, and nationalism (e.g. Layton-Henry 1982b: 1). With this definition the boundaries between conservative and (populist) radical right parties are hard to establish. However, nationalism in this conceptualization of conservatism tends to refer specifically to loyalty to the nation, which is fundamentally different from the way nationalism is understood in this study, and might better be referred to as patriotism.

In the 1980s two of the major conservative parties in the West, the British Conservative Party and the US Republican Party, changed their core ideology significantly. Whereas conservatives had traditionally been only moderate supporters of the free market, fearing the moral perversions of capitalism (e.g. materialism, socialism), Margaret Thatcher and Ronald Reagan combined social conservatism with strident neoliberalism (in rhetoric rather than practice). This new conservative consensus went by various names in the literature, including "new right," "neoconservative" and "conservative liberal" (e.g. Raniolo 2000; Girvin 1988).

Interestingly, neoconservatism and the populist radical right have been linked by many of the leading scholars in the field. Most extremely, the combination of social conservatism and neoliberal economics is identical to the definition of "the winning formula" that Herbert Kitschelt and Anthony McGann (1995: vii) provide in their influential comparative study of "the radical right." It also strongly resembles definitions employed by authors who stress the neoliberal character of populist radical right parties (notably Betz 1994). Finally, Ignazi (1992) has largely collapsed the two together in his "silent counter-revolution" argument.

Fundamentally, however, the two groups are quite far apart. First and foremost, nativism is *not* a core ideological feature of neoconservatives, although they do tend to be strong defenders of national state interests, which also largely explains their propensity towards isolationism and Euroskepticism. Second, the socioeconomic agenda is secondary to populist radical right parties, and most of them do not hold neoliberal views. Third, traditional ethical and religious values are not a defining feature of the populist radical right party family, although they are at the core of the ideologies of *some* parties.

1.6.2   Nationalists and (Ethno)Regionalists

One of the borders between party families that has led to some confusion, for example with respect to the classification of the LN and VB, is that between populist radical right parties and (ethno)regionalist parties. The latter party family goes under many names: autonomist, regionalist, ethnoregionalist, regional nationalist, moderate nationalist, and nationalist (see in De Winter & Türsan 1998). Before establishing the borders between this diffuse party family and the populist radical right, we first have to address the relationship between nationalism and regionalism.

In an ideological typology, it does not make sense to distinguish between nationalists on the basis of the existing state borders. Consequently, regionalism should not be used for parties that strive for separatism to fulfill their nationalist aspirations of a monocultural nation-state. According to Michael Keating and John Loughlin, regionalism is related to views and movements that demand "greater control over the affairs of the regional territory by the people residing in that territory, usually by means of the installation of a regional government" (1997: 5). Thus, regionalism is best limited to groups that call for more autonomy of a region within a larger state structure. So defined, there is also a clear distinction between nationalists (including populist radical rightists) and regionalists: first, regionalists accept a multinational state and, second, their call for autonomy is not necessarily culturally defined.

If we exclude regionalism from the core feature of this party family, does it still make sense to distinguish between the populist radical right party family and a separate nationalist party family? As argued above, not all nationalists are also populist radical right; some will not be authoritarian, others not populist. In short, while all populist radical right parties are nationalist, only subsets of the nationalist parties are populist radical right. The populist radical right is thus a subfamily of a broader nationalist party family.

1.6.3   Populists

In some lists of party families, a distinction is made between general "populist" or "protest" parties and particular "right-wing extremist" or "fascist" parties. For example, Klaus Von Beyme (1985) distinguishes between a "protest" and a "fascist" party family, while Jan-Erik Lane and Svante Ersson (1999) separate "discontent (populist)" from "ultra-right" parties. To a certain extent, the party family of the populist radical right is positioned in between the two. Not surprisingly, various parties that are classified as populist radical right here tend to be placed in either one or the other group in other studies. Thus, a short discussion is necessary to clarify the positioning of the populist radical right party family in terms of these two categories, and to explain some possibly contested classifications.

The first family has been caught in many different nets: alternative (Delwit 2001), antipolitical establishment (Abedi 2004; Schedler 1996), protest (Von Beyme 1985), discontent (Lane & Ersson 1999), or unorthodox (Pop-Elechus 2003). Despite the different terms, definitions and classifications, the main criterion for these party families is a core anti-establishment position. Using such a broad criterion might be useful for some studies (e.g. Abedi 2004, 2002), but it is too narrow a basis for defining a separate party family; also it reduces these parties to single-issue movements. The term "populism," however, if defined in a clear and distinct manner, does have enough leverage to discriminate among party families. Three groups of parties deserve our attention here: right-wing populists, neoliberal populists, and social populists.

Starting with the last, which is the easiest to distinguish from the family of the populist radical right, social populists combine socialism and populism as their core ideological features (see March & Mudde 2005). Clearly the similarities with the populist radical right are in the shared radicalism, notably populism. However, the differences are even more important, as the social populists are essentially egalitarian and thus left-wing. Moreover, they will not have a nativist ideological core, even if some individual parties at times clearly espouse such ideas (see 2.4.1).

The term right-wing populism is one of the most popular within the field, particularly within the German literature (e.g. Decker 2004; Eismann 2002; Pfahl-Traughber 1994). As defined here, the term denotes nonegalitarian populism, and is too imprecise to define one particular party family. However, it can be used as an umbrella term for different subgroups of parties, most often referred to as neoliberal populism and national populism. As the party family of the national populists roughly overlaps with the one termed populist radical right here, this discussion will be limited to the neoliberal populists.

Betz has distinguished between "neoliberal" (or "libertarian") and "national" (or "authoritarian") populists on the basis of the "relative weight" of liberalism and nationalism in their party ideology, implying that the two constitute the (ideal typical) poles of one dimension (1994: 108; also 1993a: 680). I both agree and disagree. While the main difference between the two is the centrality of neoliberalism and nationalism (or better: nativism), respectively, the two do not constitute the poles of one dimension. In other words, they are at least as different as they are similar. They share one core feature (populism), but their other core ideological element(s) differ(s). In essence, neoliberal populism is defined by a core ideology of neoliberalism (primarily in terms of economy) and populism. In contrast to the populist radical right, the ideological feature of nativism is either not present or not central to the neoliberal populist party family, while the same applies to neoliberalism for the populist radical right.

1.7   Conclusion

Before discussing the various aspects involved in classifying individual political parties, most notably how to categorize populist radical right parties, we needed to reformulate the way the term populist radical right relates to the other key terms used in the field. The ladder of abstraction, presented above, constitutes the basis of this discussion.

First and foremost, the populist radical right is a specific form of nationalism. Therefore, while all populist radical rightists are nationalists, not all nationalists are populist radical rightists. Most importantly, nonxenophobic nationalists are excluded, which includes many of the historic liberal nationalist movements of nineteenth-century Western Europe (e.g. Alter 1989; Anderson 1983). Secondly, elitist nationalists are excluded, which includes many of the authoritarian nationalist movements of the twentieth century, including the pre-fascists in France (e.g. Sternhell 1978; Nolte 1965) and the intellectuals of the German *Konservative Revolution* (e.g. Wiegandt 1995).

Second, the populist radical right is not merely a moderate form of the extreme right, including fascism and National Socialism and its various 'neo'-forms. There are fundamental differences between the two. Most importantly, the radical right is (nominally) democratic, even if they oppose some fundamental values of *liberal* democracy (see chapter 6), whereas the extreme right is *in essence* antidemocratic, opposing the fundamental principle of sovereignty of the people (e.g. Mudde 2006a, 2005c).

Third, the populist radical right is a special form of the broader radical right, which also includes nonpopulist ideas and movements. It makes sense to see the populist radical right as the temporary dominant form of the radical right, as a radical right reflection of the contemporary populist *Zeitgeist* (Mudde 2004). However, while populism might be a defining feature of the radical right of the current era, this does not mean the radical right always has to be populist. Even today nonpopulist or even elitist radical right movements exist, though they are far less prevalent and relevant than their populist brethren.

In this book populist radical right parties in contemporary Europe are the prime unit of analysis. However, reference to other nativist, nationalist, populist, and nonpopulist radical right parties will occasionally be made as well, at times to show the differences, occasionally to point out the similarities. But before this can be done, we must classify individual parties according to the various categories. This will be the topic of the next chapter.

2 From conceptualization to classification: which parties?

> Though formal definitions or derivations based on the history of ideas largely failed to provide a convincing concept for 'right-wing extremism', research work on political parties of the right has not had serious problems in selecting appropriate cases. (Von Beyme 1988: 3)

2.1 Introduction

Both the academic and public debate about the "extreme right" lends credence to Von Beyme's assertion that we know *who* they are, even though we do not know exactly *what* they are. However, I fundamentally disagree with the belief that "the extreme right is easily recognizable" (Anastasakis 2000: 4). Practice certainly reveals that *we* do not know who *they* are (also Mudde 2000a): while there is consensus with regard to the inclusion of some parties in this category, the proper classification of many others remains contested. Indeed, there are some special circumstances that make the implications of this assumption especially problematic for this particular party family.

Some scholars consider the Scandinavian Progress Parties to be the first of the recent wave of "right-wing populist" parties (e.g. Decker 2004; Betz 1994), whereas others exclude them from their analysis on the grounds that they are not "extreme right" (e.g. Mudde 2000a). Similarly, while the Italian Lega Nord (Northern League, LN) is included in most comparative studies of the populist radical right party family, at least one prominent scholar (Ignazi 1992; 2003) has consistently excluded it. The confusion with respect to classifying the parties in Eastern Europe is even more striking. According to some observers the Hungarian Fiatal Demokraták Szövetsége–Magyar Polgári Szövertség (Alliance of Young Democrats–Hungarian Civic Movement, FIDESz-MPS) is part of this family (e.g. Bohlen 2002; Jungwirth 2002a; Rupnik 2002), while others reject their inclusion and label the MIÉP the only major populist radical right party in Hungary (e.g. Bernáth et al. 2005; Karsai 1999).

There are different reasons for this lack of taxonomical accord but the root of the problem seems to be less related to the plethora of concepts and definitions than to the limited attention paid to the classification of political parties. Few authors have established a clear method for categorizing political parties, i.e. to establish on the basis of which criteria certain parties should be classified as populist radical right, and others should not. This chapter will draw upon earlier work on party families (e.g. Mudde 2000a; Mair & Mudde 1998) to develop an effective method of classification and discuss the various problems involved in classifying individual parties.

2.2   How to study party ideology?

Given that we have defined the populist radical right party family exclusively on the basis of ideological features, it follows that individual parties should be classified purely on the basis of party ideology as well. However, this raises several important questions: who determines the ideology of a party, on what basis, and how should the representative source be studied?

2.2.1   The classifier: parties vs. researchers

The first question to be answered is who determines the ideology and thus the categorization of a party, the researcher or the party itself? There is undoubtedly much to be said for relying on the parties' self-classification; after all, who knows a party better than the party itself? This approach has the likely advantage of producing results very compatible with the general self-understanding of the parties. Moreover, it would be cost- and time-effective.

In the literature on party families, the two criteria employed most frequently in classification, party name and transnational federations (e.g. Gallagher *et al.* 2005; Mair & Mudde 1998), assume that parties know themselves best. Both criteria work relatively well for some party families, but are of little use for classifying members of the populist radical right party family.

The criterion of party name seems particularly suited for the Christian democratic, the socialist and social democratic, the communist, and the Green party families. In these families, most members have (part of) the family name in their party name. However, with regard to conservative, liberal, or ethnoregionalist parties this criterion is far less useful. How does one classify parties with names like Soldiers of Destiny (Fianna

Fáil), Alliance for a New Citizen (Aliancia nového občana, ANO), or People's Union (Volksunie, VU)?

Establishing ideological similarity through party names is possibly even more dubious in the case of the populist radical right. What do party names like Flemish Interest (Vlaams Belang, VB), League of Polish Families (Liga Polskich Rodzin, LPR), or National Front (NF) have in common? At first glance one could surmise that their common feature is a nativist ideology based on the fact that all party names refer to the (own) nation. But when one considers the fact that the names of virtually all political parties in Flanders or Slovakia share this reference, it is obvious that this is not a very robust conclusion. What then might one read in names such as Center Democrats (CD), The Republicans (REP), or Truth (Veritas)?

Some authors have identified the refusal of populist radical right parties to call themselves "party" because of their alleged antidemocratic or antiparty position as a reliable indicator of ideological similarity (e.g. Decker 2004; Heinisch 2003; Mény & Surel 2002b). This assertion is problematic on two counts. First, there are several populist radical right parties using the term "party" in their name, such as the British National Party (BNP), the Hungarian Justice and Life Party (MIÉP) or the Greater Romania Party (Partidul România Mare, PRM).[1] Second, many non-populist radical right parties, particularly on the (center-)right, do not have the term(s) of their party family in their name; examples include the Belgian Reform Movement (Mouvement Réformateur), the Norwegian Right (Høyre), and the Polish Civic Platform (Platforma Obywatelska).

The use of transnational federations as a criterion of classification assumes that political parties will align themselves cross-nationally with ideologically similar organizations. Consequently, all members of the Liberal International are counted as liberal parties, while all members of the Party of European Socialists are classified as socialist. Unfortunately, things are not that simple. The ideological diversity within transnational party federations is quite extensive, not just in global organizations like the Socialist International, but even within geographically more confined groups like the European People's Party. According to both academics and the organizations themselves, transnational parties may have a core of political parties sharing a common ideological heritage, but "their political identity is obfuscated by the inclusion of parties, and parts of parties, that do not belong to the same political family" (Andeweg 1995: 64; also

---

[1] Paradoxically, it is particularly in postcommunist Europe that populist radical right parties use the term "party" in their name, despite the fact that it has an even more negative connotation there because of the link with "the Party," i.e. the former ruling communist party.

Bardi 1994). In short, electoral and political relevance are sometimes more important criteria for inclusion in a transnational federation than ideology, particularly when a suitable ideological representative cannot be found in a (large) country.

But even if membership in transnational federations could be seen as an indication of ideological similarity, it is an even less useful criterion of classification than party name. Currently it is only relevant to the larger party families, as most smaller ones have either geographically limited transnational federations or none at all. In the case of the populist radical right, no transnational federation exists. Even in the European Parliament there have been few examples of a pure populist radical right faction. Some alleged populist radical right parties are part of groups with members of various party families, but most are nonaligned (see chapter 7).

A third method of letting the parties classify themselves is use of their self-identification. If different parties define themselves in a similar way, their common self-definition could be a relatively simple and efficient way of categorizing a given party. Leaving aside the problem of circularity, i.e. which parties you look at influences the character of the self-identification (see chapter 1), a quick overview of the self-identification of some (alleged) populist radical right parties presents a flurry of different terms and identities.

Not surprisingly, given the limited use of the term, and the negative connotation associated with nearly all of its components in most countries, no political party defines itself explicitly as populist radical right. Only a few smaller parties will define themselves as populist; for example, the self-identification of España-2000 (Spain-2000) is "populista, social y democrático" (populist, social and democratic) on its website (www.espana2000.org), while the Bulgarska otechestvena partiya-Natsionalen suyuz (Bulgarian Fatherland Party–National Union) proclaimed that its "social policy has a populist character" (Mitev 1997: 81). In some cases populist radical right politicians have adopted the term "populism" as a *nom de guerre*. Jörg Haider, then leader of the Austrian FPÖ, said in an interview: "Populism is gladly used as a term of abuse for politicians who are close to the people (*volksverbundene Politiker*), whose success lies in raising their voice for the citizens and catching their mood. I have always considered this designation as a decoration" (in Worm 2005: 9). Similarly, FN-leader Jean-Marie Le Pen once claimed in an interview: "The FN is a national-populist movement . . . A populist movement takes care of people's interests" (in Birenbaum & Villa 2003: 47).

Also, some parties will identify themselves as "popular"; for instance, the Italian MS-FT describes itself in various pamphlets as the "alternative nazionalpopulare" (national-popular alternative). Very few will define themselves as radical, however, a still-contested term within the party family. One of the few exceptions has been Miroslav Sládek, who at the founding party congress of February 1990 defined the new Sdruženi pro republiku–Republikánská strana Československa (Association for the Republic–Republican Party of Czechoslovakia, SPR-RSČ) as a "radical right party."

Even with regard to the broad categories of left and right, the self-identifications of individual populist radical right parties differ significantly. Whereas various parties identify themselves openly and unequivocally as right-wing (e.g. Croatian Party of Rights (HSP), Popular Orthodox Rally (LAOS), Slovak National Party (SNS), VB), most members of the populist radical right party family reject a positioning in terms of left and right (e.g. CD, FPÖ, MIÉP, PRM, Slovene National Party (SNS)).[2] Finally, some parties will define themselves as part of different political families: for example, the Croatian Hrvatska stranka prava (Croatian Party of Rights, HSP) considers itself to be "neo-conservative" (HSP n.d.a), the Swiss Schweizerische Volkspartei–Union démocratique du centre (Swiss People's Party, SVP) as "liberal conservative" (in Hennecke 2003: 159), while the Russian LDPR even calls itself the "liberal democratic" party of Russia.

In conclusion, while reliance upon self-classification by parties is appealing, if only for its efficiency, it presents many fundamental problems for categorizing populist radical right parties. Consequently, researchers must confront the task themselves. The question remains how. The first step toward a solution is determining what or who represents the (core) ideology of a political party.

2.2.2   The data: what or who represents the (whole) political party?

Some scholars have categorized populist radical right parties (partly) on the basis of the special characteristics of the party *electorates*. Two different approaches can be distinguished within this group. The first group of scholars works on the basis of the famous model of cleavage politics, in which political parties are primarily seen as representatives of specific social groups (Lipset & Rokkan 1967). Consequently, party families are defined on the basis of certain sociodemographic characteristics of their (core) electorates (e.g. Kitschelt & McGann 1995). The second group does categorize party families on the basis of ideology, but defines the ideology of individual parties (in part) on the basis of the attitudes of the *voters* of these parties (e.g. Ignazi 2003).

---

[2] For example, the FN used to consider itself as "ni gauche, ni droite" (not left, not right), while the FPÖ (still) sees itself as "jenseits von rechts und links" (beyond right and left).

There are several problems involved in these two approaches. First, electorates might and do change, irrespective of whether the parties do as well. Partly as a result of their electoral success, the electorates of many populist radical right parties transformed significantly in the 1990s. However, while the "proletarization" (Betz 1994) of the party electorates was accompanied by a (slight) change in the socioeconomic policies of some parties, the latter change was rather superficial (see chapter 5). In other words, whereas the core electorate of populist radical right parties changed, their core ideology did not. Second, their electorates are far from homogeneous, which is true for different parties within the wider family, notably the more electorally successful ones (see further 9.5).

Another approach might be the categorization of political parties on the basis of the ideology of their *members* (e.g. Ivaldi 1996), but this method is also intrinsically flawed. According to John D. May's famous "special law of curvilinear disparity," rank-and-file members are the most ideologically extreme of all party supporters, compared to the voters, on the one side, and party leaders, on the other (e.g. May 1973; also Narud & Skare 1999; Kitschelt 1989). Furthermore, while the membership of a party is generally more stable than the electorate, the other problems listed above persist with this approach: party members often do not have a clear profile, and different parties will include various subgroups (the FN provides an excellent example; see 2.3).

Focusing exclusively on party membership would also give rise to some serious practical problems, most notably the lack of accurate data on the membership of these groups. The few studies that are available either have quite limited information on the members in question, or are based on a very small section of the membership, of which it is impossible to ascertain whether the selected portion is a representative sample (e.g. Klandermans & Mayer 2005; Orfali 1997).

Some studies have classified political parties on the basis of the ideo-logical views of *party leaders*. A variety of different data and methods have been employed within this approach, including official speeches, pub-lished media interviews, or original interviews with party leaders (e.g. Fennema & Pollmann 1998; Gardberg 1993). Again, this approach has some important weaknesses. First, *who* speaks for the party? In other words, who are party leaders and how does one know that the views of the leaders are representative of the (whole) party?[3] Second, these

---

[3] A dramatic example can be found in the very original work of Annvi Gardberg (1993), who interviewed all but one (i.e. Franz Schönhuber) of the MEPs of the REP to study the ideology of that party. However, by the time he had finished his study, all but Schönhuber had left the REP and now represented the Deutsche Liga für Volk und Heimat (German League for Ethnic People and Homeland, DLVH).

data might not provide a very accurate picture. The manner in which an interview is (semi-)structured seriously influences the answers of the interviewee (e.g. Schuman & Presser 1981). Also, interviews and official speeches will almost certainly produce a socially acceptable picture, i.e. what Jaap Van Donselaar (1991) has referred to as the "front-stage" of the populist radical right.

While a political party is constituted of a collective of individuals, it is not limited to its leaders or those who claim membership. A political party is more than the mere collection of the individuals involved; it is an actor in its own right. Therefore, only the party can truly represent itself, which it does through the official party literature. Indeed, the (few) authors who have analyzed the party ideologies of populist radical right parties have acknowledged this and have generally focused on party literature as the definitive voice of the party rather than reducing the party to its leadership, voters or electorate (e.g. Kolovos 2003; Ivaldi & Swyngedouw 2001; Mudde 2000a, 1995b).

However, some important limitations have to be taken into account (see also Mudde 2000a: 20–2). First, only official party publications should be included, rather than publications by individuals or organizations "close to" the party (see also Spruyt 1995). Second, only publications from the national party should be studied. Obviously, local and other sub-national publications can provide important insights, but they cannot be considered representative of the national party. Third, the selected literature should entail both externally and internally oriented literature, so as to minimize the chance of catching only the "front-stage" of the party.

2.2.3   The method: qualitative vs. quantitative

Having established which data to use, only one question remains unanswered: which method is best suited for the study of party ideology? Most comparative research on party families is based on quantitative content analysis, most notably the ECPR-sponsored party manifesto project (on populist radical right parties, see Cole 2005; in general, see Budge *et al.* 1987). Huib Pellikaan recently developed an alternative method, based on a confrontational rather than a spatial approach (on populist radical right parties, see De Lange 2007a; in general, see Pellikaan *et al.* 2003). Leaving aside the exclusive use of election programs in these studies, which is a data rather than a method problem, neither approach is particularly well suited to the study of party *ideology*. Both approaches primarily code policy initiatives, which often translate only marginally to complex ideological features. Moreover, the strict coding scheme leads to conceptual rigidity, particularly when applied over time (a major weakness of the manifesto project).

Qualitative content analysis is a far more effective approach to studying phenomena like the core features of a party ideology. It provides the proximity to the data and flexibility in operationalization necessary for studying highly complex concepts such as nativism, authoritarianism, and populism. Moreover, the "causal chain approach" can separate core from secondary ideological features on a more accurate and logical basis than simplistic quantification (Mudde 2000a: 23–4). While qualitative content analysis of a broad range of party literature is admittedly labor-intensive, various studies have shown that it can create analyses that are useful in the comparative study of political parties (e.g. De Raad 2005; Kolovos 2005, 2003; Mudde 2000a; Jungerstam 1995).

2.2.4   The problems: factions, strategies, changes

While qualitative content analysis of party literature is the best method for analyzing the ideology of an individual political party, there are nonetheless important problems with this approach to party classification that must be addressed. Political parties are aggregates of diverse yet intersecting factions (ideology- or interest-based) that are in dynamic relation to one another and to the larger political scene. Party literature may variously reflect or obscure the competing ideologies within a party as it addresses the party faithful or reaches beyond them to attract a broader audience. Consequently, we cannot always simply equate party with ideology nor ideology with party literature. This difficulty is not limited to analysis of the populist radical right but extends to the broader study of party politics. Unfortunately, this study can do little more than signal the problems and provide some provisional solutions.

The first problem with classifying political parties on the basis of their ideology is the internal heterogeneity of some political parties. Actually, this is the Achilles heel of most comparative research on political parties, which operates under the often implicit assumption that political parties are unitary actors. Only through this assumption can one speak of *the* party and classify *it* on the basis of *the* party ideology. However, as Maurice Duverger already noted over fifty years ago, "[a] party is not a community, but a collection of communities" (1954: 17). And as a general rule, one could say that the bigger the party, the larger the importance and number of these communities (better known as factions).[4]

The problem of heterogeneity might pose fewer difficulties for classifying the party on the basis of its *core* ideology, however. First of all, a

---

[4] In the late 1960s, Lipset and Rokkan noted: "Most of the parties aspiring to majority positions in the West are conglomerates of groups differing on wide ranges of issues, but still united in their greater hostility to their competitors in the other camps" (1990: 93–4).

political party is to some extent an amalgam rather than a mere sum of its internal factions. Secondly, the various factions may disagree on some issues, but will probably concur on (most) core ideological features. For example, the different factions within the FN all share a core populist radical right ideology, but each complements it with some additional, specific features (see 2.3).

Political parties that include both factions that share the populist radical right core ideology and factions that do not will still pose a challenge for definitive classification. My preferred solution is to exclude political parties that have significant ideological wings that are not populist radical right.[5] In other words, only parties with a populist radical right core ideology *and* without any significant alternative faction(s) are classified as members of the populist radical right party family.

The strategic employment of rhetoric by political parties can also present a challenge to accurate classification on the basis of ideology. Parties may appear schizophrenic if their rhetoric diverges from their ideology and the researcher is left with the dilemma of which image to trust. This problem will most often present itself as different ideological discourses in the internally and externally oriented literature. Particularly during election campaigns, political parties that do not have a populist radical right core ideology can adopt the rhetoric of the populist radical right in an attempt to win voters (e.g. Bale 2003). However, if this situation continues for a long time, it becomes increasingly difficult to decide what constitutes ideology, and what strategy. The causal chain approach (Mudde 2000a) can provide some answers by tracking the hierarchy of ideological features, but ambiguities will continue to exist.

The last two problems of categorizing political parties have been described vividly for the situation in Eastern Europe by Michael Minkenberg: "Studying the radical right in transformation countries in Central and Eastern Europe not only resembles shooting at a moving target but also shooting with clouded vision" (2002b: 361). While these problems might be more pronounced in Eastern Europe, they are certainly not limited to that part of the continent. Even with regard to various established political parties in Western Europe the problems of party change and limited information about their core ideological features create substantial hurdles in their categorization.

While parties are generally disinclined to change their ideological core, given the large potential costs involved (Downs 1957), it does happen. The development of the British Labour Party under Tony Blair (e.g.

---

[5] I am indebted to Michael Minkenberg, who suggested this solution in a discussion at a conference in Geneva in 2004.

Ludlam 2000) or of the Flemish VU in the 1970s (e.g. De Winter 1998) is clear evidence that party ideology is not inalterable. Unfortunately, it is not always easy to pinpoint exactly when a party is in which party family. The process of change (sometimes back and forth) can go on for decades, often leading to sustained periods of ideological hybridization.

The party political situation has been even more volatile in Eastern Europe, particularly during the transition phase in the first decade of postcommunism. As many authors have noted, most postcommunist parties have so far been mere vehicles of small groups of elites, which sported diffuse and highly similar ideologies and held very weak links with social groups in society (e.g. Lewis 2000; Kopecký 1995). Ideological change bore little cost for a party that mainly served the political survival of the party leader(s). In this climate, various parties went through a populist radical right stage, particularly in the first years of postcommunism when nationalism seemed to be "the *sine qua non* for political success" in certain parts of Eastern Europe (Fischer-Galati 1993: 12).

Now that we have established the best method to ascertain the core ideology of a party family, and discussed the main problems involved in classifying (some) political parties on this basis, it is time to determine which political parties belong to the populist radical right party family, and which do not. However, as the list of political parties to be classified is almost limitless, attention will be paid, first and foremost, to the so-called "usual suspects"; i.e. those parties that most authors classify under the headings of "extreme right," "radical right," "right-wing populism," etc. Obviously, all this is done within the severe limitations faced by any one researcher who studies such a broad range of parties (e.g. data, language, time).

2.3   Populist radical right parties

The most famous populist radical right party, the French Front national, considered the prototype by various scholars, was founded in 1972 (e.g. Davies 1999; Simmons 1996). Initially, the FN was not much more than a confederation of extreme and radical right *groupuscules* under the leadership of veteran radical right politician Jean-Marie Le Pen. While different and occasionally opposing factions continue to exist within the party, for example, the pagan nouvelle droite (new right) faction and the orthodox Catholic Chrétienté-Solidarité (Christian Solidarity) faction, they all share a populist radical right core ideology (e.g. DeClair 1999). The split in 1999 did not change this; rather, it added another populist radical right party to the French political system, the Mouvement national républicain

(National Republican Movement, MNR) of Bruno Mégret (e.g. Bastow 2000).

Almost equally famous is the Austrian Freiheitliche Partei Österreichs (FPÖ) and its former leader Jörg Haider. From its beginning in 1956, the party has been divided between a "national" and a "liberal" faction (e.g. Luther 1991; Riedlsperger 1998). The populist radical right takeover of the party is commonly considered to have taken place in 1986, when Haider was elected Bundesobmann (Federal Chairman) with the help of the national wing. While the FPÖ continued to include a nonpopulist radical right faction with prominent members like Heide Schmidt, at least until the split of the Liberales Forum (Liberal Forum) in 1993, Haider's grip on the party was strong and within a few years he had transformed "his" FPÖ into a full-fledged populist radical right party (e.g. Luther 2003). In 2005 Haider and his most loyal supporters, including his sister (then FPÖ-leader) and the federal FPÖ-ministers and state secretaries, founded a new political party, the Bündnis Zukunft Österreichs (Alliance for Austria's Future, BZÖ). The differences between the BZÖ and FPÖ are largely personal and strategic rather than ideological, and both parties are essentially populist radical right.

Despite its relatively poor electoral results, the German Die Republikaner (REP) is among the most well-known populist radical right parties in contemporary Europe. It originated as a national conservative split-off from the Bavarian Christlich Soziale Union (Christian Social Union, CSU) in 1983. After a short power struggle, Franz Schönhuber took the party in a populist radical right direction, inspired by the first electoral successes of the French FN (e.g. Mudde 2000a; Jaschke 1994). While the REP went through various ideological and leadership struggles, it remained loyal to its populist radical right core ideology. However, with the exception of the 1989 European election, the party has never been able to top the 5 percent hurdle in nationwide elections.

Belgium is home to two populist radical right parties, both strongly influenced by the French FN. The Front national (Belge) (National Front (Belgian), FNb) is the populist radical right in the French-speaking part of the country, contesting elections in Brussels and Wallonia (e.g. Coffé 2005; Alaluf 1998). Founded in 1985, it copied the name and logo from its successful French brother. This notwithstanding, the FNb is in many ways the opposite of the FN: it has no party organization to speak of and its leader, Daniel Féret, lacks the charisma of Le Pen. To the degree that the party has a developed ideology, it is populist radical right, with a nativism driven far more by xenophobia than Belgian state nationalism. Over the years the FNb has seen many splits, including the Front nouveau de Belgique (New Front of Belgium, FNB), another populist radical right party in Brussels and Wallonia.

In the Dutch-speaking part of Flanders, the Vlaams Belang (VB) is in many ways the antithesis of the FNb. It originated in 1978 as Vlaams Blok, an electoral cartel of two radical splits of the nationalist VU, and continues its radical push for Flemish independence against the Belgian state. After its beginning as an old-style radical right party, with some elitist elements, the VB developed into a well-organized populist radical right party in the 1980s, under the impetus of young leaders like Gerolf Annemans, Filip Dewinter and Frank Vanhecke (e.g. Mudde 2000a; Spruyt 1995). Convicted for inciting racial hatred in 2004, the party quickly changed its name, but so far not its ideology (e.g. Erk 2005).

In Denmark the populist radical right Dansk Folkeparti (DFP) is in many ways a special party. First of all, it is one of the few splits that have been able to fully overshadow its mother party. Second, the DFP was founded and is still led by a woman, Pia Kjærsgaard (see also chapter 4). Third, because of the Danish tradition of minority government, the DFP is one of the few populist radical right parties that are not formally part of the government, but that does officially weigh heavily on it. From the outset the party has been unequivocally populist radical right, despite keeping its distance from similar parties like the FN and VB (e.g. Rydgren 2004b; Hasselbach 2002; Widfeldt 2000).

While the usual suspects in Western Europe will have been well known to most readers, the situation in Eastern Europe might be less familiar. Given the few comparative sources on the populist radical right in postcommunist Europe (e.g. Mudde 2005a, 2000b; Minkenberg 2002b; Ramet 1999a), it seems a bit presumptuous to speak of "usual suspects" in this respect. This notwithstanding, all parties discussed below are identified by most authors and experts in the field as being unequivocally part of what is usually called the radical or extreme right.

The Croatian Hrvatska stranka prava (HSP) was founded in 1990 by former dissident Dobroslav Paraga and a group of associates living in- and outside of Croatia (e.g. Irvine 1997; Zakošek 1994). It presented itself as the direct continuation of the original HSP of Ante Starčević, founded in 1861. Starčević's ideal of an independent Great Croatian state (including Bosnia-Herzegovina) had also inspired Ante Pavelič, the leader of the infamous *Ustaša* state (the fascist Croat puppet state during the Second World War). Initially, the "new" HSP moved between the populist radical right and the extreme right, in part because of the activities of its paramilitary arm, the Hrvatske obrambene snage (Croatian Defence Force, HOS). Under pressure from the Tuđman regime in 1992, the HSP was forced to moderate its actions and ideology and split: the pro-Tuđman

Table 2.1 *Main populist radical right parties in contemporary Europe*

Country	– Party	High Score (Year)[a]
Austria	– Freiheitliche Partei Österreichs (FPÖ)	26.9 (1999)
Belgium	– Front national (Belge) (FNb)	6.9 (1995)
	– Vlaams Belang (VB)	16.8 (2003)
Croatia	– Hrvatska stranka prava (HSP)	6.8 (1992)
Denmark	– Dansk Folkeparti (DFP)	13.2 (2005)
France	– Front national (FN)	14.9 (1997)
Germany	– Die Republikaner (REP	2.1 (1990)[b]
Hungary	– Magyar Igazság és Élet Pártja (MIÉP)	5.5 (1998)
Poland	– Liga Polskich Rodzin (LPR)	8.0 (2005)
Romania	– Partidul România Mare (PRM)	19.5 (2000)
Russia	– Liberal'no-demokraticheskoi partii Rossii (LDPR)	22.9 (1993)
Slovakia	– Slovenská národná strana (SNS)	11.7 (2006)

Notes: [a] These are the national results in elections for (the lower house of) the parliament. In the case of the two Belgian parties this obscures their real strength, as they only contest national elections in certain parts of the country.
[b] The REP gained 7.1% in the (nationwide) European election of 1989.

faction of Ante Djapic got the official right to the party name, while the faction of the original leader founded the HSP-1861. In the end, both parties moderated their discourse somewhat, but still remained firmly within the populist radical right. But while the HSP was able to continue its parliamentary presence, although mainly through electoral coalitions with nonpopulist radical right parties, the HSP-1861 disappeared into political oblivion.

The Hungarian Magyar Igazság és Élet Pártja (MIÉP) was founded by István Csurka, a well-known populist playwright under communism and one of the founders and vice-presidents of the Magyar Demokrata Fórum (Hungarian Democratic Forum, MDF), the main opposition party at the end of the communist era and the clear winner of the first election in postcommunist Hungary (e.g. Bernáth *et al.* 2005; Szôcs 1998). After years of incidents, including various anti-Semitic statements and a challenge to the moderate MDF leadership, Csurka and several of his followers were expelled in 1993 and founded the MIÉP. The new party is unequivocally populist radical right, even if it does not have a particularly modern image and seems stuck in classic Hungarian radical right issues such as anti-Semitism and irredentism (Greater Hungary).

For a long time, ambitious Polish radical right politicians operated mainly within broader nationalist and right-wing electoral coalitions, such as the Akcja Wyborcza Solidarnošč (Solidarity Electoral Action, AWS). Shortly before the 2001 parliamentary election, some AWS backbenchers founded the Liga Polskich Rodzin (LPR), which gained a surprising 8 percent of the votes (e.g. Kostrzębski 2005; Pankowski & Kornak 2005). Its initial election results were to a large extent the result of strong support from Father Tadeusz Rydzyk and his influential Catholic nationalist Radio Maryja (Maria) media empire. However, in recent years the LPR, a populist radical right party that combines Polish nativism with orthodox Catholicism, has been able to consolidate its electoral success, despite only lukewarm support by Rydzyk. In 2006, after several months of supporting the minority government of the national conservative Prawo i Sprawiedliwošč (Law and Justice Party, PiS), the LPR joined a coalition government with PiS and the populist Samoobrona Rzeczypospolitej Polski (Self-Defense of the Polish Republic), despite internal divisions.

One of the oldest and most successful populist radical right parties in Eastern Europe is the Partidul România Mare (PRM), founded in 1991 as the political arm of the România Mare magazine (e.g. Andreescu 2005; Shafir 2001, 2000). From the beginning the party has been led by the erratic and flamboyant Corneliu Vadim Tudor, who gained a shocking 30 percent of the votes in the second round of the 2000 presidential elections. The PRM is one of the more extreme populist radical right parties, having been a key player in the *coup d'état* of some radical miners in 1999. Its discourse regularly crosses into the realm of antidemocracy and racism, even if the core ideology remains within (nominally) democratic boundaries. Authoritarianism has become increasingly central in the election campaigns of the PRM and its leader, "Vadim the Righteous."[6]

Russia is home to undoubtedly the most eclectic and erratic of all populist radical right parties, the ill-named Liberal Democratic Party of Russia (LDPR).[7] This is largely because of Vladimir Zhirinovsky, the democratically elected dictator of the party, who has been described in such unflattering terms as "political clown" (Wilkiewicz 2003: 173) and "buffoon" (Service 1998: 180). Notwithstanding the erratic behavior and bizarre statements of party leader Zhirinovsky,[8] most analysts agree that the core ideology of the LDPR has remained relatively stable and populist

---

[6] In 2005 Tudor briefly stepped back as party leader and the party added the term "popular" to its name, becoming the Partidul Popular România Mare (Greater Romania Popular Party), in a feeble attempt to gain membership of the European People's Party (EPP).

[7] The LDPR was founded as the Liberal Democratic Party of the Soviet Union in 1989 and changed its name after the demise of the Soviet Union.

[8] One author has described Zhirinovsky as "part fascist, part communist, part liberal, part imperialist, part fantasist" (e.g. Service 1998: 196). Zhirinovsky himself has claimed, among many other things: "I shall not be linked to an ideological trend and I shall remain faithful to my voters" (Williams & Hanson 1999: 276).

radical right (e.g. Shenfield 2001; Service 1998; Umland 1997b). While the boundaries of its preferred state have changed over time, Russian nativism, authoritarianism and populism have always been core features of the party ideology.

Slovakia is one of the few countries where the populist radical right has not only made it into government, but has even come out of government with additional votes. The Slovenská národná strana (Slovak National Party, SNS) was founded in postcommunist Czechoslovakia in April 1990. From the outset the party claimed to be the successor to the historical SNS (1871–1938), a nationalist party that later formed a coalition with the pro-fascist Hlinkova Slovenská ludová strana (Hlinka's Slovak People's Party), the ruling party in the clerico-fascist Slovak State of the Second World War (e.g. Fried 1997; Kirschbaum 1996; Strahn & Daniel 1994). The party's historical ties were ambiguous, however, as internal divisions led it to claim the tradition of other pre-communist parties as well (i.e. the historical SNS and the national-conservative Agrarian Party).

After Slovakia achieved national independence, internal problems increasingly divided the party, culminating in a split in 1993. When the conservatives left and formed the Demokratická únia (Democratic Union), the SNS became a full-fledged populist radical right party. Under new leader Ján Slota it became a junior party in the third Měciar coalition (1994–98), almost doubling its electoral support along the way. However, relegated to the opposition benches because of the losses of its coalition partners, the SNS soon got entangled in a vicious leadership struggle between chairman Ján Slota and vice-chairwoman Anna Malíková. The party's internal strife led to splits and mergers, but most notably perhaps, to loss of parliamentary representation in 2002. However, after long negotiations a truce was signed between the two leaders and in the 2006 parliamentary elections the SNS reentered parliament with a stunning 11.7 percent of the vote.

2.4   Nonpopulist radical right parties

Having identified the most important populist radical right parties among the usual suspects, it is now time to turn our attention to those parties that are not included in the populist radical right party family. The discussion is limited mostly to political parties that are mentioned regularly in relation to the "extreme right" (and related terms), but some unsuspected parties will be discussed as well, mostly to clarify the boundaries between party families. As far as possible, the aim is not only to argue why these parties are not populist radical right, but also to determine their party family. In most cases the party belongs to one of the families that border and partly overlap the populist radical right, as already discussed at a more general level in the previous chapter.

2.4.1   Nonradical right populists

Most usual suspects that are excluded from the populist radical right party family belong to the larger and more diffuse category of populist parties. Two subgroups are most relevant in this respect: social populists and neoliberal populists. The latter category is most closely related to the populist radical right; together they form the loose category of right-wing populism. The core ideology of neoliberal populism, as defined in the previous chapter, is the combination of primarily economic liberalism and populism.

A good if somewhat extreme example of a neoliberal populist party is the Norwegian Fremskrittspartiet (FRP), whose status has always been debated within the field. Founded in 1973 as the Anders Lange Parti til sterk nedsettelse av skatter, avgifter og offentlige inngrep (Anders Lange Party for a Strong Reduction of Taxes, Duties and Public Intervention), the party changed its name a few years after the death of its founder. Under the leadership of Carl Ivar Hagen, the FRP has been erratic in its electoral results as well as its ideological positions. The party began as an antitax party, morphed into a neoliberal party in the 1980s, and then embraced an opportunistic populism in the 1990s (e.g. Lorenz 2003).[9] Notwithstanding the protean nature of the FRP, it is quite clear that nativism does not constitute part of its core ideology.[10] Despite its occasional highly xenophobic campaigns, or its more recent defense of welfare chauvinism, the FRP is best classified as a neoliberal populist party.

Among the parties most often confused with the populist radical right, the following parties are most accurately categorized as neoliberal populist: the Bulgarian Balgarski biznes blok (Bulgarian Business Bloc, BBB), the Danish Fremskridtspartiet (Progress Party, FPd), the Dutch Lijst Pim Fortuyn (LPF), the German Schill-Partei and Partei Rechtsstaatlicher Offensive (Constitutional Offensive Party, PRO), the Italian Forza Italia (Go Italy, FI), the Polish Unia Polityki Realnej (Union

---

[9] Various authors have argued that opportunism is a key feature of (neoliberal) populist parties (e.g. Decker 2003; Lorenz 2003; Pissowotzki 2003; Mény & Surel 2002a). As we define party families exclusively on the basis of ideology, strategic features (however important for certain parties) cannot be considered in the classification.

[10] In fact, at various times in the existence of the FRP there have been struggles between nativists and the party leadership, notably Hagen, which mostly led to the nativists either leaving the party voluntarily or being expelled forcefully (e.g. Decker 2004: 106–7).

for Real Politics, UPR), the Swedish Ny Demokrati (New Democracy, ND), and the Swiss Schweizer Autopartei/Parti Suisse des automobilistes (Swiss Car Party, AP).[11] Though most of these parties have been linked to xenophobic campaigns, nativism is not central to their ideology.[12] Moreover, their xenophobic rhetoric is primarily informed by their liberalism.[13]

Finally, some parties are best classified as social populists. In the core, social populism combines socialism and populism, and is thus a form of left-wing populism rather than right-wing. One of the best-known examples of a social populist party is the Greek Panellinio Sosialistiko Kinima (Panhellenic Socialist Movement, PASOK), at least under the leadership of Andreas Papandreou (e.g. Sotiropoulos 1996; Spourdalakis 1988). Among the more relevant contemporary representatives of this party group we find the Dutch Socialistische Partij (Socialist Party, SP), the German Die Linke. PDS (The Left.PDS), and the Scottish Socialist Party (SSP) (e.g. March & Mudde 2005).[14]

A party that seems better classified as social populist than populist radical right is the Polish Samoobrona Rzeczypospolitej Polski. Founded in 1992, Samoobrona exists as both a political party and a (farmers') trade union annex social movement (e.g. Krok-Paszkowska 2003; Wilkiewicz 2003). Its diffuse ideological party program and complex organizational structure, as well as differences in the use of terminology between East and West, make any consensus on labeling the party impossible. The one thing most experts agree upon is that Samoobrona is a populist party; whether it is left- or right-wing is a matter of great dispute, however (Schuster 2005). More detailed and structured analysis of the party ideology is needed, but for the moment Samoobrona is best excluded from the populist radical right party family. Similarly, the Romanian Partidul

---

[11] It would be going too far to argue all these cases individually. For detailed analyses of the (core) ideologies of these parties, see Mitev (1997) on the BBB Gooskens (1994) on the FPd; Mudde (2007) and Lucardie & Voerman (2002) on the LPF; Decker (2003) and Hartleb (2004) on Schill and the PRO; Grassi & Rensmann (2005) and Pissowotzki (2003) on the FI; Pankowski & Kornak (2005) on the UPR; Taggart (1996) and Westlind (1996) on the ND; and Altermatt & Furrer (1994) on the AP.

[12] In this respect, Decker's (2004: 219–20) distinction between "*opponents* to" and "*sceptics* of*" multicultural society can be useful, with the populist radical right belonging to the first category and the neoliberal populists to the second.

[13] Good examples are the Islamophobic remarks of Pim Fortuyn and Silvio Berlusconi, who have both criticized Islam (interpreted as Islamic fundamentalism) as being fundamentally opposed to liberal democracy; see Akkerman (2005) and Pissowotzki (2003), respectively.

[14] Somewhat surprisingly, the SP has been one of the first Dutch parties to militate against immigration, but on the basis of socialist rather than nativist grounds, i.e. to protect the Dutch workers against capitalist oppression. Similarly, the SSP has supported Scottish independence because the party believes this increases the chances for a socialist Scotland (which remains just a first step towards global socialism).

Socialist al Muncii (Socialist Labor Party, PSM) is better labeled social populist, despite its occasional nativist discourse (e.g. Shafir 2000).

2.4.2 Nonpopulist right

This study draws a clear line between populist radical right parties and various forms of the extreme right, including neofascism and neo-Nazism. Most importantly, extreme right parties are undemocratic, and often elitist, whereas populist radical right parties are (nominally) democratic and populist. This means the exclusion of many of the parties that Ignazi has called "traditional" (2003) or "old" (1992) extreme right, such as the Austrian Nationaldemokratische Partei (National Democratic Party, NDP), the German NPD, or the Greek Ethniki Politiki Enosis (National Political Union, EPEN) – but not others, which do meet the definition of populist radical right, such as the British National Party (BNP) and the Dutch Centrumpartij '86 (CP'86).[15]

In Eastern Europe various smaller organizations are more accurately defined as extreme right. This includes political parties like the Czech Pravá Alternativa (Right Alternative), the Polish Narodowe Odrodzenie Polski (National Rebirth of Poland, NOP), the Romanian Miscarea pentru România (Movement for Romania), the Russian Russkoe natsionalnoe edinstvo (Russian National Unity, RNE) and Natsionalbolshevistskaya partiya (National Bolshevik Party, NBP), and the Ukrainian Ukrainska natsionalna assembleya–Ukrainska natsionalna samooborona (Ukrainian National Assembly–Ukrainian People's Self-Defense, UNA-UNSO).[16]

There are also some parties that are radical right but not populist. While this combination used to be quite common, the experience of semi-permanent opposition and the current populist *Zeitgeist* (Mudde 2004) have brought most radical right parties to adopt populism. Good examples of such transformations are the Belgian VB and the French FN, which both originated as nonpopulist radical right parties in the 1970s.

One of the few relevant contemporary examples of a radical right party that is not populist is the Turkish Milliyetçi Hareket Partisi (Nationalist Action Party, MHP). Founded in 1965 as the Cumhuriyetçi Köylü

---

[15] Again, these decisions are made on the basis of various primary and secondary sources and cannot be discussed here in detail. As an indication, the following literature can be mentioned: Mudde (1995b) on the NDP, Flemming (2004) and Mudde (1995b) on the NPD, Kolovos (2003) on EPEN, Eatwell (2000) on the BNP, and Mudde (2000a) on the CP'86.

[16] All extreme right political parties are marginal in both electoral and political terms. On the post-Soviet parties, see, among others, Umland (2005), Shenfield (2001) and Solchanyk (1999); on the Central and East European parties, see the various country chapters in Mudde (2005a) and Ramet (1999a).

Millet Partisi (Republican Peasant National Party), it changed its name in 1969 and remained relatively marginal until its surprise achievement of 18 percent in the 1999 parliamentary election and the consequent stint in government (e.g. Yavuz 2002; Aras & Bacik 2000). While the core ideology of the MHP includes both authoritarianism and nativism, the party does not simply follow the *vox populi*. In fact, it has strong elitist and statist beliefs: "The MHP always sides with the state when there is a tension between state and society" (Yavuz 2002: 211).

2.4.3   Conservatives

Conservatism has many permutations, some closer to the populist radical right than others. The neoconservatism that developed in Britain and the US in the 1980s in particular has been linked to the populist radical right (e.g. Ignazi 1992). Indeed, Kitschelt and McGann's famous "winning formula" (1995) better defines neoconservatism than the (populist) radical right. Crucially, while the two share authoritarianism and a concern for the national interest, nativism and populism are not core features of conservatism, while neoliberal economics is not a core feature of the populist radical right.

The obvious differences between the two political ideologies notwithstanding, much confusion remains with regard to various individual parties. For example, in an article on "the new populism," Ian Hall and Magali Perrault (2000) collapse some usual populist radical right suspects, like the Austrian FPÖ and the Slovak SNS, together with parties that are normally labeled conservative (liberal), such as the Czech Občanská demokratická strana (Civic Democratic Party, ODS) and the Hungarian FIDESZ-MPS. This is not completely without reason, as several authors have pointed out nativist and populist statements by leading members of these latter parties (e.g. Segert 2005a; Hanley 2004; Kiss 2002). Still, while populist radical right sentiments at times play an important role in electoral campaigns of some conservative (liberal) parties, they do not constitute their core ideology. Consequently, parties like the British Conservative Party, the Czech ODS, and the Dutch Volkspartij voor Vrijheid en Democratie (People's Party for Freedom and Democracy, VVD) are excluded from the populist radical right party family.

2.4.4   Ethnoregionalists

As we have seen in the previous chapter, the ethnoregionalist party family is quite diffuse in terms of the terminology used to designate criteria for membership and the resulting variety of parties it includes. While exclusion of some populist radical right parties from this family is pretty straightforward, in other cases the differences are far less obvious and significant. The key distinction within this diffuse party family is between the regionalists and the nationalists (see 1.6.2).

Regionalists can be clearly distinguished from nationalists (including the populist radical right) given the concern of the former group with autonomy for a region within a larger state structure. Consequently, various political parties can be excluded from the populist radical right party family: notably those parties that primarily call for regional autonomy to increase the power of an ethnic minority, such as the Dutch Frysk nasjonale partij (Frisian National Party), the Polish Ruch Autonomii Slaska (Movement for Silesian Autonomy), the Slovak Magyar Koalíció Pártja-Strana madarskej koalície (Party of Hungarian Coalition), and the Spanish Convergència u Unió (Convergence and Union).

The second distinction between "nationalists" and the populist radical right is more difficult. Do parties like the pan-Irish Sinn Féin (We Ourselves, SF) and the Spanish Herri Batasuna (People Unity, HB) belong in a different party family than, say, the Italian LN and the Belgian VB? The former parties would definitely claim so, even though substantial sympathy exists for them within the latter parties. Most authors seem to share the opinion that the parties should not be grouped together, as they do not even explicitly address their omission of parties like the SF and HB from the populist radical right.

The separation of these parties from the populist radical right seems mainly based on the socioeconomic left–right distinction: the "nationalist" parties are believed to be on the left, favoring strong state intervention (including nationalizations and elaborate welfare policies), whereas the populist radical right are said to be on the right, defending a dominant market model (i.e. neoliberalism). This distinction is highly overstated: not all nationalist parties are socioeconomically on the left, while many populist radical right parties are not really on the right. Moreover, it separates nationalist parties on the basis of a secondary aspect of their party ideology (see chapter 5).

Obviously, not all nationalists are populist radical rightists. Some nationalist parties are not fundamentally populist, such as the Belgian Nieuw-Vlaamse Alliantie (New-Flemish Alliance) or the Albanian monarchist Partia Lëvizja e Legalitetit (Movement of Legality Party). In fact, some self-proclaimed nationalist parties are not even truly nationalist. For example, the Scottish National Party (SNP) is better described as separatist than as nationalist. In the words of the party chronicler, "[s]elf-government/independence for Scotland has always been its fundamental aim not self-government/independence for Scots" (Lynch 2002:

Table 2.2 *Some borderline parties that are* not *populist radical right*

| Party name | Core populist radical right ideological features* | | | |
	nationalism	xenophobia	authoritarianism	populism
AP			+	+
FRP			(−)	+
LPF		(+)	(−)	+
MHP	+	+	+	(−)
NPD	+	+	+	(−)
N-VA	+		(+)	
Samoobrona			+	+
Schill/PRO		(+)	+	+
SF	+		+	+
VVD			+	

Note: *+ = core, (+) = present, not core, (−) = opposite present, but not core
For the sake of clarity, the separate features of nationalism and xenophobia, rather than the integrated feature of nativism, are included here (although they are not identical).

4).[17] This has also become true for Plaid Cymru (The Party of Wales), the main political representative of Welsh nationalism (e.g. Christiansen 1998; McAllister 1998).

Most problematic is the categorization of the SF, the political arm of the terrorist Irish Republican Army (IRA), which contests elections both in the Republic of Ireland and in (British) Northern Ireland (e.g. Maillot 2004; Feeney 2002). SF has traditionally been strongly nationalist, populist, and authoritarian – the latter both ideologically, in terms of law and order, and practically, in support for IRA actions and structure.[18] The party does not seem to be xenophobic, although nativist strands are present within the organization (mostly against English and Protestants). Paradoxically, SF presents an extremely open position regarding immigrants, notably in its highly pro-multicultural policy paper *Many Voices One Country: Cherishing All the Children of the Nation Equally. Towards an Anti-Racist Ireland* (SF 2001). As this makes the SF nationalist but not nativist, the party will not be included in the category of the populist radical right, despite its satisfaction of many other criteria.

[17] Consequently, the SNP openly campaigns for an independent yet multicultural Scotland. For example, party leader John Swinney said in his 2003 address to the National Council: "I take pride in the SNP's belief in a multicultural, inclusive Scotland."
[18] There are also striking parallels with the populist radical right in the fierce antidrug campaigns of the SF (see Maillot 2004: 90–4).

2.5   Residual cases

Having classified the so-called usual suspects, largely either as populist radical right or as neoliberal populist, two important categories of residual parties remain to be discussed: unusual suspects and borderline cases. The former are political parties not normally associated with the populist radical right, or that do not feature commonly with usual suspects like the FN and FPÖ in the literature, but that do hold a populist radical right core ideology. In the first subsection we will identify a few key cases, which actually belong(ed) to the most relevant populist radical right parties in Europe.

Borderline cases are political parties that defy unequivocal classification in terms of the populist radical right. This is not so much the result of flaws in the method of classification chosen, but rather reflects the various problems involved in studying political parties (see 2.2.4). Some parties are coalitions of highly diverse ideological factions, which fight over party domination with different levels of success over time. In other parties, significant discrepancies exist between the externally oriented party discourse, and sometimes even implemented policies, and the core ideology of the internally oriented literature. Finally, some parties have been developing in a populist radical right direction over the past decade or so, but cannot yet be considered full-fledged populist radical right parties.

2.5.1   Unusual suspects

While many authors have described Eastern Europe as a hotbed of nationalism in the early postcommunist years (e.g. Bogdanor 1995; Fischer-Galati 1993), very few have linked it explicitly to the radical right (e.g. Tismaneanu 1998). Consequently, while state politics from the Baltics to the Balkans were described as authoritarian, nativist and populist, the qualification "radical right" was normally limited to the more marginal usual suspects (e.g. Ramet 1999a). Unfortunately, few empirical studies of party ideologies at that time are available, so it is hard to classify the leading parties of that period unequivocally. This notwithstanding, it does not seem far-fetched to argue that at least some Eastern European parties, which are nonradical now, started out as populist radical right.

This was probably most pronounced in the Baltic states, specifically in Estonia and Latvia. Both newly independent states started their process of state- and nation-building confronted with a huge Russian-speaking population within their borders and a hostile Russian state just beyond them (see further 6.2.2). Particularly in the early 1990s this led to polarization between a self-conscious, nativist Estonian/Latvian parties block, on the one hand, and a marginalized and nostalgic Russophone parties block, on the other. The nativist idea of a "Latvian Latvia," combined with "anticolonization" rhetoric, was common to virtually all Latvian parties, most notably the Latvijas Nacionālās neatkarības kutības (Latvian National Independence Movement, LNNK) and the Tēvzeme un Brīvībai (Fatherland and Freedom, TB), which later merged (see Kalnina 1998). However, from the mid 1990s onward nativism became less pronounced and in both countries the main party discourses and policies slowly but steadily accepted a multicultural state (e.g. Kelley 2004).

A similar development could be noted in Yugoslavia and its main components, Serbia and Croatia. One of the first openly nativist parties in Serbia was the Srpski pokret obnove (Serbian Renewal Movement, SPO) of the later Foreign Minister Vuk Drašković. The SPO was founded in 1990 as a populist radical right party struggling for a Serbian Greater Serbia. Drašković was a fierce critic of Slobodan Milošević, whom he accused of being too soft on anti-Serbian forces (i.e. Albanian, Croatian and Slovene separatists). As a consequence of the various wars and the increased repression by the Milošević regime, Drašković moderated his authoritarian and nativist positions. While the SPO still voices nationalist and populist positions at times, these features have lost their prominence since the party became part of the pro-Western coalition after the fall of Milošević in 2000 (e.g. Bieber 2005).

Despite its dubious reputation, and well-documented links to the extreme and radical right, the Croatian Hrvatska demokratska zajed (Croatian Democratic Movement, HDZ) is seldom classified as populist radical right. It has been more common to describe the HDZ as a conservative nationalist umbrella party with an "extreme right faction" (e.g. Grdešič 1999; Irvine 1997; Zakošek 1994). But analyses of the official party literature show that it was fundamentally a populist radical right party; this was also evident in the actions of its single-party governments (e.g. Maleševič 2002; Uzelak 1998).[19] Since the death of its founder, the late President Franjo Tuđman, and the party's consequent relegation to the opposition in 2000, the HDZ seems to have transformed into a truly conservative party (e.g. Buric 2002).

---

[19] Indeed, in terms of its revisionist views on the period of the Second World War, the HDZ even closely resembles some extreme right organizations (e.g. Drakulic 2002; Goldstein & Goldstein 2002; Milentijevic 1994).

This process was strengthened by several expulsions and splits of radical individuals and factions, among them a group around Miroslav Tuđman, whose new party, Hrvatski istinski preporod (Croatian Integrity and Prosperity), remains loyal to the populist radical right legacy of the HDZ of his father. The Hrvatska demokratska zajednica Bosne i Hercegovine, originally the Bosnian branch of the party, has become more independent and radical than its Croatian mother party since the death of Tuđman (see Kasch 2002). Both parties are therefore (still) included in the populist radical right party family.

A striking, unusual case is the Democratic Unionist Party (DUP) of the infamous Reverend Ian Paisley, the nemesis of SF in Northern Ireland. Founded in 1971, the DUP is to a large extent *sui generis*: while having only a regionalist basis, contesting elections only in Northern Ireland (or Ulster), its nativism is not restricted to this regional territory. The DUP defends a British nationalism that is virulently xenophobic (notably against Catholics, but also against homosexuals and other "deviants"). Furthermore it is fundamentally authoritarian and populist. However, unlike most other populist radical right parties in Europe, the DUP is also religious fundamentalist. Its fundamentalist Protestantism makes the party somewhat similar to the Christian Right in the US, rather than to the orthodox Catholic LPR in Poland.

2.5.2   Borderline cases

In Hungary the radical right originated within the broader national conservative anticommunist movement MDF (see 2.3). However, even after the expulsion of the Csurka-group and the consequent foundation of MIÉP, populist radical right forces remained active within the national conservative camp. Since the late 1990s the previously liberal FIDESz-MPS has filled the space left by the imploded MDF, a process accompanied by increasing populist radical right rhetoric. While the boundaries between ideology and strategy have become more and more blurred (e.g. Bayer 2005), in line with the dominant literature FIDESz-MPS will still be regarded as essentially (national) conservative for the moment (e.g. Enyedi 2005; Oltay 2003).

For obvious reasons, postwar Italy has always been linked to strong "extreme right" parties. According to Ignazi (1992), the MSI was the defining party of the whole "extreme right" party family before the 1980s. While this might be true, the party very much stood for an old-fashioned extreme right, which was both antidemocratic and elitist. Even if one focuses more on the practice of the party, i.e. acceptance of democratic practice, it is at best a radical right party, lacking the core feature of populism.[20] The MSI is therefore not included in the populist radical right party family.

The Alleanza nazionale (National Alliance, AN), MSI's main legal successor, is similarly excluded from the populist radical right family but for different reasons. After some initial ambivalence, the AN transformed itself into a conservative party, in which neither nativism nor populism is prominent (e.g. Ignazi 2005; Tarchi 2003; Griffin 1996). This is not the case for the MS-FT, which claims to have remained loyal to the "fascist heritage" of the MSI but is in fact both nativist and populist. The MS-FT is therefore included in the populist radical right party family.

The classification of the Lega Nord (LN), which originated in 1991 as a coalition of regionalist "leagues" in the north of Italy (e.g. Tarchi 2002; Cento Bull & Gilbert 2001; Betz 1998; Visentini 1993), is more contested and problematic. Many scholars have included the party (initially) in the "(ethno)regionalist" rather than the "extreme right" party family (e.g. Hix & Lord 1997; Gallagher et al. 1995; Ignazi 1992). Moreover, while populism has always been a core feature of the LN and its dominant leader Umberto Bossi, authoritarianism and nativism have not. As some skeptical observers have noted, "[t]he Lega is too politically opportunistic to be ideologically coherent, hence its relatively chaotic ideological references" (Fieschi et al. 1996: 241).

The League started out as a fairly liberal party, both in terms of economics and rights, but became increasingly authoritarian in the 1990s. And while nativism has been present throughout its existence,[21] the party has often been torn between regionalism and nationalism. In conclusion, the LN might not (always) be a perfect example of the populist radical right, but it is too similar to be excluded from the party family.

The same cannot be argued for the Lega dei Ticinesi (League of Ticino, LdT), which contests elections in the Italian-speaking canton of Ticino in Switzerland (e.g. Albertazzi 2006). Although this one-man party, built around the "president for life" Giuliano Bignasca, clearly tried to skim off the success of its Italian neighbors to the south, the LdT differs from the LN in some important aspects. Most notably, the LdT has steadily maintained a regionalist stance, never aspiring to independence for the Italian Swiss. In addition, unlike the LN the Swiss League is not authoritarian. In the words of one of its foremost experts, Daniele Albertazzi, "on issues

---

[20] In his more recent work, Ignazi (2003) has qualified his thesis, labeling the MSI as the defining party of only one subtype of extreme right parties, the traditional.

[21] Originally, the LN directed its nativist sentiments mainly against *terroni*, which literally means "those of the land," a derogatory term for people from the south of Italy. In the mid 1990s the party also started targeting immigrants, and became the most vocal anti-immigrant party in Italy.

such as homosexuality, women's rights and alternative lifestyles, the LDT has little in common with the radical right, with which it is often confused" (2006: 137). The LdT will therefore be excluded from the group of populist radical right parties.

The Serbian Socijalisticka partija Srbije (Socialist Party of Serbia, SPS) is sometimes linked to the populist radical right, mostly because of the actions and speeches of its (former) party leader, Slobodan Milošević (e.g. Markotich 2000). The conclusions to be drawn from the behavior of Milošević, however, are open to debate. Looking at his political career, Milošević seems better classified as a "radical opportunist" than a "radical nationalist" (Stojanović 2003: 60).[22] Furthermore, there is a methodological problem with accepting the party's designation as populist radical right. Parties are classified here exclusively on the basis of their core ideology, which in this case is best understood as social populist (e.g. Bieber 2005). Thus, the SPS is not included in the populist radical right party family.

A similar conclusion should be drawn with regard to the Slovak Hnutie za demokratickč Slovensko (HZDS)[23] and its party leader Vladimír Mečiar. While some authors have classified this party as part of the populist radical right family (e.g. Kneuer 2005), this overstates both the importance of certain party figures and speeches, and the coherence of the party and its ideology. Despite attempts to develop an integrated political party with a consistent ideology, the HZDS has always remained a diffuse and opportunistic alliance of various factions, including a populist radical right one, under the towering dominance of party leader Mečiar (e.g. Thanei 2002; Haughton 2001).

The most problematic party to classify is the Schweizerische Volkspartei–Union démocratique du centre (SVP), which originated as an agrarian party in the German Protestant cantons of Switzerland. In recent decades the SVP has changed in terms of both its ideological profile and its electoral and geographical support basis. However, as Swiss politics is first and foremost cantonal, it is not always easy to speak of truly national parties (e.g. Kriesi 1998). In theory, and sometimes even in practice, political parties can hold very distinct ideologies in different cantons.

Ideological diffusion at the cantonal level has existed within the SVP for much of the 1980s and 1990s (e.g. Kriesi et al. 2005a; Altermatt

---

[22] In the words of Takis Pappas, "Milošević must be seen as a political entrepreneur who recognized the importance of 'cultural identity' to the Serbian nation and used it as a political resource in his bid for power" (2005: 193).

[23] In 2003 the HZDS added the prefix Ludová strana (People's Party), becoming the LS-HZDS.

& Skenderovic 1999). There are two very important cantonal branches in Switzerland in general, and within the SVP in particular: Berne and Zurich. In the canton of Berne, the capital of Switzerland, the SVP has always been a centrist governmental party with a strong liberal character. In sharp contrast, in the financially and economically strong canton of Zurich, the party has developed a more conservative and oppositional character since the mid 1970s, particularly under the leadership of Christoph Blocher. During the 1990s the Zurich branch slowly but steadily took over the national SVP, in part through the founding of various new cantonal branches loyal to Blocher (see Skenderovic 2005).

For decades the SVP has been considered as either an agrarian/center party (e.g. Gallagher *et al.* 2001; Müller-Rommel 1993) or a conservative (liberal) party (e.g. Helms 1997). Still, there is no doubt that the party has radicalized under the leadership of Blocher. The main question today seems to be whether the SVP is (neo or national) conservative, as some scholars and the party itself claim (e.g. Hennecke 2003), or populist radical right, as the new consensus asserts (e.g. Geden 2005; Betz 2004; Husbands 2000). Although classification has been hindered by the decentralized structure of Swiss politics, and the prominent position of the Berne faction, at least since 2005 the SVP has to be put in the category of the populist radical right. With the entrance of Blocher into the Swiss government that year, the moderate Berne faction lost its ability to counterbalance the populist radical right rest of the party (see, in particular, Skenderovic 2005).

2.6   Conclusion

Many debates on the populist radical right party family base the often implicit classification of individual political parties on the age-old common wisdom: if it walks like a duck, talks like a duck, and looks like a duck, it is a duck. At the very least, this chapter should have raised serious doubts about this "method." Despite the logistical and conceptual difficulties it entails, party family scholars will have to take the issue of categorization and classification more seriously. This chapter has taken a first step by identifying the best data and method to employ, and by presenting a provisional classification of most parties linked to this party family.

The classification of the usual suspects has led to some unexpected outcomes. To stay in the terminology of animal metaphors, we have found some wolves in sheep's clothing, i.e. populist radical right parties that are not recognized as such (e.g. DUP, HDZ), but even more sheep in wolves' clothing, i.e. nonpopulist radical right parties that are often perceived as populist radical right (e.g. AN, HZDS, LPF). Most of the latter belong to a separate, if somewhat overlapping, party family, that of neoliberal populism (e.g. FI, PRO, UPR). In addition, some parties within the conservative (e.g. FIDESZ-MPS, ODS, VVD) and (ethno)regionalist families (e.g. HB, SF) show striking similarities to the populist radical right, but are in essence, i.e. in their core ideology, not part of this party family.

Some remarkable observations can be made regarding the group of correctly classified populist radical right parties, too. First, several of the key parties did not originate as populist radical right; some started as clearly nonradical right (e.g. REP, SVP), as nonpopulist radical right (e.g. FN, VB), or as diffuse with a populist radical right faction (e.g. FPÖ, SNS). Second, a number of parties that originated as populist radical right have since transformed, mostly into conservative parties (e.g. HDZ, LNNK, SPO). This does not automatically mean that "the radical right has proven to be considerably more flexible and fluid than rigid classification schemes allow for" (Betz 1999: 305). Rather, it reminds us that classifications can only be valid temporarily, as political parties and ideologies can and sometimes do change over time.

This chapter has discussed only the most important and well-known parties. A more comprehensive list of populist radical right parties in contemporary Europe is presented in appendix A. In most cases only parties that have independently gained over 1 percent in the parliamentary elections at least once since the 1980s are included. In certain cases even smaller parties have been included, mostly because they will be referred to in the following chapters. Obviously, this list is very tentative, as much more work will have to be done on many individual parties to establish a correct and comprehensive classification of the whole populist radical right party family.

Part II

Issues

3   Who's afraid of . . . ?

> The Other lies at the heart of radical right politics, and for the radical right, which understands the world in terms of struggle, in terms of "us" versus "them," the Other is translated into "the Enemy."
>
> (Ramet 1999b: 4)

3.1   Introduction

Identity politics, of which the populist radical right is (just) one form, is always based upon an "us–them" distinction. To construct the native identity, one needs to delineate the boundaries with other identities, i.e. those of the nonnatives. In other words, to construct the *ingroup* ("us") one needs to construct the *outgoup(s)* ("them"). This process of ingroup–outgroup differentiation, which social psychologists and others have described as standard behavior in identity building (e.g. Brewer 1999; Tajfel 1982), has been said to be even more crucial to the populist radical right than to other actors engaged in identity politics (e.g. Geden 2005; Pelinka 2005).

Within the literature, various scholars have pointed out the dissimilarities between the ways the populist radical right differentiates between ingroup and outgroup(s) and the process of identity construction among, for example, Greens or gay and lesbian activists. First, populist radical rightists are believed to hold a Manichaean worldview: the world is divided into "good" and "bad" (e.g. Eatwell 2000; Ramet 1999b). Indeed, one of the key characteristics of populism is the dominance of morality (e.g. Mudde 2004; Taggart 2000). Consequently, the "us–them" division is transformed into a Schmittian friend–foe distinction in which the "Other" is demonized (e.g. Abts & Rummens 2005; Mouffe 1995; Gessenharter 1991).

Second, the populist radical right is said to define the ingroup mainly through the description of outgroups (e.g. Taggart 2002). In other words, whereas the defining features of the ingroup identity remain vague or unspecified, those of the "anti-figure" (Cohn 1971: xix) are described very clearly and explicitly. Hence, the ingroup is largely defined *ex negativo*, i.e. as the mirror image of the outgroups and their alleged characteristics. Consequently, a better understanding of the outgroups, or in the populist radical right's thinking the "enemies," is crucial to getting a better understanding of the worldview of the populist radical right.

In a comparative study of this scope it is hard to come up with a structure that allows for a coherent yet comprehensive presentation of the enemies of the populist radical right that goes beyond an endless list of the multitude of groups feared and hated by the various parties within this family in contemporary Europe. With some exceptions, most studies focus on only one group of enemies of the contemporary populist radical right party family, recent (non-European) immigrants. As far as other enemies are mentioned, they tend to be rather idiosyncratic, i.e. particular to that specific populist radical right party, for example Serbs for the HSP or Walloons for the VB.

As "every country has its own favorite enemy" (Von Beyme 1996: 438), each populist radical right party also sports its own particular list of enemies, largely dependent upon its national context and ideological particularities. In order to move beyond the idiosyncrasies of individual parties to establish a more general understanding of the prime characteristics and key role of enemies in the politics of the populist radical right, the chapter is structured in accordance with a *typology* of enemies applicable to the whole populist radical right party family. Within these categories, parties might include different *groups* of enemies. The next section presents this broad typology of enemies and presents examples and general characteristics of the four different types. The final section discusses three special groups of enemies and prejudices: Jews and anti-Semitism, Muslims and Islamophobia, and Roma (and Sinti) and Romophobia. Finally, in the conclusion, the description of the various groups and types of enemies is related to the self-definition of the ingroup, i.e. the "native."

3.2   A typology of enemies

For the populist radical right two categories are particularly important in terms of identity and politics: the nation and the state. These two define to a large extent who is and who is *not* "native." It thus makes sense to base a broad typology of enemies on membership in these two categories. This two-by-two table produces four types of enemies: (1) those within both the nation and the state; (2) those outside of the nation but within the state; (3) those within the nation but outside the state; and (4) those outside both the nation and the state (see table 3.1). Within

Table 3.1 *Typology of enemies*

	Nation	
State	*Within*	*Outside*
Within	(1)	(2)
Outside	(3)	(4)

each category, different groups of enemies are identified and feared on the basis of a few basic arguments and characteristics. The main aim of the following discussion is to describe these more general subgroups, rather than to lose ourselves in the details of the almost limitless singular enemies and arguments identified by the individual populist radical right parties.

Before we do this, however, it is important to emphasize that outgroups, like ingoups, are social constructs; in the famed terminology of Benedict Anderson (1983), they are "imagined." While the various enemies might refer to real existing groups, such as Muslims in Denmark or Hungarian-speakers in Romania, the characteristics of the groups will be stereotypical constructs. Consequently, some individuals who meet the objective criteria of an outgroup might be excluded from the category "enemy" on the basis of subjective criteria.[1] This also applies to ingroups: various leaders and heroes of strictly defined ingroups did not themselves meet the criteria of that ingroup (e.g. Hitler or Stalin).

3.2.1   Within the state, within the nation

The definition of enemies in this first category is based mainly on two of the three features of the populist radical right core ideology: nativism and populism. The key internal enemy of all populist radical right parties is "the elite," a broad and indeterminate amalgam of political, economic, and cultural actors. The national elite *is* criticized in both nativist and populist terms, i.e. as traitors to the nation and as corruptors of the people. In much of the propaganda of the parties, these two features are combined. For example, the Bulgarian Partija Ataka (Party Attack,

---

[1] Almost everyone who has had a conversation with people who openly espouse anti-immigrant sentiments will have noticed these inconsistencies. For example, someone will argue that all Turks have to leave the country because they are too lazy to work, but will exclude his colleague Ali. When confronted with the question why Ali, who is clearly (and objectively) Turkish, does not have to leave the country, he will argue that Ali is not a real Turk, as he is not lazy and he works.

Ataka) reduces the current situation in the country to a struggle between "national traitors" and "honorable Bulgarian patriots" (Segert 2005b), while the Romanian PRM uses the slogan "Sus Patria! Moarte Mafei!" (Up with the homeland! Down with the Mafia!), insinuating that the (other) politicians are both corrupt and antinational. In similar vein, Robert Kilroy-Silk launched his new Veritas party stating: "Our country is being stolen from us and we have never been asked for our permission . . . Elect me and a few more like me and I promise they will not get away with the lies again in the future" (*Yorkshire Post* 03/02/2005).

Various populist radical right parties make little distinction between the political and the economic elite, or in the unique language of the Ukrainian extreme right UNA-UNSO, the "bitch collaborators and goat democrats" (in Dymerskaya-Tsigelman & Finberg 1999: 5). The Russian LDPR describes the established politicians, referred to as "democrats" in quotation marks or "radical democrats" without quotation marks, as agents of the West who reap huge financial gains from selling out the natural riches of the country and who break the spirit of the nation by denouncing honest patriotism with accusations of fascism and imperialism (LDPR 1995). The latter argumentation is very similar to the attacks of German and Hungarian populist radical rightists on their elites, whom they accuse of using "re-education" (*Umerziehung*) to make Germans/Hungarians passive and self-hating (e.g. Bock 2002; Mudde 2000a; Gessenharter 1991).

In another theme of treachery, a broad coalition of elites is linked to the issue of immigration. Western European populist radical right parties are vehemently xenophobic towards (non-European) immigrants, but often consider the national elites as the true culprits of mass immigration. They see mass immigration as a conspiracy of the left-wing parties, trade unions, and big business in which the first two want to (artificially) increase their support base, and the latter their pool of cheap labor (e.g. Zaslove 2004a; Mudde 2000a). Hence, they came together to push through their egocentric agendas at the expense of the nation (and the "little man"). Similarly, Eastern European parties claim that their elites are discriminating against the "native" or "own" population in favor of "minorities" like the "Gypsies" and "Turks."

Virtually all populist radical right parties accuse the national elite of being "left-wing" and "progressive." In Western Europe they link these ideas back to the "new left" and the student revolts of May 1968: for example, Italian LN leader Umberto Bossi often refers to "those '68 fools" (see Zaslove 2004a: 107). In Eastern Europe the point of historical reference is the former communist regime: the new elites are accused of being "the old elites with new masks" (Tismaneanu 1996: 527). This is most strongly expressed in the theme of the "stolen revolution," oddly enough expressed often by populist radical right leaders who used to work for the security services of that former regime and who played no (supportive) role in that "revolution" (see Mudde 2001).

Some populist radical right parties also see the cultural elite as part of the internal enemy. This has been particularly strong within the FPÖ, which has been in a constant fight with part of the cultural elite, which reached new "heights" after the party joined the Austrian government in 2000. In its propaganda the party speaks of "cultural anarchists," "culture Mafiosi" and "social parasites" (e.g. Ahlemeyer 2006). The Romanian PRM even went as far as to publish "a list of top intellectuals who should be shot for the greater good of the country" (Pop Elechus 2001: 163).

Many populist radical right parties consider the media to be instruments of the established parties, most notably in the struggle against "the only real opposition" (e.g. FN, VB) or "the patriotic forces" (e.g. LDPR, SPR-RSČ). Particularly when in power, the populist radical right will denounce critique from the media as "traitorous" and "unpatriotic" (e.g. Heinisch 2003; Irvine 1997). Although many media do indeed openly campaign against the populist radical right, journalists will not so much follow a party line, but rather a company line or their own personal opinion. Most parties regard the media as part of one big conspiracy, in which the media is under "left-wing control" (SVP 2003: 40), and journalists are leftists, liars, and traitors: "The monopolistic media hide the true values for the people" (Csurka 1997: 260). In the case of anti-Semitic populist radical right parties, obviously, the media are controlled by "the International Jewry." In this regard, a popular word play within anti-Semitic circles is reference to the "Jew York Times," building upon the widespread linkage of New York (and the US) with Jewish domination.

In addition to the "traitors" and "corrupt(ers)," we can distinguish two more categories within the subtype of internal enemies: perverts and perverters. Perverts are people who deviate in actions or ideas from the populist radical right moral standard. Among this type of enemy one can find "sexual deviants" (e.g. homosexuals), junkies, and so-called *Sozialschmarotzer*, i.e. people who are perceived to draw social benefits without a valid reason. Importantly, the latter category does not include all people on welfare, but only those that according to the populist radical right do not need it (see also chapter 5).

Homophobia is part of many, but by no means all populist radical right parties. For example, the two Dutch parties of the 1990s, the CD and CP'86, did not take an overtly homophobic position (e.g. Mudde

2000a).[2] However, for most populist radical right parties in Catholic and Orthodox countries, homosexuals are part of the perverted internal enemy. In addition to being "a biological and social abnormality" (Le Pen), homosexuality is seen as a threat to the survival of the nation. Moreover, many parties will conflate homosexuals and pedophiles in their propaganda, making the perverted into the perverters. For example, the 1984 FN Program mentioned homosexuality only once, in the case of homosexual relationships between adults and minors. This was done under the heading of "Security" and used also to denounce the alleged laxity of the judiciary (see Lesselier 1988).

Perverters are even worse than the mere perverts, as they corrupt the pure and innocent and therefore further weaken the nation. Examples of perverters abound within the literature of the populist radical right. One group that is often singled out is the feminists, who allegedly try to pervert innocent women with their "unnatural" ideas of gender equality (see also 4.2). Another prime target is drug dealers – where the parties do not distinguish between "hard" (e.g. cocaine and heroine) and "soft drugs" (e.g. hashish and marihuana), but always exclude alcohol and cigarettes. Here it is often the youth wings of the parties that organize the most vigilant campaigns, calling for higher penalties for drug dealers.

In various Eastern European countries "pro-Western" individuals are seen as perverters. The arguments are either that they support "Western values" (ranging from materialism to human rights), leading to the degeneration of the nation, or that "the West" is an enemy of the homeland, which makes the pro-Westerners traitors to their own country. The latter argument is particularly strong within the Russian LDPR and the Serbian SRS, but can also been found in the Hungarian MIÉP and the Slovak SNS.

However, the internal enemy that is singled out for the most vehement attacks is the populist radical right competitor. Much of the party literature is filled with accusations of betrayal and corruption by people within the broader movement. This is particularly the case in countries where different populist radical right parties compete for a relatively limited

---

[2] Even within the extreme right, homosexuality has not been rejected universally. Historic examples include the (alleged) homosexuality of the top of the Nazi-German Sturmabteilung (Storm Division, SA), most notably its leader Ernst Röhm, while the issue has divided the British NF and the German neo-Nazi scene. Interestingly, Germany's most charismatic and influential postwar neo-Nazi, Michael Kühnen, was an open homosexual who died of AIDS. He distributed a remarkable pamphlet arguing that it was in accordance with natural law that leaders *should be* homosexual, so as not to be diverted by women, while the masses should be heterosexual, to ensure the survival of the nation/race (Kühnen n.d.).

share of the electorate, such as in Germany and the Netherlands, or where larger parties have lost electoral significance because of party splits, as in France and Slovakia. For example, the German REP often referred to the DVU as a *Spalter-Liste* (splitter list), accusing it of being an instrument of the established parties – notably the Christlich Demokratische Union (Christian Democratic Union, CDU) – to divide the "real patriots" (Mudde 2000a: 54). And during the short existence of the Slovak Prava Slovenská národná strana (Real Slovak National Party, PSNS), leader Slota referred to his successor in the SNS, Anna Maliková, who had thrown him out of "his" party, as "my biggest mistake" and "a mad cow" (*The Slovak Spectator* 01–07/10/2001).

But the category of (populist) radical right enemies includes even people that are or were among the party faithful. First, there is "the apostate," i.e. someone who was a committed member of the party but renounces both the cause and the party. This is the ultimate traitor, as she or he has seen the light, yet turned away from it. Second is "the infiltrator," a person who is only in the party in the service of an external enemy (e.g. the secret service or antifascists). Generally, the smaller and more radical the group, the more paranoid it is. The "outing" of infiltrators is a popular activity that often approaches the absurd. For example, Viorel Salagean, a Senator of the Romanian Partidul pentru Uniunea Naţionalnă a Românilor (Party of Romanian National Unity, PUNR), accused party leader Funar of being a spy for the Hungarian minority (Gallagher 1997).

3.2.2 *Within the state, outside the nation*

The classic enemy within this category is the ethnic minority. Generally speaking, in Western Europe the archetypical group of the enemy within the state, outside the nation, is the immigrant community, whereas in Eastern Europe more or less indigenous ethnic minorities are the usual suspects. That said, various West European populist radical right parties are also xenophobic towards nonimmigrant ethnic minorities, while an increasing number of Eastern European parties have started to target the still small recent immigrant communities. For example, one of the leaders of the Hungarian MIÉP referred to "Galician newcomers" (referring to both Ukrainians and Jews) as the source of all problems in Hungary (see Pető 2005).

Most of the literature focuses almost exclusively on non-European immigrants when addressing the xenophobia of populist radical right parties. Some authors have even adopted the term "antiimmigrant party" to label the parties, suggesting that their agendas are reducible to this single issue (e.g. Gibson 2002; Fennema 1997). There is no doubt that non-European immigrants are among the main enemies of these parties in Western Europe, particularly in their electoral propaganda. However, this is a relatively recent development, as various parties initially targeted European immigrants and have started to focus primarily on non-Europeans only since the mid to late 1980s. Their antipathy followed the immigration current in much of Western Europe, which changed from guest workers from among mainly South Europeans in the period 1950–70 to mainly North Africans and Turks since the 1970s, with a sharp increase in non-European asylum seekers since the 1980s.

Among the recent groups of asylum seekers and immigrants, Muslims have been targeted most consistently and vehemently in the propaganda of populist radical right parties (see 3.3.2). However, non-Muslim immigrants have also been victims of xenophobic campaigns, including both Europeans and non-Europeans. Whereas the latter group was always treated with suspicion and fear, the position towards the former group, mostly immigrants and asylum seekers from Eastern Europe, has changed fundamentally. During the Cold War, populist radical right parties were vehemently anticommunist, making them fairly welcoming towards asylum seekers from Eastern Europe. In the words of the Belgian VB, they were "driftwood of collapsing political systems, of which they bear no guilt" (*Vlaams Blok* 5/91). Since the fall of the Berlin Wall, however, they are no longer useful pawns in anticommunist propaganda, and have "thus" become targets of the usual xenophobic accusations (e.g. stealing jobs, being involved in crime).

In addition to the nativist arguments against immigrants in general, two seemingly "objective" arguments are used against the acceptance of asylum seekers and refugees: (1) they are not real political refugees, but "bogus" economic immigrants; and (2) there is no place for them. This is vividly captured in a pamphlet of the German REP, depicting a boat crowded with foreigners and reading "The boat is full. Stop the asylum sham."

In postcommunist Eastern Europe itself, immigrants and refugees have yet to be overtly politicized, with the notable exceptions of Slovenia in the early 1990s (e.g. Jalušič 2002; Kuzmaniž 1999; Žagar 2002). Indeed, some empirical studies show that immigrants and refugees are not (yet) perceived as a threat in Eastern Europe. According to data from the New Democracies Barometer, classic nativist feelings even decreased in most countries in the 1990s (e.g. Haerpfer 2002: 102). However, other studies show a growing disquiet about immigrants and refugees in various postcommunist countries, despite the fact that these countries still have very small (if growing) numbers of both groups (e.g. Coenders *et al.* 2004).

Notwithstanding the existing anti-immigrant potential within these societies, Eastern European populist radical right parties give a rather low priority to anti-immigrant positions in their propaganda (Mudde 2005b). While the Czech Republicans included a section on immigration in their program, in it the party merely wrote:

Who can still believe today that our country can remain true to herself, when you see that today it is an open paradise for various ethnic groups and our children are gradually raised to the sounds of primitive black and Gypsy songs. (SPR-RSČ 1999)

In Russia a single-issue party Rossijskoe Dvizhenie Protiv Nelegalnoj Immigratsii (Russian Movement against Illegal Immigration, DPNI) was founded in 2002. In its manifesto "How many Russians are there left in Moscow?," which reads like a copy of anti-immigrant positions from the West European populist radical right, the group links immigrants to all evils of society (e.g. unemployment, crime, terrorism) and calls for "the deportation of any illegal aliens from the territory of Russia" (DPNI 2004). According to the DPNI, "migrants from the Caucasus states and from Central and South-Eastern Asia are the first part of the foreign expansion." The group is closely associated with other nativist parties and extreme right *groupuscules* in the country, but it has so far not grown into a noticeable political force (Verkhovsky & Kozhevnikova 2005).

In contrast, Eastern European populist radical right parties target mainly the second largest group of enemies within the state but outside the nation, i.e. indigenous ethnic minorities. All European countries have ethnic minorities among their populations. Some are well known and established, such as the Basques in Spain (and France) or the Kurds in Turkey, whereas the existence of others, such as the Livs in Latvia, is known only to some specialized ethnographers. Whether groups are recognized as an ethnic minority, officially by the state or unofficially in academic studies and the media, depends on a variety of factors, mostly subjective rather than objective.[3] In short, as majority nations are "imagined" (Anderson 1983), so are minority nations or ethnic minorities.

In general there are three conditions that make ethnic minorities more likely targets of xenophobic campaigns, both by populist radical right parties and by mainstream forces: (1) the ethnic minority is well organized and claims minority rights or protection; (2) it is linked to the majority

---

[3] For example, whereas Czechoslovakia was considered a multinational state of two "ethnicities," the Czechs and the Slovaks, the Czech Republic is considered to be a homogeneous country, including by most Czechs, despite the historic distinction between the territories of Bohemia and Moravia and the (short-lived) political mobilization of some "Moravians."

ethnicity of a bordering state; and (3) the ethnic minority is part of the former dominating group in the country. In some cases all three conditions will come together, which has given rise to particularly high levels of "inter-ethnic" tensions and xenophobic campaigns.

A prime example of such a case is the Hungarian-speaking minority in Central Eastern Europe, most notably in Romania and Slovakia. In these countries the perception of threat from ethnic minorities is particularly high; 32 percent and 43 percent, respectively, in 1998 (Haerpfer 2002: 100). This is wiped up by the populist radical right, which uses some of its most fanatic and vulgar rhetoric against the Hungarian-speakers. For example, at a party meeting Slovak SNS leader Slota referred to Hungarians as "a disgusting and deceitful nation" (in Gyárfášová 2002: 195).

The principal accusation against these minorities is that they are not loyal to the state they live in, but instead constitute "a fifth column" of their kin state. This charge was often expressed by Slota, for example, when he stated that "what we are experiencing from our Hungarian citizens borders on treason" (Cibulka 1999: 118). Similar allegations can be found in Bulgaria toward the Turkish-speaking minority. The Bulgarska national-radikalna partija (Bulgarian National Radical Party, BNRP) refers to them as a group "with an alien national consciousness" that should be expatriated (Mitev 1997: 77).

The importance of minority mobilization is often overlooked in studies of nativist campaigns. While it is obviously not the basis for being defined as the enemy, minority mobilization can make a specific group a more prominent target of populist radical right campaigns. The mobilization does not have to be by the minority itself; in many cases, pro-minority campaigns are only noted if (prominent) members of the "ethnic" majority become involved. Alternatively, foreign actors can make claims on the basis of a domestic minority, ranging from kin-states (e.g. Russia in the Baltics or Hungary in Central Eastern Europe) to international organizations and foreign states (as is mostly the case with weakly organized minorities, such as the Roma).

The importance of minority mobilization and claiming can be seen in the case of the Chinese minority, which has been present for decades in almost all European countries. Chinese are on all counts nonnative to populist radical right parties; moreover, they are often little integrated and connected to stories of crimes (e.g. "triads" and "snakehead gangs"). This notwithstanding, Chinese are almost never targeted in populist radical right campaigns. While their numbers and growth might not be striking, neither are those of some explicitly targeted minorities (notably the Jews). What sets the Chinese apart from most other ethnic minorities is their low level of political mobilization and the absence of collective claim making on the majority population.[4]

A special category of the nonnative internal enemy is the so-called "southerners," who can be both immigrants and indigenous ethnic minorities. Various populist radical right parties identify "southerners" as a key enemy within the state, but outside the nation. The infamous Russian populist Zhirinovsky, for example, shows a fascination with "criminal southerners," referring mostly to people from the Caucasus and from Turkic countries, which borders on obsession (e.g. Umland 1997a). Similarly, the idiosyncratic populist Ivan Kramberger, who was killed by an insane person just before the Slovene parliamentary elections of 1992, called for the expulsion of "Southerners" (*Južnjaki*) from Slovenia (Rizman 1999).

In Italy the LN made itself the voice of the long-standing northern Italian prejudices towards their countrypersons from *il Mezzogiorno*, a derogative term to denote the southern part of Italy. Whether or not these *terroni* (see note 21, chapter 2) are included in the party's "nation" varies with the self-definition of the party. Originally the LN was a regionalist party, identifying itself (lukewarmly) with the Italian nation. Since the party has invented the northern land of "Padania" and the Padanian nation, it increasingly treats *meridionali* (another insulting name for southerners) as foreigners.

3.2.3 *Outside the state, within the nation*

The enemy outside the state but within the nation is something of an odd category, but can and does exist in practice. Still, even in the case that parties will identify and vilify this category of enemy, it will not feature prominently in the propaganda or identity creation of the parties. Roughly speaking, we can distinguish two main groups of enemies within this category: countrypersons having moved abroad and kindred people living often in neighboring countries.

The first group is quite small and often involves artists, intellectuals and politicians who have (temporarily) emigrated. Most of the time, these groups and individuals are accused of the same vices as the native elites within the country, i.e. corruption, leftism, and treason. For example, the FPÖ often criticizes Austrian representatives in international organizations for these vices, in particular the country's European Commissioners

---

[4] In instances where this changes, for example when Hong Kong was handed back to China and many Hong Kong Chinese demanded British citizenship or asylum status, the Chinese also become targets of nativist campaigns (see, for example, NF 1999).

(see Heinisch 2003). The only additional qualifications this category of enemies could earn by living abroad are being hypocritical (e.g. sportsmen living in tax havens and criticizing welfare cuts "back home") and cowardice ("selling out" to the host country). Such sentiments have been quite common within German parties like the DVU and REP (see Mudde 2000a).

The second group, which is both more important and more numerous, refers to members of the nation "forced" to live outside of the "nation-state." As many populist radical right parties consider the territory of their nation to substantially exceed that of their current state (see 6.2.1), they believe that many people in neighboring countries are in fact part of their nation. If this sentiment is not shared by (leading) individuals from the groups, a party claims, they will be attacked for being cowards, opportunists, or traitors.

This has been the case, for example, with moderate Hungarian-speaking intellectuals and politicians in Slovakia and Romania, who reject reunification with Hungary and identify as Slovak or Romanian citizens. For example, MIÉP leader Csurka has regularly attacked Béla Markó, the moderate leader of the Uniunea Democrată Maghiară din România (Democratic Alliance of Hungarians in Romania, UDMR), accusing him of betraying the Hungarian nation, while at the same time heralding László Tőkés, the leader of the radical faction within the party of Hungarian-speakers in Romania (e.g. Csurka 2004: 68). Similar, though less extreme, are radical Flemish nativist organizations aspiring to a reunification with the Netherlands, such as the VB (in its early years) and *Were Di* (Protect Yourself). They have been highly critical of the "unhistorical" and "progressive" Dutch people, who were (rightly) seen as being unsupportive of the Flemish struggle and uninterested in reunification.

3.2.4   Outside the state, outside the nation

The populist radical right has an inherent distrust of the "external," i.e. the outsider who is a nonnational living outside of the state. In many cases they will focus on particular outsiders, often the big neighbor or former occupier, although many consider virtually the whole "outside" with suspicion. For them the world is a hostile place, in which everyone is believed to conspire against their nation (and state). This not only includes foreign countries, particularly if historical tensions exist, but also international organizations like the EU and the UN (see chapters 7 and 8).

This paranoid worldview is particularly strong within the German and the Hungarian radical right. Regarding the latter, which includes the

MIÉP, the "*Magyar* nation" is seen as unique and surrounded by "a sea of Slavs." The reasons for the particularly hostile worldview of the German radical right, including the DVU and REP, lie in its revisionist view of the Second World War. During the Cold War, they believed that the US and USSR kept Germany divided to prevent it from becoming great again. In recent years, a similar conspiracy theory has been applied to the European Union (EU), under the guidance of France or the US (e.g. Mudde 2000a).

In Serbia, the paranoid worldview is a direct result of the international military actions against the country in reaction to the Serbian aggression in Bosnia-Herzegovina and Kosovo. As the Serbian populist radical right considers both territories key historical parts of Greater Serbia, the foreign military actions are considered proof of an "international conspiracy against Serbs" that involves almost everyone, but in particular Germany, the Vatican, the CIA, Italy, and Turkey (Pribičević 1999: 200).

With regard to the European populist radical right as a whole, the former occupiers hold a special place in its worldview. The parties accuse this particular external enemy of irredentism, i.e. the aim of reoccupying them. The fear of neighboring states and of irredentism was particularly widespread in transitory postcommunist Europe, where the borders and states were not as firmly established as in the West. However, during the 1990s the perceived threat from neighboring countries decreased sharply throughout the region, even though it remained relatively high in most countries. For example, while the group of people feeling threatened by neighboring states had dropped by roughly 40 percent in Romania, Hungary, and Poland by 1998, it still accounted for 27 percent, 23 percent, and 20 percent respectively (Haerpfer 2002: 98).

The fact that some former occupiers involve themselves with the politics of their "lost territories," mostly to guarantee the rights of "their kin," certainly goes some way in explaining these relatively high numbers. In a number of cases, leading politicians strengthened fears of irredentist claims by ambiguous statements about the borders of the nation. For example, the first postcommunist prime minister of Hungary, Jószef Antall (1990–93), declared that he was "in spirit" the Prime Minister of fifteen million Hungarians (whereas only some ten million live in Hungary); FIDESz-MPS leader Viktor Orbán made similar remarks, both as PM and as leader of the opposition. While these statements did not create the fears of Hungarian irredentism among the populist radical right in neighboring countries, they certainly lent credence to their warnings that Hungary entertained such ambitions.

Among the populist radical right in Romania and Slovakia, fears of Hungarian irredentism have given rise to huge conspiracy theories.

Already in 1992, the 4th Assembly of the Slovak SNS called upon the Slovak government, of which it was part, "to stop the penetration of the Hungarian irredentist elements and the forced Hungarisation of Slovaks in the South of Slovakia and the Hungarisation of municipal names" (in Gyárfášová 2002: 167). For the leadership of Vatra Romaneasca (Romanian Cradle) and its political arm PUNR, Romania was "the target of a conspiracy of domestic and external forces that pursue the dismemberment of its being [and] the degrading of human values that have characterized us all along our history" (in Gallagher 1997: 33). This conspiracy included also such unlikely actors as Max van der Stoel, then UN High Commissioner for Minorities, who was accused of "acting like a representative of the UDMR," the political party of the Hungarian-speaking minority in Romania.

Similarly, the fear of Turkish irredentism is strong in countries like Bulgaria and Greece, and local populist radical right parties do much to increase it even further. In the 1994 manifesto of the BNRP, for example, the party stated "that since early in 1993 the fearsome ghost of the obscure Turkish oppression has been palpably looming over our country" (in Mitev 1997: 77). Greek populist radical right parties accuse MPs who declare themselves as "Turks" as traitors who need to be stripped of their mandate; the Greek Elliniko Metopo (Hellenic Front, EM) even wants to foster closer cooperation among peoples "enslaved by expansionist Turkey (Greeks, Kurds, Armenians)" (in Kolovos 2003: 56). A similar Turkophobia can be found in Russia, particularly within the LDPR, whose leader believes that "Pan-Turkism threatens Russia" (Williams & Hanson 1999: 271).

The fear of Germany is fairly similar, particularly in the Czech Republic and Poland, where large groups of the population still consider their Western neighbor as the main external threat (Haerpfer 2002: 94). Here alleged irredentist claims come from social movements, such as the Bund der Vertriebenen (League of Expellees) and the Sudetendeutsche Landmannschaft (Sudeten German League), rather than from mainstream political parties, although the expellees hold some influence within the Christian democratic camp, particularly in Bavaria, where leading CSU politicians have supported some of their claims.

Within Poland anti-German sentiments are still widespread, particularly among Catholics and farmers (who fear land claims). Consequently, they find political voice in the two peasant parties, the PSL and Samoobrona, and through various Catholic parties, some within larger center-right electoral blocks linked to the successors of the Solidarity trade union (e.g. Lebioda 2000). Although Germanophobia is a bit less widespread among the Czech populace, the situation at the elite level is even more extreme than in Poland. Almost all established Czech parties have at times voiced anti-German sentiments, most notably the ardently Germanophobe communist Komunistická strana Čech a Moravy (Communist Party of Bohemia and Moravia, KSČM).

Still, in both cases populist radical right parties belong to the most anti-German parties in the country. Already in 1990, at a "Conference of the Polish Right," Marciej Giertych, now an MEP for the Polish LPR and the father of the party leader, declared that Poland should be the most decisive element in the self-defense of Europe against the German dominance" (Rudnicki 2000: 11–12). In the Czech Republic, Miroslav Sládek, then leader of the SPR-RSČ and not known for his subtlety, once shouted at a party demonstration that "we can regret that we killed too few Germans in the war" (*CTK* 21/06/1998).

But Germanophobia is not limited to the Eastern part of the European continent. In some Western European countries Germans are (among) the least liked Europeans, and fears of German expansionism continue to exist (e.g. in Denmark and France). While not a major issue, some regional populist radical right parties will indulge in Germanophobia at times, particularly linked to the process of European integration. For example, the Greek EM refers to the EU as "the new Roman Empire" and claims that "very soon it will be proven that the Euro, EMU and EU are geopolitical fabrications of Germany and France, enabling them to become the 'guardians' of the whole of Europe, and obey the needs of German capital for expansion and domination" (Charitos 2001).

In many Eastern European countries, Russia is still considered to be external enemy number one, despite the fact that the percentages of Russophobe people are decreasing (Haerpfer 2002: 91). Not surprisingly, populist radical right parties are among the most open and rabid anti-Russian political actors in the region. This is particularly so in Estonia, Latvia and Poland, where Russophobia extends far into the political mainstream as well. In sharp contrast, in a number of Slavic countries the Russian Federation is seen as an ally rather than an enemy. For parties like the Srpska radikalne stranke (Serbian Radical Party, SRS) Russia is the "Slavic brother" that helped defend Serbia against "Western aggression." Similarly pro-Russian sentiments can be found in the Bulgarian BNRP and the Slovak SNS (e.g. Fried 1997).

In addition to neighbors and former occupiers, a primary role in the category of external enemies within the populist radical right is reserved for the US and the international organizations allegedly dominated by it (e.g. NATO, UN, WTO). It is fair to say that, "in general, anti-Americanism is now at the top of the agenda of extreme right parties all over Europe" (Rensmann 2003: 119). Traditionally, the most fiercely anti-American

populist radical right parties are to be found in Southern Europe, in countries with a significant anti-American mainstream (e.g. Fabbrini 2002).
For example, the French FN is one of many French political parties
to espouse strong Americanophobia, as is the new Laikos Orthodoxos
Synagermos (Popular Orthodox Rally, LAOS) in Greece. The tiny Italian MS-FT is even obsessively anti-American, considering, for example,
NATO as an American instrument of the colonization of Europe.

In Eastern Europe, while Russophobe sentiments are decreasing,
Americanophobia is on the rise (Haerpfer 2002: 96). Not surprisingly,
the Former Republic of Yugoslavia tops the poll with a staggering 85
percent in 1998, while, in the short period of 1992–98, sharp increases
have occurred in Slovakia (+19 percent), Ukraine (+17 percent), Belarus
(+13 percent), and the Czech Republic (+10 percent). Particularly in the
former Soviet countries, anti-Americanism is also widespread at the elite
level, especially on the radical left and right. Both sides will support pan-
Slavic cooperation, at least partly to constitute a counter-weight to the
US (e.g. LDPR, Slovak SNS, SRS).

However, not all populist radical right parties are anti-American; in
fact, some are explicitly pro-American! Jörg Haider has long been fas-
cinated by the US, seeking inspiration at Harvard summer schools and
in the Republican Party (e.g. Höbelt 2003). The VB has become virtually the only open supporter of American foreign policy in contemporary Belgium. During the invasion of Afghanistan some party members
(including leader Filip Dewinter) demonstrated in Antwerp in front of
a banner reading: "Bush is right! Stop Islam terrorism!" And in Poland,
where Americanophobia is not widespread anyway, the LPR prefers the
US over the EU, above all because of the importance of Christianity in
the former.

3.3   Three special enemies: the Jew, the Muslim, and the Rom

Within the populist radical right, three groups perform particularly
important, if quite different, functions in the self-definition of the
ingroup. Traditionally, "the Jew" has been the personification of modernity, and through anti-Semitism all the perceived evils of modernization
were opposed (e.g. Cohn 1971). In sharp contrast, "the Rom" is the personification of "the barbarian," and through Romophobia the modernity
of the ingroup is emphasized. To a large extent, "the Muslim" is also a barbarian, although she or he is more clearly linked to modernity. Whereas
"the Rom" has not yet reached modernity, "the Muslim" lives in it, but
consciously rejects it. Interestingly, it is particularly in their Islamophobia
that populist radical right parties present themselves as fierce defenders
of liberal democracy, including various freedoms that until recently have

been secondary to these parties (e.g. equality of sexes, separation of state and religion; see also 4.2).

3.3.1   "The Jew": anti-Semitism

Anti-Semitism has always taken a special place in the wide world of prejudices. Whereas most "Others" are considered as relatively unintelligent and powerless, and their threat is primarily seen in terms of their numbers, "the Jew" is an atypical enemy, one who is clever and cunning, and whose threat lies not in the numbers of the many, but in the power of the few. Hence, the Polish anti-Semitic "joke" of 1990: "There are almost no Jews in Poland, but why do all of them have to be in the government?" (in Gerrits 1993: 111). It is also in this perspective that László Karsai's provocative but accurate observation should be read:

With a little exaggeration we could say that the famous financial guru George Soros, who maintains close, friendly relations with the leaders of the Alliance of Free Democrats, and who comes from a Hungarian-Jewish family, is worth several hundred thousand virtual Jews. (1999: 142)[5]

Hence, the (not so) "paradoxical" existence of what Paul Lendvai (1972) has coined "anti-Semitism without Jews."[6] How this classic anti-Semitic conspiracy unfolds can be read in the *Protocols of the Elders of Zion*, the notorious forgery of the Czarist secret service of over one hundred years ago, which continues to inspire anti-Semites around the globe (e.g. Bernstein 1935).

Within the typology presented above, anti-Semitism normally falls in categories 2 and 4, i.e. outside of the nation but both inside and outside of the state. Anti-Semitism is most often expressed with reference to international politics, particularly when related to Israel and the United States. A blunt example was given by PRM leader Vadim Tudor, in a speech he gave in Libya: "The United States is a colony of Israel . . . In my mind's eye I see a little mouse pulling a gigantic elephant behind it on a very long chain. This is Israel and the United States" (in *Haaretz* 07/04/2004). But in many instances the anti-Semitic conspiracy links the two groups, i.e. the internal and the external Jews, seeing (allegedly) influential Jews who live within the state as the fifth column of "International Jewry."

---

[5] Similarly, Leonard Weinberg has referred to Soros as "a godsend for far-right party leaders" (2003: 298).

[6] Dmitri Vasiliev, a former leader of the Russian extreme right grouping Pamyat (Memory), has provided an anti-Semitic "logic" for the existence of anti-Semitism without Jews: "It is not necessary to be Jewish to be a Jew . . . Everybody in power is a Jew, or their wives are" (in Lee 2000: 306).

In Western Europe open anti-Semitism has remained rare in the post-war era. Despite different interpretations of the war period between and within countries, there exists a strong consensus that the Holocaust was the epitome of evil and that anti-Semitism is unacceptable. Obviously, there can be discussion about what exactly constitutes anti-Semitism, particularly with respect to critique of the politics of the state of Israel, but clear and open anti-Semitism is not expressed commonly by the political mainstream, including most relevant populist radical right parties. The recent wave of "new anti-Semitism" that has hit Western Europe is more exclusively focused on the Arab–Israeli conflict, and is primarily expressed within the Muslim immigrant and (intellectual) left-wing communities (e.g. Taguieff 2004; Wistrich 2003).

The key proponents of (old) anti-Semitism in Western Europe were the usual suspects: marginal extremist groups, like neo-Nazis and some communists, as well as certain fringe Christian fundamentalists. Particularly within the neo-Nazi groups the most outrageous anti-Semitic conspiracies abound; virtually all leading Nazis have been "outed" as being Jewish (including Adolf Eichmann, Joseph Goebbels, and Adolf Hitler himself), while the Holocaust is said to have been invented by "the Jews" to blackmail the Germans/Europeans/whites (hence the term "Holohoax").

In some Western European populist radical right parties anti-Semitism might not be overt, but more or less coded messages indicate that it is nonetheless latent in their propaganda. For example, after a negative experience with a television interview the late British radical right politician John Tyndall, a former leader of both the NF and the BNP, said: "One glance at Mr. Lapping (the producer) was enough to convince us that his ancestors originated in lands far from those where Saxon yeomen and bowmen were bred" (in Nugent 1980: 219). More openly, the Greek LAOS has regularly referred to the alleged dark power of Israel and the Jewish lobby (see Kolovos 2003).

One of the few larger Western European parties to use coded anti-Semitic messages is the French FN, although anti-Semitism is not a core feature of its ideology. In the party literature and leadership speeches terms like "internationalists," "cosmopolitans," or "lobbies" feature with great frequency (e.g. Simmons 2003; Marcus 2000). In the case of Le Pen, anti-Semitism has often been part of his personal attacks on individual politicians. For example, he has referred to the "dual nationality" of the former Minister of Labor, Lionel Stoleru, who never made any secret of his Jewish background (e.g. Mayer and Sineau 2002; Birnbaum 1992).

The West European party most often associated with anti-Semitism is the FPÖ, and particularly its former leader Jörg Haider (e.g. Heinisch

2003; Wodak 2002). Again, while anti-Semitic statements have been made by party officials, and tolerated by the leadership, it is not a key ideological feature of the party. In addition to a strategic move to satisfy the anti-Semitic part of the party electorate and membership, Haider's willingness to tolerate anti-Semitism can best be seen as a strategy of coping with the guilt of the Holocaust (Peri 2001), which one can also find among German populist radical rightists like former REP leader Franz Schönhuber.[7]

The situation of anti-Semitism in Eastern Europe is much more diverse. In some countries, such as the Czech Republic or Slovenia, anti-Semitism is as unacceptable and marginal as it is in most Western European countries. In the largest group of countries, however, a certain tolerance towards anti-Semitism exists among parts of the masses and the elites. For example, in both Hungary and Lithuania almost one-quarter of the population can be classified as anti-Semitic (e.g. Kiaulakis 2005; Kovács 1999). In Poland, approximately half of the population declares negative feelings towards Jews and Israelis, a percentage that has remained largely stable over the past decade (Pankowski & Kornak 2005: 179).

Anti-Semitism in postcommunist Europe has a wide variety of ideological sources; some are shared with Western Europe, others are more particular to the region. Communist anti-Zionism and pan-Slavic anti-Western sentiments are particularly relevant for some smaller, mostly post-Soviet radical right groups. For example, Oleh Tyahnybok, leader of the Ukrainian populist radical right party Svoboda (Liberty), and a former member of the center-right Nasha Ukrayina (Our Ukraine) parliamentary faction of president Viktor Yushenko, called upon Ukrainians to resist the "Russian-Jewish mafia" that, according to him, rules Ukraine (*Ukrayinska Pravda* 21/07/04).

On average, Eastern European populist radical right parties are much more (openly) anti-Semitic than their brethren in the West. For example, the Serbian SRS published the infamous *Protocols* as a supplement to their official biweekly publication *Velika Srbija* (Great Serbia) in May 1994 (Sekelj 1998: 13). Of particular prominence are "Judeo-Communist" conspiracy theories, which have a long tradition within nativist circles in the region (e.g. Gerrits 1995). Volen Siderov, the virulently anti-Semitic leader of the Bulgarian Ataka party, openly preaches such conspiracy theories. At the "International Conference on Global Problems of World History," among other notorious anti-Semites and revisionists like the

[7] Interestingly, the famous "Nazi hunter" and fellow-Austrian, the late Simon Wiesenthal, defended Haider against accusations of anti-Semitism, saying that "Haider never said anything against Israel and has never said anything anti-Semitic" (in Sully 1997: 222).

Swiss Jürgen Graf and the American former Grand Wizard of the Knights
of the Ku Klux Klan, David Duke, Siderov (2002) proclaimed: "Jewish
bankers such as Schiff and Kuhn financed the Bolshevik revolution which
brought destruction and misery to the Russian people and ruined the
Russian economy, thus eliminating a powerful competitor of the Anglo-
Saxon powers."

Even more contemporary anti-Semitic conspiracies are highly present
too. In a bizarre merger of anti-Semitism and Islamophobia, the Ataka
website sported a picture of Bulgaria with small Turkish and Israeli flags
and the text "for sale" on it, indicating that the country was being sold out
to Turkey and Israel. And in some parties anti-Semitism even forms one
of the most vicious and central ideological features. Not surprisingly, this
is the case in countries where anti-Semitism is generally widespread, such
as Hungary, Poland, and Russia. One of the most rabid anti-Semites in
Eastern Europe is MIÉP leader István Csurka, who was expelled from the
then ruling party MDF in 1993 for publishing the essay "Wake Up, Hungarians," in which he accused a "dwarf minority" of frustrating Hungary's
national destiny (e.g. Pataki 1992). This has been a dominant theme in
his publications.

Like practically all anti-Semites, Csurka is convinced that "International Jewry" is involved in a worldwide conspiracy and operates through
American henchmen (see also chapter 8). But Csurka and MIÉP are able
to relate the Jewish conspiracy to virtually every topic (e.g. Weaver 2006;
Marsovszky 2002; Mihancsik 2001; Varga 2001). For example, prior to
the referendum in December 2004, when Hungarians voted on whether
to grant citizenship to ethnic Hungarians living outside Hungary, the
party paper, *Magyar Fórum* (02/11/2004), declared that those who campaigned against granting citizenship to Hungarians from abroad did so
because:

Others, foreigners, need the places that a few Hungarians arriving from beyond
the borders might take. [*These people feel that*] Hungarians should not come here,
so that there will be room for the Jews who will arrive from Russia, Ukraine and
the Near East. [*They'll do*] Anything to prevent a Hungarian from getting a run-
down farmhouse, so that the suburbs of the wealthy can be filled. (in Weaver
2006: 101)

As in many other respects, the populist radical right in Eastern Europe
also provides the most bizarre examples of anti-Semitism. The best known
is LDPR leader Zhirinovsky, who is both the perpetrator and victim of
anti-Semitic attacks (e.g. Shenfield 2001: 94–6). Allegedly, his biological
father was a Jewish Russian by the name of Edelshtein, which Zhirinovsky
long side-stepped by describing his ethnic origins in quasi-comical terms:
"My mother was Russian, my father was a lawyer." Despite, or maybe

because of, its leader's personal background, the LDPR programs reject the "pathological anti-Semitism" of the Russian extreme right movements (e.g. LDPR 1995). This implies that the party regards the various anti-Semitic remarks of its members, including Zhirinovsky himself, as normal (e.g. Shenfield 2001).

A remarkable development is the emergence of philo-Semitic statements within a few populist radical right parties. While it has been more common that nativist parties would refer positively to the "Jewish state," regarding it as the present-day example of their own preferred nativist state model, the similarities have been taken to the extreme in Serbia. During his populist radical right phase, SPO leader Drašković spoke of "the centuries long history of Jewish-Serbian martyrdom," and wrote: "It is by the hands of the same executioners that both Serbs and Jews have been exterminated at the same concentration camps, slaughtered at the same bridges, burned alive in the same ovens, thrown together into the same pits" (in Zivkovic 2000: 73).[8]

The most clear and convincing examples of philo-Semitism are found in the literature of the Belgian VB, which has never openly expressed anti-Semitism (Mudde 2000a).[9] In recent years the party has increasingly presented itself as *the* defender of the Flemish Jews and an ardent supporter of the state of Israel. In an interview with a conservative Jewish weekly from New York, Dewinter boasted that "very often we were the only political group defending Israel, both in publications and in parliament" (*The Jewish Week* 12/09/2005). The former is particularly remarkable as the Jewish community of Antwerp includes a relatively large section of Hassidic Jews, who are highly visible with their black robes and hats, and against whom much of the VB's critique of the alleged resistance to assimilation of the Muslim population could also be directed.

A probably unique combination of anti-Semitism and philo-Semitism has recently been shown by Romanian PRM leader Tudor, who until then mainly "excelled" in Jew-baiting. But to the surprise of almost everyone, including his fellow party members, Tudor radically changed his position on Jews and the Holocaust in 2004. He wrote an open letter apologizing to "all the Jews who were hurt by my exaggerations." Probably most shocking was Tudor's decision to hire a Jewish Israeli campaign manager in

---

[8] This theme was later taken up, and elaborated upon, by the Serbian–Jewish Friendship Society (Drustvo srpsko-jevrejskog prijateljstva), a bizarre collection of Serbian nativist intellectuals and members of the Serbian-Jewish community (e.g. Zivkovic 2000; Sekelj 1998).

[9] Anti-Semitism has not been part of the discourse of the Italian LN either, and its leader Umberto Bossi even declared that "the Lega is a friend of the Jews," after a Catholic theologian of Jewish descent (Luis Marsiglia) had been the victim of an anti-Semitic attack (Merkl 2003b: 31).

2002, with a close second in Eyal Arad's acceptance of the offer. Arad was supposed to help Tudor win the presidency in 2004. However, the reason that "Vadim 2004" gave for this unorthodox move was quite orthodox: "It is clear that no one can do anything in a state like Romania without American or Israeli advice" (in *Haaretz* 07/04/2004).

3.3.2 Islamophobia

At first sight, it looks like Islamophobia is the radical right's anti-Semitism of the twenty-first century. The centrality of anti-Islam sentiment in their propaganda lends credence to this assertion for most members of the populist radical right party family, particularly in Western Europe. While "the Jew" or "International Jewry" was the key enemy and scapegoat for the various types of nativist in the (early) twentieth century, particularly the Nazis, "the Muslim" or "Islam" is the key enemy of their contemporary counterparts. Moreover, like anti-Semitism the Islamophobic discourse of the populist radical right also relates to enemies outside the nation but both within and beyond the boundaries of the state. However, unlike anti-Semitism, Islamophobia is a common form of prejudice, in which the enemy is feared because of its numbers, not its qualities – in fact, Muslims (like "Gypsies" or "negroes") are mostly considered in negative terms (lazy, fanatic, etc.). In other words, whereas a few Jews could constitute a significant threat, a few Muslims could not.

Islamophobia has taken center-stage in the Western world since the fall of the Berlin Wall. The al-Qaeda attacks of 9/11, and the following developments in the ongoing "war on terrorism," deepened and extended this sentiment. As a consequence, Islamophobia is certainly not an exclusive feature of the populist radical right, but reaches deep into the political mainstream of most Western countries. However, populist radical right parties tend to stand out in both the "quality" and the quantity of their Islamophobia. For various European parties, from the Belgian VB to the Bulgarian Ataka, the main national and international threat today comes from "Islam," which they describe as an inherently fundamentalist and imperialist religion-cum-ideology.

In this world view, where Samuel Huntington's "The Clash of Civilizations" (1993) functions as a modern *Protocols*,[10] "the West" is at war with an imperialist Muslim world. Expressing a view that finds support well beyond the populist radical right, FPÖ leader Haider stated in the early 1990s: "The social order of Islam is opposed to our Western values"

---

[10] Almost all Islamophobes refer to "The Clash of Civilizations" to legitimize their views. This includes not just populist radical right parties like the fiercely Turkophobic Greek EM or the strongly xenophobic Belgian VB, but also purely Islamophobic politicians like the late Pim Fortuyn and the neoliberal populist LPF (e.g. LPF 2003).

(in Betz 2003b: 84). All major conflicts seem to fit this "Clash," including the (civil) wars in the Balkans. According to LN leader Bossi, combining anti-Americanism with Islamophobia, the "Christian Serbs" were attacked by NATO because they represented "the ultimate obstacle to the advance of the global American and Muslim empires" (in Betz 2003b: 84). The Spanish DN portrayed its vision of the clash under the heading "Europe in danger," picturing Albania, Morocco and Turkey as crabs attacking Europe.

But in addition to the attribution of various international ills to Islam, it is also the focus of pronounced domestic anxiety. LDPR leader Zhirinovsky, an Orientalist by training, stated almost fifteen years ago: "Islam does not still stand in front of the door, it already marches through the cities of Europe" (1992: 27). Some ten years later, the Greek Hellenic Front (HF) presents an even more chilling image: "The clash of civilizations takes now the form of a civil war in the interior of the Western countries" (HF 2001). This civil war is between the hospitable and naïve Europeans and the bloodthirsty Muslim immigrants in Europe, who are seen as "the fifth column of international Islam." Dramatic events like the "race" riots in France in November 2005 are placed within this broader framework. According to the FPÖ, they were an "Islamic Intifada against the French secular state" (*Neue Freie Zeitung* 10/11/2005).

Particularly among Western European populist radical right parties, Islamophobia seems to have led to a new emphasis on the Christian essence of Europe (or the Occident). Parties like the Belgian VB or the Italian LN used to largely ignore the issue of religion, but refer to the Christian roots of their own culture increasingly since the 1990s. In addition, they stress the alleged incompatibility of Islam with the basic tenets of the European or native culture. The Austrian FPÖ even overcame the long-standing anticlerical position of the third *Lager* (camp) to become one of the staunchest supporters of orthodox Catholicism, most notably in the person of Kurt Krenn, the Bishop of Sankt Pölten.

In Eastern Europe the link between (Catholic and Orthodox) Christianity and the populist radical right has always been very strong. The link is strongest in the Polish LPR, which combines Polish nativism with orthodox Catholicism at the core of its ideology, but parties like the Slovak SNS or Croat HSP are also staunchly Catholic. In the Orthodox countries the synergy between religion and nation is even more complete, as most Orthodox churches are national churches.[11] Thus, parties like the

---

[11] Traditionally, the links between state and religion have also been strong in Protestant Northern Europe, especially in the Scandinavian countries (e.g. Madeley 2006; Minkenberg 2002a). Interestingly, the Danish DFP wants the Danish Evangelical Lutheran Church to become the "National Church" of Denmark (DFP n.d.).

Bulgarian Ataka, the Romanian PRM, or the Russian LDPR define their nation as essentially Orthodox Christian.

As most of these countries are not (yet) confronted by mass immigration from Islamic countries, Islamophobia is not (yet) prominent within the discourses of the local populist radical right parties. Exceptions are the Bulgarian and Serbian parties, which consider internal Muslim minorities ("Turks" and "Albanians" respectively) as a national threat and a fifth column of a neighboring country. In a bizarre combination of Christian defense and Islamophobia, the Bulgarian BNRP demanded a ban on Muslims adopting children from Christian families (Mitev 1997).

Interestingly, there is at least one exception to the Islamophobic populist radical right in Europe, the Croatian neo-pravaši parties HSP and HSP-1861 (Irvine 1997). In the 1990s the governing HDZ struggled for the return of the Croatian Banovina of 1939, including only the "Croat" parts of Herzegovina, while the Greater Croatia of the neo-pravaši follows the borders of the wartime Independent State of Croatia (NDH), including the "Bosnian Muslim" parts of Herzegovina. And even though Croatia should be for the Croats, the neo-pravaši do not want to cleanse the country of Bosnian Muslims, whom they consider to be Croats of the Muslim faith. In fact, the HSP fiercely campaigned against Tuđman's Bosnian policy because it drove a wedge between Croats and Bosnian Muslims, who, in the eyes of Paraga and Djapic, should be natural allies in the fight against the true enemy, the Serbs. It has even been said that the HOS, the HSP militia that fought quasi-independently in Bosnia in the early 1990s, counted "numerous Muslim members" (Irvine 1997: 58).

3.3.3   Romaphobia

The most widely targeted ethnic minority in Central and Eastern Europe is the Roma, who are more commonly known under the derogatory term "Gypsies." Particularly in countries where the Roma minority is relatively numerous, such as in the Visegrad countries (Czech Republic, Hungary, Poland, and Slovakia) and Bulgaria and Romania, anti-Roma sentiment and violence are common (see Mudde 2005b; Kürti 1998). While populist radical right parties are certainly not the only political actors targeting the Roma in their propaganda, they are often the most vocal and extreme (e.g. Mudde 2005a). Thus, in much of Central Eastern Europe, Roma constitute the main enemies within the state but outside of the nation.

For the Czech SPR-RSČ the Roma have always been the main internal enemy, with the possible exception of the indigenous political elite. In its

1999 draft program, the party states: "The Gypsies . . . freely kill, rape and rob ordinary citizens . . . The vast majority of the Gypsies parasite on the society" (SPR-RSČ 1999). Vadim Tudor and the PRM espouse the most vicious and vulgar Romaphobia in Romania, a country which has a particularly dubious history in this respect. Ataka leader Sidorov even promised to "stop the Gypsy genocide against Bulgarians" (Reuters 25/06/2005). The Slovak SNS originally left the Roma largely alone, focusing mainly on Czechs, Hungarians, and Jews in the early 1990s. But under the leadership of Ján Slota, Rom-bashing became a "specialty" of the party (e.g. Fried 1997).

More remarkable is the situation in Hungary, a country with one of the largest Rom populations in the region and where nativist discourse stretches far into the mainstream. Here, Roma feature only scantily, even in the propaganda of the populist radical right MIÉP. While Csurka has made some (implicit) Romaphobic statements, claiming for example that Hungary has declined because of "genetic causes" (Barany 2002: 314), his obsessive anti-Semitism probably prevents him from playing the "Roma card" more regularly.[12]

The prejudices against the Roma are diverse and partly nation-specific, although several return in most national settings. One of the most heard prejudices is that Roma are inherently "primitive"; in this sense, the populist radical right largely works with the same stereotypes as many Western Romaphiles, but come to a fundamentally opposite evaluation. Slota has called Roma "children of nature" (in Gyárfášová 2002: 191), with whom one can only deal with "a big whip and a small yard" (in Cibulka 1999: 126).

Another key prejudice against the Roma is that they are (inherently) criminal. The discourses of Central and East European populist radical right parties are full of references to "the Gypsy mafia," "criminal Gypsy gangs," or "Gypsy thieves." SNS leader Slota has claimed that 70 percent of the Slovak Roma are criminal, obviously not substantiating that claim with any statistical material. SPR-RSČ leader Sladek, probably the most Romaphobic politician in Europe, even went so far as to state in his parliamentary opening speech of 1994 that "Gypsy children" were criminal because of the mere fact that they were born (Barany 2002).[13] Politicians

---

[12] For example, one of his most openly Romaphobic statements mainly portrayed Roma as naïve henchmen of the Jews, and was therefore primarily anti-Semitic (see Chiantera-Stutte & Petö 2003). Similar arguments can be found in other parties in Eastern Europe: for example, the Bulgarian BNRP sees the Roma as pawns of the CIA, the Open Society Institute (e.g. = Jews), and the Freemasons (see Büchsenschütz & Georgiev 2001).

[13] Other prominent members of the SPR-RSČ have made similar remarks, such as MP Jan Vik, who stated in October 1993: "We can't wait for the country to be flooded by crime.

from Slovak SNS honorary chairman and MP Vitazoslav Móric to Romanian PRM leader Tudor have called for the internment of Roma in "reservations" or "settlements" to solve the problem of "Gypsy crime." In this discourse the parties combine their nativist and authoritarian features and play into the widespread prejudices about Roma crime within their native societies.

A third prejudice depicts the Roma as social parasites. The distressingly high levels of unemployment among Roma are not regarded as a sign of discrimination by the majority populations, but are instead considered proof of the claimed parasitic nature of Roma. The Slovak SNS employed this theme in the 1998 parliamentary elections with the slogan, "Let's vote for a Slovakia without parasites." While this was one of the more subtle Romaphobe expressions of the party, the message was not lost on the average Slovak voter, despite party leader Slota's claim that the term "parasite" applied to "quite a lot of Gypsies but also to whites" (in Fisher 2000: 42).

A fourth and final prejudice is that Roma are the beneficiaries of state discrimination. This discourse parallels the anti-immigrant rhetoric of the populist radical right in the Western part of the continent, increasingly employed in the East as well. Populist radical right parties, like the Czech NS, claim that "we are discriminated against in our own country."

In addition to targeting the Roma, this prejudice is cloaked in populism in an attack on the political elite, who are held responsible for reverse discrimination in favor of the Roma at the expense of their "own people." Some parties also use it in their nativist struggle against foreign influences, particularly of "Western" countries and organizations such as the EU and the US, which pressure domestic politicians into adopting measures of positive discrimination towards Roma.

In countries where Roma (and Sinti) constitute just a tiny minority, including all Western European countries, anti-Roma sentiments are less prominent, but still latently present (e.g. Sigona 2005). This was evident in antirefugee campaigns after the fall of the Berlin Wall, which specifically targeted Roma refugees from Eastern Europe. For example, the DLVH targeted a Macedonian Roma woman in a campaign against *Schein-Asylanten* (sham refugees) in the German city of Cologne (Brück 2005: 32). However, in most cases populist radical right parties played only a minor role in the Romaphobic campaigns, which were mainly

At age three, a Gypsy will see his drunk father, his prostitute mother, and all we try to do for him will prove in vain. His parents tell him the best way of life is stealing" (in Sobotka 2003: 28).

led by mainstream tabloid media and local politicians (e.g. Grillo 2005; Nordberg 2004).

3.4   Conclusion

If one accepts German philosopher Carl Schmitt's definition of politics as the distinction between friends and foes, populist radical right parties are quintessentially political. They divide the world into friends and foes on the basis of the three key features of their ideology: nativism, populism, and, to a lesser extent, authoritarianism. In most cases, while attention is paid primarily to enemies within the state, but outside of the nation (notably immigrants and indigenous minorities), the biggest threat is often ascribed to the enemies within the state and within the nation (i.e. the corrupt and traitorous elites).

In their propaganda, foes are far more prevalent than friends. The populist radical right is a clear example of the politics of fear, which has become even more pronounced in Europe with the end of the Cold War and the terrorist attacks of 9/11. The politics of fear plays an important role in homogenizing the ingroup and polarizing the relationship towards outgroups. Given that virtually all these ingroup–outgroup distinctions have a strong moral dimension, compromise is almost impossible (after all, this would "contaminate" the pure ingroup). It is important to realize that this type of thinking is not limited to the populist radical right. The politics of fear is a key strategy in both terrorist and antiterrorist campaigns (e.g. Stern 2004). Moreover, much of the official discourse on issues such as crime and immigration is based on a politics of fear (e.g. Furedi 2005; Huysmans 2004).

However, the friend–foe distinction is also an extreme form of a more common ingroup–outgroup differentiation. As such, the various enemies and related prejudices perform different functions in defining the ingroup *ex negativo*. For example, the description of some enemies as primitive (e.g. Muslim and Roma) helps to define the ingroup as advanced and modern. Similarly, the targeting of criminal enemies (e.g. elites, dealers, immigrants, Roma) indirectly says that the ingroup is honest. The identification of parasitic enemies (e.g. Roma and *Sozialschmarotzer*) proclaims the ingroup as hard-working and social. In this way, the enemies provide implicit and intuitive substance to an otherwise vaguely defined "nativeness."

4   *Männerparteien*

It is hard now (although, unfortunately not impossible) to envisage an account of the extreme right that does not take the importance of gender seriously. Instead the great danger may now be that studies will recognise the importance of the relationship between the extreme right and women but in such a way as to obscure its complexity.   (Durham 1998: 167)

4.1   Introduction

The relationship between populist radical right parties and women has been the subject of much commentary but surprisingly little serious research. The first academic article published in a prominent English-language academic journal appeared only in 2004 (see Givens 2004). The situation is not much better in other academic sources, including edited volumes and less prominent journals. As far as women and "the extreme right" are topics of research, most academic work still focuses on historical fascism rather than on the contemporary populist radical right.

As is often the case in this field, the situation is somewhat better in the German-language literature, although even here the research is limited and, arguably, not representative. The main studies are based on in-depth interviews with a very small number of female activists within extreme right (often neo-Nazi) nonparty organizations (for a recent overview, see Hammann 2002). Moreover, the few studies that focus exclusively on women in populist radical right parties are based on a very small and highly selective number of interviews; for example, the study of "women politicians in the Austrian FPÖ" is based on fourteen leading female politicians (*Spitzenpolitikerinnen*) in the party (Rösslhumer 1999), while the often-quoted study of "the women in the REP" has an empirical foundation of interviews with just fifteen female party members (Skrzydlo *et al.* 1997). The most egregious example is the book *Women and Right-Wing Radicalism in Europe: A Study of Women in Leading Positions in Right-Wing Radical Parties in Germany, France and Italy* (Brück 2005), which is based on a mere seven "guided interviews" with women in more or less leading positions in six different parties in three countries.[1]

Solid studies of the role of women in the organizations and ideologies of populist radical right parties are practically nonexistent. The only exception is a little-known edited volume, *Extreme Right Parties – A Possible Home for Women* (Amesberger & Halbmayr 2002a), which combines English- and German-language chapters on four populist radical right parties (FN, FPÖ, SPR-RSČ and SNS) and the MSI/AN. Notwithstanding its marginal presence within the literature, this highly original and remarkable piece of scholarship is a landmark in the study of the role of women in populist radical right parties.

This chapter has two main goals. The first aim is to provide a comprehensive overview of the role of women in the ideologies and organizations of populist radical right parties in Europe. Obviously, the argumentations and evidence from the above-mentioned edited volume feature prominently in this chapter. Additionally, I have called upon many colleagues to help me find more detailed information about the situation in their respective countries. Finally, various data and insights from my own research on populist radical right parties in various countries are included.

The second aim of this chapter is to provide a revisionist account of the main "truths" that are held in the field. The key argument is that most research on the role of women in populist radical right parties is seriously flawed because of, what I will call provocatively, a "feminist bias." The main assertions are based on incorrect assumptions and a flawed research design. Regarding the former, most work in the field builds upon two erroneous assumptions: (1) gender equality is the normal situation in party politics; and (2) all women hold modern (or even feminist) views on gender roles. Regarding the research design, populist radical right parties are too often studied in isolation, and compared (implicitly) to the "normal" situation of gender parity in society, or they are analyzed in a specific subcontext of other political parties, most notably left-wing and Green parties. These feminist and selection biases have led to overstated claims of specific gender inequality and traditional gender views within populist radical right parties. But they have also been used to substantiate incorrect explanations for the (actual) occurrence of these phenomena. The conclusion will present an alternative explanation for the gender disparity within the populist radical right.

---

[1] The interviews were with one woman each of the DVU, NPD, and REP in Germany, one woman each of the MSI/AN and LN in Italy, and two women of the French FN (Brück 2005: 9).

4.2   Ideology

Much literature on the role of women in populist radical right and other nativist ideologies is written by self-declared feminist authors, most but not all of whom are women activists (e.g. Mostov 1999; Lesselier & Venner 1997; Seidel 1988a). A key feature of these studies is that authors assume that the (female) readership already knows that the populist radical right regards women as inferior to men. The (presumed) self-evidence of the populist radical right's sexism relieves the author of the burden of empirical justification; thus it is invoked through a seemingly random selection of sexist citations from a wide variety of sources and organizations rather than systematically studied. Few of the authors follow conventional academic argumentation and methods, such as defending their chosen data, or start with an open view of the possible outcomes.

Within this limited and largely homogeneous subfield, all nativists are believed to share a highly traditional view on gender roles in which women are seen and treated as second-rate citizens. In this alleged "normative cult of motherhood" (Pető 2002) women are reduced completely to mothers, who have a duty to secure the survival of the nation by providing and raising multiple offspring (e.g. Benton 1998; Nagel 1998; Yuval-Davis 1997). Whether or not this image is expressed by the populist radical right alone, or by all right-wing parties, seems one of the few points of debate within this subcommunity (e.g. Pető 2002; Capitan & Guillaumin 1997; Seidel 1988a).

The few systematic content analyses of the ideologies of populist radical right parties do not support this stereotypical view on gender relations within the populist radical right (e.g. Amesberger & Halbmayr 2002a; Mudde 2000a). Indeed, they seem closer to the opinion of Eleonore Kofman, who has argued that "there is not a single and consistent attitude to the family and its social relations among Far Right movements" (1998: 91).

As far as a consensus does exist, it is in the populist radical right parties' perception of *Frauenpolitik* (women politics) mainly as *Familienpolitik* (family politics), their opposition to the *Gleichmacherei* (equalization) of the feminists, and stringent defense of the "natural differences" between the sexes.[2] The populist radical right further argues that as women are the only sex that can give birth, and offspring are vital for the survival of the nation, women should be "protected" in their "sublime role of

---

[2] This resembles the "equal but different" position towards cultures of the *nouvelle droite* (i.e. ethnopluralism), which is also very popular among populist radical right parties (e.g. Spectorowski 2000; De Benoist 1985).

housewife and mother" (CP'86 1989). This is particularly strong in populist radical right (and conservative) parties in countries with low birth rates, such as Croatia, France, and Russia; the FN has declared *dénatalité* as one of the greatest threats to the French nation (see Davies 1999: 120–4). However, beyond this rather minimalist combination of patriarchal family values and antifeminism, which are indeed shared by many right-wing parties (notably conservatives), lies a more nuanced and diversified world of party positions.

The academic literature distinguishes between a "traditional" view, in which women are seen exclusively as mothers, and a "modern traditional" view, in which women (want to) work but remain primarily responsible for the family and the home (Amesberger & Halbmayr 2002b).[3] In the traditional view, women are discouraged from working and are treated as either mothers or mothers-to-be. The exclusive goal of relevant policy measures is to provide a favorable climate for women to become mothers and housewives. This is done by both negative and positive policies. The traditional parties will not support initiatives that make it easier for women to work (e.g. child care provisions), and even propose legislation to make it more difficult (e.g. through special taxes). Instead, they will exclusively support policies that keep the mother at home, such as the contentious *Kinderbetreuungsscheck* (child care check) of the Austrian FPÖ, salaries for housewives, and tax breaks for (large) families (e.g. Amesberger & Halbmayr 2002a).

However, many populist radical right parties hold a more "modern traditional" view on women. They prefer women to be housewives, and support several of the above-mentioned measures, but they also accept that women have a career. Most parties would probably agree with the Russian LDPR's entry on "women" in the party's political ABC:

The good option would be when a woman, before she turns 30–35 years old, invests more energy in the upbringing of the young generation in the family and in the strengthening of the family as such. And after that, she can start working, first maybe a couple of days a week, and then gradually she moves towards a full working day [*sic*]. (LDPR n.d.a)

Still, there is quite some difference within this group of parties regarding how much women should be encouraged to work. While some parties limit themselves to not opposing the professional activity of women, others call for more state-supported facilities to help women combine

---

[3] In many parties one can find both views being supported by different factions (not strictly men against women), even though in most cases the issue remains secondary to all. For an account of the confusing struggles on this particular issue within the British NF, see Durham (1991).

raising children and holding a job (e.g. Agir, MNR, SNS, SPR-RSČ). The DVU program explicitly states that "the combination of work and raising children must be promoted," e.g. through "better opportunities in extra-familiar care" (DVU n.d.: point 4), while the Austrian BZÖ wants to increase the offer of child care and the building of multigenerational houses (*generationengerechten Wohnungsbau*) to facilitate working parents, stating that "the occupation of women is self-evident" (BZÖ 2005: 6–7). Finally, some parties also call explicitly for equal pay for equal work in their programs (e.g. FPÖ 2005: 18; 1997: 24; REP 1990: 22).

Similarly, not all populist radical right parties see eye-to-eye on the issue of gender quotas. Most parties are skeptical about, if not outrightly hostile to, any quota, particularly for ethnic minorities but also for women, arguing that positive discrimination is also discrimination. Against the "authoritarian politics" of quotas (MNR 2002), these parties put "quality" and "competences" as the only criteria in selecting representatives. In the words of Anke Van dermeersch (2002), a former Miss Belgium and prominent MP of the Belgian VB, "we don't need positive discrimination because we want to be judged on the basis of our competences and merits and because we are also not a poor minority that needs gifts from the men." The South Tyrolean Die Freiheitlichen (The Freedomites, F) even devotes one of its ten points to the issue: "Self-conscious women instead of quota women [*Quotentanten*]! NO to women quota" (F n.d.).

But not all populist radical right parties reject "quota women" (e.g. FPÖ, REP). Some have accepted temporary measures of positive discrimination for women, including in their own party. The first program of the German REP included a special section, entitled "Equal Rights for Men and Women," in which the party pledged to award "an appropriate number of political mandates within the party" to women (REP 1983: 5). That this was not mere talk is shown by the fact that the share of women within the leadership of the REP was at an estimated 20 percent, "by all means respectable" compared to other German parties (Rommelspacher 2001: 207).

On feminism the views are not always the same either. Whereas some parties and activists reject everything about feminism, others acknowledge the important achievements of the first wave of feminism, such as equality in education and voting as well as improvement of working conditions and rights. What they claim to oppose is the "extremist" feminists of the second wave, who are believed to be Marxists, pursuing a "class struggle of the sexes" based upon antimale and unnatural policies (e.g. Rommelspacher 2001: 209; Kofman 1998). For example, the North Rhine-Westphalia branch of the REP declared: "The German women's movement has a tradition of which we can be proud. However, it has obviously nothing to do with the dogged equalization [*Gleichmacherei*] of man and woman of the contemporary self-proclaimed emancipists [*Emanzen*]" (in Brauner-Orthen 2001: 64). And the Turkish MHP stated in its 1993 program that "we strongly oppose feminist attacks upon the family and its social functions" (in IHF 2000: 452).

In postcommunist Europe, feminism carries the dual stigma of being linked to both "the fanatical man-haters of the West" and "the imposition of communist rule," which is not just limited to the populist radical right (Rueschemeyer 1998: 293; also Mostov 1999). Consequently, SNS leader Anna Maliková would start her quite progressive call for more gender equality in Slovak politics with the statement: "I'm not a feminist, but . . ." (in Gyárfášová 2002: 183). Still, this does not necessarily mean that Eastern European populist radical right parties are more traditional than those in the West. For example, the election platform of the Croatian HSP calls for the "equal treatment [of women] in social, political, and economic life" (HSP n.d.b).

Even abortion is not universally rejected within the European populist radical right. The Czech SPR-RSČ explicitly defended women's right to choose, while the Austrian FPÖ and Dutch CD did not discuss abortion in their election programs (e.g. FPÖ 2005; Havelková 2002; Mudde 2000a). While the (large) majority of the population in these countries favors the legality of abortion, this does not necessarily effect the positions of populist radical right parties. For example, the Dutch CP'86 staunchly opposed abortion, referring to it as "the mass murder of the unborn child" (CP'86 1990: 12.9). And in Eastern Europe, which as a consequence of the communist legacy is in large majority pro-choice (e.g. CDC 2003), most populist radical right parties are vehemently antiabortion – they are also more openly and staunchly Christian than their comrades in the West. HDZ leader and Croatian President Tuđman, who believed that giving birth to at least four children was "the sacred duty" of Croatian women, called women who have abortions "mortal enemies of the nation" (in Mostov 1999: 55).

Interestingly, many female activists within populist radical right parties live very different lives than they and their parties promote (e.g. Brück 2005; Amesberger & Halbmayr 2002a; Rommelspacher 2001). While few parties strictly oppose divorce, it is clearly seen as a last resort, particularly when children are involved (e.g. CD 1998). Nonetheless being divorced does not appear to preclude women from successful careers within populist radical right parties – Australian One Nation Party (ONP) leader Pauline Hanson, twice divorced, even defined herself as "a mother of four children, a sole parent" (in Winter 2002: 203). Similarly, while most parties (strongly) prefer marriage over other forms of relationships, nonmarried women can hold high positions – Anna Maliková was unmarried and without children when she became leader of the Slovak SNS.[4] And many female populist radical right politicians themselves combine a full career with the motherhood of one or more (often young) children.

Finally, there are many women (and men) within populist radical right parties who do not share the party view on gender roles (e.g. Brück 2005; Hammann 2002; Rommelspacher 2001). Various authors quote from interviews with (particularly young) women in parties who do not see themselves primarily as mothers and aspire to full(-time) working careers (e.g. Rösslhumer 1999). Some also believe that their party shares these more modern ideas, despite the official traditional position espoused in the literature. A young female economics student from the tiny Deutsche Liga für Volk und Heimat (German League for People and Homeland, DLVH), for instance, argued: "Every woman can do what she wants with us. With us, most are working, and I study . . . I also wouldn't want, when I have finished my studies, to play the housewife, who stands at the stove [am Herd] at home and cooks all day. I will work afterwards, of course" (in Kernbach & Fromm 1993: 184). Consequently, some authors refer to these female activists as "neofeminist" or "postfeminist" (e.g. Brück 2005).

In the end, what is most important to note is that, like so many other issues, gender relations are secondary to the populist radical right. Consequently, they are instrumentalized in the primary nativist struggle, although in conflicting ways. As Kofman noted for the Western European parties:

On the one hand, sexual and gender relations of European populations are seen to be more progressive than the traditional and globally misogynist ones characteristic of immigrant communities in Western Europe . . . On the other hand, the more permissive and liberal relations, and the consequent lower birth rates of the indigenous population, threaten the ability of the nation to survive. (1998: 93)

It is indeed quite ironic to see populist radical right parties defend the equal rights of men and women as a key value of their ideology. After years of complete silence on this topic, the struggle against "Islam," which in the populist radical right view is identical to Islamic fundamentalism (see 3.3.2), has brought the parties to the struggle for women's rights, sometimes even criticizing feminists for doing too little for immigrant women

---

[4] This was not undisputed within the party, as was made clear by the previous leader, Ján Slota, who said about his rival that she has not been able "to deliver even one Slovak soldier" (in Gyárfášová 2002: 183).

(e.g. Brück 2005). For example, during the Austrian "headscarf debate" in the mid 1990s, Haider accused socialist Minister for Women's Affairs Johanna Dohnal, a long-standing and prominent feminist, of not caring about "the real discrimination of women" (Amesberger & Halbmayr 2002c: 293). Similarly, the Zurich branch of the SVP wrote in a position paper on immigration:

In Europe, we fought for centuries for liberal and democratic values, for the separation of state and church, and *gender equality*. It is a particular irony of history that the same left-wing and liberal forces, who led this fight, are today the most eager to advocate generous immigration policies – policies that threaten the basic occidental values. (in Betz 2003a: 199; my italics)

4.3 Party women

One of the least studied subfields of the populist radical right is party membership in general, and the role of women therein in particular. There are many reasons for this, most notably the almost complete lack of large data sets, mostly a result of the suspicion and secrecy of the parties themselves (see also chapter 11). While the received wisdom is that women form a tiny minority within populist radical right parties, few studies have provided empirical evidence for this claim. This section analyzes the representation and roles of women at three different levels within the populist radical right party family: leadership, representatives, and general membership.

4.3.1 Leadership

The number of female party leaders within the populist radical right might not be that staggering in absolute or even relative terms; compared to other party families it is certainly not remarkably low(er). In fact, although reliable comparative data are lacking, it seems to be comparatively high. This is not so much to the credit of the populist radical right, but rather to the shame of other party families.

There has been no single female party leader in the two major parties in Australia, Canada, and the United States (see Davis 1998). In the Anglo-Saxon world, the only female leader of a major party and Prime Minister has been Margaret Thatcher, leader of the British Conservative Party (1975–90). In most of Continental Europe the situation is not as extreme, but it is hardly much better. For example, there has been only one female leader of a relevant political party in postwar Germany: Angela Merkel of the CDU, who recently became the first female *Bundeskanzlerin*. France has seen no female leader of a major party yet, though socialist Edith

Cresson was France's first and so far only female Prime Minister (1991–92).[5] So throughout Europe, including Scandinavia where women are relatively well represented in parliaments and governments, female party leaders still constitute only a tiny minority (e.g. Henig & Henig 2001).

It is quite surprising then that several populist radical right parties have had women as party leaders at some stage: these include Petra Edelmannová of the Czech Národní strana (National Party, NS) (since 2003), Ursula Haubner of the FPÖ (2003–05), Anna Maliková (now Belousosová) of the Slovak SNS (1999–2003), and Susanne Riess-Passer of the Austrian FPÖ (2000–02). Some parties even had founding female leaders: Pia Kjærsgaard is one of the founders and so far the only leader of the highly successful Danish DFP, and Pauline Hanson founded and initially led the Australian ONP. While these still constitute exceptions to the rule of male leadership that also prevails within the populist radical right, they do not stand out as particularly rare relative to the lamentable absence of women in the upper ranks of most other party families.

There are various other examples of women in leading positions. For example, in the few cases where populist radical right parties joined coalition governments, women have largely been part of the administration. In Eastern Europe, one of the two SNS ministers in the 1994–98 Slovak government was a woman, i.e. the Minister of Education and Science, Eva Slavkovská. Previously, she had also been the First Deputy Chairperson and parliamentary leader (1993–94). The Romanian PRM had a female State Secretary of Romanians Abroad in 1995–96, Mitzura Domnica Arghezi, who was also former executive party secretary and president of the Permanent Section of the Romanian Parliament to the Parliamentary Assembly of the Francophony. In the 1998–2000 Serbian coalition government, the SRS originally had four (out of fifteen, i.e. 26.7 percent) female ministers: Jorgovanka Tabaković, Minister of Economic and Property Transformation; Rada Trajkovic, Minister of Family and Child Care; Gordana Pop Lazić, Minister of Local Self-Government; and Maja Gojković, minister without portfolio. Gojković is one of the founders of the SRS, and in addition to occupying various positions within the party (e.g. vice-president and general secretary), she is also currently mayor of Novi Sad, the second biggest city in Serbia.

Similarly, the few populist radical right parties that made it into government in Western Europe have at times had remarkably high levels of

[5] She served at a time when the president, François Mitterrand, was from the same party, which meant that her position was actually not as strong as that of some other prime ministers. That said, in 2000 she was still one of only three female prime ministers in the postwar history of ten major West European countries, including three Scandinavian ones (see Henig & Henig 2001).

female representation.[6] During much of the first Schüssel Government (2000–03), two of the six FPÖ-ministers were women and Susanne Riess-Passer was also vice-chancellor. In the second (or possibly better: third) Schüssel Government, Ursula Haubner (Social Security, Generations and Consumer Protection) and Karin Miklautsch (Justice) are two of the four BZÖ ministers. Even the LN, probably the most male chauvinist populist radical right party in Western Europe, both in terms of rhetoric and representation, appointed a woman to a high position after their successful 1994 elections: Irene Pivetti, only 31 years old at the time, became the youngest ever president of the Chamber of Deputies in Italy (Cento Bull & Gilbert 2001).

Obviously, this is not to argue that women are well represented within the populist radical right leadership. In fact, it is absolutely clear that leading women are a minority within these parties. However, in this respect populist radical right parties do not differ from other political parties, not even on the left. As far as party leaders and ministers are concerned, politics is still very much the business of (older, white, middle-class) men. As this overview demonstrates, women are not absent from leading position within populist radical right parties, as is often suggested, and their underrepresentation might actually be no worse (or even less bad) than in other party families. Whether or not this is indeed the case, and to what extent, can only be established unequivocally when more data become available.

What *is* a striking phenomenon within the populist radical right party family, however, is the number of leading female politicians who are directly related to male leaders. There are various categories of related female leaders: wives, lovers, sisters, daughters. The most high-ranking woman in the Dutch CD was Wil Schuurman, the partner and later wife of party leader Hans Janmaat. Similarly, Sabina Funar was the first wife of a post-1989 political leader, then PUNR leader Gheorghe Funar, who entered Romanian politics at a senior level (Gallagher 1997). Somewhat surprisingly, in parties that stress traditional family values, (not that secret) lovers of party leaders can also achieve high party positions. This has been the case with Laura Rajisglová, the lover of SPR-RSČ leader Sládek, who was one of the party's MPs. Rarer has been the involvement of sisters of party leaders; the most well-known case is the short tenure of Ursula Haubner, Jörg Haider's sister, as FPÖ-*Bundesobfrau*. The most common involvement of female relatives

---

[6] Obviously, this claim is relative, and compares the share of female ministers of populist radical right parties with that of other political parties in Europe (on general figures, see Ramet 2005).

of party leaders, however, is that of daughters. Two of VB-founder Karel Dillen's three daughters have been party representatives as have the two daughters of FN-founder Jean-Marie Le Pen. In both cases one daughter was the leading female politician within the party for a period; allegedly Le Pen was even grooming his favorite daughter, Marine, as his successor until a dispute between them in 2005 (Henley 2005; Rogge 2005).

In some parties wives will stand in for their husbands in cases where for legal reasons they cannot run themselves. The FN in particular has employed this substitution strategy; various wives of leading members have stood in elections to replace their suspended husbands. Le Pen, whose decision to have himself replaced by his (second) wife in the 1999 European elections was instrumental in the party's subsequent split, even came up with an ideological justification for this approach. In an interview with the French newspaper *Libération*, he argued: "It's true that in the Front National we have a culture of the couple, a family culture, and that in the history of our families it is the women who take the place of the men when they are at war or are unable to be there" (in Mayer & Sineau 2002: 77).

4.3.2   Representatives

The image of the populist radical right as a male-dominated realm extends to its representation, both within the party and within the political system. The parties are believed to have fewer female representatives than other political parties and even these few are thought to be largely irrelevant. In other words, if women are included within the party organs, they are believed to be noninfluential. The same beliefs are held with regard to female representation in state organs and the positioning of female candidates on party lists; i.e. either the number of female candidates is low or, in electoral systems where districts play an important role, their number is high in the most difficult districts.

Again very few empirical data are available. One of the few documented cases is the *Bundespräsidium* (federal presidency) of the German REP, which consisted of 18 percent women in 1993 and 23 percent in 1995 (Birsl 1994: 120). In the case of the French FN, the share of women in the *comité central* (legislature) was 15 percent in 1996 and 17 percent in 1998, whereas the figures for the *bureau politique* (executive) were 5 percent and 7 percent, respectively (Allwood & Wadia 2000: 62). In 1997 the proportion of women in the different organs of the Austrian FPÖ were 11 percent in the federal party presidium (*Bundesparteipräsidium*) and roughly 17 percent in the federal party's executive committee (*Bundesparteivorstand*) and leadership (*Bundesparteileitung*) (Amesberger & Halbmayr 2002c: 356–7).

While it is already very difficult to get reliable information on female representation in the party organs, it is nearly impossible to find data that enable a comparison between the populist radical right and other parties. The literature yields only four cases; interestingly three from the East and only one from the West.

The data on French parties in the 1990s are very sketchy and must be treated with great caution. Survey data of party congress delegates in 1990 show that the FN had the lowest proportion of female delegates (18 percent) of all French parties (Lesselier 2002: 129). However, relative to other parties the numbers are not that striking: the socialist PS had 19 percent, the Gaullist RPR 24 percent, the communist PCF 29 percent and the green Les Verts 30 percent female delegates (see table 4.1). On the other hand, party ideology does seem to play a significant role with regard to the inclusion of women in the higher party organs. On average, the FN fares poorly in this respect when compared with left-wing parties (PCF, PS, and Les Verts), but appears quite typical where right-wing parties (RPR and UDF) are the standard. In fact, in terms of female representation in party organs and on party lists the FN is fairly similar to the other French right-wing parties (e.g. Allwood & Wadia 2000).

In Hungary female representation in the leadership of all parties was very low throughout the 1990s. Consequently, the 7 percent of MIÉP was hardly shocking when compared to the other Hungarian political parties. Only two parties had significantly higher figures, i.e. the two big parties, the conservative FIDESz-MPS and the social democratic MSzDP, whereas virtually all other small parties had similar or even lower scores, including the progressive liberal SzDSz with 6 percent (Montgomery & Ilonszki 2003: 115).

In Croatia the share of women in the leading committee of the HDZ was 16 percent and that of the HSP 18 percent (IHF 2000: 127–8). While this was clearly lower than in the liberal HS (40 percent) and the social democratic SDP (30 percent), it differed little from the conservative liberal HSLS (20 percent) and even exceeded that of the center-right HNS (13 percent) and the peasant party HSS (7 percent). In Slovenia, finally, the situation was fairly similar in 1993: with just 12 percent the SNS had one of the lowest shares of female representation in the party presidency (Antić Gaber 1999: 10). Only the social democratic SDSS (10.5 percent) performed worse, while the pensioner party DSPS (13.3 percent) came close.

Table 4.1 *Female representation in organs of the major French parties (1990s)*

Party Year	Legislature (%)	Executive (%)	Secretariat (%)
FN			
1996	15	5	
1998	17	7	1
PCF			
1996	25	23	14
1999	28	30	20
PS			
1990	21	19	7
1994		26	9
1999		30	29
RPR			
1990		24	
1994		0	
1999		13	
UDF			
1995	5		
1999	14		
Les Verts			
1992	34	27	
1996	35	45	
1999		47	

Source: Adapted from Allwood & Wadia (2000: ch. 2)

Regarding female representation in representative state organs, draw-ing a general picture is even more difficult. The fact that many populist radical right parties have few if any representatives in (national) par-liaments strongly influences the relative weight of one individual. For example, for certain periods the FN (1989–93) had a 100 percent female representation in the national parliament, as they had only one MP, who happened to be a woman. In many more cases it was the other way around, i.e. a 100 percent male representation, the male party leader (e.g. CP/CD leader Hans Janmaat 1982–86 and 1989–94; VB leader Karel Dillen 1978–87). However, this phenomenon is not unique to the populist radical right. As Milica Antić Gaber has stated, reflecting on the (nonlinear) relationship between party size and female represen-tation in general: "The only certainty is that the chances of women's

Table 4.2 *Female representation in populist radical right party factions in the European Parliament (1979–2009)*

Country / Party	1979–1984 No.	%	1984–1989 No.	%	1989–1994 No.	%	1994–1999 No.	%	1999–2004 No.	%	2004–2009 No.	%
Austria												
FPÖ									1	20	0	0
Belgium												
FNb							0		0			
VB					0		0	0	0	0	0	0
Denmark												
DFP									0		0	0
France												
FN			1	10	1	10	1	9	0	0	2	29
Germany												
REP					1	17						
Greece												
LAOS											0	0
Italy												
AS											1	100
LN							0		0	0	0	0
MS-FT									0		0	
Poland												
LPR											1	10
UK												
DUP	0		0	0	0	0	0	0	0	0	0	0

Note: Boxes are only empty when the party did not have *any* (male or female) representation during that legislature.
Source: European Parliament, www.europarl.europa.eu (accessed April 2005).

election increase with the chances of the party winning additional votes" (1999: 20).

The picture is particularly striking in the European Parliament, where populist radical right parties have always been poorly represented (see table 4.2). At first sight, the striking number of all-male factions seems to support the received wisdom that women are not well represented within populist radical right parties. However, it should be noted that in most cases the all-male factions are *one*-male factions. The only exceptions are all factions of the LN and VB, and the 1999–2004 faction of the FN. That said, even in cases where women are represented in the populist radical

right factions in the European Parliament (EP), the percentages
are not particularly impressive, with the possible exceptions of the
29 percent of the current FN faction and the 20 percent of the former
FPÖ faction (1999–2004). The case of the Italian Alternativa Sociale
(Social Alternative, AS) is an outlier, explained by the fact that it was an
electoral alliance around Alessandra Mussolini, who is the only MEP.[7]

When the populist radical right is compared to other party families, the
picture becomes even less pronounced. While the percentages remain
well below the average female representation within the EP, these figures were also far removed from 50 percent. For example, the percentage of female MEPs was 16.8 percent in the first directly elected
European Parliament of 1979–84 and increased to one-quarter in 1994
(Norris 1997: 211). This upward trend has continued, although it is
not perfectly linear; in the current EP (2004–09) female MEPs constitute 30.2 percent (www.europarl.eu.int/presentation/1_1_en.htm). Again,
levels of female representation differ sharply between parties and party
families; on average the percentages are a lot higher in the left-wing
party families (particularly the Greens) than in the right-wing party
families.

Researchers have established "a strong link between the proportion
of women elected in each country to the European and national parliaments" (Norris 1997: 212). This is also the case for populist radical right
parties, where the picture is not much different in national parliaments.
Virtually all one-person factions are male, a phenomenon by no means
exclusive to the populist radical right as the vast majority of leaders of all
political parties are male. When the factions are bigger, however, women
remain significantly underrepresented. The only time the Dutch populist
radical right had more than one seat in the parliament, i.e. the CD in the
period 1994–98, one of the three members was a woman (and the partner
of the leader). This is actually still a comparatively high proportion. The
only time the FN had more than one MP in the Assemblée Nationale, in
the 1986–89 term, only one out of thirty-five of its parliamentarians was
female (2.8 percent).

At first glance, the situation in Central and Eastern Europe does not
appear particularly different from that in Western Europe (see table
4.3). The most striking trend in the 1990s was that there was no trend.
Female representation ranged from 27.8 percent in the case of the Czech

---

[7] The AS is an electoral coalition, so far only successful in the 2004 European elections,
consisting of three tiny groups that try to combine modern politics with loyalty to classic
Italian fascism: Alessandra Mussolini's Azione Sociale (Social Action), Forza Nuova (New
Force), and Fronte Nazionale (National Front).

Table 4.3 *Female representation in populist radical right parliamentary factions in Central and Eastern Europe, 1992–2005*

Country	Populist radical right party (year of election)	% of female MPs (party)	% of female MPs (country)	(%) Difference (party − country)
Croatia	HDZ 1995	4.8	4.6	0.2
	HDZ 1992	3.5	4.1	−0.6
	HSP 1995	0	4.6	−4.6
	HSP 1992	0	4.1	−4.1
Czech Republic	SPR-RSČ 1996	27.8	14.0	13.8
	SPR-RSČ 1992	0	9.5	−9.5
Hungary	MIÉP 1998	7.1	8.3	−1.2
Poland	LPR 2005	14.3	20.4	−6.1
	LPR 2001	26.3	20.2	6.1
	ROP 1997	1.3	13.0	−11.7
Romania	PRM 2004	12.8	11.1	1.7
	PRM 2000	11	12	−1
	PRM 1996	15.8	7.3	8.5
	PRM 1992	0.0	3.8	−3.8
	PUNR 1996	0.0	7.3	−7.3
	PUNR 1992	6.7	3.8	2.9
Russia	LDPR 2003	5.6	9.1	−3.5
	LDPR 1999	0.0	7.8	−7.8
	LDPR 1995	2.0	10.2	−8.2
	LDPR 1993	7.9	13.4	−5.5
Serbia	SRS 2003	4.9	9.6	−4.7
	SRS 2001	8.7	10.8	−2.1
Slovakia	SNS 1998	21.5	12.7	8.8
	SNS 1994	11.1	14.7	−3.6
Slovenia	SNS 1996	25.0	7.8	17.2
	SNS 1992	16.7	13.3	3.4

Source: Adapted from OSCE/ODIHR (2004); Antić Gaber & Ilonszki (2003); Matland & Montgomery (2003); Saxonberg (2003); CoE (2002); Havelková (2002); www.cedp.ro; www.lpr.pl (accessed April 2005).

SPR-RSČ in 1996 to 0.0 percent of various populist radical right parties at some time, including the same SPR-RSČ in 1992. This also shows that levels of representation differ sharply, and as much between parties and countries as between legislative periods. Both SNS parties had large differences in the share of female MPs in their respective terms: 8.3 percent for the Slovene and 10.4 percent for the Slovak parties, respectively. In Poland, the difference between the LPR in 2001 (26.3 percent) and the ROP in 1997 (1.3 percent) demonstrates that there is no discernible trend at the country level.

Clearly the proportion of female representatives of populist radical right parties varies dramatically over time; indeed, this is true of political parties in general, including bigger mainstream ones. Consequently, the relative over- and underrepresentation of women in these parties changes regularly. In the Central and Eastern European parliaments of the 1990s female representation in parliamentary factions of populist radical right parties was more often below than above the parliamentary average (roughly two-thirds and one-third, respectively).

The underrepresentation of female parliamentarians might be extraordinary compared to the percentage of women within the whole (adult) population, but it is far less staggering if compared to some of the other political parties. Unfortunately, very few studies include these comparisons, and empirical data are thus scarce. Moreover, many scholars compare populist radical right parties only with left-wing parties, notably social democrats and Greens, which are well known for their support for gender equality (e.g. Matland 2003; Jalušič & Antić Gaber 2001; Norris 1993). Even these left-wing parties often face large gender disparities both in their representation and party membership.

The differences between the populist radical right and *right-wing* parties are even smaller, and in some cases nonexistent. Even the 2.8 percent of female MPs of the FN in the 1986–89 parliament was more than the 1.9 percent of the Gaullist RPR (Mayer & Sineau 2002: 78). Similarly, while the 11 percent female MPs of the Romanian PRM in 2000–04 was just below the average (of 12 percent), only one party exceeded this level of female representation: the self-declared social democratic PDSR with 22 percent. The other three parties, all mainstream right-wing, were with 2–4 percent well behind the PRM (CoE 2002). With 28 percent female representation, the SPR-RSČ outperformed all other Czech parties, including the social democratic ČSSD with 18 percent and the communist KSČM with 23 percent (Saxonberg 2003: 166). In Slovenia, the SNS has consistently been among the parties with the highest percentage of female MPs (Antić Gaber & Ilonszki 2003).[8]

---

[8] In contrast, at 21.5 percent the relatively high percentage of the Slovak SNS was still the lowest of all parliamentary parties in that country – paradoxically, while being the only

Again the role of family members of male party leaders is striking. Often party lists are filled up with the names of partners and siblings of male candidates. An investigative article in the left-wing Flemish daily *De Morgen* (10/05/2003) paints a sobering picture. Of the 106 female VB-candidates for the federal elections of 2003, twenty-nine were married to a leading party member, seven were a girlfriend or lover, five were family, and no less than twenty-five (almost one-quarter!) were employed as secretaries within the party. Additionally, seven of the women had been elected in earlier elections, but had immediately given up their mandate for a nonelected male candidate.

Once more, the French FN is the most extreme proponent of the instrumentalization of female partners for party purposes, particularly regarding municipal assemblies. As Nonna Mayer and Mariette Sineau have noted cynically, but correctly: "The hierarchy of the sexes was generally respected: when the husband was mayor the wife was only a municipal councilor or at best a deputy-mayor. When the woman herself was elected mayor, it was only to substitute her husband because he had been declared ineligible to exercise his function as a result of fraud" (2002: 81–2).

In short, women are undoubtedly underrepresented in the parliamentary factions of populist radical right parties, but the picture is less apparent than is often assumed. While the situation is particularly grave when compared to the percentage of women in the population as a whole, it is far less striking when one compares it to the percentages of women in other parliamentary parties (e.g. Lovenduski & Norris 1993; Randall 1987). For example, according to the Inter-Parliamentary Union the average share of female MPs in a cross-section of Western democracies was a mere 16.5 percent around 1990, while the share of female candidates in national elections accounted for 21.3 percent (in Norris 1993: 310). For April 2005 the same organization recorded an average of 18.9 percent in the single and lower houses of the parliaments in "Europe-OSCE member countries" (IPU 2005).

While these general averages are already well below gender equality, they obscure the complexity of the situation. Various studies have shown that party ideology plays an important role in explaining strategies for (female) candidate selection and the share of female representatives in party and legislative bodies (e.g. Caul 1999; Lovenduski & Norris 1993). However, the difference is not so much between populist radical right

relevant Slovak party with a female leader and "the most generous party regarding its share of women on its candidate list" (Gyárfášová 2002: 181).

parties and the rest, but rather between (new) left-wing parties and the rest:

Social democratic and Green parties are far more likely to believe intervention in the recruitment process is necessary and appropriate, hence positive discrimination is justified to bring about short-term change. Parties of the right and centre are more likely to rely upon rhetorical strategies, and possibly affirmative action, in the belief that women should be encouraged to stand, and party members should be encouraged to select them, but the recruitment process has to involve 'fair' and open competition. (Norris 1993: 320)

Thus, while the differences between populist radical right and left-wing, particularly Green, parties may be striking in terms of female representation, the populist radical right are clearly parties of the right, and not always very radical at that. In fact, many of the populist radical right parties are (well) ahead of (some of) their right-wing competitors in terms of female representation.

In conclusion then, the most important points to note are that: (1) in virtually all European countries and political parties women are (strongly) underrepresented in major representative bodies; (2) the percentage of women within representative bodies can vary dramatically among different institutions and legislatures, as well as within parties; and (3) unequivocal conclusions about differences between populist radical right parties and their competitors, most notably small and right-wing parties, are hard to draw.

4.3.3   Members

Although there are some studies of members of populist radical right parties, most are very limited in scope, i.e. covering only a particular subset of members of one party. Comparative studies, either within one country or cross-nationally, are virtually nonexistent. And the few studies that do exist do not focus specifically on gender aspects (e.g. Klandermans & Mayer 2005). As is so often the case when few empirical data are available, wild speculations abound.

Regarding the situation in Germany, Kerstin Hammann estimates the share of women and girls within radical and extreme right groups at "only a few percent" (2002: 38), whereas Barbara Kernbach and Rainer Fromm put it at between one-quarter and one-third and growing (1993: 185). Somewhat in the middle, but equally unsubstantiated by empirical data, Joyce Marie Mushaben speaks of "roughly ten per cent of the membership" (1996: 252), while Birgit Rommelspacher believes the share to be "approximately around 20 per cent," adding that "[t]he more extreme the parties are, the lower admittedly is the share of women" (2001: 207). According to the parties themselves, the percentages were 20 percent for the REP and 33 percent for the DVU (see Fromm & Kernbach n.d.: 6).

Where more or less reliable data are available, the picture is unequivocal: women constitute only a (small) minority of the membership of populist radical right parties. In the Austrian FPÖ the share was 26.4 percent overall, although significant differences existed between the various regional branches, ranging from a low 20 percent in Burgenland to a high 33.9 percent in Vienna (Luther 2003: 205). According to the spokesman of the Slovak SNS, approximately one-third of the party membership was female (Gyárfášová 2002: 182), while the Belgian VB stated in 1995 that it had two female members for every seven male members (22 percent). The party acknowledged that this was well below the percentage of women in the two big mainstream parties, which have a relationship of 2:3 (or 40 percent women), suggesting that maybe it could "take women as our next target group in the upcoming membership drive" (in Buelens & Deschouwer 2003: 5).[9]

Slovenia is one of the few countries for which comparative data on female membership in all major political parties are available (see table 13.3 in Antić Gaber 2003: 274). However, the data should be treated with great care, as they are based on estimates from the parties themselves. The Slovenska nacionalna stranka (Slovene National Party, SNS) has the lowest share of women among its members, estimating it at 18 percent in 1993. The other political parties estimated percentages ranging from 20.3 percent for the center-right SDS to 61.7 percent for the Christian democratic SKD. Given that both parties are considered to be right-wing, party ideology does not seem to influence female party membership in Slovenia in a traditional way. The situation is quite similar in Slovakia, where the SNS has by far the lowest share of female members (25 percent), followed by the social democratic SDSS (30 percent), the most progressive of the parties included in the study (see Mallok & Tahirović 2003: 691). Interestingly, the party with the highest share of women, the Christian democratic KDH with 56 percent, shares many of its conservative Catholic views on gender with the SNS.

In the Netherlands the situation is somewhat different. Based on a survey of a random sample of members, scholars established that only 16

---

[9] In the run-up to the local elections of October 2006, the local VB branch in the town of Aalst announced its intention to distribute 30,000 leaflets under the motto "free women in a free city" with the explicit aim of getting women more involved in politics (*Het Nieuwsblad* 03/02/2006).

Table 4.4 *Gender distribution of the membership of major Dutch parties*

	CD	VVD	CDA	D66	PvdA	GL
Male	84	72	80	73	62	67
Female	16	28	20	27	38	33
Total	100	100	100	100	100	100
N	204	300	265	362	292	n.a.

Source: Table 6.1 in Esser & Van Holsteyn (1998: 80)

percent of the membership of the CD was female. Moreover, this was the lowest percentage of all major Dutch parties (see table 4.4). Interestingly, the differences from the Christian democratic CDA, the party with a traditionally strong female electorate, are quite small; additionally, two orthodox Protestant parties are not included, one of which did not allow women to become members until 2006 (the SGP), while the other (the CU) most likely has a low share of female members.

Denmark is a particularly interesting case: Scandinavian countries are well known for their progressive gender relations and the DFP is one of two significant populist radical right parties worldwide that was founded by a woman. This notwithstanding, the DFP has the second lowest proportion of female members of all major parties in Denmark. However, their share of 30 percent is quite close to the average of all parties (33 percent) and does not stand out from the two other right-wing parties: a bit less than the conservative KFP with 32 percent, and slightly better than the conservative liberal Venstre with 29 percent (see Pedersen *et al.* 2004: 371). It is only in comparison with the 41 percent of the Christian democratic K and the 46 percent of the radical left SF that the disparity is striking.

The single comprehensive cross-national study of members of populist radical right parties published to date confirms the more general impression that many women join populist radical right parties because of their male partner (Klandermans & Mayer 2005). Interestingly, this was not what Kathleen Blee (2002) found in her study of women in the Ku Klux Klan in the US. On the basis of even more sketchy data, Kernbach and Fromm argue that women no longer enter as "mere appendices of their boyfriends or husbands, but on their own initiative" (1993: 185). However, this difference might be explained by the type of organization women join. Membership in smaller and more extreme organizations requires a far higher level of commitment than the largely passive membership in a populist radical right party. Consequently, one would expect more (individually) motivated people (male or female) to join the smaller and more personal extreme right groups than the larger and more anonymous populist radical right parties.

Despite the underrepresentation of women in the membership of populist radical right parties, and the low priority given to achieving gender equality within them, many parties do have specific suborganizations for women. In the above-mentioned study, four of the five parties had a specific women's organization (Amesberger & Halbmayr 2002a).[10] However, in none of the cases was the organization particularly dynamic or important. As far as they were active, the women's groups would combine relatively emancipatory aims (rather than demands), including the strengthening of the political self-consciousness of women, with antifeminism and a modern traditional view on gender roles (see also Fromm & Kernbach 2001: 72).

4.4 Female voters

The only group of populist radical right women that has received substantial attention from academics outside of the feminist community is the female electorate of populist radical right parties. It is with regard to this group that most theories have been advanced and some studies have appeared in major academic journals (e.g. Gidengil *et al.* 2005; Givens 2004).

4.4.1 The gender gap: the data

Various studies have demonstrated that women vote for populist radical right parties far less than men. Interestingly, this is the only sociodemographic variable that is consistently relevant in practically all European countries (Norris 2005). From Austria to Russia and from France to Slovakia, the electorate of populist radical right parties is constituted by roughly two-thirds men and one-third women (e.g. Evans & Ivaldi 2002; Gyárfášová 2002; Lubbers 2001; White 1997; Betz 1994; Falter 1994). Indeed, the differences have been so striking that some authors have spoken about *Männerparteien* (male parties) with regard to the populist

---

[10] Strictly speaking, this refers to only three populist radical right parties, as this study excludes the Italian MSI/AN (see chapter 2). A fairly singular organization, not included in that book, is the Republikanische Bund der Frauen (Republican League of Women, RBF), the official women's organization of the German REP. It was founded in 1995, twelve years after the party itself, and includes both men and women! According to the group, 70 percent of the members were women and all leading positions were held by women in the mid-1990s (Sturhan 1997: 122–4).

radical right (e.g. Brück 2005; Decker 2004; Geden 2004; Hofmann-Göttig 1989).

While the underrepresentation of women has been consistent both temporally and geographically, there are some important exceptions: in the 1993 French parliamentary elections the FN had a 50–50 electorate (e.g. Mayer & Sineau 2002: 70), while in the 1992 Italian parliamentary elections the LN had a 51–49 (male–female) support (Betz 1994: 143).[11] Eastern Europe has on average shown similar overrepresentation of men, but with even more striking exceptions. In the 1995 parliamentary elections in Croatia "roughly equal numbers" of men and women voted for the HDZ and HSP (Irvine 1998: 230). But most striking is the gender composition of the electorate of the Polish LPR: with 67 percent female voters it resembles the gender basis of a Green rather than a populist radical right party (Siemieńska 2003: note 2). Given that the LPR belongs to the most traditional and conservative parties within the party family, combining populist radical right ideas with orthodox Catholicism, this seems particularly puzzling.

Like most sociodemographic variables, gender is a very general category, often allowing for almost as much variation within the group as between groups. Research suggests that while the general statement that women vote less for populist radical right parties is correct for most female subgroups, it does not hold for all. Electoral studies show that a complex interplay of variables is at work, of which gender is an important one. However, combined with other variables gender has different effects.

For example, in Austria, far more less-educated men than women under forty-five voted for the FPÖ, yet no such difference exists between higher educated men and women over forty-five (Hofinger & Ogris 1996). Similarly, studies make a distinction between various subgroups within the female FN electorate, with age and religion as important distinguishing variables (Mayer & Sineau 2002: 71ff.). In Slovakia, two groups of women could be distinguished on the basis of occupation that are particularly prone to support the SNS: clerks and housewives, on the one hand, and unemployed and retired women, on the other (Gyárfášová 2002: 173).

---

[11] The 2002 parliamentary elections in France showed only a small gender gap for the FN and no gap for the MNR (Evans & Ivaldi 2005: 354), although the latter might have been in part the result of the very small number of MNR voters in the study. Interestingly, if only women had voted in the first round of the 2002 French presidential elections, Le Pen would not have made it into the second round, coming third with 14 percent after Chirac with 22 percent and Jospin with 16 percent. If only men had voted, however, Le Pen would have come first with 20 percent, against Chirac with 17 percent and Jospin with 16 percent (Mayer 2002: 339). I thank Alexandre Dézé for alerting me to this striking fact.

4.4.2 The gender gap: the explanations

It is important to note that female voting behavior differs from that of men not only with respect to populist radical right parties. As Anton Pelinka has noted: "The proximity and the distance to the political center correlates with gender specific voting" (2002: 15). More specifically, relative to men, women vote more for "center" parties and less for "radical" parties. In short, the central question is: "Women vote differently – but why?" (Amesberger & Halbmayr 2002b).

Most empirical research available shows no significant gender differences with regard to voting motivations of the electorate of populist radical right parties (e.g. Gyárfášová 2002; Rommelspacher 2001; though see Amesberger & Halbmayr 2002c). This suggests a very obvious answer to the question why fewer women support these parties than men: fewer women than men hold populist radical right views.[12] Until well into the 1990s this was the conventional view within feminist circles: women had "a certain resistance towards the radical right ideology" (Dobberthien in Siller 1997: 9). Feminist scholars have presented many (highly ideological) explanations for this alleged fact: the innate mother instinct makes women more caring than men; as victims of (male) oppression themselves, women sympathize with other marginalized groups; women are more social and less competitive (either by nature or nurture), etc. (e.g. Birsl 1994). However, empirical studies have proven these explanations to be nothing more than "indefensible wishful thinking" (Siller 1997: 25): there is no significant gender gap in terms of populist radical right attitudes.

Most survey data show that the difference between men and women in terms of nativist attitudes is far from striking, if at all present. While in some West European countries (e.g. Germany and Portugal) men are somewhat more negative towards people from other nations, races or cultures, in others (e.g. France) women are more xenophobic (e.g. Winkler 2003).[13] In a study of twenty-two countries from both parts of Europe as well as the non-European West, the authors find that "[w]omen scored slightly higher on resistance to immigrants than men, but there were no

---

[12] While accepting the feminist critique that this mere statement assumes that women are the exception, rather than men, the fact that populist radical right parties attract only a (small) portion of their potential support, i.e. people (women *and* men) with populist radical right attitudes (see also chapter 9), justifies the "male-centered" approach here.

[13] Other studies have found that even in Germany women are more nativist: for example, an 1989 Infas survey found that almost twice as many women (15 percent) as men (8 percent) supported the slogan "Ausländer raus" (Foreigners out) (see Siller 1997: 25; also Ottens 1997).

differences with regard to resistance to refugees" (Coenders *et al.* 2004: 104).[14]

Moreover apparent gender differences usually disappear in multivariate analyses, i.e. they are largely an artifact of other variables (cf. Coenders *et al.* 2004; Givens 2004; Winkler 2003). In short then, the observation of Mayer and Sineau with regard to the French FN can be extended to populist radical right parties in general: "the paradox of the woman's vote for the Front National is that even when they are authoritarian, nationalist and racist, women are less likely than men to vote for the Front National, a party propounding those values" (2002: 75). So far explanations of electoral behavior have not been able to explain this sharp difference in voting, which continues to exist even in the case of similar attitudes.

The so-called theory of the "central tendency" (Hofmann-Göttig 1989) merely describes the tendency of women to vote for center parties, without providing a clear explanation of the reasons why this is so. Other scholars point to the recent changes in gender roles and the consequent insecurities among (some) women as a reason for populist radical right voting (e.g. Hammann 2002: 72–3). However, this is an adaptation of the more general modernization paradigm (see chapter 9), which at least theoretically applies roughly the same way to men and women.

The theory of "antifeminism," which argues that women do not vote for populist radical right parties because their "antifeminine" or "sexist" ideology abhors female voters, makes intuitive sense, but has both empirical and logical flaws. Most notably, it assumes that women hold progressive (or even feminist) views on gender relations; an assumption not substantiated by empirical research (e.g. Wilcox *et al.* 2003b; Conway *et al.* 1997). Moreover, female voters have been the backbone of the electorates of the Christian democrats and conservatives in postwar Europe, parties that also tend to hold (modern) traditional views on gender (e.g. Amesberger & Halbmayr 2002a).[15] While the position of populist radical right parties will definitely be abhorrent to some women, it is most likely to deter women who are not particularly susceptible to right-wing views anyway. Therefore it is of limited value as a general explanation for the strikingly low share of women in the electorate of these parties, compared

---

[14] Surveys of political and social attitudes in Eastern Europe also show that fewer women than men support democracy (e.g. Haerpfer 2002: 54–6).

[15] While the overrepresentation of women in the electorates of conservative parties has been declining in the West (Harrop & Miller 1987: 204–7), it is (still) very strong in postcommunist Europe (Pető 2002). Also, in Eastern Europe, almost all political parties hold at best a modern traditional view on women, so differentiation between parties on this point is difficult (see Binder 2003).

to both that of men in populist radical right parties and that of women in other right-wing parties.

Studies of some Western European parties have suggested that part of the answer may lie in the role of institutionalized religion as an intervening variable that prevents part of the populist radical right heartland from voting for populist radical right parties (Mayer 2002; Gidengil & Hennigar 2000). Most empirical research demonstrates that people who are actively religious, i.e. regularly attending church and integrated into the religious subculture, vote for populist radical right parties at a much lower rate than the general public (e.g. Billiet 1995; Falter 1994). As older women are generally more religious than older men, they vote for Christian democratic parties more than for populist radical right parties. However, religion does not always act as a buffer against populist radical right voting; indeed, in countries like Croatia, Poland and Slovakia religion seems to strengthen it. Consequently, in these countries the populist radical right fares particularly well among older women (e.g. Amesberger & Halbmayr 2002c). In short, while religion as an intervening variable might account for the underrepresentation of *some* female voters in *some* countries, it leaves much unexplained.

Ursula Birsl has summarized the findings of German research as follows: "The reticence of women towards extreme right parties and right-wing violence is not the result of their being the 'peaceful sex', but rather of that their attitudes are expressed differently because of sex specific socialization" (1996: 61). I concur fully and would argue that the main effect of different socialization in this regard is the significantly lower level of political efficacy among women.[16] As Vicky Randall recognized (reluctantly): "Of all the charges brought against women's political behaviour, apparently the most solidly founded is that they know less about politics, are less interested and less psychologically involved in it than men" (1987: 79). Obviously, this generalization requires qualification, as levels of political efficacy differ between various groups of women, but the general point is beyond dispute (e.g. Lovenduski 1986; Sapiro 1983).

The theory advanced here, which holds that political efficacy accounts for much of the disproportionate representation of (wo)men in populist radical right parties and their electorates, builds upon empirical insights from and theoretical reading by some prominent election researchers, who have also made major contributions to the study of the populist

---

[16] To be absolutely clear, I do not claim that all women are less confident with regard to politics, but simply that there are significantly more women than men with low levels of political efficacy. In line with Birsl, I believe these differences to be the result of nurture (i.e. socialization) rather than nature (i.e. inborn characteristics).

radical right. In his analysis of the surprising (short-term) electoral success of the German REP, Dieter Roth (1989; also 1990) advanced an explanation that has been labeled the "delayed effect theory" (Amesberger & Halbmayr 2002b). He explains the more conservative voting behavior of women by the lower level of political interest among women, which leads them to vote for established parties rather than for new parties (see also Gidengil *et al.* 2005). Empirical evidence that even the more "feminine" Green parties were initially ignored by female voters lends credence to this theory.

However, empirical research also shows that after some time the electorates of Green parties developed into the mirror-image of populist radical right parties; whereas the populist radical right consists of *Männerparteien*, the Greens are *Frauenparteien* (see Betz 1994: 143). Nonna Mayer (2002) has explained the predominance of male support for the populist radical right by pointing to the supply-side of the parties. While agreeing with the general point, I would argue that *perception* is more important than *reality* in this regard. In Mayer's own words, it is the "extremist image" rather than the "conservative positions on gender issues" that keeps women from voting for the populist radical right. This interpretation is consistent with both the low-efficacy argumentation of the delayed effect theory and empirical attitudinal research, which shows that men and women hold fairly similar views on all aspects of the populist radical right except extremism and violence, which are rejected far more by women than by men (e.g. Rommelspacher 2001; Roth 1990).

The low efficacy theory is also able to account for most empirical exceptions where either no or a reverse gender gap exists.[17] As mentioned above, the electorates of parties like the HDZ and HSP in Croatia or the LPR in Poland did not have significantly lower shares of women, while these parties are clearly populist radical right and particularly conservative in their gender views. However, what sets them apart from the other populist radical right parties in Europe is that they are not perceived as extremist or violent and even have a mainstream image: in the case of HDZ and HSP this is true in general, while for the LPR this applies mainly to the (large) orthodox Catholic subculture.[18] This could also explain the incongruent effect of religion on potential populist

[17] Incidentally, if the low efficacy theory is correct, women should be even less willing than men to confess to voting for the populist radical right in surveys, which might explain some of the difference; i.e. women might be even more underrepresented in surveys than in the electorate itself.

[18] This could explain also why there was no gender gap in the electorate of the Flemish VB before the introduction of the *cordon sanitaire*, the collective ostracism of the VB by the other Belgian political parties, and a (growing) overrepresentation of male voters afterwards. Similarly, with the "normalization" of the Italian AN in the 1990s the gender

radical right voters: where institutionalized religion speaks out against these parties, religious voters will be underrepresented in the populist radical right electorate (e.g. France, Germany), but where (parts of) the clerical hierarchy actively supports these parties, they will be overrepresented (e.g. Croatia, Poland, Slovakia).[19]

4.5 Conclusion

Although hard and reliable data are not always available, the evidence presented in this chapter points overwhelmingly in the same direction: at all levels (leadership, membership, electorate) there are fewer women than men within populist radical right parties. However, this underrepresentation should be placed in the proper context. While the level of representation is well below the proportion of women in society, this is true for almost all political parties, left, right and center. If compared to other political parties, the populist radical right still falls well short of the levels of female representation in many left-wing parties, most notably the Greens and New Left, but is on a par with that of other right-wing parties, notably conservatives.

Little is known about the ways in which women make their careers within populist radical right parties, but being female does not appear to be uniformly disadvantageous. In a comparative study of women and politics, Randall noted: "A woman's relationship to a particular man may give her access to considerable indirect political power" (1987: 122). Evidence seems to suggest that association with powerful men may confer substantial career opportunities on women in the populist radical right. With the notable exception of most female party leaders, almost all leading populist radical right women are related to party leaders. This includes mostly wives and daughters, but can also extend to lovers and sisters.

Interestingly, the degree of underrepresentation of women seems to be inversely related to the level of participation in the party. Compared to other (right-wing) political parties, women feature relatively prominently in the leadership of populist radical right parties; of particular note is the number of female party leaders. In the representative bodies populist radical right parties seem to perform as well or as poorly as other right-wing parties, while the share of women in the membership seems to

gap has drastically decreased, despite the fact that the AN even strengthened the already traditional view on gender relations of the MSI (see Riccio 2002).

[19] Research shows that the majority of listeners to Radio Maria are rural, elderly *women* (Stankiewicz 2002: 272). In the US, the electorate of populist radical rightist Pat Buchanan, who is supported by many leaders of the religious right, also shows virtually no gender gap (Weakliem 2001).

fall behind that of their right-wing counterparts (which might be at least partly an effect of their relative newness). Finally, in terms of the electorate the differences between the populist radical right and other right-wing parties are most striking. At this level populist radical right parties are genuine *Männerparteien* (male parties).

While explanations of the resistance of women to the populist radical right abound, most are blinkered by a feminist bias, which overestimates the support for feminist values among women as well as the real and perceived impact of the male chauvinism of the populist radical right. As far as empirical research is available, it shows that there are few gender differences in terms of populist radical right attitudes or objective motivations to vote for populist radical right parties. The puzzle is that while men and women have fairly similar attitudes with regard to the populist radical right *ideology*, they behave very differently with regard to populist radical right *actions* (Amesberger & Halbmayr 2002b; Siller 1997).

I have suggested an alternative explanation: the different socialization of men and women leads – among other things – to a lower level of political efficacy among women; this in turn explains why more women than men vote conservatively, i.e. for established center parties, and shy away from parties that are new and perceived as extreme. For people with lower efficacy, general perceptions have a greater influence on their behavior. Consequently, populist radical right parties that are stigmatized outsiders will attract fewer voters with low efficacy, resulting in disproportionally fewer women (FN, REP, VB), while those that are not, or that are even part of the mainstream in their country, will not face this problem (e.g. HDZ, LPR).

Finally, this theory can also explain the different effects of religion upon populist radical right voting. In countries where the populist radical right is denounced by the religious authorities, religious people holding populist radical right attitudes (mostly older women) will vote less for the populist radical right (e.g. France and Germany), yet in countries where these parties are supported by (parts of) the clerisy, there will be greater congruence between populist radical right attitudes and support for these parties among religious people (e.g. Poland, Slovakia).

5   It's *not* the economy, stupid!

Neoliberalism and right-wing populism go hand in hand.

(Butterwege 2002: 918)

All the great patriots and nationalists in Europe are merely Trojan horses of Big Business.   (Thompson 2000: 98)

5.1   Introduction

The academic literature on the populist radical right puts strong emphasis on the alleged neoliberal economic program of the party family. According to numerous authors, neoliberal economics is an essential feature of the parties' ideology and success. At first sight, it is not surprising that the populist radical right is linked to neoliberal economics. After all, contemporary understanding of "the right" in (empirical) political science is first and foremost in economic terms, standing for a trust in the market over the state, i.e. neoliberal economics (see also 1.5).

Few scholars have provided substantial empirical evidence for the alleged neoliberal content of the socioeconomic programs of the populist radical right. In fact, as is so often the case in the field, the claim is just assumed to be correct and broadly accepted. However, systematic analysis does not substantiate these claims; even in their early days most populist radical right parties at best expressed neoliberal *rhetoric* without fronting a consistent neoliberal *program*. Could it be that the populist radical right parties were just trying to fit the neoliberal *Zeitgeist* of the 1980s? Does the populist radical right actually share a coherent and collective (socio)economic program? And, if so, is this a core feature of their ideology?

In this chapter, the thesis that neoliberal economics constitutes a defining element of the populist radical right is rejected on the basis of two empirical arguments: (1) many key representatives of the party family do not hold neoliberal views on the economy; (2) the economic program is a secondary feature in the ideologies of populist radical right parties. In fact, it is also secondary to their electorates. Most of the time, populist radical right parties use their economic program to put into practice their core ideological positions (nativism, authoritarianism, and populism) and to expand their electorate.

5.2   The secondary literature: neoliberal dominance

At least until the beginning of the twenty-first century, the academic literature was dominated by the conventional wisdom that populist radical right parties espouse a neoliberal economic program. Indeed, for many authors neoliberalism was one of the core features of the populist radical right program and one of the main reasons for their electoral success. While this view was initially popularized by Hans-Georg Betz, Herbert Kitschelt developed it into a comprehensive conceptual and theoretical model. Largely due to the influence of these two leading scholars, the predominance of neoliberal economics in the ideology and success of populist radical right parties has become an established fact in much of the literature, irrespective of language or (sub)discipline (e.g. Höbelt 2003; Jungerstam-Mulders 2003; Thompson 2000).

Interestingly, both Betz and Kitschelt are German scholars, who made most of their respective careers in the United States and came to the study of the populist radical right after studying the Greens. To different degrees, they see the populist radical right as the antithesis of the Greens, i.e. a right-wing (partly) materialist backlash against a left-wing postmaterialism. Consequently, neoliberal economics features very prominently in the primary works of both scholars on the topic. Betz identifies one of two subtypes of radical right-wing populism as "neoliberal populism" (1994: 108), while Kitschelt's famous "winning formula" is a combination of "extreme and economically [speaking] rightists, free-marketeering as well as politically and culturally authoritarian positions" (Kitschelt & McGann 1995: vii). For both scholars this economic program is also a key reason for the electoral success of populist radical right parties, although this is most explicit and elaborated in Kitschelt's theory.[1]

---

[1] In recent work, Kitschelt has (somewhat half-heartedly) moderated his position: "While the Kitschelt 'winning formula' fits our two cases well, it is necessary to amend it to take account of the softening of the neoliberalism of many new radical right parties during the 1990s. It is probable that the 'winning formula' does not require a consistent neoliberalism, but rather a compromise that is sufficiently free-market to appeal to petty bourgeois voters, but does not alienate working-class support by attacking the welfare state too vigorously, while at the same time promising protectionism favorable to both" (McGann & Kitschelt 2005: 163–4; also Kitschelt 2004).

More recently, some authors have qualified the predominance of neoliberal economics within the populist radical right.[2] In fact, Betz himself had already noted that "[w]ith a few notable exceptions, starting at the end of the 1980s, national populist elements have increasingly come to predominate over neoliberal ones" (1994: 108). According to others, there was nothing new about this. They argued that the economic program of populist radical right parties like the FN or VB had always included nonliberal elements (e.g. Eatwell 2003; Bastow 1997), or that neoliberalism had never been more than a rhetorical veneer over an essentially welfare chauvinist program (e.g. Mudde 2000a).

Some authors, particularly within the German literature, have come to recognize two distinct socioeconomic directions within "the extreme right," i.e. the neoliberal program of the (alleged) "new" parties, such as the REP, and the national-social(ist) program of the "old" parties, such as the DVU and the NPD (e.g. Ptak 1999; Backes 1996). Although important differences exist regarding the categorization of parties and the details of the socioeconomic programs, this distinction comes quite close to that made by Ignazi (1992), i.e. between the "old" (in 2003: "traditional") and the "new" (in 2003: "postindustrial") extreme right, and that of Kitschelt and McGann (1995), between the "new radical right" and "welfare chauvinist" parties. The basis of all these distinctions is that "new" right-wing extremists (in our terms: populist radical rightists) are neoliberal and *thus* successful, whereas "old" right-wing extremists (in our terms: the extreme right) are welfare chauvinist (or literally national-socialist) and *therefore* unsuccessful.

The predominance of the neoliberal perspective has led to some remarkable conclusions, especially with regard to Eastern Europe. Radoslaw Markowski, representing the view of many scholars in the region, concludes that populist radical right parties in Central and Eastern European countries (CEECs) are fundamentally different from those in the West. Referring explicitly to Kitschelt's terminology, he states that "there is no single party that resembles the New Radical Right of the West. All of these CEECs parties are definitely opting for state protectionism and economically leftist ideas. Neoliberal stances are totally missing" (Markowski 2002: 28; see also Thieme 2005; Butterwege 2002). This conclusion is largely correct with respect to the socioeconomic program

---

[2] As so often in a vibrant field of study, some of the points in this chapter have been made in recent studies that appeared while I was working on my book. This is most strongly the case in the very interesting recent book chapter by Steffen Kaillitz (2005), which I only managed to read during my revisions. However, I do believe that this chapter still adds some further elaboration, both empirically and theoretically, to his work and that of other colleagues.

of the parties in the East, but it also erroneously accepts the flawed interpretation of the parties in the West.

5.3   The primary literature: nativist economics

At first sight, the predominance of neoliberalism in the secondary literature seems to be confirmed by the parties themselves. Many referred
positively to "neoliberal economics" or "free market economics," at least
throughout the 1980s. Jean-Marie Le Pen, for example, claimed to be
a Reaganite *avant la lettre*, having developed the economic program two
years before it made the former US president famous (Bastow 1997: 61).
Similarly, the magazines of the VB would hold Reagan and Thatcher up
as icons in the 1980s (e.g. Mudde 2000a), while the (then Czechoslovak)
SPR-RSČ presented itself as the sole defender of the free market in the
early 1990s (Pehe 1991). Moreover, as far as economic policies would find
their way into campaign materials, they would primarily be calls for lower taxes and less state regulation, the classic hobbyhorses of neoliberals.

However, particularly since the 1980s, several populist radical right
parties have presented themselves in a completely different light. For
example, in sharp contrast to its neoliberal populist predecessor, the
FPd, the Danish DFP from the beginning "marketed itself as a welfare-
friendly party that carried the legacy of the classical social democracy"
(Bjørklund & Andersen 2002: 132). And most East European parties
campaign strongly on social issues and around key concepts such as social
justice; for example, the Bulgarian Ataka presents its preferred economic
model as "social capitalism" (Ataka 2005).

Moreover, in sharp contrast to the common claim in the literature
on political parties in general, and that on the populist radical right in
particular, systematic content analyses of the socioeconomic program
of populist radical right parties hardly ever support the predominance
of neoliberalism (e.g. Mudde 2000a; Alaluf 1998; Govaert 1998; Roy
1998; Bastow 1997). Instead, these studies find a predominance of what
could best be termed "nativist economics." Scholars have further noted
important changes in the economic programs and a rather peculiar combination of policies that support neither a purely liberal nor a purely
socialist economic program (e.g. Betz 2003a; Eatwell 2003; Minkenberg
2000; Bastow 1997).

5.3.1   *State* and *market*

Like other political parties in contemporary Europe, virtually all populist
radical right parties have accepted the fundamentals of capitalism and

the market economy. However, there is significant variation in the level of state involvement in the economy preferred by populist radical right parties. In fact, the party family spreads a significant part of the whole dimension between the two poles of *laissez faire* and state economy. Interestingly, this is also one of the few issues on which an East–West divide can still be noted, even if it is far from perfect.

The most pro-market member of the party family is the borderline case of the Swiss SVP, which began agrarian and developed through neoconservative, into a populist radical right party (e.g. Skenderovic 2005). It is the only party to defend an unqualified "liberal economic order" (SVP 2003: 56). Its election manifesto reads as a strong defense of the free market: "The overburdening state interventionism in the end leads to the downfall of the Swiss economy" (SVP 2003: 56). According to the party, this is already happening in Switzerland and there is only one cure: less state, more market. "The economy goes badly today, because the state intervenes more and more, makes restrictions and redistributes money, instead of creating a favorable general framework for the businesses" (SVP 2003: 56).

The other major party that has traditionally been closest to *laissez faire* market economics is the Austrian FPÖ, which has always struggled to integrate a liberal and a nativist wing (e.g. Riedlsperger 1998; Luther 1991). Like that of liberal parties, the FPÖ propaganda is full of references to "freedom" and "liberty": the books of (then party leader) Jörg Haider, for example, carry titles such as *Liberated Future beyond Left and Right* (1997) and *The Freedom that I Mean* (1993). However, the economic model that the party supports is not so much a "free" market economy, but rather a "fair" market economy (*faire Marktwirtschaft*). While the fair market economy is clearly seen as more market-oriented than the current economic model of Austria, which is allegedly perverted by clientelism and socialism, it is also explicitly posited against neoliberalism. As Haider explains:

A 'fair market economy' is the answer to the coldness of turbo-capitalism and creates partnership instead of force by chambers [*Kammerzwang*]. Competition does not have to mean that only the winner survives. Businesses that exploit their employees, tolerate inhuman working conditions and do not invest in continued education [*Weiterbildung*], have no future. (1997: 10–11)

As is clear from the German title of Haider's 1997 book, which literally includes the title of Anthony Giddens' book *Beyond Left and Right*,[3] as

---

[3] Giddens' book is also included in the list of "books, which have inspired me," as is Tony Blair's book *My Vision* (Haider 1997: 248).

well as from many interviews with the party leader, Haider and the FPÖ were strongly influenced by the "Third Way" of New Labour (see also Thompson 2000). But despite the fact that Tony Blair's party is a strong supporter of the market economy and of liberalizing measures like deregulation and privatization, as to a lesser extent are Haider and the FPÖ, the ideology of the "Third Way" is better described as social liberal than as neoliberal (e.g. Freeden 1999).

Traditionally, third-way ideologies have been associated with an economic program that rejects both the free market and the state economy. Instead, they entailed "a strong, organic, hierarchically organized corporatist state, with a leader at the top" (Bastow 1998: 57; also Spicker 2000). Particularly during the Cold War the "Third Way" was a neutral economic and political position, opposing both American liberalism and Soviet socialism. Both the third way label and its positions have been popular among many ideological groups, including extreme right circles such as national revolutionaries and solidarists (see Bastow 2002; Griffin 2000). However, some populist radical right parties have also flirted with it; the Belgian VB used to support a "solidaristic" model, the Greek Hellenism Party (KE) called for a democratic model where "the economy is in the hands of the demos, i.e. the people," the Italian MS-FT presents itself as "the national-popular alternative to liberal-capitalism," while the Polish LPR supports "national solidarism" (e.g. Kolovos 2003; Mudde 2000a).

If anything, the populist radical right's view on the relationship between market and state is closest to that of Christian democracy.[4] In German terms, it resembles the CDU/CSU model of the "*soziale Marktwirtschaft*" (social market economy) more than the "free market" of the liberal FDP. Several populist radical right parties also literally refer to their preferred model as social market economy (e.g. BZÖ, MIÉP, REP, Slovak SNS). Essentially, the social market economy supports the capitalist economy, but wants the state to moderate its inherent detrimental social effects. In direct violation of free marketism, this includes state dirigisme and protectionist measures.

Haider's newest project, the BZÖ, has among its key focal points the guarantee of the *social* market economy. Despite the change in terminology, however, the BZÖ's "social market economy" is not much different from the FPÖ's "fair market economy": a combination of a basic free market with low taxes and various protectionist measures for small businesses, shopkeepers, and farmers. Similarly, Le Pen has stated that the FN supports "Rhenish capitalism which tries to reconcile a certain

---

[4] In fact, this is not unlike New Labour's "Third Way," as several scholars have argued (e.g. Huntington & Bale 2002; Spicker 2000).

level of economic performance with an acceptable level of social well-being" (in Simmons 2003: 31–2). Some parties even defend an essentially Keynesian economic model, arguing that "[t]he state should in times of recession execute extensive investments as well as lower taxes and duties" (DVU n.d.: point 5).

However, whereas the state involvement of Christian democrats is mainly informed by the Christian concept of charity (*charitas*), the populist radical right's prime motivation is nativist. The economy should be at the service of the nation and only the nation. Or, in the words of the Greek Eoniko Komma (National Party, EK), "the national state has the duty to define the conditions of the economic procedures so that these activities benefit the whole of the people and the general interests of the country" (in Kolovos 2003: 50).

Consequently, the populist radical right holds a relatively positive view of the market within the nation-state, but it regards the European and global markets with great suspicion. In the words of the FN, "globalization leads to company relocations, thus to unemployment, and Maastricht brings about the deregulation of public services, thus insecurity" (in Bastow 1998: 60). This nativist suspicion also applies to the welfare state, which is supported in principle, but should be provided only to needy members of the nation.

Many parties call for the protection of the welfare state at its present or previous high levels, including the increase of some social benefits (notably pensions) and the introduction of new provisions (e.g. parental wage or *Kindercheck*). However, they also want to limit access to welfare provisions. Arguing that the welfare state has become a "hammock" rather than a "safety net," they want to exclude the so-called *Sozialschmarotzer*, i.e. those who can work but prefer to "live off" the state, to reserve "social provisions for those who really need them" (CP 1980). However, this only applies to needy people from the own nation. To ensure the translation of this principle into policy, the parties call for a distinction within the welfare system between "natives" and "aliens" (see 5.3.4).

5.3.2 Protectionism

The centrality of nativism to populist radical right parties significantly impacts their economic programs. The national economy should be at the service of the natives; hence it should be under the strict control of the nation and the international free market should be approached with great suspicion. In fact, many parties are close to a model of national capitalism, in which the market is principally accepted but international free trade is largely rejected. The aversion to international interference extends to the EU as well, at least since the 1990s, when most populist radical right parties became increasingly EU-skeptic (see chapter 7). The late REP leader Schönhuber clearly linked the themes of external and internal protectionism in his critique of the then European Communities (EC): "who benefits from the EC? Primarily the Euromultinationals, big business, but not small-scale craftsmen, farmers or workers" (in Fieschi *et al.* 1996: 244).

Most Western European populist radical right parties try to find a balance between protection of the national economy and access to external markets. For example, the FPÖ argues, "[t]o counter the foreign sell-off of Austria's economy we have to give priority to building an effective Austrian capital market" (1997: 21); and consequently calls for some (relatively limited) protectionist measures. In the same vein the British BNP supports the "[p]rotection of British industry by the *selective* exclusion of foreign manufactured goods from the British market (BNP 1994: my italics), while the German DVU demands, "through subsidies the state should keep the coal-mine, shipbuilding and steel industry alive and competitive, as is also done abroad, as we should not become even more dependent on foreign interests" (*Deutsche National-Zeitung* 12/02/1988).

The preference for a national(ist) capitalist system is most strongly expressed by populist radical right parties in Eastern Europe. The Czech Republicans argued that "[i]t is not tolerable that landless liberalism based on the invisible hand of the market liquidates the fundamentals of the national economy" (SPR-RSČ 1999). Similarly, the Slovak SNS proclaimed in the introduction of its 1996–97 program:

The SNS prefers the concentration of capital, means of production and property to be in the hands of national subjects, which is the only guarantee of Slovakia's economic power. The SNS does not support, and will never support, the sale of any wealth into the hands of anonymous, supra-national and cosmopolitan subjects who misuse their economic power for political influence. (in Fried 1997: 103)

This has inspired some parties to call for quite radical policies. The Bulgarian Ataka favors a policy of national preference with regard to the local business community: "Bulgarian businessmen need to have an advantage over foreigners; Bulgarian business, private or state, should always be helped by the state" (Ataka 2005). István Csurka, the leader of the Hungarian MIÉP, goes a step further, expressing a drastic desire for autarchy. As always led by his anti-Semitic worldview, he proclaims:

We need to adopt a self-defense policy. We need our own projects, own road constructions, own education, and own army. And for that we need money that is ours and does not come from loans . . . money that serves only Hungarian purposes and comes from Hungarian work. (in Mihancsik 2001: 160)

While the Eastern European parties are the most extreme in their demands to protect the nation against foreign economic dominance, all European populist radical right parties are characterized by an essentially nativist approach to economics. Some parties explicitly express this support; for example, the Slovak PSNS (n.d.) considers "economical nationalism" a cornerstone of its ideology, describing it as "the advertisement [promotion] of buying domestic products and the support of domestic production and agriculture." Two sectors of the national economy are singled out for national protection by all parties: small businesses and agriculture.

For the populist radical right, small businesses are "the backbone of our economy and ensure our stability" (SVP 2003: 36; also Haider 1997: 128). The key argument is that small businesses employ far more people than big multinationals do and they invest their profits in the national economy. Hence, virtually all parties call for state protection and both direct and indirect support for small businesses (e.g. SPR-RSČ 1999; CD 1989). Their advocacy of these policies is entirely logical given that for the populist radical right "small business growth is the key to success in the future" (SD 2005).

In the populist radical right view the agricultural sector is also deemed vital to the survival of the nation. In the words of the German REP (n.d.), "[a]griculture is an essential and elementary component of our national economy. It should secure our nourishment and keep us from political dependence and blackmail." As a result, various parties demand that the national agricultural sector become self-sufficient (e.g. BNP, FN, FPÖ, LPR). In the words of the Finnish Isänmaallinen Kansallis-Liitto (Patriotic National Alliance, IKL), "the position of agriculture and foodstuff production have to be secured in such a way that self-sufficient food supplies can be guaranteed in all circumstances in the country" (IKL n.d.). The reason is given by the Polish LPR (2002): "A nation that fails to nourish itself will never be truly free (is destined to be enslaved)." The Italian MS-FT even launched a campaign under the motto: "Consume national products. Save your country. Eat Italian."

While the EU Common Agricultural Policy (CAP) could initially count upon some support within the party family, the continuing reforms have been a major reason for the growing populist radical right opposition against European integration (Bastow 1997). Some parties even demand the "re-nationalization of agricultural policy" (FPÖ 1997: 29). Opposition to the European agricultural program has been particularly strong in some of the new member states in the East, nowhere more so than in Poland. Although not the main defender of Polish farmers, given the competition from the PSL and Samoobrona, the LPR clearly addresses the CAP in its program: "We will protect the Polish market from unfair foreign concurrence" (LPR 2003: IV.10).

In Eastern Europe, the protection of the agricultural sector has an additional sensitivity: privatization of land ownership. As land was state-owned under communism, and tilled by state-owned and operated mass farms (i.e. *kolkhozes* and *sovkhozes*), the transformation from state social-ism to market capitalism involved the mass privatization of land. Most populist radical right parties did not so much reject land privatization *per se*, although they would criticize the (alleged) corruption involved; rather, they rejected the sale of "native land" to foreigners. The Hungarian MIÉP campaigned with the slogan "Hungarian land must be kept in Hungarian hands," while the Bulgarian Ataka called the sale of land to foreigners "anti-Bulgarian" (*Sofia News Agency* 26/06/2005) and argues that "Bul-garian land should never ever be sold to foreigners" (Ataka 2005). The Polish LPR even submitted a "citizens' motion" to the Sejm, calling for a referendum on the sale of land to foreigners. The party claimed the motion was supported by some 600,000 signatures (*RFE/RL Newsline* 16/10/2002).

5.3.3   Deregulation and privatization

Much of the work that defines the populist radical right as essentially neoliberal refers to three key demands in the propaganda of *some* parties (particularly the FPÖ and LN): lower taxes, deregulation, and privatiza-tion. The first is not particularly convincing as an indicator of a neolib-eral ideology, as the call for lower taxes is an almost universal political demand, especially among opposition parties. The latter two, support for deregulation and privatization, require some consideration.

There are numerous examples of calls for deregulation in the literature of populist radical right parties. The SVP is probably the strongest and most consistent opponent of state intervention, fighting "the corset of state regulations and restrictions" and calling for "a minimum of state and a maximum of market" (SVP 2003: 9, 36). Other parties will differ not so much in the frequency of calls for deregulation, as in the consistency of their calls. While endlessly criticizing and ridiculing the red tape that stifles the national economy, particularly regarding European regulations, they also call for new strict regulation to protect the national economy against foreign competitors (see below). In short, the populist radical right might think that there are too many rules in certain areas; it also believes that there is too little regulation in others. This can hardly be seen as strong evidence for the existence of a (core) neoliberalist ideology.

Regarding privatization the situation is even less convincing. Calls for the privatization of companies or economic sectors are quite rare in the literature of populist radical right parties. In Western Europe this might be explained by the fact that few sectors are still in the hands of the state; this is particularly true for EU member states. When such demands are found in the party literature, such as the FPÖ call for "genuine privatization" (1997: 21), the prime motivation seems to be political rather than economical (see below). Moreover, there are also parties rejecting "forced privatization" (CD 1998: III.1).

In contrast with true neoliberal ideology many populist radical right parties attach all sorts of limiting conditions to their calls for privatization. One could say that they support nativist privatization in which the privatized companies remain largely in the hands of the natives and "vital sectors" of the economy, i.e. those deemed essential to the survival of the nation-state, are excluded from (open) privatization; in the words of the Greek LAOS, "liberalism with state control on issues of national importance" (in Kolovos 2003: 67). In some cases, parties will even call for a (re-)nationalization of companies within these strategic sectors.

According to the Czech SPR-RSČ (1999), 51 percent of all that is privatized has to be in the hands of national capital, including everything related to the strategic industries (railways, mines, energy). Their demands are not much different from the French FN's advocacy of a *capitalisme populaire* (popular capitalism) in which 70 percent of the shares of public enterprises to be privatized will be in the hands of French families. The party further wants the state "to maintain the big services which are essential for the functioning of the nation, for its security, under the control of the public powers, that is to say, energy production, public transport, communications and telecommunications and the arms sector" (in Bastow 1998: 65). The list of the Polish LPR is even more exhaustive (e.g. LPR 2003: IV.4).

On average, Eastern European populist radical right parties are more antiliberal and protectionist than their brethren in the West. Because of the legacy of state socialism, postcommunist Europe has seen an unprecedented level of privatization, in terms of both scope and speed. This process was strongly linked to corruption and patronage, both in fact and in the perception of the population (e.g. Karklins 2005; Holmes 1997). Moreover, in many cases the privatization led to major companies being sold off to foreign companies, including some from traditional "enemies" (such as Germany, Russia, and the United States).

Seen in this context, it is not surprising that the Eastern European parties have been more skeptical about privatization. As one author perceptively summarized this position, the populist radical right has "tended to support a gradual transition to a market economy with significant state intervention in the economy in the foreseeable future" (Irvine 1995: 148). This state intervention should not just protect certain key sectors of the economy, but also weak groups within the nation. As LDPR leader Zhirinovsky once expressed it,

I am in favor of a diversified economy, in favor of market relations. But a market economy is not for every body. Pensioners, invalids, mothers with large families, children and youth are not adapting to it. They need social defense, and the president must defend them. (Williams & Hanson 1999: 270)

Postcommunist populist radical right parties are highly critical of the way liberal economics has been introduced in the transition period; the so-called "shock therapy," which they believe has had severe material and nonmaterial detrimental effects upon the nation. According to the Czech Republicans, "[t]here hasn't been any privatization. Everyone understands that it was nothing less than a simple robbery of the state property" (SPR-RSČ 1999). In line with this assessment, the Slovak PSNS has opposed "the sellout of the national economy" (*RFE/RL Newsline* 09/10/2001), while the Croatian HSP-1861 has called for the introduction of a Law of Denationalization (HSP-1861 1997b). In the post-Soviet space the parties tend to be even more radical antiliberal, at times bordering on anticapitalism. Even the seriously misnamed Liberal Democratic Party of Russia, which tries to present a more Western image (at times), denounces the introduction of the market economy by previous Russian governments as "the criminal experiments of the radical democrats" (LDPR 1995).

5.3.4   Welfare chauvinism

Most populist radical right parties would agree with Haider's short and simple description of the socioeconomic policy of his *Freiheitlichen*: "social, not socialist" (1997: 226). In a Europe where extended welfare states are the norm, both in the East and in the West, no political party dares to propose the full dismantling of the welfare state. At the same time, most parties, including those on the center-left, argue that the system has become too elaborate and expensive to maintain and that at least some cuts will have to be made to keep it affordable. Within the populist radical right the extent of cut-backs advocated by particular parties varies substantially, in part relative to the extent of the existing welfare provisions in the country.

Some parties are much closer to the Christian democratic and conservative position on welfare than to the socialist and social democratic position. The former is based on the importance of charity, implying a privilege extended by the state and society, while the latter proceeds from the idea of solidarity, meaning an obligation to be met. This is particularly the case with Western European parties like the Austrian FPÖ and the Italian LN, both of which inspired Betz's ideal type, "neoliberal populism" (Betz 1994). Haider used to argue that social policy (*Sozialpolitik*) is not necessarily a competency of the state and that "help to self-help in the private sector can be more effective, economic and social" (1997: 226–7). Similarly, in Switzerland the SVP calls for more "individual responsibility" with regard to "social insurances" (2003: 9), while the Freiheits-Partei der Schweiz (Freedom Party of Switzerland, FPS) argues that "[m]arket economical foundations – in particular stimuli to an open competition – have their worth for the insured, the insurants, and the medical professionals" (1999: 4.2.4).

Other populist radical right parties find the concept of solidarity far less problematic, and present themselves explicitly as "social" parties. The FN distributes pamphlets and posters with the slogan "Le social, c'est le Front National" (The social, that's the National Front). The Slovak SNS summarizes its party program in three principles, of which "the social principle" is one; the "national principle" and the "Christian" principle" are the other two (SNS n.d.). Furthermore, its party program states that "the SNS promotes economic and social ethics based on solidarity" (SNS 2002: 20). There are even parties that want the state to guarantee full employment (e.g. DN, FN, HSP-1861), a demand normally only found among socialist (not even social democratic) parties.

Some authors have accused the populist radical right of "social demagogy" (e.g. Ptak 1999) and "social paranoia" (Rensmann 2003: 116). While this may be an overstatement and definitely reflects a normative bias, many of the parties do campaign with slogans that clearly express an "economic populist" program reminiscent of Latin American populists (e.g. Mudde 2001; Weyland 1999). The Croatian HSP-1861 contested the 1997 local elections with the message "Work for Unemployed – Justice for All – Food for the Hungry" (HSP-1861 1997b). And PRM leader Tudor used the slogan "Food, heating, medicine, law!" to call upon the Romanians to "vote for the tribune" in the 2004 presidential elections.

However, the solidarity of the populist radical right has very clear boundaries. First of all, it does not include so-called *Sozialschmarotzer*, i.e. all those who can work but prefer social benefits, even if they are "native." "The system of the social welfare state can only be preserved if the allocation of benefits goes primarily to those in social need" (FPÖ 1997: 24). Second, and more important, the benefits of the welfare state should be limited to the "own people."

In this nativist interpretation of the welfare state, fairly generous social benefits are to be guaranteed for the native needy (mainly pensioners and the sick), while "aliens" are to be excluded. This is not just argued on the basis of nativist arguments, but also on "common sense" financial grounds. The argumentation is that the welfare state can only be sustained at the required level when it is limited to the "own people." Or, in the words of a 1980s pamphlet of the German REP: "Saving the social state: expelling sham refugees (*Asylbetrüger*)! Solving unemployment: stopping immigration!"

This welfare chauvinist model has been most elaborated by the FN and the VB, the latter often imitating its French sister party. In the infamous seventy-point program, an expansion of the fifty-point program of the FN (1991), the VB presents a highly detailed "apartheid regime" with respect to, among others, the welfare state. For example, the party wants "national preference" with respect to general social services, jobs, and social housing (Dewinter 1992: 11–12; also FN 1991: E). Moreover, as part of its "deterrent politics," the VB wants to limit child and unemployment benefits as well as property rights for "non-European aliens" (Dewinter 1992: 27–8).

A similar but far less elaborate approach is suggested by some Eastern European parties that want to redesign their social benefits programs to exclude ethnic minorities, most notably the Roma. For example, in its proposal to abolish income tax for families with five children or more, the Czech Republikáni Miroslava Sládka (Republicans of Miroslav Sládek, RMS) excludes "those groups of the population which use child allowances as the source of their living and bring disadvantages to citizens of high integrity and those people who are economically active," a reference to Roma obvious to any Czech citizen (in Report 2002: 27).

In conclusion, the populist radical right supports an ambiguous economic program that entails a "mixture of market liberalism and welfare chauvinism" (Betz 1994: 174). However, most importantly, they support a nativist economic model, i.e. an economy that (solely) benefits the "natives" and that is protected against "alien" influences.

5.4   Economics: secondary and instrumental

The idea that neoliberalism predominates within the economic program of populist radical right parties is not the only misperception within the literature. Equally erroneous is the contention that economics is primary to the ideology and success of this party family. In fact, as careful analysis of the programs and surveys of the electorates of these parties makes clear, socioeconomic issues are secondary to the populist radical right party family. Their socioeconomic principles proceed from the core tenets of their ideology (i.e. nativism, authoritarianism, and populism) rather than determine them, and can be and are consequently instrumentalized to attack competitors and attract voters.

5.4.1   The party perspective

At first sight, the secondary nature of the socioeconomic agenda can already be observed from the relatively little attention it receives in the programs and propaganda of populist radical right parties (cf. Mudde 2000a; Roy 1998; Spruyt 1995). Some leading members in more successful parties started to recognize this in the 1990s. Bruno Mégret, then still the number two of the FN, said in 1996: "Today we are recognized as competent in the area of insecurity or immigration: tomorrow we must conquer a third important domain, the economic and social" (in Bastow 1998: 63). Similarly, Gerolf Annemans was the driving force behind the elaboration of the socioeconomic program of the VB, which was developed at the thematic conferences "Vlaanderen werkt!" (Flanders works!) in November 1996 (VB 1996) and "Ondernemend Vlaanderen" (Entrepreneurial Flanders) in November 2005 (VB 2005a).

While members of the party family differ somewhat with respect to the content of their socioeconomic program, they are in full agreement regarding its importance within their broader ideology and program: (socio)economics is a secondary issue (Betz 2003b; Mudde 1999). The Schweizer Demokraten (Swiss Democrats) have expressed this general standpoint clearly in their election program: "the economy is not an end in itself, but rather serves the true needs of the people of Switzerland" (in Olson 2000: 32). Similarly, the Greek EK states that "the economy is not the end-goal but the means" (in Kolovos 2003: 50).

Populist radical right parties define their (socio)economic policy on the basis of their core ideology, particularly nativism, and instrumentalize it accordingly. Even in the case of those parties that have more sophisticated economic programs, and which come closer to the neoliberal stereotype, the economy remains a secondary, highly instrumentalized issue. In the words of Michael Minkenberg, "market liberalism was never a key component of right-wing ideology . . . it was a tactical tool to be abandoned as soon as the political winds changed and protectionism and welfare chauvinism seemed more promising" (2000: 173–4).

For example, whereas the early programs of the Italian LN included various neoliberal demands, particularly in the 1990s, they first and foremost served the higher goal of the party, nativism (sometimes in the shape of regionalism). Consequently, if nativist and neoliberal goals clashed, such as over the issue of immigration, the LN always chose the former (cf. Cento Bull & Gilbert 2001). In the same way, "the use and distribution of economic resources was claimed not on the grounds of a neoliberal agenda of more or less state, but as a matter of political rights questioning the whole edifice of the Italian state" (Gomez-Reino Cachafeiro 2002: 99). Similar arguments and strategies can be found among many populist radical right parties, hiding nativist demands under a neoliberal veneer.

In the case of the FPÖ, one of the few parties that remained somewhat loyal to its neoliberal rhetoric of the 1990s despite the proletarization of its electorate, many calls for privatization and other alleged neoliberal measures clearly have another, more important motivation. At least until the late 1980s, the Austrian political system, known as *Proporzdemokratie* (proportional democracy), meant that virtually all aspects of life were dominated (and distributed) by the two parties, including the economy. And through their grip on the economy, which in reality was not as big as the FPÖ made it out to be, the two parties had disposal over a huge system of patronage, which gave them an important electoral and political advantage over the FPÖ. Proposals for revision of the economic system therefore were to a large extent attempts to weaken the party's main political competitors, i.e. the two established parties (SPÖ and ÖVP), and to create a level playing field in the electoral and political arenas (e.g. Betz 2003b; Heinisch 2003).

The purely instrumental nature of the FPÖ's interest in the economy is clear from many of Haider's statements, including the following: "We want to see real competition between the public and the private sectors instead of a monopoly of politicized housing cooperatives which hand out apartments. This whole party book system must be a thing of the past" (in Tiersky 2001: 233). Likewise, the party manifestos make various references to this issue: "Through a program of genuine privatization, the withdrawal of political parties and associations from the economy, the reduction of influence of interest groups and their restriction to their real tasks, the power of party functionaries in the public economy should be eliminated" (FPÖ 1997: 21; also 14).

While "overpromising" (Papadopoulos 2000) is common to all political parties, at least during election time, opposition parties tend to have an advantage over those in government, as they have no track record against which to judge the likelihood of their delivering on their commitments. As most members of the European populist radical right party family are (semi-)permanent opposition parties, they are unconstrained by political inhibitions in pursuing their vote-maximizing strategy to the fullest (Deschouwer 2001). Consequently, they can get away with highly contradictory points in their programs. The Czech SPR-RSČ was one of the few Eastern European populist radical right parties to be confronted by a *cordon sanitaire*, although an unofficial one, and provides a good example of this opportunistic use of its socioeconomic program. In the words of one scholar:

The main contradiction of all its election manifestos was the call for a drastic decrease of taxes and a reduction of the state apparatus, on the one hand, and the call to generously support practically all weaker social groups, on the other: pensioners, young families, women with small children, state care for socially weak citizens, building of social housing, subsidies for agriculture, railways, sports, free education at all levels, financial support for inhabitants of economically impaired regions, etc. (Havelková 2002: 240–1)

5.4.2 The voter perspective

An indirect way of determining whether socioeconomic issues are primary or secondary to the electorates of populist radical right parties is to look at their class base. If the electorate of a party has a highly homogeneous class base, it is concluded that economics does play an important role to its voters. In contrast, if the electorate is cross-class, particularly including groups with opposing economic interests (objectively defined), it is taken for granted that economics is largely a secondary issue. Indeed, various studies have shown that these parties do have cross-class electorates, combining an overrepresentation of two opposing groups: the self-employed and blue-collar workers (e.g. Evans 2005; Ivarsflaten 2005).

However, an alternative explanation is also possible. As populist radical right parties present a schizophrenic socioeconomic agenda, i.e. using both neoliberal and welfare chauvinist rhetoric, both groups might actually (think they) vote for the right party on the basis of their preferred economic position. And as long as these parties remain in (total) opposition, they will not have to choose between differing positions and can continue to promise the world to all groups.

Not much is known about the socioeconomic attitudes of the electorates of the populist radical right. Usually, these are measured by socioeconomic position (class) or occupation, assuming that (all) individuals with a certain position or occupation hold the same socioeconomic views (e.g. Kitschelt & McGann 1995). Studies of the electorates of various populist radical right parties show that their voters do not stand out from those of other right-wing parties in terms of their socioeconomic views; in fact, they are slightly less neoliberal (e.g. Mayer 2005; Ivarsflaten 2002). Pippa Norris comes to a fairly similar conclusion in her comparative study, although she qualifies her inference, noting that "the full range of economic attitudes toward the role of markets and the state were only poorly gauged" in the particular survey she used (2005: 260).

Interestingly, Flemish research finds that rather than neoliberal or socialist, most voters of the VB hold socioeconomic views that are best labeled "economic populist" or "right-wing egalitarian" (Derks 2005: 21). Similarly, the FPÖ electorate has a lower percentage of "social state traditionalists" and "market liberal individualists" than the Austrian electorate as a whole, yet a higher proportion of "welfare state chauvinists" (Plasser & Ulram n.d.: 5). This indicates that the views of the electorate and the parties of the populist radical right are in fact not as different as is often claimed.

The only way to clearly establish whether economics is secondary to the electorate of the populist radical right is by probing into voter motivations. Unfortunately, very few studies use these questions to test their hypotheses. Some studies of political priorities among voting groups do indicate that socioeconomic concerns are secondary to the electorates of the populist radical right. For example, in 1992 securing social security and pensions had a high priority for only 36 percent of FPÖ voters, which was below the Austrian average (42 percent) and only the fifth most-mentioned priority (even after "improve environmental protection"; Betz 1994: 66). In the 2002 presidential elections in France, "unemployment" ranked a shared third in the list of major concerns of Le Pen voters and fourth for Mégret voters (Perrineau 2002: 9).

The few studies that do ask for the motivations of voters provide strong evidence that only a tiny minority of the electorate of (Western) European populist radical right parties select their party primarily on the basis of economic self-interest (e.g. Swyngedouw 2001; Fetzer 2000). They also clearly show that, in contrast to the electorates of most mainstream parties, socioeconomic issues are only secondary to the voters of populist radical right parties (e.g. Mayer 2005). Similar results have been found in countries outside of Europe, such as Australia (e.g. Goot & Watson 2001) and the United States (Weakliem 2001).

5.5   Conclusion

This chapter challenges one of the most widespread and fervent misperceptions in the field, i.e. the importance of neoliberal economics to the ideological program and electoral success of the populist radical right party family. Comparative study of the party literature of the European populist radical right family shows that (1) their economic program is not neoliberal and (2) economics is not a primary issue to the party family. In fact, the bulk of the parties hold a fairly centrist position on the dominant state–market axis, relatively similar to that of the Christian democratic family. However, most importantly, for the populist radical right the economy should always be at the service of the nation. They defend a nativist economic program based upon economic nationalism and welfare chauvinism.

As economics is a secondary issue to the populist radical right party family, the parties instrumentalize it to pursue their primary ideological agenda, i.e. nativism, authoritarianism, and populism. Liberal arguments are used to weaken the power of mainstream parties (e.g. privatization of party-controlled state institutions), while social measures are supported to protect or strengthen the nation (e.g. agricultural and family subsidies). Additionally, as most populist radical right parties are vote-maximizing parties in semi-permanent opposition, they "overpromise" to attract as wide a support basis as possible: e.g. tax cuts for the companies and middle class and increased social benefits for the (native) socially weak.

While many commentators have considered this to be the Achilles heel of the populist radical right, some empirical research suggests that this schizophrenic presentation of their socioeconomic agenda pays off (at least in the short run). By presenting neoliberal *and* welfare chauvinist policies and rhetoric, populist radical right parties are able to attract different groups of voters with distinct economic preferences (e.g. Immerfall 1998). It might be true that this could potentially be a problem when they implement their policies in government (e.g. Ivarsflaten 2005), but in most cases this is merely a theoretical problem, as the parties are far removed from actual political power. Until that moment, the populist radical right has much to gain by keeping economics a secondary issue that is first and foremost of strategic value in their larger ideological struggle.

6   Populist radical right democracy

Whose democracy is it anyway?   (Maryniak 2002: 107)

6.1   Introduction

Although the populist radical right is not antidemocratic in a procedural sense, as argued in chapter 1, core tenets of its ideology stand in fundamental tension with *liberal* democracy. Various authors have discussed this tension, although mostly at an abstract level without much reference to concrete positions of the parties in question (e.g. Betz 2004; Decker 2004; see also Lipset 1955). To understand the nature and scope of this tension, we must examine the societal and systemic consequences of the three key features of the populist radical right: nativism, authoritarianism and populism.

The following sections will discuss the populist radical right parties' views on nativist democracy, authoritarian democracy, and populist democracy, respectively. In the conclusion the populist radical right view of democracy will be constructed and compared to the key features of liberal democracy in general, and the way they are implemented in contemporary European countries in particular. This exercise should also help provide a clearer insight into the key question on the mind of many authors and, indeed, readers: how dangerous are populist radical right parties for liberal democracy?

6.2   Nativist democracy: it's our country!

The key concept of the populist radical right is nativism, the ideology that a state should comprise "natives" and that "nonnatives" are to be treated with hostility. Like all ideologues, nativists are torn between the ideal and the practice, the dream and the reality. While they dream of a utopian monocultural state, i.e. a "pure" nation-state, most parties would settle for a more attainable ethnocracy.

6.2.1   Monoculturalism: the utopia of the pure nation-state

The single most striking similarity in the propaganda of populist radical right parties worldwide is their main slogan: "Britain for the British" (NF), "Bulgaria for the Bulgarians" (Ataka), "Netherlands for the Netherlanders!" (CP'86), "Slovenia for the Slovenes" (SNS), etc. These slogans summarize the core goal of every nativist: "Our own state for our own nation." According to nativists, true democracy is only possible within a true nation-state. As Koen Koch (1991) has elaborated, the full nationalist doctrine includes two additional elements: internal homogenization and external exclusiveness. Or, in the words of the foremost scholar of nationalism, "all Ruritanians, as far as possible, into the sacred Ruritanian homeland, and all or virtually all non-Ruritanians, *out* of it!" (Gellner 1995: 6). In today's world, we find few populist radical right parties that will openly call for both.

The essence of internal homogenization is caught in the infamous slogan of German right-wing extremists: "Deutschland den Deutschen, Ausländer raus!" (Germany for the Germans, foreigners out!). Not only should "our state" be ruled by (people of) "our nation," "we" should be its exclusive inhabitants. This nativist aim remains the ideal of most members of the populist radical right party family today, but very few parties openly profess it without qualification. All parties continue to call for the expulsion of certain groups of nonnationals, mostly illegal aliens and criminal "foreigners" (sometimes including naturalized immigrants). But particularly among the more relevant parties in Western Europe the undeniable reality of multiethnic society has sunk in and some degree of ethnic diversity within the nation-state is grudgingly accepted (see 6.2.2). So, while the Belgian VB called for the return of second- and third-generation "aliens" in its infamous seventy-point program (Dewinter 1992: 29–30), recent manifestos no longer include this demand (e.g. VB 2005b, 2004b).

In Eastern Europe calls for internal homogenization were not uncommon in the years following the collapse of communism. In a region with a history of population transfers, the call of the Bulgarian BNRP to drive all the "Turks" out of Bulgaria and replace them with "Bulgarians" from Moldova and other countries might not even have sounded completely absurd to many Bulgarians (Eminov 1997). And in the former Yugoslavia some nativists did not stop at calls for population transfers, but openly supported genocide. Leading politicians of Croatian and Serbian populist radical right parties called for the forceful expulsion and, if necessary, killing of Serbs and Croats, respectively (e.g. Irvine 1995). Campaigning in 1992, SRS leader Šešelj stated:

Albanians should be driven out of Kosovo to Albania, similar actions should be taken with the Muslims in Sandžak, Hungarians who were our brothers-in-arms may remain, but the Hungarians who followed Ágoston (the independent Hungarian leader) have no place in Serbia, and (all) Croats must be expelled from Serbia (in Bugajski 1994: 150).

Only a few populist radical right parties in Western Europe openly express the wish for external exclusiveness, i.e. all people and territories of the nation should be part of the state (Koch 1991). Initially, both the Belgian VB and the Dutch CP'86 aspired to a Greater-Netherlands in which the Netherlands, Belgian Flanders (including Brussels), and French or South Flanders (the area around the city of Lille) would be "reunited" (e.g. Mudde 2000a). However, in recent years the VB no longer calls for reunification and appears content with Flemish independence and "an as close as possible connection with the Netherlands and South Flanders" (VB 2004b).

Similarly, German parties like the DVU and REP would call for "true" German reunification, including not just *Mitteldeutschland* (Central Germany), i.e. the former German Democratic Republic or East Germany, but also the "real" *Ostdeutschland* (East Germany), referring to areas in the current Czech Republic, Poland, Russia, and Ukraine that were part of the German empire in 1937. Interestingly, calls for a new *Anschluß* with Austria are not made (openly) by these parties (e.g. Mudde 2000a). And in Greece, the tiny HF wants to liberate all "enslaved Greek Fatherlands" and reunite them with Greece (in Kolovos 2003: 56).

In Eastern Europe borders are generally more contested than in Western Europe, nowhere more so than in the former Yugoslavia. Not surprisingly, populist radical right parties in this region express some of the most grandiose territorial ambitions. Like all Croatian nativists, the HSP-1861 has not given up on "its historical parts" and supports "as close as possible coordination and creation of confederate or federal state communities between the Republic of Croatia and the Republic of Bosnia and Herzegovina." The motto "Croatia up to river Drina, BiH up to Adriatic Sea" (HSP-1861 n.d.a: article 10) sums up the party's vision of the true Croatian state. This Greater Croatia overlaps significantly with the utopias of other nativists, most notably the Serbs. In fact, the Greater Serbia supported by the SRS includes most of the same territory. And while HSP-1861 leader Doroboslav Paraga called for the destruction of Serbia until there is nothing left but "Belgrade and its surroundings," SRS leader Vojislav Šešelj wanted the territory of Croatia to be reduced to "as much as one can see from the tower of the Cathedral on Zagreb" (in Irvine 1995: 149–51).

Even in relatively peaceful Bulgaria populist radical right parties espouse irredentist views. The 1994 election manifesto of the BNRP proclaimed that "even in a United Europe the BNRP will plead for and seek ways of ethnic unification of all Bulgarians and Bulgarian lands on the basis of historical facts and arguments, thus endeavouring to stem denationalization and the suppression of the Bulgarian self-consciousness" (Mitev 1997: 77). This would not be appreciated in neighboring countries like Greece and Macedonia, particularly among the populist radical right there. Similarly, MIÉP's irredentist demand for the reconstitution of the sixty-four counties of Greater Hungary clashes with the ideals of nativist parties in Romania, Serbia, Slovakia, and Ukraine, while Greater Albania utopias envisioned by parties like the Albanian Balli Kombëtar (National Union) or the Kosovar Lëvizja Kombëtare për Çlirimin e Kosovës (National Movement for the Liberation of Kosovo) clash with nativist aspirations in Greece, Macedonia, Montenegro, and Serbia.

In some cases, irredentism seems to run counter to the nativist ideal. Zhirinovsky's self-proclaimed "Drang nach Süden" – "I dream that Russian soldiers will wash their boots in the warm waters of the Indian ocean and switch to summer uniforms for good" (McCauley & Sagramoso 1994: 447) – would create a Greater Soviet Union that would make Russians a numerical minority in their own state.[1] The now defunct SPR-RSČ, which was the only Czech political party to keep the term "Czechoslovak" in its party name after the split of the country in 1993, called for a Czechoslovak state including Subcarpathian Ruthenia, which had been part of the First Czechoslovak Republic (1918–38) and was annexed by the Soviet Union after the Second World War.[2] This was despite the fact that the party acknowledged the separate identities of Czechs and Slovaks. Indeed, the party wanted to accommodate this diversity in a new constitution that would consist of four regions: Bohemia, Moravia and Silesia, Slovakia, and Subcarpathian Ruthenia (e.g. Pehe 1991).

Most parties do not (openly) demand external exclusiveness, but some do consider their country responsible for "kin" outside of their borders. For example, the FPÖ wants Austria "to act as a protector for German minorities on the territory of the former Austro-Hungarian Monarchy" (FPÖ 1997: 11, 13). Similar sentiments can also be found in nonpopulist radical right parties, particularly in the postcommunist East. Virtually all Hungarian political parties consider the Hungarian state to be the

---

[1] Over the years Zhirinovsky's dream state has had many different borders, although one constant has been that the preferred Russian state was always closer to the former Soviet Union than to the current Russian Federation.

[2] Since the break-up of the Soviet Union in 1991, the territory of Ruthenia has been part of Ukraine.

protectors of the Hungarian speakers in neighboring countries. The conservative FIDESz-MPS even proposed the notorious Status Law when in government, calling for dual citizenship for "Hungarians abroad" (e.g. Kántor *et al.* 2004). Less far-reaching is the preferred involvement of the Danish DFP: "Outside Denmark's borders we would like to give financial, political and moral support to Danish minorities" (DFP n.d.).

The DFP also takes a remarkably moderate approach to some territories of the current Danish state. On its website the party states: "We wish to see the Danish State Community preserved for as long as the Danish people have a wish to do so *and the Greenland and Faeroese peoples wish to remain in the Community* (DFP n.d.; my italics). The FPÖ is only willing to grant the power of choice to those "Austrians" currently outside of the state: "There must remain the possibility of South Tyrol to join the Republic of Austria in a free exercise of its right to self-determination" (FPÖ 1997: 13).

6.2.2   Ethnocracy: the art of the possible

The concept of ethnocracy has been around for at least three decades, although it was originally used mainly as a derogatory term (Yiftachel 2000). It has been applied with reference to multiethnic (nominal) democracies – including Northern Ireland, Sri Lanka, and, most notably, Israel (e.g. Yiftachel 2000, 1998; Butenschøn 1993). In recent years the term ethnocracy has been employed with reference to various new post-communist democracies (e.g. Smith 1999) and populist radical right parties (e.g. Betz & Johnson 2004; Griffin 1999a; Mostov 1999).

Because of the particular cultural and historical context of certain regions of Eastern Europe, notably the Balkans and Baltics, ethnocratic ideas were widespread among both the elites and the masses during the period of transition. In fact, in the early 1990s it was often impossible to make a clear distinction between the "mainstream" and the populist radical right on this issue. Various new states officially installed ethnocratic regimes; paradoxically building in part on the Soviet tradition of "titular nations" (e.g. Beissinger 2002). In these "ethnic democracies" the populist radical right parties were part of the political mainstream and among the staunchest supporters of the system.

A good example of such an ethnic democracy was Estonia in the early 1990s (e.g. Melvin 2000; Smith 1999; Smith *et al.* 1994).[3] With

---

[3] The situation was quite similar in the neighboring state of Latvia. However, it is incorrect to speak of a "Baltic model," as Lithuania, the third Baltic state, did not follow the ethnocratic model.

a Russian-speaking population of around 40 percent at the time of independence in 1991, the Estonian elite introduced a Citizenship Law based on the so-called "restorationist principle," which granted automatic citizenship only to citizens of the First Estonian Republic (1918–1940) and their descendants. The rest of the population, roughly one-third, were regarded as Russian citizens, who had the choice between leaving Estonia for their "homeland" Russia (the preferred option even though many had been born and raised in Estonia), and applying for residence and work permits in Estonia. Although the 1992 Citizenship Law did not restrict citizenship exclusively to Estonian speakers, for example some 80,000 Russian speakers got automatic citizenship, nevertheless it did lead to the complete political dominance of Estonian speakers.

The naturalization process has been seriously revised since then, not least because of EU pressure, but important ethnocratic elements persist within Estonian democracy today. In the early 1990s the ethnic model of Estonian democracy was supported by all relevant Estonian parties; parties of the Russian speakers were not politically viable because their natural electorate was excluded from citizenship. Not surprisingly, nativist and populist radical right organizations have been among the most vocal opponents of the liberalization of the Estonian ethnocracy. Within the first postcommunist government (1992–95) leading members of both the national-conservative Isamaa (Fatherland) and the populist radical right Eesti Rahvusliku Sõltumatuse Partei (Estonian National Independence Party, ERSP) would vehemently defend the strict Citizenship Law and voice strongly xenophobic anti-Russian statements. Outside of government, calls for an even stricter ethnic policy, e.g. exclusion of all Russian speakers from Estonia, came from small populist radical right parties like the Eesti Rahvuslaste Keskliit (Estonian Central Union of Nationalists) and Parem Eesti (Better Estonia).

Since the mid 1990s, populist radical right parties have not been electorally relevant in Estonia, although some of their former leaders are active within more mainstream parties such as the Isamaaliit (Fatherland Union), into which the ERSP largely integrated, and the Eestimaa Rahvaliit (Estonian People's Union) (see Poleshchuk 2005). Moreover, the "second generation" of Estonian populist radical rightists, notably the Eesti Iseseisvuspartei (Estonian Independence Party), is more concerned with the perceived threat from the West, i.e. the EU and NATO, than from the East, i.e. the Russian bear and its citizens in Estonia (see Kasekamp 2003).

But ethnocracies are not limited to unstable regions (afar) or new countries in the East. The most pure form of ethnocracy was the South African apartheid regime, a complex legal and political system of discrimination and segregation, which guaranteed the "white" minority complete dominance over the majority "black" and "colored" populations. Another important example of a state with strong ethnocratic elements was the Federal Republic of Germany, before the recent change in citizenship laws from an exclusive *ius sanguinis* to a combination with *ius soli* (Wimmer 2002; Brubaker 1992). Not surprisingly, populist radical right parties in those countries were among the most loyal supporters of the legal system (and the most ardent opponents of changes).

In most European countries the nativist goal of a monocultural state and the contemporary reality of a multicultural society create significant problems for the populist radical right. Like many within the populist radical right party family, the Croatian HSP-1861 deals with this tension by stressing different and contradictory goals with no regard for their apparent incongruity. While in article 8 of its basic principles the party "supports the protection of the rights of the minority groups," in article 11 it considers that "every acknowledgement of the constitutional right to any other ethnic group in the Republic of Croatia is contrary to the interests and aspirations of the Croatian people" (HSP-1861 n.d.).

The underlying idea of article 11, i.e. that a democratic nation-state belongs to one ethnic group and that other ethnic groups can only live there if they accept this group's dominance, is a prime example of "national preference," the guiding principle of all populist radical right parties and the basis of ethnocratic rule. It comes pretty close to George Orwell's famous dictum from his classic work *Animal Farm*: all animals are equal, but some animals are more equal than others. While the parties stress the legal equality and protection of all citizens, they also clearly stress the predominance of their own nationals. Throughout the continent, populist radical right parties stress that their country should be first and foremost for "our nation": the Belgian VB uses the slogan "Eigen volk eerst!" (Own people first!), the French FN "Les Français d'abord!" (The French first!), and Spain 2000 "Los españoles primero!" (The Spanish first).

The second key feature of ethnocracy in the programs of most populist radical right parties is an ethnic *Leitkultur* (leading culture). For nativists culture is an essentialist and rigid category; it must be preserved and cultivated, while adaptation and relativism are believed to lead to decline and ultimately death. While various minorities can be accommodated within the state, there can be only one official national culture. The Danish DFP expresses this as follows: "Denmark belongs to the Danes and its citizens must be able to live in a secure community founded on the rule of law, developing *only* along the lines of Danish culture" (DFP n.d.: my italics). Consequently, populist radical right parties reject multiculturalism and instead proclaim the strengthening of the "own" culture a national priority.

Today almost all populist radical rightists accept the possibility of assimilation of nonnationals, usually referred to (incorrectly) by the less negative term "integration." Few are as open-minded and accommodating as the British Veritas party, however, which states in its General Election Manifesto: "We believe in a society of many colours, many faiths and many ethnic backgrounds – but one culture" (Veritas 2005a). While few parties explicitly mention color or race, there is a tacit understanding that the own nation is white. Also, some parties still distinguish between European and non-European foreigners, arguing that the former share a kind of meta-culture and can therefore assimilate, whereas the latter have no cultural affinity with the host nation (and preferably state) and thus have no business residing there. Others have given up on this distinction, forced by the reality of large numbers of "third generation non-European immigrants." Instead, they have started to distinguish primarily upon the basis of religion, arguing that Islam is incompatible with liberal democracy or "European civilization" and that Muslims can therefore never assimilate into the host nation (except when they give up Islam).

Populist radical right parties further oppose special facilities for cultural minorities, which they consider hindrances for assimilation and hotbeds of fundamentalism. In recent years, the most strident demands to eliminate state protection and support of cultural pluralism have been directed toward the Muslim community. For example, the VB wants to revoke the official recognition of Islamic honorary services and drastically limit the number of mosques, in a claimed effort to fight back Muslim fundamentalism and ghetto-building (e.g. Dewinter 1992). Similarly, the BNRP called the plan of the Bulgarian government to include Turkish in the school curriculum "betrayal of national interests" (in Perry 1991: 7). The most notable exceptions have been support for facilities to help minorities "return" to their homeland, which has been proposed mainly with regard to refugees and guest workers (e.g. Dewinter 1992).

6.3   Authoritarian democracy: follow the rules!

For the populist radical right, order is the basis of freedom. It believes that society should be structured according to strict rules and that the rule of law should be upheld at all costs. From a policy perspective this leads not only to an extensive focus on law and order, but also to ascribing an important role to the state in installing "crucial values" such as authority, compliance, order, and respect (e.g. Altemeyer 1981). Whereas most populist radical right parties are careful not to cross the line between democracy and dictatorship, they do regard contemporary democracies as too soft and weak, incapable of defending themselves against the many threats that lie within and beyond their borders.

The key issue of the authoritarian program of the populist radical right is the fight against crime through "an uncompromising (*kompromissloses*) approach against criminals" (SVP 2003: 44). In this regard, many parties call for a "zero tolerance" policy on crime, inspired by the experiences in New York under former Mayor Rudolf Giuliani. All parties want more policemen, with better equipment and salaries, less red tape, and greater competence. They also want policemen to regain their high standing in society, though the parties normally do not indicate how this is to be achieved. In the words of the German DVU, "[t]o ensure the security of the citizens, we need a police that is capable to act and sufficiently equipped, that should no longer be whipping boys [*Prügelknaben*] of a failed politics" (n.d.: point 8).

The populist radical right further calls for a significant strengthening of the independence of the judiciary and police force. They want both institutions to be free from (party) political influence. Regarding the judiciary, many parties claim that the judges are politically appointed and thus serve their partisan political masters, while the police are seen as being hindered in their work by political correctness and lack of political backup because of the cowardice of the established parties. In the words of the Czech Republicans' 1996 election program, "[t]he current corrupted government garniture with its degenerated 'humanistic' attitude toward criminals is neither willing nor able to ensure an honest citizen's safety and to protect his property" (in Dvořáková & Rataj 2006).

Other frequently expressed calls relate to the elaboration and transformation of the prison system and citizens' right to self-defense. Most parties will call for the building of more prisons, with prescription that they be (more) basic and impose a strict(er) regime – e.g. no television sets in the cells, no social services, multiple persons per cell. Somewhat paradoxically, given their stress on the state's monopoly of violence, several populist radical right parties defend citizens' right to bear and use arms. Obviously, this is a huge issue in the US, where the Constitution's Second Amendment is one of the most contested issues in politics (largely because of the powerful lobby of the National Rifle Association), but some European parties also support this right, despite the lack of tradition in the region.

The right to bear arms is most important to populist radical right parties in Switzerland, the only European country with a tradition in this respect. Several members of the highly fragmented Swiss populist radical right party family are strongly opposed to any limitations on the right to bear arms; at least for the Swiss population, certain limitations on the right of foreigners are actually encouraged (see FPS 2003). In Britain the BNP has defended the issue in almost American terms: "The Armed People – the ultimate protection against invasion or tyranny" (BNP 2005). And in Italy, the LN initiated a controversial law, passed in January 2006, which gives Italians the right to shoot in "self-defense" at intruders in businesses and homes (*De Tijd* 26/01/2006). Similar proposals have been put forward recently by the VB in Belgium.

Another authoritarian claim of the populist radical right party family is captured well by the Swedish SD: "We want to help the victims – not protect the criminals" (SD 2005). For the populist radical right, "the protection of society must rate higher than the rehabilitation of the criminal" (FPÖ 1997: 19). The claim is that the current legal system is excessively focused on understanding and rehabilitating the perpetrator at the expense of the victim; what the Czech SPR-RSČ disapprovingly refers to as the "humanization of imprisonment" (in Dvořáková & Rataj 2006). For the populist radical right the victim, defined as both the individual(s) concerned and society as a whole, should be at the center of the legal system.

Consequently, they advocate tougher laws and increased sentences. Moreover, they want to eliminate all laws that ensure early release, particularly when it is not conditioned upon the good behavior of the prisoner. The BNP (2005) goes so far as to demand that "[c]riminals should be made to serve their full sentences, with time added for *bad* behaviour." The ultimate sentence varies across parties. Many members of the populist radical right party family call for the (re-)introduction of the death penalty (e.g. Ataka, HF, LAOS, MIÉP, NS, SPR-RSČ), while only a few parties are openly against capital punishment (e.g. FPÖ, REP). Several do not mention the issue in their election manifestos (e.g. DVU, LPR, SVP), sometimes because they are internally divided on the issue (e.g. VB, Veritas). Interestingly, the British Veritas party states:

We have no 'party line' on 'issues of conscience', like the death penalty, abortion, euthanasia, and fox-hunting. On these issues, we invite voters to question their VERITAS candidate on where he or she stands. Our candidates will give a truthful answer. In Parliament, we would allow a free vote on these controversial issues. (Veritas 2005b)

For most of the parties that do not support capital punishment, life imprisonment is the ultimate penalty. However, they do demand that "[l]ife imprisonment must mean what it says" (FPÖ 1997: 19).

The maximum penalty is demanded with regard to two crimes in particular: selling and smuggling drugs, and engaging in terrorism. For many parties, drugs are the scourge of contemporary (youth) society and should be fought by all means. The parties, and particularly their youth movements, campaign tirelessly against any attempt to tolerate or legalize drugs – including the differentiation between "soft" and "hard" drugs, which is considered misleading (alcohol is excluded, obviously). In these campaigns, drugs are related to all "ills" of the current age: immigration, insecurity, progressiveness, teenage sex. A number of parties call for forced detoxification for junkies and the death penalty for (major) drug dealers (e.g. BNP, CP'86). However, a few others want to combine policies of liberalization and repression by supporting free distribution of drugs to junkies under medical observation to minimize their crimes and the consequent insecurity of the citizens (e.g. Agir n.d.).

Despite the populist radical right's emphasis on the protection of the rule of law in theory, there are reasons to doubt their commitment to it in practice. While in power, populist radical right parties have shown their authoritarian face. Without exception they have introduced, or tried to introduce, legislation that would both extend the list of criminal offences and increase the punishments to be meted out. In most cases the targeted "criminals" were not so much external enemies of the "own nation," but those within it, most notably political opponents. From Austria to Romania and from Croatia to Italy bills were introduced with clear intent to stifle internal political opposition (e.g. Pelinka 2005; Kelley 2004). In some cases they also targeted foreign opponents; for example, the SNS demanded the proscription of the Soros Foundation from operating in Slovakia after the Hungarian-born American philanthropist George Soros openly criticized the Slovak government (Cibulka 1999).

The parties often attacked their political opposition indirectly, through legislation allegedly defending "the State." A good example of this was the "draconian Law for the Security of the Republic" (Cibulka 1999: 119), which the SNS submitted to the Slovak parliament in 1995. In its original form, the law would have rendered virtually every critique of the Slovak government a criminal offence, thus making normal political opposition an extremely dangerous affair. Similar laws have been proposed and passed by other governments with populist radical right participation. In all these cases the laws meant a serious infringement of various fundamental freedoms, including those that, when in opposition, the populist radical right always champions (e.g. demonstration, press, speech). Thomas Johansson, chairman of the small Swedish Nationaldemokraterna (National Democrats), has summarized this type of instrumentalist approach to freedom of speech as follows: "We must have an open and free debate, but it must be combined with discipline and national loyalty" (Johansson n.d.).

The populist radical right considers the internal opposition of "nonnationals," most notably "ethnic" (and sometimes religious) minorities, another big danger. As discussed above, they have great difficulties with the whole concept of minority rights within "their" state, while many at the same time call for protective rights of their own kin in neighboring countries. The Czech RMS states that it "will not tolerate the existence of so-called Gypsy political parties, which are solely parties of a single ethnic group" (in Report 2000). The VB is strongly opposed to Muslim mobilization and called for a ban of the tiny but notoriously militant Arab nationalist annex Islamic fundamentalist Arabisch-Europese Liga (Arab European League), while simultaneously campaigning for "real" freedom of speech, in reaction to the court case that led to the effective banning of the Vlaams Blok and the consequent founding of the Vlaams Belang (e.g. Erk 2005).

Intolerance towards ethnic mobilization and rights is particularly strong in countries with (sizeable) minorities from former occupying countries. Here, the populist radical right supports the prohibition of all political parties that are "overtly or covertly organized on a minority basis" (HF in Kolovos 2003: 55). In fact, the Macedonian Dviženje za Semakedonska Akcija (Movement for All-Macedonian Action) has demanded the outlawing of all Albanian parties because of their alleged threat to the constitution (Bugajski 1994: 114), while the Romanian PRM has regularly pushed for the banning of the "anti-Romanian organization UDMR" (in Shafir 1996: 96).[4] SNS leader Slota even went so far as to demand that "the activity of the Hungarian minority in Slovakia must be outlawed" (in Zitny 1998: 38).

Particularly after 9/11, populist radical right parties have increased their authoritarian stance on Islam and the Muslim community. Most European countries have reacted to the terrorist attacks in New York (and later Madrid and London) by introducing far-reaching antiterrorist measures (e.g. Haubrich 2003). Several of these measures at least partly target the (radical) Muslim community, but the populist radical right has denounced them as too little, too late. Parties like the VB and LN have called for strict(er) controls of mosques and Islamic centers and even the closing of the borders for Muslim immigrants (e.g. Betz 2003a). In a clear reference to "Muslim fundamentalists," the BNP (2004) argues that "any immigrants who have the audacity to preach hatred of our society should be deported – no prolonged appeals procedures; no expensive legal aid at our expense – just deported."

---

[4] In many Eastern European countries such claims are not without legal basis, given that constitutions often have a nativist element to them. For example, Article 1.1 of the Romanian Constitution states that "Romania is a sovereign, independent, unitary, and indivisible National State," while Article 4.1 elaborates that "The foundation of the State is based on the unity of the Romanian people" (Andreescu 2005: 195).

In the tumultuous early period of postcommunism, some populist radical right leaders clearly left the realm of democracy and entered the terrain of dictatorship. Vadim Tudor, the "righteous" (*justiţiar*) leader of the Romanian PRM, called for a two-year period of authoritarian rule to make Romania (again) into a country of "unity in abundance" (in Shafir 1997: 392). And the even more erratic Zhirinovsky said in the same period, despite his party's official support for liberal democracy: "In a multiethnic state like Russia the form of government of parliamentarism remains a utopia, and a life-threatening one for all ethnic communities (*Völker*) at that . . . Russia can only be saved by a dictatorship" (Zhirinovsky 1992: 30).

The populist radical right party family is highly divided with respect to militarism (also Mudde 2000a, 1995a). There are some parties that espouse traditional militaristic values or call for the building of a large(r) and strong(er) national army (e.g. DVU, LDPR). The LAOS even wants Greece to "gradually become a nuclear power" (in Kolovos 2003: 66). However, particularly within Western Europe many parties are not proponents of militarism or are even antimilitaristic. This is particularly strong in countries and regions where, for historical reasons, nationalism and pacifism are interlinked, such as Flanders and Germany.

Most parties support compulsory military service, although some oppose it (e.g. FPÖ) or accept a more general social service (e.g. REP). Rather than being an expression of militarism, compulsory military service is seen as a civic duty, i.e. as both an individual's opportunity and a state's necessity. In the words of the German REP:

Military service, also in the form of a general compulsory military service, is a command of a democracy correctly understood. [A person] who has the right to decide with others upon the fate of the state in elections, votes and freedom of speech, has fundamentally the duty to participate in the protection of the state. Military service is service to our country, to our ethnic community [*Volk*], to our liberal state, and to the maintenance of peace. (REP 1983: X)

For many parties the protection of the state entails not only a military struggle against an external enemy, but a cultural and political struggle against an internal enemy as well. In this respect, they speak of ideological and practical vigilance against "subversive actions" and "antinational elements" within their "own state" (e.g. communists, Islamists). This is also to be achieved by the (re)creation of a national *esprit civique* (Agir n.d.).

6.4   Populist democracy: power to the (own) people!

Recent years have seen an explosion in literature on populism, much of it stressing the tense relationship between populist democracy and liberal democracy (e.g. Mény & Surel 2002a; Taggart 2000; Canovan 1999). A core element of populist democracy is the belief that the *volonté générale* should be implemented without any restrictions. Nothing is more important than the general will of the people. This applies not only to politicians and political institutions like parties, parliament and governments, but also to laws and even to the constitution.

As populism is essentially a monist ideology, it is inherently opposed to division and pluralism. In Europe's democracies, which are first and foremost party democracies (Gallagher *et al.* 2005), the main targets are established political parties. In line with the populist radical right's revisionist rather than revolutionary creed, Haider stated, obviously before his party entered the Austrian government, "there exists no alternative to democracy, but there very well exist alternatives to the ruling parties" (Probst 2003: 120). The populist radical right does not merely want to change the players, however; they also want to change some rules of the game. The Spanish DN has expressed in extreme terms, and poor English, what most (larger) populist radical right parties voice more moderately: "The big parties monopoly over political life is to be broken . . . Same opportunities for every party. Creation of new ways of political representation to enhance the existents. Referendum and popular initiative to hold elections must be promoted" (DN n.d.). In essence, populist democracy is based upon three key features: plebiscitary politics, personalization of power, and primacy of the political.

6.4.1   Plebiscitary politics

One of the crucial claims of the populist radical right is expressed by Le Pen's mantra "rendre la parole au peuple" (return the word to the people). According to all populist radical right parties, with the temporary exception of those in government, the contemporary political system in their country is not really democratic. They claim that the political elite (in the singular) controls all power through the system of representative government and the practice of cartelization. Only through the introduction of elements of plebiscitary democracy can power be given (back) to "the people."

Plebiscitarianism is one of many ideological approaches to democratic representation. It purports to radically curtail the distortion and mediation of citizen preferences by compromised political organizations, offering to substitute direct connections between the people and the policies or social results they seek. These direct connections are the recall, the initiative and the referendum. (Barney & Laycock 1999: 318)

The most popular instrument of plebiscitary democracy is the referendum. Virtually all populist radical right parties call for its introduction or increased use. While matters pertaining to national sovereignty in particular are considered to be legitimized only through referendums, notably with regard to European integration, most parties want every major (and sometimes even minor) decision to be potentially scrutinized by "the voice of the people." The Bulgarian Ataka even created an objective, numerical cut-off point: issues that concern at least 10 percent of the people could be subject to a referendum (Ataka 2005).

Many parties will go a step further and support (the introduction of) a people's initiative, i.e. a bottom-up version of the referendum. Being fundamentally suspicious of the political elites, they want the power to decide upon the use of the referendum to lie with the people, not with the government or parliament. In essence, the parties want the people to have the right to call for a referendum on practically any issue. They see the people's initiative as "a construction kit for detours around corrupt policy intersections, clogged and fouled by parties and organized interests" (Barney & Laycock 1999: 319).

The formal requirements of these initiatives tend to be set quite low, although many parties do not go into details in their discussion of them. One of the exceptions is the British BNP, which has developed a radical bottom-up model.

Accordingly, we propose as a vital check and balance on the political class the introduction of Citizens' Initiative Referenda on the Swiss model. Under this, individual citizens only have to collect the requisite number of electors' signatures on any given petition – the wording of which they decide themselves – in order to compel either the local or national government to hold a referendum on the subject.

If passed by between 50%–66% [*sic*] of those voting, such a referendum result would in turn trigger a full-scale council/parliamentary debate on the subject, with heavy moral pressure on the politicians to follow the wishes of the majority. If passed by more than 66% of those voting, however, the result of such a referendum would automatically be binding on the authorities, who would have no choice but to accept the will of the people and enact their wishes as law. (BNP 2005)

In countries that already allow for referendums, populist radical right parties have been active initiators. This is true most notably for the Swiss SVP; leader Blocher even founded a separate movement to mobilize around referendums, the Aktionsgemeinschaft für eine unabhängige und neutrale Schweiz (Action Society for an Independent and Neutral Switzerland, AUNS). Similarly, the Austrian FPÖ launched a series of people's initiatives, each designed to highlight one of its core issues: party patronage and privileges (1987), the 'foreigners question' (1993), and the public broadcasting system, which the FPÖ portrays as a domain of the SPÖ and ÖVP (1989). The FPÖ promoted its third core issue, its anti-EU stand, in two initiatives (both 1997) which followed the obligatory constitutional referendum on allowing Austria's accession to the EU . . . With the exception of the public broadcasting system, all the FPÖ's initiative issues struck a responsive chord in the mass public. (Müller 1999: 311)

Some parties also support some form of recall. The FPÖ, for instance, argues that "[p]remature removal from office either of the federal president, [or] provincial governors or mayors should be possible in a referendum after a qualified initiative from the relevant parliament or municipality" (FPÖ 1997: 17). And the Bulgarian Ataka wants to create the possibility of the recall of MPs who do not do what they promise, based on a petition of voters (Ataka 2005).

There seems to be some regional variation with regard to support for plebiscitary democratic initiatives within the populist radical right party family. While nearly all family members in the West, including extra-European territories, put the introduction and the use of these measures at the center of their propaganda, and base much of their political argumentation on plebiscitarianism, there are various Eastern parties that do not put much emphasis on it (e.g. LPR, Slovak SNS). However, as is so often the case, the intra-European divide is not complete; parties like Ataka, MIÉP, and PRM do support plebiscitary initiatives, and for those like the NS and SPR-RSČ they are even quite central to their program.

6.4.2   Personalization of power

While there is an element of truth in the statement "direct democracy and populism meet in their fundamental aversion of the principle of representation and intermediate bodies" (Puhle 2003: 26), this does not mean they are inherently at odds with liberal democracy. Moreover, rather than being against representation *per se*, populists are primarily against representation by the wrong people, i.e. "the corrupt elite" (Mudde 2004). Because of the intrinsic monism of populism, any form of political pluralism is treated with suspicion. This is also the basis of its aversion to intermediate bodies, which are generally seen as artificial divisions or representatives of "special interests." The monism of the populist radical right is particularly visible in its call for a more personalized political system.

Most populist radical right parties call for an increase of the powers of the main political figure in their system, be it the president (e.g. EK, FN,

NS, REP) or the premier (e.g. CD, LN). Some parties even call for the introduction of a (super)presidential system, in which the president centralizes and personalizes the *vox populi* (e.g. HSP, KPN, LPR, SPR-RSČ). Not all populist radical right parties are well versed in political systems. The Czech Republicans called for the introduction of a directly elected president with more powers, which they presented as "a presidential system like in France" (SPR-RSČ 1999).

However, a party like the FPÖ calls for the popular election of "provincial governors or mayors as well as administrative heads of the relevant territorial legal entities," on the one hand, but wants "to enhance the National Assembly vis-à-vis the executive," on the other (FPÖ 1997: 16–17). Regarding the latter, the party demands the introduction of the parliament's right to elect the cabinet and to have an effective no confidence vote, as well as the abolition of "governmental legislation."

6.4.3   Primacy of the political

A key notion of populist democracy is the primacy of the political. As elaborated in chapter 5, for the populist radical right party family, politics clearly has primacy over the economy. However, in the populist ideology the will of the people cannot be limited by anything, not even the law. "From the populist point of view, legalism and the rule of law hinder the full realization of the rule of the people" (Blokker 2005: 382).

There are some clear examples of European populists expressing this opinion. For example, Andrzej Lepper, leader of the social populist Samoobrona, has stated forcefully: "If the law works against people and generally accepted notions of legality then it isn't law. The only thing to do is to break it for the sake of the majority" (in Maryniak 2002: 103). Similarly, FI leader and Italian Prime Minister Silvio Berlusconi has regularly questioned the authority of the Milan judges ("red robes") to convict him, arguing that they represented no one, whereas he himself was the voice of the people (e.g. Ruscino 2002). A somewhat similar argument has been used by leaders of the Belgian VB; after gaining another electoral victory a few months after its conviction for inciting racial hatred, the party proclaimed that it had been "convicted by *a* Belgian judge, acquitted by *the* Flemish voter" (my italics).[5]

However, with the exception of some slogans, the subordination of the judiciary to the will of the people does not feature in much of the official party literature. Most parties rather stress the importance of a politically independent judiciary; in most cases the populist radical right

---

[5] Note also that the reference is to a *Belgian* judge, yet to the *Flemish* voter.

faces a fairly hostile political environment and it believes that the judiciary is controlled by its political opponents. Yet, once in power the populist radical right has been less supportive of this independence. In fact, they have strongly criticized unfavorable judicial rulings and tried to curtail the judiciary's independence and power by introducing new laws or by appointing partisan judges (e.g. Kelley 2004; Ruscino 2002).

6.5   Populist radical right democracy vs. liberal democracy

Populist radical right democracy is a combination of nativist, authoritarian, and populist democracy. While no party calls for a pure populist radical right democracy, and probably no two family members defend an identical form of democracy, the whole party family supports an ethnocratic regime with strong authoritarian and plebiscitary elements. This essentially monist interpretation of democracy is at odds with some fundamental aspects of liberal democracy.

It is obvious that a nativist democracy, whether based upon forced monoculturalism or ethnocracy, opposes key elements of liberal democracy, most notably the protection of minorities and the centrality of individual rights. Regarding its authoritarianism, no inherent contradictions exist, but in practice various parties push the limits of the rule of law (*Rechtsstaat*) in favor of a state of security (*Sicherheitsstaat*) (Mudde 2006). Convinced that the nation is under an imminent threat from aliens (varying from immigrants to Islamic terrorists), the populist radical right believes that the state should no longer be obstructed in its defensive actions by principles like the right to privacy or legal counsel.

The relationship between populist democracy and liberal democracy is somewhat more subtle. Many authors will agree that "[a] plebiscitarian approach to direct democracy might [thus] easily undermine rather than support the democratic cultural goods (tolerance, compromising skills, other-regarding perspectives) produced through deliberative representational practices" (Barney & Laycock 1999: 334; also Abts & Rummens 2005). Referendums are also believed to weaken political parties and fragment party systems, thus undermining key institutions of contemporary democracies. However, empirical proof for these assertions is hard to come by (e.g. Ladner & Braendle 1999). Similarly, the critique that personalization of power leads to antiliberal regimes, as has happened in Latin America (e.g. Werz 2003b), ignores the fact that various strong liberal democracies with powerful political leaders exist within Europe (e.g. Britain and France).

Most problematic is the radical interpretation of the primacy of the political, particularly with respect to the judiciary. Within the populist idea the "general will" of the people is the basis of democracy and cannot be limited by anything. Consequently, populists will defend an extreme form of majoritarian democracy, in which minority rights can exist only as long as the majority supports them. Similarly, constitutional provisions are valid only as long as they have majority support. While these aspects are generally not expressed in the party literature – which in fact rather stresses the opposite (political independence of the judiciary) – the practice shows that once in power the populist radical right clearly follows these ideas (see also 12.3). This has led to some serious (attempts at) infringements of constitutionally protected liberal rights (e.g. in Austria, Croatia, Italy, and Slovakia).

As a general rule then, we can conclude that populist radical right democracy is fundamentally at odds with liberal democracy because of its monism, most strongly expressed in its nativism and populism. Consequently, the more liberal a democracy is, the more antisystem the populist radical right will be. Similarly, we can posit that the more ethnic and plebiscitary a democracy, the more pro-system the populist radical right. Hence the strong support for the constitution of populist radical right parties in Croatia, Estonia, Germany (until the revision), Israel, Switzerland, or Turkey. This again shows that if one wants to use the term populist radical right in a (nearly) universal way, i.e. not limiting it to liberal democracies, the antisystem criteria cannot be included in the definition (cf. Ignazi 2003).

This leads us to the normative question: how dangerous is the populist radical right? Various authors have argued that populist democracy in general is non- or even antidemocratic (Abts & Rummens 2005). However, this is only accurate if the term democracy is used exclusively for the subtype *liberal* democracy; which is what most authors also implicitly or explicitly do. Similarly, the argument that the populist radical right is antipolitical holds only for certain (liberal) definitions of politics (cf. Schedler 1997). In fact, one could equally argue that the populist radical right is extremely political, in the sense that it believes in the primacy of politics over all other forces, including economics and history (e.g. Decker 2004).

Another popular view, particularly among scholars of and from Eastern Europe, holds that the populist radical right might not constitute a major challenge to the established democracies in the West, but does represent a fundamental threat to the fragile new democracies in the postcommunist East (e.g. Thieme 2005; Bayer 2002). According to some authors, this is at least in part a result of the greater strength of the populist radical right in the East. Josef Bayer has posited that "[r]adical right parties are fringe phenomena in Western democracies, whereas they are used as possible smaller coalition partners or majority providers in Central and Eastern Europe" (2002: 267). A quick look at the situation in the two parts of Europe quickly disproves this statement: while no populist radical right party provides government support in the East in January 2006, three Western European countries have parties from this family in government (Austria, Italy, and Switzerland).

A more convincing argument is based on the allegedly weaker democratic culture of postcommunist countries. István Gyarmati, senior vice-president of the East-West Institute and a former Hungarian deputy defense minister, has expressed this view forcefully:

There is a general trend in Europe which is the re-emergence of the extreme right, as various radical elements look for solutions outside the system . . . But in Central Europe, this is more dangerous than in Western Europe, because in Central Europe, democratic thinking and the democratic public are not quite so stable. (*New York Times* 12/05/2002)

While his view is broadly shared within the academic literature, the empirical evidence does not fully substantiate this claim either (Mudde 2005b). Inter-regional differences in terms of democratic quality do exist, but they are not always larger than intra-regional variations. For example, it is debatable whether in terms of "democratic thinking" Estonia or Slovenia have more in common with Bulgaria or Romania than with Finland or Austria (e.g. Pollack *et al.* 2003; Plasser *et al.* 1998).

In conclusion then, while the populist radical right does not constitute a fundamental challenge to the democratic procedural system itself, clear tensions exist between its interpretation of democracy and liberal democracy. On various fundamental procedures and values, populist radical right democracy and liberal democracy clash in both theory and practice. At the core of this tension is the distinction between monism and pluralism: whereas populist radical right democracy considers societies to be essentially homogeneous collectives, liberal democracy presupposes societies to be made up of groups of fundamentally different individuals.

7 "Europe for the Europeans"

"Nationalistes de tous les pays unissez-vous!" [Nationalists of all countries unite!]
(Jean-Marie Le Pen (FN))

"Das einzige, was viele rechte europäische Parteien gemeinsam haben,
ist das, was sie trennt." [The only thing that many right-wing European
parties have in common is that which divides them.]
(Franz Schönhuber (REP))

7.1 Introduction

International cooperation among populist radical right parties has thus far
received little academic attention. Some scholars have studied the internationalization of the extreme right, notably neo-Nazi and racist groups
(e.g. Kaplan & Weinberg 1999), and there have been a few publications
on the cooperation among populist radical right parties in the European
Parliament (e.g. Stöss 2001; Veen 1997). However, overall this topic has
been the domain of antifascists and freelance journalists, and there has
been virtually no systematic empirical challenge to their often grotesque
misrepresentations of a "brown network" based largely on bizarre conspiracy theories (e.g. Svoray & Taylor 1994).

As far as European cooperation between more or less relevant populist radical right parties is concerned, opinions differ quite substantially. Some scholars believe that "[t]he attempts at cross-linking
[*Vernetzungsbemühungen*] of the extreme right in Europe have increased
in the last years, and particularly the development of an extreme right
Europe ideology is presently taking concrete shape – despite all national
specifics and differences" (Salzborn & Schiedel 2003: 1209). Others are
more cautious, arguing that it does not seem correct "to speak of one
European right-wing extremism in the sense of a political actor. Its degree
of institutionalization is limited, and all attempts to solidify its form – not
to speak of establishing binding structures or even international organizations – have always failed" (Stöss 2001: 2). The latter group of authors get

support from unexpected corners; for example, Germany's most famous populist radical right politician, the late Franz Schönhuber, admitted with regret that "it is a fact that the European Right does not exist" (2000: 56).

This chapter will critically assess these different claims by analyzing the relationship between populist radical right parties and European cooperation from three perspectives: (1) the views of populist radical right parties on the European Union; (2) their European utopias; and (3) their cooperation in Europe.

7.2   The European Union: sepsis and rejection

Given the predominance of nativism in the ideology of the populist radical right, it comes as no surprise that most parties hold negative views on the European Union. However, this has not always been the case. Many Western European populist radical right parties were supportive of the process of European integration during the 1980s. This applied most notably to the relatively moderate parties, such as the Dutch CP and the German REP (Mudde 2000a); the latter had emerged from the Euroenthusiast CSU and initially considered "European unification . . . the historical task of our generation" (REP 1983: X).

But even more radical parties, like the alleged prototype, the French FN, started out as Euroenthusiasts. In the 1985 party program, Le Pen wrote, "The European Union will remain utopia as long as the Community doesn't have sufficient resources, a common currency and a political will, which is inseparable from the ability to defend itself" (in Simmons 2003: 3). Consequently, the party called for

a common European defence and nuclear strategy, a common foreign policy, common immigration controls, a common antiterrorist policy, a common (as opposed to single) currency, and the establishment of an external European border under supranational control and of a clearly defined 'European citizenship'. (Fieschi et al. 1996: 240)

Obviously, this was all to be done under the leadership of France. After all, "France is too much of a model for too many countries, starting with their neighbours" (Le Pen in Fieschi et al. 1996: 240).

In most cases, the turning point came with the Maastricht Treaty in 1992, which meant a change in both the parties' position on the European issue and its salience. Whether mainly targeting the "neoliberalism" or the "socialism" of the EU, virtually all populist radical right parties believe that with the Maastricht Treaty "the E.U. has taken a significant step further towards becoming an intrusive supranational body" (FPd 1998).

The German REP even described the Maastricht Treaty as "Versailles without weapons" (*Der Republikaner*, Sonderausgabe I, 1989), while Le Pen compared it to the "infamous Treaty of Troyes" (in Fieschi *et al.* 1996: 248).

Even among parties in countries that were still outside of the European Union in 1992, Maastricht is seen as the turning point. István Csurka, leader of the Hungarian MIÉP, believes that "when the common Europe of Maastricht arises, then the Hungarian ethnic community (*Volk*) cannot continue to exist as an independent subject" (Csurka 1997: 260). And the Slovak SNS refers to "the perverse thinking behind Maastricht" (in Boisserie 1998: 299). The fiercely anti-EU Swiss SVP sees the Treaty as the point where the EU decided upon "a centralist structure" (SVP 2003: 22).

Like in the old member states, most populist radical right parties in the accession countries were initially pro-European, but became increasingly negative about the drive towards EU membership by the various post-communist governments. Indeed, in some countries it even became an opportunity for various small groups to overcome their differences and unite in the face of this overwhelming enemy. In Poland, for example, various tiny populist radical right and other nativist parties came together in the Porozumienie Polskie (Polish Agreement), with the explicit aim of resisting the accession of Poland to the EU (Stadtmüller 2000). A similar process took place in the Czech Republic, culminating in the emergence of the highly active, if still electorally irrelevant, NS.

Some party leaders came out openly against EU membership. Referring to the EU in the wake of the sanctions against Austria, MIÉP leader Csurka said in the Hungarian parliament that Hungary "must not join an organization that restricts national sovereignty" (*RFE/RL Newsline* 07/02/2000). However, in most cases the parties would do their best not to be perceived as fundamentally anti-European, given the pro-European conviction of the majority of the population. They would imply that their opposition was temporary and could be changed depending upon the economic and political development of the EU and their home country. In a "Memorandum" summarizing the main conclusion of their "Euro-critical Congress," the Czech NS summarized this position as short and simple: "In today's situation we say NO to the accession to EU" (NS 2003).

Various parties tried to win sympathy for their negative standpoint on EU membership by linking it to the recent anticommunist struggle in their country. For the Czech Republicans, for example, "[t]he idea of the EU is in many respects similar to the ideology of communism" (SPR-RSČ 1999). These parties portrayed the EU as a modern-day version of the old Soviet Union, or its economic organization COMECON. Csurka wrote in his weekly *Magyar Fórum*: "The European Constitution is a new Soviet system of centralization that was prepared in the West" (in Weaver 2006: 102). And Anna Maliková, then SNS chairwoman, said that the EU-14 boycott of Austria reminded her of the Soviet "doctrine of limited sovereignty" (*RFE/RL Newsline* 21/02/2000).

Interestingly, similar analogies have been made by leaders from West European parties. Umberto Bossi, leader of the Italian LN, has repeatedly referred to "the Soviet Union of Europe," which, in line with the infamous Judeo-Communist conspiracy theories, is seen as "a nest of freemasons and Communist bankers" (in Quaglia 2005: 286). Similarly, Le Pen has raised the alarm against a Europe that is "overstretched, similar to the Soviet Union, cosmopolite, cut off from its Christian roots, and flooded by Islam" (in Schmid 2005: 8).

The EU is also linked to that other superpower, the US, as the alleged model of European integration, i.e. a federalist "United States of Europe." Some parties also see the US as the true power behind the EU. Bruno Mégret, leader of the MNR, considers the current EU as "the Trojan Horse of the Americans" (in Bastow 2000: 8). And according to MIÉP leader Csurka, "[t]he American world power, which is becoming increasingly the world power managing the world's financial affairs, pushes the whole European Union to create a common Europe that contradicts the basic nature of each country" (in Kriza 2004; also Csurka 2000).

In general, party positions on European integration can be categorized on the basis of two dimensions: diffuse and specific support (Kopecký & Mudde 2002). Diffuse support denotes agreement with the underlying ideas of European integration, i.e. an integrated market economy and pooled sovereignty. This dimension divides the Europhiles and the Europhobes. Specific support entails the belief that the EU is a good reflection of the underlying ideas of European integration, or is at least developing in the right direction. This separates the EU-optimists from the EU-pessimists. On the basis of these two dimensions, four types of party positions can be distinguished: Euroenthusiasts, Europragmatists, Eurorejects, and Euroskeptics (see table 7.1). While populist radical right parties can be found in all types, the vast majority are at least EU-pessimist.

7.2.1   Euroenthusiasts

Many populist radical right parties in both parts of Europe started out as Euroenthusiasts, i.e. expressing support for both the underlying ideas

Table 7.1 *Typology of party positions on European integration*

		Support for European integration	
		Europhile	Europhobe
Support for the EU	EU-optimist	Euroenthusiasts	Europragmatists
	EU-pessimist	Euroskeptics	Eurorejects

Source: Kopecký & Mudde (2002: 303).

of European integration and the EU itself, but grew increasingly skeptical during the 1990s. At the beginning of the twenty-first century, few parties still support the direction of European integration. One of the notable exceptions is the Austrian BZÖ, the new party of Jörg Haider, which considers the EU as "the answer to negative phenomena of globalization" and even supports "an integration process of different speeds and dynamics of developments" (BZÖ 2005: 3–4).

7.2.2   Europragmatists

The Europragmatists' position at first looks somewhat paradoxical: they do not believe in the underlying ideas of European integration, but they do support the EU. Not surprisingly very few European political parties fall into this category, and this is the same for the populist radical right. One of the examples of the few in this category is the Romanian PRM.

In the 1990s the party still saw the EU as a Hungarian conspiracy to regain Transylvania, the northern part of Romania inhabited by a sizeable Hungarian-speaking minority, which Hungary lost as a consequence of the Trianon Treaty of 1920. In his typical bizarre style, Tudor once said: "No trespassing, dear Magyar irredentists and highly cherished Romanian traitors, we do not believe in your variant of the common European Home" (in Schuster 2005: 39). And though the party ideology remains clearly opposed to the underlying ideas of European integration, the PRM now sees no other choice than to accept EU membership. According to party leader Tudor, "[t]his is no capitulation, but *realpolitik*" (in Shafir 2001: 106).

7.2.3   Eurorejects

Within the old member states, i.e. the former EU-15, only a few populist radical right parties are openly Euroreject. These are mostly found in the traditional Euroskeptical countries, Britain and Denmark (e.g. BNP and

Veritas, and DFP), but tiny Euroreject parties also exist in traditionally Euroenthusiastic countries like Spain (e.g. DN). The key arguments these parties use are nativist, i.e. the EU is seen as an infringement of or a threat to national independence, but also (populist) democratic, e.g. pointing to the more broadly criticized "democratic deficit" of the EU. In the singular case of the orthodox Protestant DUP, the EU is rejected on the basis of its alleged Catholic domination. According to party leader Rev. Ian Paisley, "the European Union is a beast ridden by the harlot Catholic Church, conspiring to create a Europe controlled by the Vatican" (in Ronson 2002: 243).

The Euroreject parties from the old EU member states want their country to get out of the EU (e.g. BNP, DN, DFP, DUP, Veritas). The Danish DFP simply states that it "opposes the European Union" (DFP n.d.), while the Veritas program explicitly includes the demand that the UK "withdraw from the EU" (Veritas 2005b) – in fact, the latter party claims that "[a]ll our policies are . . . based on our intention to leave the EU immediately" (Veritas 2005b). The British Freedom Party desires the same, but wants the people to decide the issue in a national referendum (FP 2005). For the Greek HF, everything hinges upon whether or not Turkey enters the EU: ". . . if it ever is accepted, then Greece should leave the European Union!" (Voridis 2003). The fact that there is no procedure to leave the EU does not seem to bother these parties. According to Matti Järviharju, leader of the Finnish IKL, this problem will solve itself anyway as "[t]he EU will disintegrate because of internal problems and the [IKL] will participate in this process to regain Finnish independence" (in Hynynen 1999: 140).

Despite the often fierce critique of the EU, and of the consecutive governments' pursuit of EU membership, few populist radical right parties in the accession countries openly rejected their country's entrance into the organization. In some of the few cases where parties did come out against EU membership, their positions were largely informed by Germanophobia. In the Czech Republic, for example, parties like the NS and SPR-RSČ rejected EU membership because it would allegedly make the country "fully dependent upon Germany as the biggest country in the EU" (SPR-RSČ 1999). Similarly, LPR party leader Maciej Giertych claimed that "[i]t is Germanophiles and sympathizers of freemasonry who are pulling us forcibly into this Eurokolchoz" (in Taras 2003: 8). Consequently, the party came to the conclusion that "Poland can only develop well outside the EU" (LPR 2003: XI. 8).

Among populist radical right parties in the countries (still) outside the EU, Eurorejection seems more widespread than Euroskepticism. All members of the highly fragmented party family in Switzerland are open and vehement Eurorejects. Indeed, it is one of the key points of the governing SVP, which "fights the accession to the EU" in both words and deeds (SVP 2003: 17). The Bulgarian Ataka also rejects the EU, even if Bulgarian membership is a foregone conclusion, and the party has in recent months adopted a "maybe, if" position – which does not change anything essentially, as EU membership under the party's conditions is not realistic. And although Zhirinovsky has at times hinted at aspiring toward Russia's entry into the EU, the LDPR does not officially seek membership for the country.

7.2.4   Euroskeptics

The majority of populist radical right parties believe in the basic tenets of European integration, but are skeptical about the current direction of the EU. This includes most of the formerly Euroenthusiastic parties of the old member states (e.g. FN, LN, REP), which continue to argue their European credentials, but at the same time consistently criticize the EU. A good example is provided by the Belgian FNb, which somewhat pathetically claims that it has been pro-European since its founding, but proceeds with a tirade against the EU, referring to "the McCarthy of ultra-liberalism" and "the eurokapos of the Europe without borders" (*Le National* 121/2005). This is quite similar to the VB, which combines an abstract pro-European rhetoric with fierce attacks on "Eurocratic palaces and their extravagant lackeys" (Mudde 2000a).

Most populist radical right parties in the accession countries have been ambivalent and inconsistent in their position on EU membership; a phenomenon more broadly expressed within Central and East European political circles (e.g. Beichelt 2004; Kopecký & Mudde 2002). While considering themselves part of European history and civilization, they were skeptical about the EU, which reminded many too much of the past. In the Polish context, Antoni Macierewicz, MP for the LPR, expressed it as follows: "We don't reject the EU, we've been part of Europe for 1,000 years, but the Europe we're being presented with now has the face of [former communist dictator] Jaruzelski" (in Maryniak 2002: 104). The Hungarian MIÉP campaigned under the slogan "In this way, no," arguing that it did not oppose EU membership *per se*, but that Hungary was not yet ready economically (*RFE/RL Newsline* 09/12/2002). In the end, whereas the LPR rejected EU membership, MIÉP accepted it (bitterly).

In the countries that are not (yet) EU member states, several populist radical right parties express Euroskeptic positions too. They do not openly take a position on membership *per se*, but will critically discuss the current state of affairs and preconditions. Few parties are as cautious as the Croatian HSP. Even though the official declaration of their fifth party meeting in 2004 was entitled "Croatia in Europe," it did not once mention the EU. This notwithstanding, the declaration is a clear and consistent plea for the unconditional sovereignty of the Croat state against any curtailment of it by membership in "international associations" (HSP 2004).

More commonly, parties claim not to be against EU membership but their propaganda will espouse almost exclusively negative views on the EU. An alternative strategy is to profess a (weak) pro-membership stand, but at the same time argue that either the country is not yet ready for membership, or the EU is proposing unfair demands to the country; both points logically lead to a rejection of EU membership, now and in the foreseeable future.

Most populist radical right parties outside of the current EU demand major revisions in the current treaties and stress the comparative importance of other geographical areas. For example, the Bulgarian Ataka program states: "Negotiations with the EU are not more important than the standard of living and the life of Bulgarians. If trade with India is more beneficial for BG than trade with France, relations with India should win. The same goes for China, Japan, Russia and the ex-Soviet Republics" (Ataka 2005). And in line with its pan-Turkic ideology, the MHP expresses a preference for cooperation with the "Turkic" countries in the post-Soviet area, and demands major revisions in the current customs agreement between the EU and Turkey (Akgun 2002).

7.3   European utopias

While most populist radical right parties constantly criticize the process of European integration in general, and the EU in particular, many of them support some alternative form of European cooperation. In the words of the Swedish SD: "European cooperation is a good thing, but the establishment of a new European superstate is not" (SD 2005). Consequently, many parties have campaigned with slogans like "No to Maastricht – yes to a Europe of Fatherlands!" (FN), "Yes to Europe, No to this EC" (REP), or "Yes to Europe, No to Brussels" (DN).

Yet, though virtually the whole party family agrees that the current EU is bad and should be either reformed fundamentally or abolished, there is no "common ideal of Europe" (Chiantera-Stutte & Pető 2003). In fact, populist radical right parties differ deeply on what kind of Europe should come in the place of the current EU. On the other hand few parties have given the issue much thought; this is particularly the case in the East (e.g. Ataka, LPR, SRS).

Table 7.2 *Typology of nationalisms and views of the European Union*

Type of nationalism	Main objective	View of EU as alliance of
Traditional	Ensure congruence of political and cultural boundaries (nation-state)	States
Substate	Strengthen political representation for homeland *vis-à-vis* state	Nations
Transsovereign	Create institutions to link nation across state boundaries	Nations
Protectionist	Preserve national culture in face of immigration/social change	States

Source: Csergő and Goldgeier (2004: 23)

The most humble European ambitions are expressed by Euroreject parties. Veritas (2005a), for example, states that "[w]e will replace the Treaties on European Union with a free trade agreement." At least this vision is fairly concrete. Most parties express their European "vision" in extremely general and vague terms. A good example is the Czech Euroreject NS, which describes its preferred form of European integration in the following noncommittal terms: "free development of national states co-operation with equal rights" (NS 2003).

Against these minimum interpretations stand some quite bizarre maximum ambitions, mostly expressed by tiny (populist) radical right groupuscules. For example, the Greek HF, a virulently anti-American party, proclaims that "Europe, caged by the false pacifism and the egalitarian ideals of the Left, seems incapable to fulfill its destiny: to become a great world power, equal to its traditions and history, equal to the Athenian, Roman and Byzantine empire, equal to leaders such as Alexander the Great, Napoleon the Great and Peter the Great" (Voridis 2003).

Obviously, most populist radical right parties fall between the maximum utopia of a new empire and the minimum project of a free trade zone. All reject a federal "United States of Europe," but many support some form of "Confederal Europe." In short, they want a more limited form of European cooperation than the current EU, involving only specific policy fields and no significant loss of sovereignty. The shape of this new Europe leads to a variety of different terms and visions (e.g. Fennema and Pollmann 1998; Hafeneger 1994; for a more historical overview, see Griffin 1994).

Some authors see a relationship between the type of nationalism and the type of European integration particular parties support. The most elaborate typology of this correspondence was constructed by Zsuzsa Csergő and James Goldgeier, who distinguish between four types of national-ism and two types of EU (see table 7.2). While undoubtedly creative, its usefulness is limited by the fact that the different types of nationalism are not actually discrete in practice or in theory, and in some cases par-ties synthesize elements that logically suggest different visions of the EU. The Belgian VB, for example, combines "substate" and "protectionist" nationalism. The model is further undermined by the fact that nearly every nativist party defends (at least) the other two forms.

This is not to say that there is no relationship between the type of nationalism and the view on European integration of a populist radi-cal right party, but clearly the link is relative rather than absolute. The relationship is elusive because the models of European cooperation actu-ally favored by the parties are obscured by the plethora of terms used within the party family to indicate them: "Europe of the Fatherlands" (e.g. FN), "Europe of Nations" (e.g. AS), "Europe of Ethnic Commu-nities [Völker]" (e.g. VB), "Europe of Regions" (e.g. Agir), "Europe of Nation States" (e.g. Slovak SNS), "Europe of Fatherlands and of Peo-ples" (e.g. EK), and "Europe of Fatherlands and Nations" (e.g. FL). Behind this terminological chaos lie differences of opinions on various aspects of European integration, most notably the constituting members, degree of integration, geographical borders, and reasons for European cooperation.

7.3.1 Constituting members

One of the most significant ideological divisions within the populist radi-cal right party family is between ethnic and state nationalists, although the difference is largely a matter of degree (Mudde 2000a; Rensmann 2003). This division has important consequences for the parties' views on Euro-pean cooperation (e.g. Fennema & Pollmann 1998; Hafeneger 1994). Most self-professed ethnic nationalist parties prefer a Europe of Nations or Europa der Völker. Both models more or less build upon the nations or "ethnic communities" of Europe, rather than the currently existing states, and fit the ideology of parties like the VB. Self-declared state nationalist parties, such as the FN and MNR, prefer Charles De Gaulle's Europe des Patries (Europe of Fatherlands) model, which is based on the existing "nation-states" (e.g. De Gaulle in Tiersky 2001).

The preference for "nation-states" or "nations" has practical as well as theoretical consequences. Most notably, it has been a continuous source of tension in the collaboration between populist radical right parties at the European level (e.g. Stöss 2001). Even in the most recent attempt at Euro-pean cooperation in Vienna, in November 2005 (see 7.4.3), organizer

Andreas Mölzer had to change his reference to "European ethnic communities [*Völker*]" to "European nations" after protest from French and Spanish populist radical rightists (*Kurier* 14/11/2005).

The effects of the ideological distinction are most clearly visible in the relationship between the French FN and the Belgian VB. Although the two parties have always worked together very closely, with the VB copying much of the propaganda of the FN, the issue of state versus ethnic nationalism has long strained the relationship. In the early days of the VB, many leading members were highly skeptical about cooperating with a party that was both French and state nationalist, therefore rejecting the "minority rights" of the Flemish living in the northwest of France (e.g. Mudde 2000a). At the same time, the FN never really sympathized with the VB's call for an independent Flemish state, and at various times lent support to populist radical right groups with a Belgicist ideology, such as the FNb and its splits.

7.3.2   Forms of integration

Most populist radical right parties denounce the current form of European cooperation and affirm what they do *not* want in the future: loss of independence, a European super-state, federalism. As far as they do address their preferred form of European cooperation, the most common model is confederalism. Many parties explicitly call for a European Confederation, although often without providing many details on either the exact relations between the Confederation and the member states or the policy fields in which the confederation should be active.

The Spanish DN simply states: "as an alternative to E.U., we propose a European Confederation" (DN n.d.), while the Greek LAOS and Italian AS want a Europe of Nations (*Europa Nazione*) built upon a confederation of nation-states that are free and sovereign (AS n.d.; LAOS n.d.). The short-lived Slovak PSNS called for "Eurosovereignism, i.e. the sovereignty of national governments and the maintenance of cooperation among European smaller traditional national states" (PSNS n.d.). The FPÖ, seemingly influenced by Christian-democratic views on European integration, believes that "Europe's diversity calls for forms of political cooperation which envisages different confederations on different levels" (FPÖ 1997: 10). This European confederation should be based upon the principle of subsidiarity (see also VB 2004a).

Most parties mainly emphasize what Europe should *not* do: "The independence of states should be restricted only by what is absolutely necessary to reach specific goals" (FPÖ 1997: 10). Some will also identify these "specific goals," i.e. the exact policy areas on which they prefer European cooperation: Le Pen, for example, at one time expressed a preference for "political, economic, and even military cooperation" (in Tiersky 2001: 193). Even fewer will also discuss in more detail the content and degree of that cooperation.

Given the initial support of European integration among most populist radical right parties, their positive attitude toward some kind of economic cooperation comes as little surprise. Although they remain vague on the details, the general idea of a more or less open internal market protected from extra-European competition seems widely shared. However, member states should still play an important role, "since the nation states are the only corrective against the power of multinational concerns" (Haider in Tiersky 2001: 233). For the FN, the integrated market could even include "a common currency as a unit of account," but without the abolition of national currencies and national budgetary independence (Le Pen in Tierksy 2001: 193).

Several parties also want cooperation in the field of "collective security" (SNS 2002), notably military cooperation. While some want a European army to exist in partnership with NATO (e.g. FPÖ), most populist radical right parties prefer Europe to be independent from NATO, which they believe to be "an instrument of America rather than the international community" (AS 2005). Thus, European military ambitions are particularly strong among the anti-American populist radical right parties in Eastern and Southern Europe (e.g. AS, DN, FN, MS-FT).

A few parties even call for a "social Europe." For example, the short-lived Belgian Agir hoped for "the will to realize a social Europe in a perspective of progress" (Agir n.d.), while for the Italian AS, "[t]he new European state . . . is allowed to intervene and correct the antisocial economic tendencies that are part of liberalism" (AS 2005). However, for many other parties this is clearly a bridge too far. The moderately Euroskeptic VB argues in this respect: "The social domain is a typical area specific to the ethnic community [volkseigen] that should belong fully to an independent Flanders. There can be no one European social policy for the Vlaams Blok" (VB 2004a: 70).

7.3.3   Borders

Like most mainstream politicians, the populist radical right struggles with the question of the borders of Europe. However, unencumbered as they are by indeterminate notions of citizenship and a relativist understanding of political boundaries, the populist radical right has little difficulty defining the essence of the continent. For them Europe is a "civilization," a "meta-culture," shared by the various different and independent

European nations. Most parties will see the roots of this civilization in three traditions: the Christian, Hellenistic, and Roman. Some refer (also) to the more mystic concept of the Occident (*Abendland*), although the practical differences do not seem to be very significant (e.g. Fennema & Pollmann 1998).

Before the fall of communism, some populist radical right parties were happy with the borders of the EC at that time. The German REP, for example, wanted the EC to consolidate with the inclusion of Portugal and Spain (REP 1983: XI) and extend membership no further. However, since 1989 virtually all populist radical right parties have come to accept that the EU was too limited in geographical scope. Where the exact borders of "Europe" should be, however, is a matter of discussion within the party family, mostly informed by what is considered to be the binding factor of the continent (culture, religion, etc.).

Nearly all parties argue that "Europe" should include all the "Christian" or "occidental" nations of Eastern Europe. Thus, there was broad support among the populist radical right for the enlargement toward Central Eastern Europe (including Croatia and Slovenia) and the Baltic countries; many of the new countries had been seen as "oppressed nations" during Soviet times and their independence was greeted with great enthusiasm. When actual accession came closer, the enthusiasm of several Western European populist radical right parties tempered, and some started to demand "guarantees for political and economic stability" of the new states before acceptance of membership (AS 2005).

Some disagreement exists about the inclusion of the Orthodox countries. As far as most parties are concerned, all Christian countries in Europe are welcome. Even the BNP's objection to the inclusion of Bulgaria and Romania is not based on their religion, but rather on a classic nativist fear of a mass influx of "eight million Sinta [*sic*] gypsies" (BNP 2005). The biggest problem is Russia, which is a Christian country, but according to several populist radical right parties not a fully European one. Most populist radical rightists will draw the line at the Urals (e.g. AS, REP), excluding contemporary Russia from EU membership.

The exclusion of Turkey, on the other hand, finds full consensus. In essence, all parties agree that Turkey should be excluded from the EU "as it does not have a common ethnological and cultural denominator and moreover, contains extreme Islamic elements" (LAOS n.d.: 14). "Turkey has no place in Europe as it was and still remains anti-European and non-European" (FL in Kolovos 2003: 60). In the simple terms of the Italian F: "Turkey for the Turks. Europe for the Europeans." Various populist radical right parties campaign specifically on this issue; the French MNR put out a special pamphlet entitled *Europe, Yes – Turkey, No!*, while the

Belgian VB has created a single-issue front-organization, the Comité 'Nee tegen Turkije' (Committee 'No to Turkey').

In conclusion, most members of the populist radical right party family consider Europe to be a (meta-)civilization based upon the Greek, Roman, and Christian civilizations. While no full consensus on the exact border of "Europe" exists, most parties would probably agree with the REP's statement that "[g]eographically Europe ends at the Mediterranean, at the Bosporus, and at the Ural" (REP 2003).

7.3.4   Reasons for European cooperation

While it might be an overstatement that European cooperation is anathema to nationalist parties, there is an inherent tension between them. Not surprisingly, in the worldview of the populist radical right, the construction of the "ingroup" is largely the result of the perceived threat from the "outgroups" (see also chapter 3). In the words of FN leader Le Pen:

In order for Europe to be a reality, there must be a genuine European sentiment; that is why we have expressed the wish to go beyond patriotism, beyond our respective feelings of national patriotism, to achieve a European patriotism. Which is to say that there will be no Europe unless it is destined to become a Nation. This nation can only be brought about through the need to defend itself against the external threats confronting it – and God knows, the threats to Europe are real enough. (in Fieschi et al. 1996: 238–9)

While it is true that many populist radical right parties see European cooperation as an alternative to "Western integration" (Veen 1997), i.e. NATO, there are important exceptions. Some parties believe that European cooperation should go hand in hand with Atlantic cooperation (e.g. FPÖ), arguing that Europe itself is (still) too weak to fight the enemies of "the West" (i.e. Islam), whereas others even prefer military cooperation with the US in NATO over a European army (e.g. DFP, LPR). The idea of an independent and neutral Europe is particularly strong among the populist radical right in anti-American countries like France, Greece, and Italy. Here, a strong Europe as counter-weight to a hegemonic US gives rise to some of the more intense models of European cooperation.

Some parties, like the Slovak SNS, see European cooperation as a way to protect nation-states against the destructive effects of globalization.

The process of globalization in the world requires as the necessary counter-reaction the strengthening of the role of the state in order to secure defense and promotion of national interests. The SNS, in collaboration with other patriotic parties in Europe, will promote such a conception, set up within the European Union, which will create conditions for a strong position of the nation states in promoting their interests. (SNS 2002: 9)

Similarly, the Austrian BZÖ argues that a "Europe founded on values and social stability is the answer to negative phenomena of globalization, which holds dangers for people, their identity and security" (2005: 3–4).

7.4   European party cooperation

Most accounts of a "Nationalist International" border on quasi-paranoid conspiracy theories. The evidence for the "brown network" is generally pronouncement of guilt by association: an individual from party x knows individual y, who has published in fascist magazine z, thus party x is fascist (see, for example, Perner & Purtscheller 1994). In reality, *no* "'Populist International', with closely similar parties comparing notes and coordinating tactics across frontiers" exists (Lloyd 2003: 88). All attempts to come to an official "Nationalist International" have led to largely inactive, limited (most relatively successful parties refrained from membership), and short-lived initiatives: this applies as much to the extreme right Europäische Soziale Bewegung (European Social Movement) of the 1950s as to the populist radical right Euronat of the 1990s.

7.4.1   The problem of international contacts

Within the populist radical right party family, international contacts have been largely individual, i.e. personal relationships between leading party members in different countries. In many cases, these contacts were at best condoned by the party leadership (e.g. Stöss 2001). This meant that the party would not hold official ties with the other party, but would not forbid its (leading) members to have such contacts. This has been the case particularly with relations between populist radical right parties that are relatively integrated into their national political mainstream and those that are (still) treated as political pariahs in- and outside of their country.

A good example of this ambiguous approach has been the way in which the Austrian FPÖ has related to other populist radical right parties. Already before Haider took over the party in 1986, some radicals within the party held personal contacts with populist radical right and even extreme right parties in Germany, while the FPÖ itself always kept its distance.[1] This did not change much after the party itself became populist radical right, much to the frustration of like-minded parties abroad.

---

[1] The best-known example is Otto Scrinzi, who, with pauses, was MP for the FPÖ in the period 1966–79, attended various meetings of the DVU and was awarded the Andreas-Hofer-Preis by that organization in 1982 (Lasek 1993).

In his 1993 book, written shortly after the FPÖ left the Liberal International, preempting an official expulsion, Haider devotes the whole last chapter, entitled "Europe's Freedom needs united forces," to European cooperation. In it, there is not a word about other populist radical right parties.[2] Instead, Haider dreams of a "Freedomite Union" (*Freiheitliche Union*) consisting mainly of (individuals from) conservative liberal parties from Central Europe, including the Czech ODS and the German FDP and CSU (Haider 1993: 303). Frustrated by rejections from the conservative liberals, and worried about negative domestic consequences of alliances with foreign populist radical right parties, the FPÖ increasingly gave up on attempts to establish European cooperation with like-minded parties (e.g. Höbelt 2003). Haider's 1997 book mentions nothing about cooperation with other parties. And in an interview with the Hungarian daily *Népszabadsag* (12/02/2000), he even claimed: "The Austrian Freedom Party doesn't seek any relationships with foreign parties." This notwithstanding, in the following years leading representatives of, among others, the MIÉP, MNR and VB met on different occasions in Austria.[3] Officially, these meetings were personal initiatives of hard-liner Andreas Mölzer, organized without the consent of Haider. However, it is clear that Haider knew about the meetings and even condoned them (e.g. OTS 2005). In fact, he met personally with Filip Dewinter (VB) and Mario Borghezio (LN) to discuss the possibility of a unified list in future European elections (Heinisch 2003; Salzborn & Schiedel 2003).

After the fall of the Berlin Wall, several Western European populist radical right parties tried to establish contacts with perceived like-minded parties in the East. In a number of cases personal contacts already existed, as some populist radical right individuals and parties had been active supporters of (nationalist) anticommunist dissidents. Many in the West believed that with the fall of communism, and the consequent disintegration of various multinational states, nativism would be the ideology of the future in Eastern Europe. Some populist radical rightists hoped to break through their political isolation in Western Europe by finding new friends in the East, where "political correctness" was not obscuring the image of their party.

The Russian LDPR of Vladimir Zhirinovsky was a particular favorite of the Western populist radical right parties. With its stunning electoral

---

[2] The only exception is the Italian LN, which at that time was not widely perceived as populist radical right.

[3] At least two occasions are known, namely November 2001 and July 2002 (see Salzborn & Schiedel 2003). Carl Hagen, leader of the Norwegian neoliberal populist FRP, has claimed that he had also been invited but had rejected the invitation (see Lorenz 2003: 195).

victory in the 1993 parliamentary elections, the party had become the second biggest faction in the Russian parliament. Consequently, Zhirinovsky was courted by both DVU leader Gerhard Frey and FN leader Le Pen (e.g. Hunter 1998a; Parfenov & Sergeeva 1998). Not free of opportunism, Zhirinovsky enjoyed all Western interest, populist radical right or otherwise, as long as there were financial benefits for him and his party. However, after a few years of fairly good relations between Frey and Zhirinovsky, even this mutually beneficial relationship (i.e. political relevance for the DVU and Frey, financial benefits for LDPR and Zhirinovsky) fell victim to the age-old scourge of nativist internationalism: disputes over territory. After the erratic Zhirinovsky had announced that he wanted to make Germany as small as Austria, populist radical right Germans and Russian were no longer "friends for ever," as the DVU–LDPR cooperative slogan had sounded before (e.g. Spannbauer 1998).

A similar fate befell the LDPR in most Eastern European countries, where it had also been popular since its electoral victory. During the 1990s, Zhirinovsky made appearances in a host of countries, including Hungary, Poland, and Slovenia. In addition, local branches of the LDPR were founded in Belarus, Bulgaria, Estonia, and Latvia, all independent in name, but fully subordinate to the Russian mother party (e.g. Mudde 2000b; Bell 1999). In 1996 the party hosted an "international congress of patriotic parties and movements" in its Duma offices at which members of radical right groups from Austria, Belarus, Germany, Greece, Hungary, Serbia, and Ukraine discussed plans to create an international "patrintern" of patriotic parties (*RFE/RL Daily Digest* 26/04/1996). Nothing came of it.

Similarly, no enduring connections were formed with other Central and Eastern European populist radical right parties, with the possible exception of the relationship with the Serbian SRS. The Slovak SNS, like its "Slavic brothers," has mostly been ambiguous about its relations with the LDPR: while party leader Slota declined to invite Zhirinovsky to Bratislava, deputy chairman Juraj Molnar did attend the 1994 LDPR party congress in Moscow as "an observer" (Cibulka 1999: 119). However, in 1997 the Slovak SNS officially announced the cessation of all contacts with the LDPR (Gyárfášová 2002). In contrast, RMS leader Miroslav Sládek was among the international participants at the LDPR's 1st World Congress of Patriotic Parties in Moscow in January 2003 (Report 2002: 26).

7.4.2   The FN and Euronat

During the last two decades of the twentieth century the FN and its leader have been at the center of attempts to build a "Nationalist International" (e.g. Fromm & Kernbach 1994: 13–16). Officially, Le Pen would argue that a counter-weight was needed for the "international cosmopolitan movement" (in Fried 1997: 102). Most observers, however, saw mainly financial and power motives behind his actions. International cooperation between populist radical right parties was to lead to a (strong) faction within the European Parliament (EP), which would ensure the FN the crucial financial support that it lacked because of its weak representation at the national level in France, and to secure its leading position within populist radical right Europe.

Initially, the FN developed its closest relationship with the Italian MSI, the party that was Le Pen's role model for the FN (e.g. Veugelers & Chiarini 2002; Ignazi 1992). Due to changes in the leadership and strategy within the MSI and the emergence of new potential partners, the FN decided to exchange the MSI for the German REP in the European Parliament (see 7.4.3). This led to a deep mutual hostility between the two former allies that continues up to this date.

While the FN was able to establish itself as the leading force of populist radical right party cooperation in Western Europe, many of the more successful parties kept their distance from both the party and its leader. In the case of the Austrian FPÖ the reasons were primarily strategic and personal: Haider, as an office-seeking politician, wanted to avoid the stigma of the antisystem pariah party FN, but was also involved in a battle of egos over populist radical right dominance with Le Pen. In the case of the Scandinavian parties, including the populist radical right DFP, the main rationale seems to be a real belief that the FN was another type of party, i.e. linked to a nondemocratic tradition (e.g. Simmons 2003; Bjørklund & Andersen 2002).

During the 1990s Le Pen visited various Eastern European countries, often performing as the prominent foreign guest speaker at rallies of the local populist radical right party. Among the parties that invited him to their country are the Hungarian MIÉP, the Polish Alternatywa Partia Pracy (Alternative Labor Party) and Prawica Narodowa (National Right), the Serbian SRS, and the Slovak SNS (e.g. Mudde 2005b; Ramet 1999a; Hunter 1998).[4] While Le Pen visited various parties abroad, the FN also hosted various delegations of foreign parties at its conventions and festivities (such as the annual *Bleu Blanc Rouge*). According to one British participant, delegations from thirty foreign organizations (including one from Japan) attended the FN's major rally in Nice in 2003 (Turner 2003). However, he also notes how problematic the relationships between some national delegations are: for example, the Hungarian MIÉP and the

---

[4] In some cases Le Pen was not able to enter the country, for example after pressure from antiracist organizations (as was the case in Poland in 2001).

Romanian PRM "contented themselves with ignoring each other," while the Croatian and Serbian nationalists "actually came to blows."

There are many rumors about financial support from the FN to smaller European parties. According to one source, the French party gave SEK 500,000 (*ca.* EUR 55.000) to finance the printing of the brochures of the Sverigedemokraterna (Sweden Democrats, SD) for the 1998 parliamentary elections (en.wikipedia.org/wiki/Sverigedemokraterna). A similar service was provided to the LDPR in its first electoral campaign (Parfenov & Sergeeva 1998). One journalist has reported that a foundation linked to Bernard Antony's Chrétienté-Solidarité (Christian Solidarity) channeled USD30,000 in cash to Croatian towns under the control of HSP leader Paraga (Hunter 1998a: 24). However, he also argued that most of the FN's East European connections were primarily financially motivated, i.e. to ensure a faction in the EP (and thereby party financing) and to profit from oil sales (Hunter 1998b).

In 1997 Le Pen announced the establishment of a European National Union (ENU), or Euronat, by paraphrasing the famous Marxist dictum: "Nationalists of all countries unite!" The new organization was meant to become a pan-European confederation of populist radical right parties under the leadership of the FN. Despite the many references to the organization, particularly in the more nonacademic literature, Euronat has so far led a rather shadowy existence. Among the parties identified in the literature as members of ENU/Euronat are the Bulgarian BNRP, the Finnish IKL, the French FN, and the German REP (e.g. Simmons 2003; Bell 1999; Hynynen 1999). Allegedly, some Scandinavian Euronat-member parties founded a "Nord-Nat" in 1997, which included the Swedish SD and the Finnish IKL (Kalliala 1998: 127).

In January 2006 the official website of the FN did not even refer to Euronat; it only includes links to websites of some "mouvements politiques à l'étranger" (political movements abroad): the Belgian VB, the British BNP, the Greek HF, the Italian MS-FT, and the Swiss SVP (www.frontnational.com/liens.php). However, the website of the Greek HF, one of the self-professed members of Euronat, provides an interesting overview of what it considers "European nationalist parties" and lists its affiliation to the "three largest alliances of nationalist parties in Europe," i.e. Euronat, the Union for Europe of Nations (UEN), and Independence-Democracy; the latter two are factions in the European Parliament (see 7.4.3).

According to the HF, the following parties were members of Euronat on January 1, 2006: the Belgian FNb and VB, the French FN, the Hungarian MIÉP, the Dutch Nieuw Rechts (New Right), the Portuguese Partido Renovador Nacional (National Renewal Party), the Romanian

PRM, the Slovak SNS, the Spanish DN, and the Swedish SD (www.e-grammes.gr/ideology/europe_en.htm). This list might be only partially accurate, however; on the same day the Slovak SNS website listed the members of the UEN "Europartneri" (Europartners) and did not even mention Euronat (www.sns.sk/europartneri.php).

The Front National de la Jeunesse (Youth National Front, FNJ), the youth movement of the FN, has been involved in various attempts at institutionalizing international cooperation among (populist) radical right youth groups. Among these are the Mouvement de la Jeunesse d'Europe (Movement of the European Youth), founded in 1987 as the youth organization of the parties represented in the Group of the European Right at that time (Stöss 2001: 17), and the Bureau de Liaison des Jeunes Européens (Liaison Bureau for the European Youth), established in 1993. Following the grown-ups, the FNJ founded the Euronat Jeunesse in 1998 (Report 2000: note 31). According to one of its websites, the organization counts the youth branches of the following parties among its members: the VB, the HF, the IKL, the Italian Forza Nuovo (New Force), the Portuguese Aliança Nacional (National Alliance), the PRM, the Slovak SNS, the DN, and the SD (fnj.69.free.fr/euronat.htm).[5]

7.4.3   The European Parliament

The European Parliament is one of the few arenas in which the populist radical right has been able to establish some structured cooperation. In part motivated by the institutional discrimination against nonaffiliated MEPs, populist radical right parties have always tried to come to some kind of group affiliation, even though not necessarily a (homogeneous) populist radical right one. However, it is important to remember that the party family has always been weakly represented at the European level, and cooperation within the EP has therefore remained limited to a small group of parties (e.g. Salzborn & Schiedel 2003; Stöss 2001; Lord 1998; Veen 1997; Fieschi et al. 1996).

Since the first directly elected European Parliament did not count any MEPs from the populist radical right,[6] the first official radical right grouping was the "Groupe des Droites Européennes" (Group of the European Right) in the 1984–89 European Parliament. It included MEPs from the populist radical right French FN (10), the extreme right Greek EPEN

---

[5] According to another source, the Republikánska mládež (Republican Youth), the youth movement of the Czech SPR-RSČ, joined in May 1999 (Havelková 2002).

[6] There were four MEPs of the radical right MSI and one from the neoliberal populist FP; the latter rejected cooperation with radical right parties and instead joined the "Faction of European Democrats for Progress" (Stöss 2001: 17).

(1), the radical right Italian MSI (5), and the unionist Northern Irish Ulster Unionist Party (1).[7] The Group was completely dominated by the FN and its leader Jean-Marie Le Pen.

In the next parliament (1989–94) the FN (10 MEPs) exchanged the Italian MSI (4) for the German REP (6), after the two parties rejected cooperation because of a dispute over the status of Alto Adige/South Tyrol (e.g. Stöss 2001; Mudde 2000a; Fennema & Pollmann 1998). Le Pen thought that the Italian MSI was a dying relic, while the German REP was a party of the future like the FN, and believed his assessment to be confirmed in the electoral strength of the two parties. As the Belgian MEP for the VB, party leader Karel Dillen, also strongly supported the Germans, Le Pen decided to drop his old partner. Even though this group was ideologically more homogeneous than the previous one given that it comprised exclusively populist radical right parties, Dillen insisted on calling it the "Technical Faction of the European Right," indicating the pragmatic considerations underlying the collaboration.[8] As a consequence of internal problems within the German party, the Technical Faction soon exchanged the REP for the DLVH, the new populist radical right party that all but one (REP leader Schönhuber) of the German MEPs joined. Continued internal difficulties ultimately led to the *de facto* end of the Technical Faction in 1991 (Veen 1997).

The German populist radical right parties were severely punished for their internal chaos in the 1994 European elections and lost representation in the EP. Even though the MSI (now AN) increased its number of MEPs to eleven, and both the FN and the VB got an extra member, the populist radical right was unable to constitute an official faction. The AN refused to join the FN and VB, partly because it had entered the Italian government and did not want to be associated with pariah parties, partly because these parties had chosen the REP over them in 1989. The LN continued to keep its distance, and changed affiliation from the regionalist Rainbow Group to the Liberal Democratic and Reformist faction (ELDR). A second disappointment came with the entrance of Austria to the EU in 1996, when the six members of the Austrian FPÖ also refused an alliance. This left the populist radical right with fifteen MEPs from three countries: DUP (1), FN (11), FNb (1), and VB (2). Given the requirement of twenty-six members or twenty-one from two countries, the group was not large enough to constitute an independent faction.

---

[7] Interestingly, the group did not include Rev. Ian Paisley, leader of the populist radical right DUP, and MEP from 1979 till 2004.

[8] Dillen saw major ideological differences still between the parties, most notably between the "state nationalism" of the FN and the "ethnic nationalism" (*volksnationalisme*) of the REP and the VB.

After 1999 the situation became even more confusing. The AN had moved away from the radical right at this point, while the LN increasingly looked for contacts with populist radical right representatives (notably the FPÖ). The FN, badly hurt by the split of the MNR, was left with just six MEPs; the VB had won one and was fronting three, while the FPÖ lost one and kept five. The Danish DFP, the Italian MS-FT, and the Northern Irish DUP all had one MEP. Together the populist radical right had more than enough seats to constitute an official faction, but the DVP and FPÖ did not want to cooperate; the first joined the UEN, among others with the MEPs of the AN, and the latter remained independent. With no chance of forming a populist radical right ideological faction, members of the FN and VB looked for more pragmatic alternatives.

In July 1999 twenty-nine previously unattached MEPs constituted the "Technical Group for Non-Attached Members – Mixed Group," shortly known as TDI or Mixed Group (see Settembri 2004). It was dissolved by the EP two months later, after the departure of eleven MEPs, and reinstated again two months after that. In October 2001 it was again dissolved, this time for good. The Mixed Group is a good example of the institutional pressures on nonattached members and the strategic calculations leading to opportunistic alliances among the more marginal parties within the Parliament. While the core comprised the usual suspects of the populist radical right (e.g. FN, LN, MS-FT, and VB), it also included the MEP of the radical Basque Euskal Herritarrok (Basque Citizens) and the seven members of the Italian radical liberal Partito Radicale (Radical Party).

The situation has become even more inscrutable in the new parliament, which now also includes members of Eastern Europe. Currently, eight parties that are classified as populist radical right in this study are represented in the parliament: DFP (1), DUP (1), FN (7), FPÖ (1), LAOS (1), LN (4), LPR (10), and VB (3). Additionally, the Italian AS (1) and MS-FT (1) are borderline cases. Together they have enough members (30) to constitute a separate faction, but instead they are scattered over various groups. Twelve populist radical right MEPs are members of the largely Euroreject Independence/Democracy Group; this includes the single member of the LAOS, the three members of the LN, and seven of the ten (former) MEPs of the LPR.[9] The single MEP from the DFP has remained loyal to the Euroskeptic UEN. The other populist radical right MEPs are unattached, though with the exception of the DUP close cooperation exists between them.

---

[9] In February 2006 the LN was suspended from the ID Group and subsequently left the faction.

This group of unattached MEPs is the source of the latest attempts at European party cooperation. After the split of Haider and his BZÖ, the Freiheitliche Akademie (Freedomite Academy, FA), the think tank of the FPÖ, could finally organize an international meeting of European populist radical right parties with the full backing of the party. High-ranking representatives of eight parties from seven countries discussed future cooperation in Vienna, November 11–13, 2005: the Austrian FPÖ, the Belgian VB, the Bulgarian Ataka, the French FN, the Italian Azione Sociale and MS-FT, the Romanian PRM, and the newly founded Spanish Alternativa Española (Spanish Alternative). The Danish DFP, the Italian LN and the (conservative) Polish PiS sent official greetings to the meeting (Mölzer 2005a).

In sharp contrast to earlier gatherings, which were largely inconclusive, this meeting ended with some concrete and quite far-reaching decisions (FA 2005). First of all, the delegates decided to establish a "Contact Forum for European Patriotic and National Parties and Movements," with a permanent office in Vienna. Second, they agreed to conduct annual meetings, ongoing and intensive exchanges of information, and common actions at the European and international level (*Kurier* 14/11/2005). Third, Mölzer (2005b), the main instigator of the initiative, announced that "already in 2007 the establishment of a right-wing democratic faction in the European Parliament will be possible." This presupposes that Bulgaria and Romania will join the EU in 2007 and the MEPs of Ataka and PRM will join the unattached populist radical right MEPs. Fourth, the participating parties adopted the "Vienna Declaration of Patriotic and National Movements and Parties in Europe," an eight-point populist radical right program that should be the basis of future cooperation in the EP.

1. The establishment of a Europe of free and independent nations within the framework of a confederation of sovereign nation-states.
2. The renunciation of all attempts to create a constitution for a centralist European super-state.
3. The clear rejection of a boundless enlargement of European integration to geographical, cultural, religious and ethnic non-European areas of Asia and Africa, such as Turkey.
4. The effective protection of Europe against dangers like terrorism, aggressive Islamism, superpower-imperialism, and economic aggression by low-wage countries.
5. An immediate immigration stop in all states of the European Union, also in the area of so-called family reunion.
6. A pro-natalist family policy, which aims at the advancement of large numbers of children within the traditional family of the European ethnic communities [*Völker*].

7. The solidarist [*solidarischen*] struggle of European ethnic communities against the social and economic effects of globalization.
8. The restoration of the social systems of the member states of the European Union and social justice for the European ethnic communities.

While it is far too early to conclude that Europeanization has hereby finally also reached the populist radical right party family, as it has other party families (e.g. Ladrech 2002), the Vienna meeting has definitely taken the European cooperation of populist radical right parties to a new level. The next meeting was planned for Sofia, Bulgaria in 2006. However, given the chaotic developments within Ataka, the host party, it remains to be seen whether this meeting will actually take place.

While the process of European integration and the structure of the European Parliament provide strong institutional pressures toward party cooperation, the populist radical right family has yet to consolidate its efforts in that arena. This is mostly the result of domestic considerations: parties that are (no longer) isolated in their own country do not want to be associated with pariah parties in the EP. The most recent efforts at collaboration seem to confirm this, as they include mainly populist radical right pariah parties. But even if all populist radical right parties in the EP were to unite, they would account for only a small subgroup of the whole party family, as most member parties are simply not represented at the European parliamentary level.

7.5   Conclusions

The past twenty-five years have seen many developments in European politics in general, and the process of European integration in particular. These developments have not been without effect on the populist radical right party family. While the relevant member parties were quite Euroenthusiastic during the 1980s, the vast majority of the family has given up on the EU at the beginning of the twenty-first century. Nonetheless, most populist radical right parties continue to believe in some form of European cooperation, although much disagreement remains with respect to the various details of the desired European Confederation.

There are different explanations to account for the populist radical right's "u-turn" from Euroenthusiasm in the 1980s to Euroskepticism since the early 1990s. In the literature on Euroskepticism, two key motives are identified, ideology and strategy, and much debate exists over which is the most important (e.g. Batory 2002; Kopecký & Mudde 2002; Taggart & Szczerbiak 2002). Particularly within this party family, ideology is clearly more important, although it often overlaps with strategy. Nativism and European integration have a strained relationship. However, the u-turn was mainly caused by external factors. First of all, the end of the Cold War led some parties to reconsider their international alliances; in many cases they had chosen "the West" as the lesser of two evils. Second, as was the case with various other Euroskeptics, most notably within the conservative party family (e.g. Conservative Party, ODS), populist radical right parties saw the Maastricht Treaty as the confirmation of a long-feared federalization of Europe. And to some extent the EU changed, leading the parties to reevaluate their position with respect to it.

Obviously, strategic considerations have also played a role at times. Populist radical right parties do not appear to be particularly led by the views of their electorate in their stance toward the EU (e.g. Chari *et al.* 2004). Like in many party families, significant differences exist between the European positions of some member parties and their supporters (e.g. Kopecký & Mudde 2002). For example, the electorate of the PRM is "overwhelmingly in favour of . . . EU integration" (Schuster 2005: 14): no less than 70 percent of the people who voted for Vadim Tudor in the 2000 presidential elections were pro-EU, compared to 60 percent of the Iliescu voters (Pop-Elechus 2001: 165). Even in the case of the vehemently Euroreject LPR only a tiny majority of 52 percent of its supporters was against EU membership; it is still the only Polish party with a majority against membership (Schuster 2005: 14). Recently, some populist radical right parties have moderated their European position to become *koalitionsfähig* (such as the LN and VB) or as a consequence of government participation (e.g. FPÖ, Slovak SNS).

The explanation for the lack of European party cooperation seems a lot easier to determine. The received wisdom on the subject is aptly summed up by David Cesarani: "there is a fundamental incompatibility between a nationalism, particularly in its far-right version, which accentuates national difference or racism and posits irresolvable differences between people and nations in the attempt to create transnational alliances" (in Schulze 1998). The European visions of the populist radical right, however disparate, clearly nuance this common-sense argument. As another commentator observed perceptively: "The supranational union of nationalist parties is a contradiction in itself, but not necessarily a complete one" (Veen 1997: 73). Though often not elaborated in detail, most parties combine their nativism with support for some form of European cooperation, based on the belief in a shared European culture (or civilization) and the fear of huge external threats that the own nation-state cannot fight off alone (e.g. Islamic fundamentalism, US domination).

Much of the lack of European party cooperation therefore is attributable to far more mundane factors, such as a lack of infrastructure (notably funding and organization), the ego of some key leaders (e.g. the struggle between Haider and Le Pen), the unstable position of most parties, and the low saliency of the European issue (e.g. Stöss 2001). As far as nationalism plays a role in frustrating attempts at European cooperation, it is not so much the purported nationalist egocentrism, but the clashing visions of ethnic and state nationalism and the border disputes as a consequence of different nationalist ambitions (e.g. Fennema & Pollmann 1998).

Finally, the EU also plays an important role in the (lack of) development of a populist radical right transnational party federation. Because of the high threshold for representation in the EP, only a few populist radical right parties make it into the parliament. Moreover, even fewer do so for several legislatures. This prevents the party family from profiting from the institutional pressures and rewards of group formation within the EP. However, initiatives from within the Parliament might provide a new opportunity for the populist radical right party family. The suggestion of electing a number of MEPs on the basis of European party lists has led to new initiatives within the party family (particularly from the FPÖ and the VB). The future will have to reveal whether the recent meeting in Austria was indeed the birthplace of a transnational populist radical right party.

8   Globalization: the multifaced enemy

The only true opponents of the globalization are the nationalists, who already for years denounce the ongoing process that has led to globalization being a fact today.   (Comité Nationalisten tegen Globalisering n.d.)

8.1   Introduction

"Globalization" is undoubtedly one of the most overused words of the late twentieth and early twenty-first centuries. According to its proponents, all things good are the direct consequence of globalization, while its opponents link all things evil to that same phenomenon. Consequently, globalization seems so omnipresent that one struggles to comprehend its meaning. This is not helped by the fact that the term is more easily used than defined. Many academic and nonacademic observations obscure both the meaning and the significance of the phenomenon.

Conceptual precision notwithstanding, political actors clearly perceive globalization as one of the most significant phenomena in European politics of the twenty-first century. It is not surprising that globalization is also linked to the populist radical right, one of the other most debated developments in contemporary European politics. Summarizing very crudely, the two are connected in two fundamental ways. On the one hand, globalization is seen as one of the main causes of the recent electoral success of populist radical right parties in Europe (see chapter 9). On the other hand, populist radical right parties are among the most vocal opponents of globalization. The latter aspect, which so far has received scant attention in the literature (Dechezelles 2004; Leggewie 2003; Simmons 2003), will be addressed in this chapter. The focus will be on different forms of globalization and the various reasons the populist radical right opposes them.

8.2   The many faces of globalization

Is there anything these days that is not believed to be caused by globalization? Global warming, Americanization, terrorism, unemployment, bad television, good music . . . everything is alleged to be the result of that one, overpowering phenomenon. But what does globalization really mean? What *is* globalization (cf. Brune & Garrett 2005)?

There are numerous definitions and meanings, but no consensus around any of them. According to the well-known British social scientist David Held:

> Globalisation today implies at least two distinct phenomena. First it suggests that many chains of political, economic and social activity are becoming world-wide in scope and, second, it suggests that there has been an intensification of levels of interaction and interconnectedness within and between states and societies. (1999: 340)

To a certain extent then, one can speak of *globalizations* (e.g. Berger & Huntington 2002), referring to the various dimensions of the process: the economic, the cultural, and the political.[1]

Obviously, globalization is neither neutral nor random. Not all political entities play a similar role in world politics. British youth are not copying the culture of, say, Ecuador, anymore than Uganda is setting the agenda for economic cooperation. According to most accounts of globalization, be they positive or negative, the whole process is dominated by the United States. Political globalization is linked to a monopolar world system under American dominance, economic globalization is believed to be ruled by US-based multinational corporations and US-controlled/dominated institutions like the World Bank, and cultural globalization has led to the alleged dominance of "the American way of life" of Coca-Cola, McDonald's, etc.

Throughout the world, globalization has led to a multitude of local reactions, ranging from the Zapatistas in rural Mexico to squatters in European inner cities, from indigenous people in Asia to Islamic fundamentalists in Africa (see Starr 2000). This battle for hegemony is captured pithily in the title of Benjamin Barber's famous book *Jihad vs. McWorld* (1995). Simply stated, the struggle is between an imperialist monocultural "West" ("McWorld") and a "non-Western" fundamentalist backlash or defense ("Jihad") against it. But within the Western world there is also opposition, and not only from the "official" antiglobalization movement,

---

[1] Decker (2004: 195ff.) makes a similar distinction with regard to "modernization," discussing the various relations between populism and economic, cultural and political modernization in more general and theoretical terms.

which has organized some colorful and eventful demonstrations against meetings of "institutions of globalization" in cities like Seattle, Prague, or Gothenburg. Political parties, most notably of the populist radical right (though also green and radical left), are challenging various aspects of globalization as well.

The next sections discuss the three distinct forms of globalization and the main points of opposition of the populist radical right party family with respect to each of them. While there are many different voices among populist radical right parties on this issue, some parties are in accord on certain points and various strains of antiglobalization discourse can be distinguished within the larger party family.

8.3   Economic globalization: opposing neoliberalism and immigration

The primary objective of the process of economic globalization is the creation of a capitalist global market. Clearly, the aim and process are not new: the European Union is rooted in a similar idea, if somewhat less ambitious in geographical scope. Moreover, world trade has existed from time immemorial. What makes the current process of economic globalization different is the level or intensity of integration and cooperation (e.g. Brune & Garrett 2005; Held 1999). In addition to the simple trade, international actors and states are today bound by a variety of rules, and organizations that enforce them – such as the International Monetary Fund (IMF) and the World Trade Organization (WTO).

The rise of global capitalism has led to vehement protests in the streets of cities worldwide. Obviously, many radical left organizations oppose this project as part of their anticapitalist struggle. In electoral terms, however, these groups remain relatively insignificant in Europe, as they are still scarred by the collapse of "real existing socialism" in the East (e.g. March & Mudde 2005). It is populist radical right parties that are leading the struggle against economic globalization in the parliaments of Europe. Their opposition stems from the predominance of nativism in the parties' ideology; it takes precedence over all economic concerns (see also chapter 5).

In the 1980s, several key populist radical right parties used neoliberal rhetoric, which led various commentators – including leading scholars (e.g. Schain et al. 2002b; Kitschelt & McGann 1995) – to mislabel them as neoliberal or right-wing in economic terms. However, systematic analysis of the ideologies of several parties shows that their economic policy was far from (neo)liberal. Rather, it was based on economic nationalism and welfare chauvinism: i.e. the economy should serve the nation and should be controlled by it, while a welfare state is supported, but only for the "own people" (Mudde 2000a; also chapter 5).

Consequently, it is not surprising that populist radical right parties are very critical of economic globalization. First and foremost, a global market means that foreigners can influence the national economy. István Csurka, leader of the Hungarian MIÉP, expressed this point as follows: "The World Bank does not have machineguns, but every request is at the same time an order for such small countries with GDPs smaller than that of Toyota" (Csurka 1997: 261). Or, in the words of the extreme right German NPD, "[t]he essential core feature of globalization is the destruction of national and social control mechanisms. Therewith globalization destroys the political capabilities of states" (NPD 2002: 12).

Second, the populist radical right considers economic globalization harmful to national interests. For example, the British BNP states: "Globalisation, with its export of jobs to the Third World, is bringing ruin and unemployment to British industries and the communities that depend on them" (BNP n.d.). Some parties link the national threat of economic globalization to the growing power of the US. The party program of the German REP states: "additionally globalization means largely Americanization, as the US have the largest economic power at their disposal" (REP 2002: 14).

Economic globalization itself, however, is not a major issue in the propaganda of most populist radical right parties. Indeed, some parties seem to try to accommodate it within their nativist ideology, obviously at the cost of ideological clarity. In the 1997 election program of the Austrian FPÖ the term globalization is mentioned only once, as a challenge to young people. Article 2.4 of chapter 16 ("The right to an education") states: "Tougher competition, globalization and new technologies mean ever growing challenges for our youth. To master these challenges freedomite politics aims to educate young people in a modern and practical way as they are our future" (FPÖ 1997: 32). However, in the short program of Haider's new party, the BZÖ, globalization is mentioned only negatively. Indeed, it is one of the main reasons why the new party has adopted a more pro-European position (BZÖ 2005; see further 7.3.4).

Of the more relevant populist radical right parties, the French FN is the most vocal opponent of (economic) globalization. The issue is at the centre of the FN's larger political struggle (see most notably Simmons 2003; also Betz 2002b), reflecting the greater importance of antiglobalization in French politics in general.[2] Similarly, the FN-split MNR has devoted

[2] One commentator even argues: "Globalization helps us understand the results of the [first round of the 2002 French presidential] election because it further reinforces something

special studies to economic globalization, calling it "the new menace . . . which strengthens the mortal risks that threaten a large number of [our businesses]" (MNR n.d.). Even in the French-speaking part of Belgium more attention seems to be paid to globalization than outside of the Francophone world. The short program of the tiny FNB explicitly mentions (economic) globalization, though in a fairly vague sense: "Globalization and collectivism are two stumbling blocks that have to be avoided" (FNB n.d.).

In Eastern Europe economic globalization is generally mixed with the broader ills of marketization and privatization as well as with anti-Semitic and pan-Slavic conspiracy theories. MIÉP leader Csurka devotes much attention to the economic aspects of globalization: "Today a common enemy exists for all nations of Europe, that is the globalization, that are the large banks and multis, which strive for the formation of a unitary world market" (Csurka 1997: 261). Similarly, the Slovak SNS argues that "[g]lobalisation, especially the economic one, is pushed through by a narrow group of the powerful and it is directed at the domination of the world" (SNS 2002: 9). And in an extreme form of pan-Slavic conspiracy theories, Volen Siderov, the leader of the Bulgarian Ataka, sees globalization as a form of "unbridled capitalism" that is "colonizing the Orthodox East" (Siderov 2002).

Outside of Europe, opposition to economic globalization is more central to populist radical right politics. The Australian ONP of Pauline Hanson strongly opposes the international free market, and even argued that "Australia should seek industrial self-sufficiency."[3] And in the US presidential election of 2001, populist radical right candidate Pat Buchanan stated that one of the main differences between Bush/Gore and himself was their support of economic globalization versus his protectionist stand. According to Buchanan, "what is failing the world is not capitalism but globalism" (in Simmons 2003: 2). This is because globalization is not simply a process or policy, but one of the most evil anti-American conspiracies around. In his tellingly titled lecture "A Den of Thieves," delivered at Boston University in 2000, the presidential candidate explained a recent rise in gas prices in the US:

that has been going on for years: There seems to be a new cleavage emerging from the blurred lines of French politics that we could call the globalization cleavage . . . This new split has been confirmed by the recent elections: Almost 50 percent of the entire electorate voted for overtly antiglobalization candidates, whether on the far right or the far left" (Meunier 2002).

[3] The program of One Nation could be found in various parts in the forums of its website www.onenation.net.au. This particular quote is taken from the subsection at forums. onenation.net.au/index.php? act=ST&f=6&t=131&s=7345bacc615fe7d9071eac7e5e-333f06 (accessed 22/05/2003).

Friends, this price explosion is not the result of the free market forces. It is the work of a global price-rigging conspiracy, by oil-exporting nations, to hold oil off the market, to force prices to the sky, to loot America. . . . Friends, this is the dark side of globalization. This is the hidden price of "interdependence"(Buchanan 2000).

In addition, various extreme right groupuscules oppose economic globalization. This is strongest among the various neo-Nazi, national revolutionary, national Bolshevik, and (International) Third Position movements, which all declare themselves to be anticapitalist (e.g. PoP 2002). The NPD, one of the least irrelevant among them, expressed its opposition in the following terms: "The NPD rejects the free-market extremism of the EU and GATT" (NPD 2002: 14). Similarly, the Spanish Democracia nacional (National Democracy, DN) opposes "pro-globalization organizations: NATO, World Bank, FMI [sic], EU" and believes that "[o]nly real nation-states as Spain have a chance in [the] fight against world capitalism forces" (DN n.d.).

For anti-Semitic populist radical right parties like the Greek LAOS economic globalization is part of a broader Jewish conspiracy: "globalization . . . stems from and is supported by the great multinational companies . . . which to a large percentage belong to Zionist interests, and their headquarters are in the USA, the policy of which they dictate" (LAOS n.d.: 5).

There are two main topics through which economic globalization does feature at the core of populist radical right campaigns (though often implicitly): immigration and the EU. Particularly since the 1980s immigration has become a major issue in European politics and a key issue for the populist radical right (e.g. Betz 1994; Von Beyme 1988). While their nativist language directs much of their hatred at the immigrants themselves, most parties agree that mass immigration is a consequence of economic globalization. In the words of the Spanish DN, "[i]t is obvious that the phenomenon of immigration ought to be understood in the context of capitalist globalization" (DN 2002: 63).

Some parties even go so far as to see the immigrants as victims of international capitalism; without truly feeling or expressing compassion and solidarity. This is particularly strong among parties with an anticapitalist tradition, such as the Italian radical right MSI and initially, though to a lesser extent, its successor the AN (e.g. Ter Wal 2000). Some populist radical right groups (e.g. LN, MSI-FT and CP'86) are even calling the mass immigration of guest workers to Western Europe a form of "new slavery" (see Dechezelles 2004; Mudde 2000a; Fennema & Pollmann 1998).

For most Europeans, including those in the member states, the European Union was a nonissue for decades. This only changed with the fall of the Berlin Wall in 1989, and, more importantly, the signing of the Maastricht Treaty in 1992. While various populist radical right parties had been moderately pro-European integration and the European Communities (EC) in the first years of their existence, this changed radically in the 1990s (see chapter 7; also Mudde 2000a). Confronted by an "ever closer union" (Dinan 1994), the populist radical right party family started to see the EU as a major threat to the sovereignty of their nation.

To be sure, *economic* integration was generally a minor concern, although the introduction of the euro led to some of the most radical anti-European campaigns within the EU. These were not always dominated by populist radical right parties, however. In Britain the Conservative Party's "Keep the Pound" campaign completely overshadowed the similar "Keep our Pound" campaign of the BNP. A similar fate befell the NPD's "Rettet die DM" (Save the Deutsch Mark) campaign, which was eclipsed by campaigns by neoliberal populist parties like the Bund freier Bürger (Association of Free Citizens, BFB) of Manfred Brunner.[4]

8.4   Cultural globalization: resisting Americanization

Caused in part by economic globalization, in part by technological innovation (e.g. satellite, internet), national cultures have become more and more interconnected and open to foreign influences. Whether one watches the Flemish television channel VT4 or the Czech channel Nova, foreign series and movies fill a large part of the programs of television channels in much of Europe.

Today, many television programs are made with the aim of selling them or their format to various countries; this ranges from programs like *Big Brother* and *The Weakest Link*, which have local versions in various countries (twenty and fourteen, respectively), to the series *Baywatch*, which has an estimated weekly audience of more than 1.1 billion people in 142 countries spread over all continents except Antarctica (*Holland Herald* 02/2006)! Similarly, Japanese and British designers are a hit on the catwalks of Paris and Milan, while various internet-only radio stations play music to audiences around the globe. My own most remarkable experience with cultural globalization was being kept awake one night in a hotel in Erdenet, a small city in the north of Mongolia, by the music of the 1980s German pop-duo Modern Talking.

---

[4] Initially, Burger contemplated the name "D-Mark Partei." But even after the replacement of the DM with the euro, a Pro-DM Partei exists in Germany. It is currently linked to the neoliberal populist Schill Party.

Within this "global village," American culture is clearly dominant. Trends that spring up in the cities of the United States develop with an ever decreasing time lag in the cities (and even rural areas) of Europe, Latin America, and Asia. This does not only apply to the entertainment industry, but also to the media (see the recent rise in 24-hour news television channels around the world), and even eating patterns. For many the hamburger fast-food chain McDonald's epitomizes cultural as much as economic globalization (e.g. Ritzer 2004; Smart 1999).

Not surprisingly then, the struggle against "American cultural imperialism" is particularly virulent in European countries with traditionally strong anti-American sentiments, such as France and Greece (e.g. Fabbrini 2001). Again, the populist radical right is certainly not the only opponent, and not always the most relevant. In Greece for example, anti-Americanism is traditionally strong in the extreme left Kommunistiko Komma Elladas (Communist Party of Greece), one of the few unreformed communist parties in Western Europe that still has parliamentary representation (e.g. March & Mudde 2005).

In most European countries, however, populist radical right groups are at the fore of the fight against cultural globalization because they believe that globalization leads to the homogenization of culture(s) around the world. In line with their nativism, they fear that the "ancient" European cultures will fall victim to "Americanization" or, in the words of parties like the Belgian VB and the French FN, "Cocacolonization," and no cultural differences will be left.

Some groups are clearly inspired by the ideology of "ethnopluralism" as developed by the intellectual *nouvelle droite* movement of the French philosopher Alain De Benoist. They claim to be the true defenders of multiculturalism. The tiny French extreme right Group d'Union et de Défense (Unity and Defense Group), for example, argues: "One-worldism is thus essentially the enemy of multiculturalism in the sense that it treats the world as a single human community, while true multiculturalism stems from the existence and celebration of different human communities" (in Griffin 1999b). And the Slovak SNS sees globalization as "an unnatural phenomenon, because our universe emerged, evolved, and exists in the state of diversity" (SNS 2002: 9).

Similarly, the populist radical right is fond of declaring that its enemies, the "multiculturalists" and other "leftists," are the real racists. The general argumentation is that they support the mixing of cultures at the cost of the "cultural genocide" (Csurka) of the European "native cultures." Some parties have made a link to the issue of globalization, arguing that "globalizers are the true racists in so far as they deny the diversity of cultures and peoples" (LN pamphlet in Cento Bull & Gilbert 2001: 131). According to the same source, we are dealing with a global utopian conspiracy in which cultures are to be "squashed together – along the lines of the American melting pot – into a One World Order where universal peace will reign."

Populist radical right parties have attacked "one-worldism" not just for leading to cultural homogenization, but also for creating the *wrong* culture. The Dutch CP'86 described the aspiring "Americanized" culture as materialist and hedonist, full of "consumer slaves who are devoid of culture" (*Centrumnieuws* 02/1992). Antimaterialist sentiments were an important ideological feature among the right-wing extremists of the pre-war times (see Fennema 1997) and other parties have also invoked them in their rejection of American(ized) culture; the president of the Greek HF claims that the "antiracist" organizations, which include the many actors of globalization, "want to construct a multicultural pulp, where the only characteristic of a person would be his/her consumer capability" (Voridis 2002). For Csurka this is one of the most comprehensive and imminent threats to the Hungarian nation:

Now we have to protect the Hungarian life from the global (first of all) American mass culture in any possible way. Not only the speech, the language, the city and street landscape are in danger of death but the traditional Hungarian way of life, the system of traditions and values too. The American life ideals, the materialism and the selfish consumer way of life affect mostly the young people today, but the next generations will learn the internet, multiplex, shopping mall living manners from their parents. (in Kriza 2004)

In addition to moral concerns, various parties fear the increasing use of English terminology, particularly among youngsters. The German DVU wants to counter "the mass copying of foreign words" by introducing a state protection system modeled on that of the Académie française (DVU n.d.). In Flanders, language issues have traditionally been at the heart of the concerns of local nationalists. The initial target was the use of the French language, but in recent times the continuing spread of English is considered at least as threatening. Militants of the VB and other groups, notably the Nationalistische Studentenvereniging (Nationalist Students' Association) and the Taal Aktie Komitee (Language Action Committee), have been active in spraying the text "Nederlands" (Dutch) over billboards with English-language advertisements throughout Flanders. But in the French-speaking part of Belgium also the populist radical right calls "for the protection of the languages of the [European] cultures faced with the Anglo-American imperialism" (Agir n.d.).

8.5   Political globalization: fighting the NWO

The political process of globalization has generated the most extreme reactions. It has led to a variety of bizarre conspiracy theories centered around the idea of the "New World Order" (NWO). Populist radical rightists around the globe fear the ever-growing international political cooperation between states, in particular the involvement of the United Nations (UN). Within Europe, the process of European integration has been the clearest example of supranational political cooperation.

Undoubtedly, the UN has become more active since the end of the Cold War, which had often crippled decision-making in the Security Council. In the 1990s the UN was involved in peace operations in fourteen different countries, ranging from Haiti to Tajikistan. Although the number of peacekeepers actually decreased sharply during that period (CLW 1999), operations like those in Iraq[5] and Kosovo showed the UN's assumption of an increasingly proactive course, even willingness to infringe on the sovereignty of established states.

Similarly, since the signing of the Maastricht Treaty in 1992, the EU has become more and more (seen as) a political, rather than merely an economic project. Whereas in the 1980s many populist radical right parties mocked the EU for its incompetence and preoccupation with details (determining the correct shape of a banana, for example), the organization has become associated with attempts to design common policies on such far-reaching issues as border patrol and immigration since the 1990s. In short, the EU has become a serious player in European politics, much to the dismay of the populist radical right.

Since the vision of populist radical right parties on European integration in general was discussed in the previous chapter, the focus here is exclusively on the link between European integration and political globalization, at least as it exists in the minds of some populist radical right politicians. For example, FN leader Le Pen has described the EU as a "link to one-worldness" (1992: 206) and speaks of "the forces of *Euromondialisme* and the New World Order" (in Simmons 2003: 26). In more anti-Semitic terms, MIÉP leader Csurka called European integration "in reality a cosmopolitan homogenization" (in Blokker 2005: 386), while the Polish LPR opposes the "cosmopolite-liberal EU."

---

[5] Obviously, I refer here to the first military campaign against Iraq (1990–91), following that country's invasion of Kuwait. The more recent second campaign instead showed a weakening of the importance of the UN, which might turn out to be structural rather than temporal.

The NWO and the UN mainly preoccupy the populist radical right in the US. An alliance ranging from the militias to the Christian Right, and from the right-wing of the Republican Party to the neo-Nazis, believes in a multitude of interlinked conspiracy theories of black helicopters, secret concentration camps, and world domination (e.g. Herman 2001; Rupert 2000). The European populist radical right tends to be less paranoid, but they are also negative overall towards the increased activity of the UN and the idea of the NWO; the latter term gained prominence mainly after former US President George Bush's alleged "slip of the tongue" in a speech in 1991 (e.g. Tuominen 2002). However, many European parties do not go into much detail and oppose in quite general terms "the dogmas of globalization and international unification" (LPR 2003: I.3).

Conspiracy theories can nonetheless be found in the propaganda of some groups. The tiny extreme right England First organization, linked to the infamous International Third Position (ITP) movement, expresses opinions on "internationalism" that are almost identical to those of many of its American brethren: "We are opposed to all ventures, such as the E.U., N.A.T.O. and the U.N., which seek to make England an impoverished province in the New World Order. We also oppose Big Business, Freemasonry and other N.W.O. vested interests" (EF n.d.). Le Pen, during a visit to SRS-leader Šešelj in Serbia, called the US "the armed arm of the New World Order" (in Schmidt 2003: 106).

Clearly inspired by "The Clash of Civilizations" (Huntington 1993), the Russian LDPR considers all major international economic (e.g. IMF, World Bank, G-7) and military organizations (e.g. NATO, WEU) as instruments in the construction of a New World Order by the "Western-Christian civilization" (LDPR 1995). It is obvious to the party which country is the main force behind this NWO: "The United States, as the leader of the Western world, actively uses the fruits of globalization and attempts, with more or less success, to impose its will all over the world pretending that this is the will of mankind" (LDPR n.d.b). The party explicitly identifies Israel as "an ally of this civilization" (LDPR 1995).

However, for the LDPR the current "clash of civilizations" is little more than the most recent version of an ancient Western struggle against Russia. Initially, the party presented a fairly passive remedy for its paranoid diagnosis of the current state of world affairs: "The historical experience dictates in the case of geopolitical danger the necessity of a partial or total closure of the state with the aim of [creating] a breathing space and a solution to the internal social, economic and other problems" (LDPR 1995). Recently, the LDPR envisioned a more proactive and heroic role for Russia:

Today it is exactly Russia that can become a center of power and influence, which is able to destroy the balance of power in the world unfavorable to the majority of the people of our planet. . . . Russia can become the leader of the countries of the Third World, which are supporting a fair world order. (LDPR n.d.b.)

Like many West European populist radical right parties, the French FN was (reluctantly) pro-American during the Cold War, but changed its position to a radical anti-Americanism after the fall of the Berlin Wall. In a special issue of the party journal *Identité* Le Pen explained the party's turnaround:

It is by considering this construction of the New World Order that our change in attitude about the policies of the United States must be understood. When the Cold War was at its worst, and the Red Army was threatening, NATO had its raison d'être. The American presence contributed to contain Soviet expansionism, and to assure our liberty. Now things have changed. NATO is being reconverted into the mailed fist of the New World Order. Far from being 'Europeanized' . . . it imposes on the nations of Europe an Americanization of their diplomatic and military concepts . . . The White House has become the Trojan Horse of globalization. (in Minkenberg & Schain 2003: 167–8)

Some parties even share the most paranoid conspiracy theories of the American groups. For example, the CP'86 believed that all major international organizations (like the UN, IMF, Council of Churches, etc.) "are manipulated also by the American CFR (Council for Foreign Relations) which wants to bring about a one-world government" (CP'86 1990: 29.2). Maciej Giertych, a prominent MP of the LPR, believes that the Bilderberg Group is a "behind the scenes world government" (in Buchowski 2004: 899). And the FN even includes Greenpeace in the list of shady anti-French organizations; it is considered to work primarily against France's improvement of its nuclear deterrent (Simmons 2003: 18).

For other parties, such as the DVU and MIÉP, political globalization and the NWO are simply the newest actors in an age-old Jewish conspiracy (e.g. Bock 2002; Mudde 2000a). In the words of Csurka: "Sixty years after the end of the European war the world is again involved in a war in which the only victor is struggling to spread its own sphere of interest over the entire world at the Jews' command or (more mildly) their instinct to rule the world" (in Weaver 2006: 105). Similarly, PRM leader Corneliu Vadim Tudor, in the well-established tradition of Romanian anti-Semitism, believes that proponents "from the U.S. and Israel" are imposing globalization by brutality upon Europe with the aim of constituting a "World Government" that can "monitor Europe" (in Shafir 2001: 106).

8.6   Conclusion

To the populist radical right, globalization is a multifaceted enemy. As this chapter has shown, "globaphobia" is indeed an essential feature of the populist radical right (Held & McGrew 2000: ix). In essence, all three major subtypes of globalization are feared and rejected on the basis of the same nativist beliefs: they threaten the independence and purity of the nation-state. Globalization is mainly seen as a process of Americanization. With regard to economic globalization, populist radical right parties particularly oppose neoliberal economics and mass immigration. Cultural globalization is rejected because it is believed to annihilate the cultural diversities of nations and create the wrong culture, i.e. the American culture of materialism and nihilism. Political globalization, finally, has given rise to the most bizarre and extreme conspiracy theories within the populist radical right, all linked to US domination. Still, not all major parties believe in a conspiracy centered on a mythical New World Order (NWO).

Despite the fact that the populist radical right parties are the most ideologically pure and electorally successful opponents of globalization, at least within Europe, they are not normally associated with the so-called antiglobalization movement. Indeed, the populist radical right and the so-called antiglobalization movement will often mobilize against each other, rather than work in concert. Although there have been voices within the antiglobalization movement that call for a rapprochement among all opponents of globalization, including religious fundamentalists and radical nationalists (e.g. Starr 2000), most activists remain encamped by ideology (e.g. Hari 2003).

There are two reasons for the existence of this "paradoxical mobilization" (Dechezelles 2004): first, the antiglobalization movement that has made the headlines in the media in recent years generally considers itself to be left-wing and progressive, and significant elements within it, most notably the violent anarchist "Black Block," are explicitly "antifascist." Therefore, even if populist radical rightists (or other nativists) would like to join their demonstrations, there is a fair chance that this would lead to a hostile reception by the (other) "antiglobs."[6] The second reason is that for most populist radical right parties (opposition to) globalization is not (yet) a central issue in their ideology and propaganda. The term itself is scantily used in the party programs, and not much more in the

---

[6] This was felt, for example, by Czech skinheads who tried to join the antiglobalization demonstrations in Prague in September 2000, and were consequently chased through the city by (mainly German) antifascists.

internal party papers. While issues like mass migration and the decreasing sovereignty of their nation are at the core of these parties' propaganda, they are seldom linked explicitly to the process of globalization.

Eliding the issue might be a conscious decision on the part of these parties. After all, globalization has something deterministic about it; many mainstream parties and politicians argue that globalization cannot be stopped, so we simply have to make the most of it (e.g. Blyth 2003). The populist radical right rejects this (economic) determinism, instead propagating the return of the primacy of the political (see 6.4.3). By largely ignoring (though not denying) globalization, they do not have to address the question whether mass immigration and loss of sovereignty *can be* countered in the era of globalization. In a sense, their whole world vision clearly defies the inevitability of globalization.

But will populist radical right parties (continue to) profit from their opposition to the consequences of globalization? It is clear that they will not be able to stop the process – indeed, it is doubtful whether there has been a period without globalization in the past two thousand years (e.g. Keohane & Nye Jr. 2000). However, this is mainly relevant for the few populist radical rightists that are in government. Those kept in permanent opposition, either because of a so-called *cordon sanitaire*, such as the VB, or electoral insignificance, like the BNP and MIÉP, can continue claiming that they could solve it, if only given the chance.

More important is what the other political parties will do, i.e. the center-right and the center-left. Currently most European center parties are either explicitly pro-globalization, or they see the process as inevitable and unstoppable.[7] Particularly among the more conservative (including some Christian democratic) and socialist parties one would expect an increasing unease with the consequences of globalization, both national and global. In time, they could steal some of the thunder of the populist radical right. However, as these other political actors are better termed *anderglobalisten* (different globalists), including most of the antiglobalization movement, the populist radical right parties are indeed the true *anti*-globalists.

---

[7] Obviously, there is some variation in the views on globalization among the center parties. Even among the social democratic parties there are "hyperglobalists," following the lead of New Labour, and more globalization-skeptics, such as the French Parti Socialiste (see, for example, Clift 2002).

Part III

Explanations

9 Demand-side: in search of the perfect breeding ground

> There is widespread agreement in the literature that the upsurge of radical right-wing activities has to be seen in the context of a combination of global and domestic structural change . . . There is less agreement, however, on the exact link between right-wing mobilisation and sociostructural change.
>
> (Betz 1999: 301)

9.1 Introduction

Given the explosion of literature on populist radical right parties in the past two decades, it comes as no surprise that explanations for their success abound. Nearly every author on the subject provides some reason for the electoral success of the party family in contemporary Europe, however implicitly or generally it may be presented. Most scholars' understanding of the phenomenon has been highly influenced by classic theoretical work in the social sciences, especially that concerning (historical) nationalism and fascism. Interestingly, only very little attention has been paid to the electoral failure of populist radical right parties, even though these cases are (far) more numerous (De Lange & Mudde 2005).

In addition to the pure theoretical work, which remains fairly general and underdeveloped, the bulk of articles in refereed academic journals dealing with the topic have involved empirical tests of various aspects of these theories. Overall, the conclusions largely contradict each other, which furthers both the debate and the stream of publications. The most important source of disagreement is the difference in research designs and data used in the studies: often (micro) individual behavior is explained on the basis of (macro) state-level variables (and vice versa), leading to the well-known ecological fallacy. And even when these factors are used as "context variables," they do not correspond to the theoretical argument (i.e. national-level data to explain local contexts).

While it is impossible to present a complete overview of the literature on explanations of the electoral failure/success of populist radical right parties, Roger Eatwell's "Ten theories of the extreme right" (2003) is one of the best comprehensive overviews and will be partly followed here. Like Eatwell, I will differentiate between demand-side and supply-side variables and distinguish between macro-, meso-, and micro-level explanations in the discussion of the literature. In addition, the important distinction between electoral breakthrough and persistence will be addressed (Coffé 2004); these are two related but distinct processes that cannot always be explained by the same combination of variables. The key aim of this part of the book is to assess critically the theoretical and empirical basis of the various explanations posited in the literature on the two regions of contemporary Europe. However, I will also introduce some new data and variables that I believe help explain the electoral failure and success of populist radical right parties in general.

This first chapter focuses exclusively on the demand-side of populist radical right politics, i.e. the search for the perfect breeding ground for these parties in the literature. However, the demand-side is only one aspect of (party) politics: a demand for populist radical right politics does not necessarily result in its emergence and success at the party system level. The supply-side translates demand into practical party politics. Two aspects of the supply-side will be distinguished in subsequent chapters; that external to populist radical right parties (chapter 10) and that internal to them (chapter 11). Obviously, the demand-side and the two dimensions of the supply-side cannot be distinguished so neatly in practice; they partly overlap and influence each other.

9.2   Macro-level explanations

Nearly all demand-side theories of party politics in general, and populist radical right party politics in particular, are situated at the macro-level. They point to broad economic, historical, social processes that take place at the national, supranational and sometimes even global level. Most theories are far from original; their provenance is generally either from studies of previous forms of nationalism (including fascism) or analysis of mainstream electoral politics (cf. Husbands 2002). Their strength is that they can potentially explain similar developments in very different settings. Their main weakness is that they normally cannot account for different developments in very similar settings.

9.2.1   *Modernization(s)*

In accounts of the electoral and political successes of populist radical right politics in contemporary Europe the term "modernization" is never far away. According to almost all prominent studies the rise of the populist radical right party family is directly and explicitly linked to "process(es) of modernization." In short, the parties are seen as opponents of modernization that attract the so-called *Modernisierungsverlierer* (losers of modernization) (e.g. Decker 2004; Minkenberg 1998; Betz 1994). In this respect, scholars stay within the mainstream of historical nationalism studies, which has explained the development of European nationalism since the end of the eighteenth century by the effects of modernization (see, most notably, Gellner 1983). Moreover, the arguments are reminiscent of Seymour Martin Lipset's theory of "status voting" to explain the "radical right," initially advanced in the 1950s (e.g. Lipset 1969, 1955).

In the contemporary setting, the modernization thesis has been elaborated in various forms and has been linked to many different developments and processes: globalization, risk society, post-Fordist economy, postindustrial society, and many more (e.g. Swank & Betz 2003; Loch & Heitmeyer 2001; Holmes 2000; Minkenberg 1998; Beck 1992). In the literature on Eastern Europe the modernization thesis is mostly linked to the (double or triple) transition from state socialism to capitalist democracy (e.g. Anastasakis 2002; Beichelt & Minkenberg 2002; Minkenberg 2002b; Linz & Stepan 1996). Irrespective of the specific form of modernization, all theses have serious theoretical and empirical problems.

Theoretically, they tend to remain vague about the exact effects of modernization, particularly at the micro-level. How does the macro-level process of globalization exactly lead to the micro-level action of voting for a populist radical right party? Some authors try to connect the macro- and micro-levels by linking the process of modernization to the famous cleavage theory of Lipset and Rokkan (1967), arguing that it has either created a new cleavage or gave new meaning to the main old cleavage (e.g. Kriesi *et al.* 2005b; Minkenberg 2000; Kitschelt & McGann 1995; Kriesi 1995; Betz 1994). Still, even here the translation of macro-level processes to micro-level behavior remains either vague or dependent upon significant actions at the meso-level, and the supply-side, most notably from political parties (cf. Sartori 1990).

The globalization thesis is particularly weak in terms of empirical evidence (e.g. Rosamond 2002; Keohane & Nye Jr. 2000; Amin 1997). First of all, whether or not globalization is something new is hotly debated. Second, even among authors who believe that contemporary globalization is indeed unprecedented, at least in its intensity and scope, no consensus exists with regard to exactly when it started. Third, the global nature of the process to which the thesis attributes causality limits its traction in explaining national differences. One could argue that different countries are influenced in different ways and to different degrees by the process depending on their relative position in the world economy, but this mainly distinguishes central and peripheral countries, i.e. "First" and "Third" World (e.g. Wallerstein 2004), leaving the substantial variation within (Western) Europe unexplained.

The postindustrial and postmodern theses are also fraught with theoretical and empirical problems (e.g. Wendt 2003). Nonetheless they do seem to provide at least some potential for intra-European differentiation. Most notably, Kitschelt and McGann (1995) use the postindustrialism thesis to exclude the South European countries (Greece, Portugal, and Spain), which all have very weak populist radical right parties. However, they have been criticized for their operationalization of postindustrialism by John Veugelers (2001), who does not find a strong correlation between the defined combination of open economy and welfare provisions at the state level. Yet, he does find a strong relationship between economic openness and a country's demand for populist radical right politics (see also Veugelers & Magnan 2005; Swank & Betz 2003). The question is whether this relationship also holds for the postcommunist region, where societies are (far) less "postmodern" and economies (far) less "postindustrial."

In the literature on Eastern Europe, while there is no doubt that the transformation process has yielded significant "shocks" to its societies, undoubtedly more intense and varied than those generated by the "silent (counter-)revolution" in the West, the exact relationship to populist radical right voting is not always clear. Moreover, although various transformational paths can be discerned within the group of postcommunist countries (e.g. Kopecký & Mudde 2000; Von Beyme 1999), they were all subject to a largely similar process, yet few experienced (continued) electoral success among populist radical right parties (e.g. Mudde 2005b, 2000b; Von Beyme 1996).

So far, the various modernization theories have mainly been tested by proxies: the voting behavior of groups deductively identified as (potential) losers of modernization has been evaluated for evidence of disproportional support for the populist radical right among these groups relative to the larger society. The findings of the various studies are highly contradictory. Much (cross-national) empirical research suggests that the core electorates of populist radical right parties are indeed "modernization losers" (e.g. Robotin 2002; Fetzer 2000; Kriesi 1999; Betz 1994). However, some (single country) studies have found both losers and winners of modernization among the populist radical right electorates (e.g. Gyárfášová 2002; Irvine & Grdešič 1998).[1] Most important, however,

---

[1] Interestingly, some studies find a gender effect with regard to the modernization theory (see also chapter 4). However, while some contend that the theory is better suited to explain the voting behavior of women (e.g. Havelková 2002), others consider it more appropriate for men (e.g. Amesberger & Halbmayr 2002c).

is the fact that even if most voters of populist radical right parties are actually "modernization losers," defined either objectively or subjectively (cf. Minkenberg 2000), only a small minority of the "immense army" (Thieme 2005: 354) of losers of modernization vote for a populist radical right party.

Modernization theories (in whatever form or shape) seem correct intuitively but are too general and too vague to be considered useful explanations of recent populist radical right party successes. There is no doubt that these processes do lead to important societal changes, which in turn have political effects. Nonetheless, "modernization – industrialization and all its concomitant changes – will go on giving rise to differential political and cultural mobilization" (Nairn 1995: 95). Why this mobilization is populist radical right in certain countries and periods, and liberal nationalist or even nonnationalist in others, has to be explained by other theories.

9.2.2 Crises

Emphasis on the vital role of "crisis" is a constant in studies of both historical and contemporary nativism and populism (e.g. Taggart 2000; Weyland 1999), including studies on populist radical right parties. Hanspeter Kriesi has even referred to them as "movements of crisis" (1995: 23). So far, the term "crisis" has proven of limited use analytically because, although intuitively it may be easy to comprehend, it proves quite difficult to specify. Most authors do not even bother to try to articulate what constitutes a crisis, they simply state that a certain process has led to one, assuming that both the meaning of the term and the existence of the crisis are self-evident. Others define the term so broadly that virtually every period can be interpreted through the lens of crisis. Finally, a number of authors seem to determine the existence of a crisis largely on the basis of the success of populist actors, which makes the relationship tautological.

The definitional and operationalizational deficiencies in the crisis literature should not lead to an *a priori* rejection of the whole research in this field. In fact, in many instances the empirical research itself is quite sound, focusing on statistically significant correlations between various economic and political independent variables and the dependent variable of populist radical right party electoral success. The key problem in this literature is the relationship between these variables and the overarching concept of crisis. So, rather than evaluating the economic and political crisis theses as such, this section will assess the relevance of the empirical work done in this field to the further understanding of the electoral success of populist radical right parties.

Ever since the rise of historical fascism, radical right successes have been explained by reference to economic crises (e.g. Zimmermann 2003;

Bayer 2002; Zimmermann & Saalfeld 1993; Stöss 1991). Empirically, most studies have tried to test the economic-crisis-thesis by looking for correlations between electoral success of populist radical right parties and levels of unemployment, at the national or regional level. The conclusions are, as ever, contradictory: few find (strong) positive correlations (e.g. Thieme 2005; Kreidl & Vlachová 1999; Jackman & Volpert 1996), most (weak) negative correlations (e.g. Arzheimer & Carter 2006; Jesuit & Mahler 2004; Pop-Elechus 2003; Wendt 2003; Lubbers 2001; Knigge 1998), and some no significant or contradictory correlations (e.g. Givens 2005, 2002; Chapin 1997).[2] Additionally, there are studies that find a mediated effect through the level of state welfare provisions (Swank & Betz 2003) or immigration (Jesuit & Mahler 2004; Golder 2003).

The finding that populist radical right parties fare less well in countries with a higher level of unemployment is not as puzzling as it might seem at first. In times of higher unemployment, socioeconomic issues will normally have greater salience in the political debate. This profits those political parties that have established "ownership" over issues like employment and socioeconomic policies (see chapter 10). As populist radical right parties are seldom considered particularly competent in this area, and rather profit from issues like crime and immigration (see below), the rise in salience of socioeconomic issues decreases their electoral appeal. This might be partly softened when high levels of unemployment are combined with high levels of immigration (Golder 2003), as this increases the possibility of combining the two issues, which can at least partly benefit those populist radical right parties that have established ownership over the immigration issue.

Béla Greskovits (1998, 1995) rejects the simple economic-crisis-equates-populist-success-thesis on the basis of the Latin American experience. Instead, he argues that populist episodes usually begin immediately after a deep economic crisis.[3] This would explain why Eastern Europe was not overtaken by populist politics in the first period of postcommunism. And if he is correct in his analysis of the structural similarities between (early) postcommunist Eastern Europe and postpopulist Latin America, "[t]he age of demagogic economic populism in Eastern Europe may still be on the horizon" (Greskovits 1995: 106). However, in this model the future success in Eastern Europe would be of a "neopopulist" nature (Weyland 1999; Knight 1998), in our terms neoliberal populism,

---

[2] Some of the contradictory results might be explained by differences in data and methods used in the studies.
[3] Lipset already argued that "status insecurities and status aspirations [i.e. the sources of radical right success, CM] are most likely to appear as sources of frustration, independent of economic problems, in periods of prolonged prosperity" (1955: 188).

rather than populist radical right. As the economies of the more advanced democracies in Central Eastern Europe have only recently overcome their initial postcommunist downfall (Szelenyi 2006), the coming decades will prove Greskovits right or wrong.

As Andreas Schedler noted, "[i]n the field of political science it has become commonplace to affirm that we live in times of political crisis" (1997: 2). Almost every period has its own alleged political crisis, be it the "end of ideology" of the 1950s and 1960s (e.g. LaPalombara 1966; Bell 1960), which incidentally resurfaces every so many years, the (conventional) participation crisis of the 1970s (e.g. Inglehart 1977), or the party crisis of the 1980s (e.g. Daalder 1992; Kuechler & Dalton 1990). In most cases, the arguments for the existence of a political crisis lacked both theoretical clarity and empirical substance.

In the 1990s surveys showed record low levels of political trust in European democracies almost across the board (e.g. Norris 2002; Pharr & Putnam 2000). While for most Western European democracies this indicates a (significant) drop in trust, in Eastern Europe the levels have never been particularly high, but are nevertheless decreasing. Whether these figures indicate that Europe is in political crisis today, at least in terms of "specific support" (e.g. Dahl 2000), is difficult to decide without clear definitions. The even more obvious problem is that we are not, whatever newspapers and antifascists claim, experiencing a Europe-wide populist radical right wave of electoral success. True, the 1990s have been the most successful postwar period of populist radical right parties (e.g. Wilcox *et al.* 2003a), but they have been successful in only a minority of European countries.

As part of the political crisis thesis, authors have studied the correlation between political dissatisfaction and the electoral support of populist radical right parties at the national level. As is so often the case with macro-level analyses, the results go in different directions: some find a significant positive relationship (e.g. Knigge 1998), others do not (e.g. Norris 2005). While most countries with successful populist radical right parties have experienced growing levels of political dissatisfaction, there are important exceptions. For example, Denmark saw a growing level of political *trust*, from 40 percent in 1991 to 65 percent in 2001, one of the highest in Europe, at the same time that the DFP made significant gains in electoral support (Andersen 2002: 14).

While most research on Western Europe links political crisis to specific support for democracy, i.e. the practice of democracy, given that "general support" for democracy, i.e. for the ideal ("democracy is the best political system"), has been both constant and very high (e.g. Dahl 2000). This is not the case in all parts of Eastern Europe, and some literature on

Table 9.1 *Democratic support and electoral success of populist radical right parties in Eastern Europe*

| Country | Support for democracy and its alternatives | | Electoral success populist radical right |
	Democratic support	Antidemocratic support	
Czech Rep	74	11	medium
Albania	73	18	low
Estonia	68	17	low
Slovenia	64	16	medium
Hungary	63	24	medium
Poland	62	14	medium
Slovakia	61	16	high
Romania	60	27	high
Bulgaria	52	37	low
Russia	48	43	high

Source: Averages calculated on the basis of Pickel & Jacobs (2001: 6).

this region relates the concept of political crisis to the levels of general support for democracy. Table 9.1 provides an overview of the average national support for democratic and antidemocratic ideas per country in a selection of Eastern European countries. With the exception of Russia, the populations of all postcommunist new democracies clearly support democratic ideas much more than antidemocratic ones.

The Eastern European countries are categorized into three groups on the basis of the average electoral success of populist radical right parties in national parliamentary elections in the period 1990–2005.[4] The first group includes countries with successful parties, gaining an average of over 5 percent of the national vote in the parliamentary elections of the postcommunist period (i.e. Romania, Russia, and Slovakia). The second group contains countries with moderately successful parties, averaging between 2 percent and 5 percent of the national vote over the whole period (i.e. the Czech Republic, Hungary, Poland, and Slovenia). The third group includes countries with unsuccessful parties, scoring an average of less than 2 percent (i.e. Albania, Bulgaria, and Estonia).

Some signs of a relationship between democratic support and electoral success for populist radical right parties are visible: five out of the

[4] Because of their unique character, i.e. an electoral battle between the former communist party and an umbrella party of opposition groups (e.g. Pop-Elechus 2003), the "founding elections" (i.e. the first postcommunist elections) are excluded.

ten countries fit the hypothesized inverse relationship (Albania, Hungary, Poland, Russia, and Slovenia), while three others come close (Estonia, Romania, and Slovakia). Only the Czech Republic and Bulgaria really go against the expected relationship. With regard to support for antidemocratic alternatives and electoral success of populist radical right parties the relationship is less straightforward. Only four countries more or less fit the hypothesized positive relationship (i.e. Albania, Estonia, Hungary, and Russia).

But even if a causal relationship does exist, and it is in the alleged direction (cf. Van der Brug 2003; Thijssen 2001), the theoretical argumentation remains weak. While the argument makes sense at the micro-level, i.e. people express their dissatisfaction by voting for the protest parties *par excellence* (see 9.6), it is far less compelling at the macro-level. Why would people in countries in political crisis vote for populist radical right parties?

More recently, the political crisis thesis has been operationalized in terms of the level of "cartelization." In their now famous article on the "cartel party," Richard Katz and Peter Mair (1995) argue that party competition has developed from strict government opposition to cartel-outsiders. According to them and others, this process of cartelization goes a long way in explaining the increased levels of political resentment and the success of populist (radical right) parties (e.g. Blyth & Katz 2005; Blyth 2003; Taggart 1996). So far, most studies have addressed mainly whether the cartel party and the process of cartelization exist, rather than whether it stimulates electoral success of populist (radical right) parties (e.g. Detterbeck 2005; Poguntke 2002; Helms 2001). Some of the few studies that discuss the link between cartel politics and populist radical right parties in Europe simply confirm their dual occurrence (Bottom 2004; Müller 2002). In the comparative studies that do address the relationship between cartelization and electoral success of the populist radical right within Europe, the cartel party thesis is found to be "of limited value" in its strict interpretation (Helms 1997: 49; also Jungerstam-Mulders 2003). Similarly, outside of Europe, Murray Goot (2006) has found no support for the thesis with regard to the rise of the Australian ONP.

The political crisis thesis is sometimes also studied through the more general phenomena of clientelism and corruption, although not all authors connect the phenomena explicitly. Kitschelt in particular, has included clientelism and corruption in his analyses of radical right support (e.g. Kitschelt 2002; Kitschelt & McGann 1995). His contention is that, in combination with other variables (e.g. postindustrialism and convergence of the main parties), a patronage-based party system and political economy will encourage medium support for right-authoritarian parties and strong support for populist antistatist parties (Kitschelt & McGann 1995: fig. 1.2; also Helms 1997). The thesis is confirmed empirically in a different study of several exclusively West European cases (Veugelers & Magnan 2005).

Other authors have linked political crisis to particular political systems, i.e. consociational or consensual systems (e.g. Papadopoulos 2005; Dehousse 2002; Evans & Ivaldi 2002; Andeweg 2001; Kriesi 1995). They argue that these systems have been more prone to populist resurgence because of their lack of party alternation or choice between clear political alternatives (i.e. left and right). At first sight, this seems to be supported by the data: Austria, Belgium, Netherlands, and Switzerland are broadly considered to be the prime representatives of the consensual system (e.g. Lijphart 1984), and all have been linked to large populist electoral success. However, even if consensual systems in crisis do produce populist reactions, they do not necessarily produce populist *radical right* reactions (e.g. LPF in the Netherlands).

Moreover, if we take a look at the European countries where populist radical right parties have been most successful since 1990 – Austria, Belgium, Croatia, Denmark, France, Italy, Romania, Russia, Serbia, and Slovakia – a link to one specific political system is not readily discernible (also Lijphart 2001). In addition, we should be careful to distinguish between the causes of political crisis in different regions, most notably the East and West. As Radoslaw Markowski has argued, "Western dissatisfaction with democracy and populist/radicalist trends are ontologically different phenomena (at least partly) from the manifestations of similarly dubbed processes in [the] East-Central part of the continent" (2002: 28). Most importantly, while the political systems are well established in most West European countries, they are fairly new phenomena in the East. Consequently, frustrations in the East may be less the result of actual material conditions than of unmet expectations (Učeň 2002).

9.2.3   Ethnic backlash

A third theoretical school of macro-level explanations comes from an intellectual tradition fairly similar to that of the modernization thesis, most notably history and nationalism studies. It sees populist radical right parties first and foremost as a defensive response of the majority population to a perceived "ethnic" threat (e.g. Wendt 2003; Veugelers & Chiarini 2002). In short, the main perceived threat is from (non-European) immigrants in the Western part of the continent and (domestic) ethnic minorities in the East (see chapter 3).

The horrific nativist violence in parts of the Balkans (e.g. former Yugoslavia) and the Soviet Union (e.g. Chechnya), and to a lesser extent the (largely) nonviolent separations of the Baltic states and Slovakia, gave new favor to the age-old "myth of global ethnic conflict" (Bowen 1996), so persuasive in academic circles since at least the end of the Second World War. In its most basic form, this myth states that ethnic diversity hampers democracy and leads to (ethnic) conflict, either violent or nonviolent. It is prevalent not only in nationalism or nonwestern studies, but also in much classic comparative political science (see, for example, Almond 1956).

The ethnic-backlash-thesis is quite pervasive in the academic literature on Eastern Europe. Particularly in the first years of postcommunism, scholars would argue that ethnic nationalism had always been the "dominant political force" in Eastern Europe (Bogdanor 1995: 84) and that it was thus only logical that "once again nationalism is the *sine qua non* for political success in Eastern Europe" (Fischer-Galati 1993: 12). In this view, the totalitarianism of the communist regimes had created an "unnatural" situation, an historical abbreviation, by "putting a lid" on the natural nationalism.[5] Postcommunist politics in Eastern Europe would inevitably be dominated by nationalism, given the historical legacies and the continuing ethnic diversity.

The thesis has been dominant with regard to Western Europe as well, yet in a less theoretical and more implicit form. While only few authors use the theoretical insights of ethnic politics from nonwestern studies explicitly (e.g. Wendt 2003), much of the literature sees West European populist radical right parties first and foremost as a majority response to the perceived threat of mass immigration (e.g. Husbands 2001; Fennema 1997; Von Beyme 1988). While historical determinism might be less dominant in this literature, the underlying assumptions are the same as those of "the myth of global ethnic conflict."

Empirical research produces highly contradictory results, depending on choices of datasets, indicators, units of analysis, etc. With regard to Western Europe, some authors find a clear positive correlation between the number of foreign-born citizens and the electoral success of a populist radical right party in a country (e.g. Golder 2003), while others do not (e.g. Wendt 2003). Similarly, some studies show a significant positive correlation with the number of new immigrants (e.g. Swank & Betz

---

[5] Some authors have even claimed that (most of) the communist regimes were essentially nationalist, thereby following Eastern European tradition. For example, the famous Polish dissident Adam Michnik stated that "[n]ationalism is the last word of Communism" (1991: 565). For a powerful critique of the nationalist determinism literature, see William W. Hagen's insightful essay "The Balkans' lethal nationalisms" (1999; also Bowen 1996).

Table 9.2 *Number of asylum applications and electoral success of populist radical right parties per country, 1989–1998*

Country	Asylum applications	Populist radical right
Germany	1,905,800	medium
France	**327,350**	**high**
United Kingdom	314,630	low
Netherlands	296,140	low
Sweden	264,650	low
Belgium	**152,720**	**high**
Austria	**131,290**	**high**
Spain	79,230	low
Denmark	71,160	high
Italy	54,410	high
Norway	48,390	low
Greece	26,080	low
Czech Republic	17,720	moderate
Hungary	17,080	moderate
Finland	**15,340**	**low**
Poland	**12,370**	**low**
Ireland	**10,630**	**low**
Portugal	**5,350**	**low**
Romania	3,260	high
Luxemburg	2,790	moderate
Slovakia	2,270	high
Bulgaria	**2,080**	**low**
Slovenia	610	moderate

Source: UNHCR (1998: 85).

2003; Lubbers 2001; Knigge 1998) or asylum seekers (e.g. Wendt 2003; Lubbers 2001) at the national level, but others find a negative (cor)relation or none at all (e.g. Dülmer & Klein 2005; Jesuit & Mahler 2004; Kriesi 1995).

Few pan-European analyses are so far available (though see Norris 2005). A quick look at the relationship between the number of asylum applications and the electoral success of populist radical right parties in a broad range of Eastern and Western European countries in the period 1989–98 suggests that there is no clear relationship (see table 9.2). Countries are again classified into three groups: high electoral success of the populist radical right (5 percent or more), moderate success (between 2 percent and 5 percent), and low success (under 2 percent). Only eight of the twenty-three cases fit the expected positive relationship.

One problem with using these rough data is that they do not account for the huge differences between countries. Obviously, 100,000 asylum

Table 9.3 *Number of refugees per 1,000 inhabitants and electoral success of populist radical right parties per country, 1999–2003*

Country	Refugees per 1,000 inhabitants	Electoral success of the populist radical right
Serbia & Montenegro	39	**high**
Sweden	16	low
Denmark	13	**high**
Germany	11	medium
Norway	11	low
Bosnia-Herzegovina	9	**high**
Netherlands	9	low
Switzerland	8	**high**
Austria	4	high
Croatia	4	**medium**
United Kingdom	4	low
Finland	2	low
France	2	high
Luxemburg	2	low
Belgium	1	high
Hungary	1	**medium**
Ireland	1	low
Slovenia	1	low
Bulgaria	0	**low**
Czech Republic	0	**low**
Estonia	0	**low**
Greece	0	**low**
Italy	0	high
Latvia	0	**low**
Lithuania	0	**low**
Poland	0	high
Portugal	0	**low**
Romania	0	high
Russia	0	high
Slovakia	0	high
Spain	0	**low**

Source: 2003 UNHCR Statistical Yearbook

seekers would have a more noted effect upon the population if the country itself had, say, 300,000 inhabitants rather than 30,000,000. Consequently, the following indicator is very useful, as it relates the number of refugees to that of the inhabitants of the host country. This time the period is 1999–2003, but again no clear relationship with the electoral success of the populist radical right can be observed (see table 9.3).

Fourteen of the thirty-one countries (45 percent) fit the hypothesized positive relationship; the same percentage applies to countries with

Table 9.4 *Ethnic diversity and electoral success of populist radical right parties in Eastern Europe, 1990–2005*

Country	Majority–minority groups		Electoral success populist radical right
	Percent own ethnic[6]	National threat	
Latvia	52	yes	low
Estonia	62	yes	low
Serbia	**66**	**yes**	high
Ukraine	73	yes	low
Croatia	78	**yes**	high
Lithuania	80	**no**	low
Russia	83	no	high
Bulgaria	85	yes	low
Slovakia	87	**yes**	high
Romania	89	**yes**	high
Slovenia	91	no	moderate
Hungary	92	no	moderate
Czech Rep	94	no	moderate
Poland	98	no	moderate

successful parties. However, regarding the latter, there is a difference between countries in the West (50 percent) and in the East (40 percent). Moreover, the two Eastern European countries that do fit the hypothesis, Serbia and Montenegro, and Bosnia-Herzegovina, are very distinct cases, having experienced civil war during this period. Therefore, the fact that the success of the populist radical right parties in the three "normal" postcommunist countries is not explained by the relative number of refugees warns against putting too much value on this variable, at least in the Eastern European context.

The most obvious explanation for this is that mass immigration (including refugees) is not (yet) an important social phenomenon in the postcommunist states of Eastern Europe. Here, it makes more sense to study the ethnic backlash thesis by focusing on the majority mobilization against large groups of (domestic) ethnic minorities, mostly ethnic nationals of former "occupying" states and Roma (see also chapter 3). However, once more the data do not show a strong relationship (see table 9.4).

As can be seen from the second column of table 9.4, there is no apparent relationship between the size of the minority population (measured inversely through the size of the majority population) and the level of

---

[6] These figures are taken from: *Eastern Europe and the Commonwealth of Independent States* (London: Europa, 1992), 1st edn. The figures come from very different sources and times, but the assumption is that the percentages have not changed dramatically over the last decade(s).

electoral success of the populist radical right. In fact, only one case (Serbia) fully fits the expected inverse relationship. This would not even change if we were to include the variable of state continuity, contrary to the finding in other, more impressionistic, studies (e.g. Von Beyme 1996).

But the size of the majority population does not necessarily show whether there is one or more powerful ethnic minority against which the "threatened" majority might feel it has to protect itself. Hence, I have also constructed a "national threat" indicator, measuring whether the country in question has a significant minority of a former "occupier" within its state borders. Whether the minority is significant does not merely depend on its numbers, but also on its demographic concentration and political organization. Again, no clear relationship can be found. Only five of fourteen countries (36 percent) fit the hypothesis.[7] However, four of the five countries (80 percent) with a successful populist radical party also include a "threatening" minority group. Given that this accounts for only half of the countries with a "national threat," this variable is at best a necessary but not a sufficient condition.

Quite inconclusive results are found with regard to the relationship between the electoral results of the populist radical right and the level of ethnic polarization in a country. Ethnic polarization is operationalized as "the difference between the positions taken by members of the ethnic majority and members of the ethnic minorities on issues concerning minority rights" (Evans & Need 2002: 659). The countries are divided into three categories: low (differences of less than 0.5), moderate (between 0.5 and 1), and high (more than 1). Of the three countries with a high level of ethnic polarization, two have unsuccessful populist radical right parties (Estonia and Latvia). Only Slovakia (high, high) and Ukraine (low, low) perfectly match the hypothesized relationship (see table 9.5).

This is not to say that no relationship exists between any of these variables and ethnic politics or nativism more generally. Indeed, in most of the countries with unsuccessful populist radical right parties strong ethnic and nativist rhetoric can be observed within the mainstream parties, most notably in the early postcommunist years in the Balkans and Baltics (see chapter 2) and more recently in Hungary (FIDESZ-MPS). In fact, this might be one of the reasons why populist radical right parties have not been successful in these countries, as will be elaborated in the next chapter.

In conclusion, despite its prominence in the literature, implicitly on the West and more explicitly on the East, the ethnic-backlash-thesis lacks

---

[7] Admittedly, the "moderate" category is difficult to fit, given that the "national threat" category is binary, but one would rather expect a threat than no threat.

Table 9.5 *Ethnic polarization and electoral success of populist radical right parties in Eastern Europe, 1990–2005*

Country	Level of ethnic polarization	Populist radical right success
Estonia	high	low
Latvia	high	low
Slovakia	**high**	**high**
Bulgaria	moderate	low
Lithuania	moderate	low
Romania	Moderate	high
Czech Rep	low	moderate
Hungary	low	moderate
Poland	low	moderate
Russia	low	high
Ukraine	**low**	**low**

Source: Evans & Need (2002: 662)

convincing empirical evidence. Populist radical right parties have had significant electoral victories in highly homogeneous countries (like the Czech Republic, Italy, or Poland) and failed in highly heterogeneous countries (like the Baltic states or Luxembourg). Furthermore, it rests on some questionable theoretical assumptions, most notably the equation of ethnic diversity with ethnic conflict. In the form of the immigration thesis, predominant in the literature on Western Europe, the situation is not much better. While mass immigration certainly played a role in the electoral breakthrough of some parties, often as a catalyst (Mudde 1999), it largely fails to explain the often huge temporal and regional differences in electoral support within single countries.

9.2.4   Authoritarian legacy

One of the most influential theories on historical fascism is linked to the famous thesis of the "authoritarian personality" (Adorno *et al.* 1969). Inspired by Freudian theory, various authors have argued that people with a particular personality are susceptible to the radical right and that this personality is the result of an authoritarian upbringing (e.g. Reich 1970). While the theory has been mostly applied at the micro-level, some studies on new democracies have lifted it to the macro-level, arguing that Europe's new democracies are particularly vulnerable to populist radical right parties because of the authoritarian upbringing under the former regime.

While the authoritarian legacy thesis has been applied only marginally to the new democracies in Southern Europe, possibly as a consequence of the striking lack of populist radical right success, the literature on post-communist Europe is full of these references (e.g. Tismaneanu 1998; Braun 1997). A good example is the following conclusion of Alina Mungiu-Pippidi, in her attempt to explain grassroots nationalism in post-communist Europe: "The complex of attitudes related to communist socialization, labeled residual communism, has the strongest influence in determining nationalism" (2004: 71–2). Some even go so far as to speak of a "double authoritarian legacy," referring to both the pre-war right-wing authoritarian ("fascist") and the postwar left-wing authoritarian ("communist") regimes (e.g. Anastasakis 2000). The obvious problem with this general thesis is that it cannot account for the striking absence of populist radical right success in most of the postcommunist world or for the intra-regional differences (Mudde 2002a).

9.3   Meso-level explanations

The meso-level is the most neglected level of political analysis, and studies on populist radical right parties are no exception to this general rule (e.g. Coffé 2004; Eatwell 2003). It is also the most difficult to delineate; it covers roughly everything between the macro- and micro-levels. According to Roger Eatwell, "[t]he meso [level] is concerned with local organizations to which individuals belong, or through which they gain knowledge and norms, such as the family, school, or party" (2000: 350).

Very little research has been done into the workings of the meso-level. Regarding the role of the school, most surveys show that there is a significant inverse relationship between the level of education and populist radical right voting. However, the argumentation is not so much that certain types of schools teach their pupils populist radical right attitudes, but rather that all schooling decreases these attitudes, and the more schooling an individual gets, the more populist radical right attitudes are replaced by "democratic" or "tolerant" values.

There is little doubt about the crucial importance of the family in the socialization of human beings, but because of well-known difficulties involved in researching this process, not that much is known on the topic. In the 1950s and 1960s Adorno's theory of the authoritarian personality was a popular explanation of historical fascism. He argued that people who had been brought up by an authoritarian father were predisposed to authoritarian attitudes, which were believed to be the support base of "fascism." While the authoritarian personality has largely survived as a personality type, the Freudian theory explaining its construction has been discredited on both theoretical and empirical grounds (e.g. Martin 2001; Stone *et al.* 1993).

A related theory states that populist radical rightists come from populist radical right families. A recent comparative study indeed found that many activists of populist radical right groups were raised in such families (Klandermans & Mayer 2005). However, these findings are very difficult to extrapolate to party electorates, as we know that members and voters hold very different values and have very diverse backgrounds (e.g. May 1973). Moreover, the theory can hardly explain the recent dramatic rise in populist radical right support – except by arguing that in the 1960s populist radical right families gave birth to far more children than other families – let alone account for short-term fluctuations in this support.

The relatively few studies that have focused upon the meso-level, if one can truly include these, have mostly tested macro-level theories at the subnational level. In many cases, the analysis was done at the regional level, which is often more resemblant of the macro- than the meso-level, for example in the case of the German states (e.g. Givens 2002; Karapin 2002; Lubbers 2001; Chapin 1997) and French regions (e.g. Minkenberg & Schain 2003; Givens 2002), several of which are larger than many EU member states. But there have also been studies at the local level of electoral districts (Dülmer & Klein 2005; De Neve 2001), municipalities (Coffé *et al.* 2006; Bjørklund & Andersen 2002), and even at the sublocal level of city boroughs and districts (e.g. Thijssen & De Lange 2005; Swyngedouw 1992; Witte 1991). As with the macro-level studies discussed above, the conclusions diverge seriously, depending on the data, indicators, and units of analysis used.

Although initial empirical results at the meso-level seem to provide the same confusion as studies at the macro-level, there are important reasons to devote more attention to this level. As the meso-level is closer to the individual, the link between "social context" and individual behavior, so weak in most macro-level analyses, can be more convincingly rendered (e.g. Johnson *et al.* 2002). This is particularly true the lower the level of analysis; i.e. it is more plausible that the attitudes of the family or even the socioeconomic and demographic characteristics of the neighborhood in which a person lives have an impact on her/his (voting) behavior than do the general characteristics of the (large) city or region in which s/he lives.

Consequently, much more empirical work should be done at the meso-level applying more diverse research methods (including multisited ethnography; see Holmes 2000). Moreover, this research should focus on the supply-side of politics too, including the history of a specific area, the role of the local media and opinion-makers, and the activities of the local populist radical right party (e.g. Eatwell 2000). Some initial, relatively impressionistic observations from studies in several English towns and city districts definitely provide inspiration for more fundamental research, despite the high cost and considerable difficulty involved (e.g. Eatwell 2004; Copsey 1996).

9.4   Micro-level explanations

While most explanations are developed at the macro-level, many empirical tests are carried out at the micro-level. The vast majority of articles on populist radical right politics published in international refereed journals try to explain why people vote for populist radical right parties. Often unhindered by the problematic theoretical linkage between macro-level explanations and micro-level actions, they look for correlations between individual attitudes and voting behavior. This section will critically assess the insights of these studies, focusing on two main sets of micro-level explanations: populist radical right attitudes and insecurity.

9.4.1   Populist radical right attitudes

The most self-evident explanation of the electoral success of populist radical right parties is that many people hold populist radical right views. In this approach, populist radical right parties are like other ("normal") parties, in the sense that they are voted for by supporters rather than protesters (see also 9.6). Despite the overwhelming logic of this argumentation, only a few studies have actually tested it empirically. Moreover, those that did have used some highly questionable proxies, rooted in the spatial interpretation of the party family so prevalent in quantitative studies.

The most common empirical test of the "support thesis" has been through a literal spatial interpretation of the "extreme right," i.e. the most right-ward position on the (in)famous left–right scale. There are obvious advantages to this method: left–right scales are part of every election study in the world and, particularly in Western Europe, almost all respondents are able to place themselves on them (Klingemann 1995). Various scholars have found that respondents who place themselves on the extreme right end of the scale are (far) more likely to vote for "extreme right" parties (e.g. Betz 1994; Bauer & Niedermayer 1990; Schumann & Falter 1988). While there are some differences in the cut-off points used in these studies, the results seem convincing. Indeed, even in multivariate analyses "extreme right ideology" proves to be the most important variable in explaining the electoral failure and success of populist radical right parties (e.g. Van der Brug *et al.* 2005, 2000; Van der Brug & Fennema 2003).

Despite the overwhelming empirical evidence, the relevance of these findings has to be questioned on more fundamental grounds. Putting aside the issue of endogeneity, even if there is a relationship between voting for populist radical right parties and left–right self-placement, we cannot assume (1) ideology is the most important factor in voting for a populist radical right party, let alone that (2) a populist radical right ideology is. First of all, these studies simply find a correlation and not causation; i.e. they do not find that these people have voted for populist radical right parties *because of* their ideology (or in this case, left–right self-placement). Second, the meaning of the left–right scale is quite vague and differs significantly between and even within countries (e.g. Ignazi 2003; Fuchs & Klingemann 1990). The predominant understanding of the scale, insofar as there is any consensus with regard to its meaning, is in traditional socioeconomic terms (Downs 1957). However, under this construal populist radical right parties are not positioned at the extreme right end of the scale (see chapter 5).

More accurate are the few studies that have operationalized the "extreme right" ideology on the basis of the relevant literature by constructing a scale, in the tradition of the famous F-scale (Adorno *et al.* 1969). Unfortunately, studies that operationalize the populist radical right ideology as a syndrome are extremely rare and their relevance is weakened by the small numbers of voters of populist radical right parties in their data sets (e.g. Meijerink *et al.* 1998; De Witte *et al.* 1994). Interestingly, the findings are not always in line with the general expectations: (1) the majority of supporters of populist radical right parties are not "extreme right," while (2) the majority of "extreme right" people vote for mainstream political parties (e.g. Eith 2003; Billiet & De Witte 1995).

Most empirical research studies the different features of the populist radical right ideology in isolation. According to the consensus in the literature on Western European parties, the main reason for their support is a nativist position on the immigration issue. John Veugelers and Roberto Chiarini, after pointing to the various disagreements within the field, assert "[o]ne point is beyond debate, however: far-right parties of Western Europe stand out in terms of their preoccupation with immigration and their marked intolerance toward racial and ethnic minorities" (2002: 83). Indeed, some authors even treat populist radical right parties (*de facto*) as single-issue parties; hence the term "anti-immigration parties" (e.g. Gibson 2002; Fennema 1997).

Many studies have substantiated the claim that the electorates of these parties are only distinguishable from those of the other parties in their political system with regard to their negative attitude towards immigration (e.g. Norris 2005; Mayer 2002; Van der Brug et al. 2000; Billiet & de Witte 1995; Betz 1994). These findings are corroborated in Eastern Europe, where the electorates of populist radical right parties tend to stand out in terms of nativist attitudes towards ethnic minorities, although the differences with some other parties (e.g. HZDS in Slovakia or PDSR in Romania) are not always significant (e.g. Pop-Elechus 2003; Robotin 2002; Ramet 1999a). The importance of nativist attitudes to the electorates of populist radical right parties has also been reported outside of Europe (e.g. Denmark & Bowler 2002; Gibson et al. 2002). In short, most electoral studies show that within the electorates of populist radical right parties more people are nativist (*quantity*) and they are more nativist (*quality*) than within the electorates of other parties.

Similar results have been reported in studies on authoritarianism, which is often the second most important attitudinal variable in explaining populist radical right voting, after nativism (e.g. Mayer 2005; Lubbers 2001; Minkenberg 2000). And in one of the few cross-national studies of the postcommunist region, Mungiu-Pippidi even found that "authoritarianism proves more powerful [than nationalism] in explaining the vote for radical nationalists" (2004: 64). Additionally, various studies have pointed to the importance of "law and order issues" for the electorates of populist radical right parties (e.g. Bjørklund & Andersen 2002).

The third and last core feature of the populist radical right, populism, has so far been little operationalized in empirical studies at the mass level. Many studies simply limit populism to antiestablishment sentiments and then assume that the populism of populist radical right parties is attractive to people who hold negative attitudes toward the political system (political resentment). Indeed, many studies do find that (Western) European populist radical right parties are particularly supported by people with strong antiestablishment sentiments, or that their electorates stand out from those of other parties in terms of their antiestablishment sentiments (e.g. Norris 2005; Fieschi & Heywood 2004; Ignazi 2003; Lubbers 2001; Betz 1994). Similar findings have been reported for non-European democracies, for example in Australia and New Zealand (e.g. Denmark & Bowler 2002).

In this respect, populist radical right parties do not only have to compete with other "protest" parties, like the radical left or neoliberal populists, but also with abstention (obviously, this is less the case in countries with compulsory voting, like Belgium, Greece, and Luxembourg). Many studies show that within the group of people with high levels of antiestablishment sentiments and other types of political resentment roughly two options exist: exit (abstention) or voice (vote for a populist radical right party or another "protest party"). Little research has been done into the variables that affect this choice, if only because nonvoters are very difficult to catch in survey research. However, Elisabeth Gidengil and her colleagues found that "[a]ntipartyism is more likely to result in an 'antiparty' vote than in abstention. Those who are more involved and more informed are especially likely to work for change within the system" (2001: 491). This also lends some support to the thesis that political efficacy benefits the populist radical right (e.g. Eatwell 2003, 1998; see also chapter 4). However, it does not explain why these voters would prefer a populist radical right party over another "protest party."

In conclusion, empirical research provides ample evidence for the argument that populist radical right attitudes are widespread within the electorates of populist radical right parties. However, several qualifications have to be made regarding this more general statement. First, most of the core features of the populist radical right ideology are measured by proxies, i.e. very rough indicators of these very complex concepts, which in some cases are highly questionable (notably populism). Second, the populist radical right ideology is a *combination* of three features (authoritarianism, nativism, and populism), yet in almost all empirical research the features are studied in separation. Third, populist radical right attitudes might be more prevalent and intense within the electorates of populist radical right parties, but they are very widespread within the electorates as a whole. As a consequence, the relationship between populist radical right attitudes and the support for populist radical right parties is far from perfect.

An even more fundamental problem with most of these studies is their failure to show that these people have voted for populist radical right parties *because of* their populist radical right attitudes (Mudde 1999). In fact, the few studies that do look into voter motivation produce far less convincing results. For example, even though "the immigration issue" (as a proxy of nativism) is the key motivation for people supporting the Belgian VB, only a minority of 33 percent support the party *because of* this reason. Similarly, only 14 percent of these voters mention "political resentment" (as a proxy of populism) as their prime motivation (e.g. Swyngedouw 2001: 236). Together, these two proxies for part of the populist radical right ideology still account for only a minority (47 percent) of VB voters. Similarly, in the 1980s the largest group within the FN electorate voted for that party because of the immigration issue, but they accounted for only 39 percent of overall support in 1984 and 46 percent in 1986 (Mitra 1988: 51–2). The other issues that were mentioned could not easily be linked to populist radical right attitudes.

9.4.2   Insecurity

"The preoccupations of the populist electorate can be encapsulated in one word: insecurity" (Dehousse 2002: 4). According to many authors, populist radical right parties are first and foremost supported by insecure people (e.g. Christofferson 2003). The theoretical argument goes along the following lines: as a consequence of the macro-level developments discussed above (i.e. globalization, mass immigration, economic and political crisis), large groups of the population have become insecure about various aspects of their life: identity, job, life as a whole. They seek salvation in the "simple messages" of the populist radical right, which promises a clear identity and protection against the changing world.

Micro-level survey research in various European countries also substantiates that supporters of populist radical right parties feel more insecure about the future. Some French studies even show that "insecurity" is a major motivation for people to vote for the populist radical right. In the first round of the French presidential elections of 2002, it was the most frequently mentioned motivation for 74 percent of the Le Pen voters and 68 percent of the Mégret voters (Perrineau 2002: 9). However, in (earlier) studies that allowed respondents to choose only one motivation, just 18 percent of the FN voters named insecurity as the main reason for their choice (Mitra 1988: 52). Unfortunately, in most studies the type of insecurity is not specified and the sentiments can thus refer to a broad spectrum of motivations (e.g. cultural, economic, financial, personal, political) – even though the most common meaning of the term seems to relate it to crime.

One of the few research projects that clearly distinguishes among different forms of insecurity is the EU-sponsored "Socio-Economic Change, Individual Reactions and the Appeal of the Extreme Right" (SIREN). To the astonishment of the researchers, the analyses show that "[j]ob insecurity and deprivation temper ERPA [extreme right party affinity], while a more comfortable situation seems to strengthen ERPA" (De Weerdt et al. 2004: 81). This seems to provide some support for the related thesis of welfare chauvinism, or in the terms of Lipset (1955: 191) "prosperity-born bitterness," i.e. that populist radical right parties are supported by people who want to hold on to what they have in the face of the perceived threats of globalization (i.e. mass immigration and the postindustrial society).

The security thesis is also, often implicitly, linked to the theoretical argument that the populist radical right is essentially a materialist "counter-revolution" against the economic insecurities produced by globalization and modernization (e.g. Bjørklund & Andersen 2002;

Minkenberg 2000).[8] Most often this is part of the larger modernization thesis and tested at the macro-level (see above). If applied to the micro-level, the search is for a correlation between "losers of modernization" and voting for populist radical right parties. While some studies find such correlations, with regard to either objective or subjective losers of modernization (e.g. Mayer 2002; Robotin 2002), no research has shown that (1) the electorate of populist radical right parties holds welfare chauvinist attitudes, *and* (2) that these attitudes are central in their party choice.

As far as micro-level analyses are concerned, results do not seem to provide strong evidence for the thesis that economic insecurity plays a dominant role in the motivation of voters of the populist radical right (see also 5.3). Some studies do indicate that welfare chauvinist attitudes are more widespread among the electorate of populist radical right parties than in society as a whole, but they do not show that these attitudes are the prime motivator for the party choice (e.g. Plasser & Ulram n.d.). These findings are collaborated by studies on non-European populist radical right parties (e.g. Denmark & Bowler 2002; Goot & Watson 2001).

Christopher Wendt has tested the insecurity thesis at the macro-level for Western Europe, correlating the national electoral success of populist radical right parties with national crime rates per 100,000 inhabitants. He finds that "crime rates do rather poorly in every period, though there is a positive relationship" (Wendt 2003: 38). A similar conclusion is reached with regard to Eastern Europe (Pop-Elechus 2003). However, Kreidl and Vlachová (1999) find a clear significant positive relationship between crime rate and voting for a populist radical right party at the regional level in the Czech Republic, whereas Coffé and her collaborators find no significant correlation at the municipal level in Flanders (Coffé *et al.* 2007).

At the micro-level the results are not much better. While the importance of "law and order issues" is often noted in (electoral) studies on populist radical right parties, "crime" seems to play only a marginal role in motivating people actually to vote for a populist radical right party. True, these issues have a high priority among the electorates of these parties. However, they often come second or even third in finally deciding which party to vote for (after xenophobia and political resentment; e.g. Betz 1994). For example, "crime" was mentioned by just 4.8 percent of the VB electorate as the prime motivation for their vote (Swyngedouw 2001: 236).

---

[8] This differs from Ignazi's meaning, who clearly sees the silent counter-revolution as, first and foremost, a postmaterialist phenomenon, just like the silent revolution (e.g. Ignazi 1992; Inglehart 1977).

9.5   One electorate or many?

One of the fundamental problems of most empirical studies on the electoral support of populist radical right parties is the underlying assumption of one homogeneous electorate. In other words, the hunt is on for *the* populist radical right voter, even though empirical studies of the electorates of populist radical right parties have shown that *he* does not exist. True, the electorates of these parties have been converging over the past decades, most notably as a consequence of proletarianization (Betz 1994), but important variations remain between parties and countries. In fact, if one looks at the stereotypical voter of a populist radical right party, as described in the literature – a young, male blue-collar worker (e.g. Arzheimer & Carter 2006; Evans & Ivaldi 2002) – *he* constitutes only a minority of the whole electorate of the populist radical right party family in Europe.

In fact, the electorates of populist radical right parties in Europe are heterogeneous, just like those of other political parties. Logically, they become even more diverse the more successful a party becomes. Already in 1984, French researchers had distinguished five subgroups within the FN electorate: xenophobes, traditional Right, Catholic Fundamentalists, Young Workers, and Prodigal Sons of the Left (in Mitra 1998: 58–60). In recent analyses, Nonna Mayer distinguishes four subgroups on the basis of their previous electoral behavior (1998: 16–17). The four sub-electorates show substantial differences in terms of sociodemographic characteristics and attitudes. One can even distinguish two (part) opposites, i.e. left-wing *lepénistes* versus right-wing *lepénistes* and supporters versus *ninistes* (see also 9.6). In Austria, researchers distinguish between at least two "sociopolitical types" within the electorate of the FPÖ: "welfare state chauvinists" and right-wingers disillusioned by the system (*Systemverdrossene Rechte*) (Plasser & Ulram n.d.: 5).

The existence of subgroups within the populist radical right electorates is relevant because of their (potential) effects on empirical research into the causes of electoral success. Most electoral studies employ methods that look for linear relationships. However, if various subgroups are present within the electorates, of which some share opposing values on the same variable, the analysis will find no (significant) correlation for that variable. Take, for example, the variable age, one of the most widely used demographical variables in electoral studies. Several populist radical right parties are supported disproportionally by both the youngest and the oldest cohorts of the general electorate (e.g. Arzheimer & Carter 2006). As a consequence, the variable age might not turn out to be significant in electoral analyses of these parties, even though it clearly plays a role.

While some of these problems, such as the effect of heteroscedasticity described above, could be overcome by advanced statistical methods, the analysis of subelectorates unfortunately presents new and less easily surmounted problems, most notably the fact that the small number of voters for populist radical right parties in election studies often does not allow for further differentiation (e.g. Evans *et al.* 2001).

9.6   Protest vs. support

One of the main debates in the field is whether the vote for populist radical right parties is essentially an expression of *support* or *protest* (e.g. Perrineau 2002; Schumann 2001; Shafir 2001; Williams 1999; Van Holsteyn 1990). Particularly in the media the interpretation changes regularly, depending on the "mood of the people." For example, whereas voters of the Dutch CP were mainly denounced as "racists" in the early 1980s, voters of the almost identical CD in the early 1990s were described as "protesters" who had a legitimate grievance, even if they expressed it through the wrong channel (Mudde & Van Holsteyn 2000). In academia the characterizations tend to be more stable, but different schools exist, one stressing the predominance of "xenophobia" (i.e. support) and the other of "political resentment" (i.e. protest), to use the two most prominent explanations of electoral success of populist radical right parties (Betz 1994).

As is often the case, empirical studies produce highly contradictory results, largely due to the striking differences in operationalizations. For instance, in the most influential studies on this point (Van der Brug & Fennema 2003; Van der Brug *et al.* 2000) the concept of protest vote is not operationalized directly, but as the residue unexplained by the other variables (for a critique, see Bergh 2004; Thijssen 2001). And even these most ardent believers of the support thesis had to qualify their original position by distinguishing between "two separate groups" of populist radical right parties, one voted for more on the basis of support, and the other (also) on the basis of protest (Van der Brug & Fennema 2003).

A more accurate operationalization of "the protest vote" starts from the understanding that: (1) two actors are central in the definition of any voter, the individual and the party; and (2) there are two general ways to define the protest voter, depending on which of the two actors is considered central. The first defines the protest vote on the basis of the party, i.e. a protest voter is an individual who votes for a "protest party." Here, the motivations of the party are definitive; what exactly defines a protest party is another issue of dispute, however (e.g. Fennema 1997). The second defines on the basis of the voter, i.e. a protest voter is an individual who uses her/his vote to express protest (e.g. Bergh 2004;

Decker 2004: 188–95). In the latter the ideology of the party is secondary and the choice for a party is, at least in part, instrumental.

I agree with those who argue that protest voting should be defined primarily on the basis of the voter, "since they are the ones who are protesting" (Bergh 2004: 376). After all, most protest parties also have an ideology that is supported by at least some part of their electorates. On the basis of a voter-centered definition one could further distinguish between different types of protest vote(r)s. For example, on the basis of the "object of protest," Johannes Bergh (2004) differentiates between "system protest," directed against the political system as such, and "elite protest," aimed specifically at political elite(s).

The relationship between the protest voter and the party voted for can be quite varied. In the most general sense, the party is simply a means to an end, i.e. a whip to punish one or more established parties. Won-Taek Kang (2004: 84) refers to an "exit-with-voice" option, i.e. protest voters leave their traditional party (exit) but rather than not voting at all (exit in Hirschman's terms) they vote for another party (voice). In this interpretation, the party is not chosen for its program or its policy potential, but for the pain it causes the established parties. Obviously, pariah parties, as most populist radical right parties are, will profit in particular from these voters. Some parties have understood this very well and address these voters directly. A leaflet of the German DVU stated: "For every DVU representative who gets into the regional parliament of Brandenburg, one of the others gets the chop. This way the voting ballot [*Stimmzettel*] becomes a thinking ballot [*Denkzettel*]. Only right-wing protest really hews in" (in Stöss 2005: 143).

The protest voter can choose a party that, at least on some issues, supports his/her preferred policies in order to indicate these preferences to the established parties. Here the difference between protest and support votes becomes more difficult to establish. Conceptually, it would make sense to define this distinction on the basis of the *relationship* between the voter and the party that receives the vote: the "support voter" trusts the party for whom s/he votes to govern and implement its policy agenda, whereas the "protest voter" primarily sees the voted party as a vehicle to punish other (established) parties or push them in the right direction. This could also explain the finding that in certain party systems moderate voters prefer extreme parties; i.e. expecting a watered-down policy as a consequence of coalition formation, "voters often compensate for this watering-down by supporting parties whose positions differ from (or are often more extreme than) their own" (Kedar 2005: 185).

Empirical analyses have measured protest voting either by negation or by proxy. In the former, a protest vote is the same as the absence of a support vote, i.e. an ideological vote (notably Van der Brug *et al.* 2000; Van der Brug & Fennema 2003). However, this would count a protest vote with the aim of policy balancing as a support vote. Not surprising then that these studies tend to confirm the support vote thesis, although some also acknowledge that some populist radical right parties might be voted for mainly on the basis of protest. Most studies measure the protest vote by proxy, i.e. they do not so much study the motivations of the voters but their attitudes. If voters are negative about the political system or the political elitest, they are presumed to express "system protest" and "elite protest" respectively (see also 9.4.1).

According to electoral research, "[t]he supporters and/or voters for extreme right parties are by far the most alienated vis-à-vis the democratic institutions and their functioning" (Ignazi 2003: 213). Almost half of the electorate of the two populist radical right candidates in the 2002 French presidential elections, Le Pen and Mégret, were "*ninists*" (neither right, nor left). "*Ninists* essentially vote against all existing parties, out of protest and despair, and beat all the records on our indicators of political distrust" (Mayer 2005: 9). In Austria, between 39 percent and 66 percent of the FPÖ electorate in the 1990s named the desire to "send a message" as one of its major motivations and saw the FPÖ as a "new broom" to dust out Austrian politics (Ignazi 2003: 119).

Both types of studies are limited by a conceptualization of protest that precludes the empirical possibility of overlap between a support vote and a protest vote. However, someone with populist radical right attitudes can vote for a populist radical right party both because he shares the ideology (i.e. support) and because he rejects mainstream politics (protest). Which of the two prevails can only be determined by establishing the position of the voter with respect to the party of choice.

Some data clearly show that the vote for a populist radical right party was first and foremost a vote *against* the other (established) parties, rather than *for* the populist radical right party. This was the case, for example, in the early stages of the FN: in the presidential elections of the late 1980s a majority of Le Pen voters did not want him to become president (Bell 2000). Similarly, in 1983, 23 percent of CP voters did *not* want that party to participate in government, while in 1993 this group represented 34 percent of CD voters (Mudde & Van Holsteyn 2000: 157). In the Greek parliamentary elections of 2004, just 17 percent of the LAOS supporters said they had voted for "the best choice" and 8 percent for "the least bad choice"; a stunning 75 percent said they had expressed a "protest vote."[9]

[9] The data are from a V-PRC poll and unfortunately do not include the operationalization of the category "protest vote" (personal communication by Ioannis Kolovos).

Yet there are also (indirect) indicators of the predominance of the support vote. In this respect, it is important to point out the extremely high levels of voter loyalty among the electorates of successful populist radical right parties. For example, 79 percent of the people who had voted for the Romanian PRM in the 1996 parliamentary elections did so again in 2000 (Shafir 2001: 100). The Austrian FPÖ had between 77 percent and 81 percent loyal voters in the period 1986–1999 (www.sora.at). Other studies report similarly high percentages, roughly between 75 percent and 90 percent, for the Belgian VB, the Danish DFP, and the French FN (Evans & Ivaldi 2002: 76). Obviously, successful parties will have higher percentages of loyal voters than unsuccessful parties,[10] but percentages of (over) 80 percent loyalty clearly point in the direction of at least partial "support" rather than merely undirected "protest."

Populist radical right parties will most likely have both groups of voters within their electorates. While smaller parties will have predominantly support voters, particularly in low-intensity elections, larger parties will have a more diverse electorate, including large groups of protesters. Moreover, many individual voters will occupy both positions, i.e. sharing populist radical right attitudes but also protesting against the established parties (e.g. Eith 2003; Shafir 2001; Van Donselaar & Van Praag 1983). Importantly, the groups are not static and most protest voters will either develop into support voters (loyalty) or change parties (exit). In essence, the key to the electoral persistence of populist radical right parties is their ability to transform protest voters into support voters (e.g. Schmidt 2003; Betz 2002b; De Witte 1998). The high percentages of loyal voters within the electorates of parties like the FN and VB show that the more successful parties have indeed managed to do exactly that. It is particularly in this respect that the internal supply-side becomes important (see chapter 11).

9.7   Conclusion

Electoral studies have focused primarily on the demand-side of populist radical right party politics, i.e. determining the most fertile breeding ground for populist radical right parties. In this respect, it is (self-)evident that mass social changes like the "silent revolution" (Inglehart 1977) and

---

[10] Interestingly, even unsuccessful populist radical right parties can achieve relatively high levels of voter loyalty. Despite the fact that the Czech SPR-RSČ saw its electorate almost halved in the 1998 parliamentary elections, still 50 percent of its 1996 electorate had again voted for the party (Vlachová 2001: 485). With regard to party identification, the distribution of 1996 SPR-RSČ voters was not much different from the other Czech parties, except in the categories "very strong" and "very weak," which were both comparatively high (Vlachová 2001: 487).

the development of multicultural societies (at least in Western Europe) play a role, as do Hans-Georg Betz's famous two motives, xenophobia and political resentment. However, how macro-level factors exactly influence micro-level behavior remains largely undertheorized.

Even if we can establish a clearer theoretical argumentation specifying how macro-level processes like globalization create micro-level attitudes like nativism and populism, much remains to be explained. Most of the macro-level processes affect European countries in roughly similar ways. Not surprisingly then, most European countries – particularly when considered as the East and West region – have a fairly similar demand-side, i.e. quite similar levels of theoretically relevant attitudes (most notably xenophobia and political resentment). Hence, the macro-level explanations cannot account for the striking differences in populist radical right electoral success between countries with fairly similar breeding grounds.

Europe-wide semi-permanent processes and systems like globalization, modernization, and multicultural society by and large ensure the continuous generation of nativist, authoritarian, and populist sentiments. This means that the populist radical right party family will continue to operate in a favorable breeding ground for years to come. As the recent years have already made abundantly clear, this does not necessarily mean that these parties will also (continue to) gain electoral victories in all European countries.

In other words, the demand-side might explain why and which people constitute the *potential* electorate of populist radical right parties, but they do not (necessarily) explain why and who actually *votes* for these parties. As Renaud Dehousse (2002: 4) has stated with some exaggeration, "the protest vote is only the *tip* of the iceberg." According to one study, populist radical right parties in Western Europe (1989–99) mobilized between 13 percent (CD in 1999) and 70 percent (FPÖ in 1999) of their electoral potential, with most parties achieving the support of less than half of their potential voters (Van der Brug *et al.* 2005: 547). While the operationalization of "potential voters" was very broad in this particular study,[11] the general conclusion seems valid: populist radical right parties, like all political parties, are able to mobilize only a part of the group of people that consider voting for them.

Demand-side theories are not able to explain this poor level of mobilization, i.e. the metaphorical tip of the iceberg. In other words, a fertile breeding ground is a *necessary* but not a *sufficient* condition (Van der Brug *et al.* 2005). Macro-level theories can explain the existence of

---

[11] On the ten-point scale they used to probe into the potentiality of respondents to vote for a party, the authors selected a rather low cut-off point of 6 (rather than, say, 8).

certain micro-level attitudes, which in turn create the breeding ground for (populist radical right) parties. It is the meso-level, however, that can explain why some attitudes become more important in voter motivation than others. The supply-side of populist radical right party politics is crucial to understanding meso-level processes; thus, it will be the focus of the next two chapters.

10 External supply-side: political opportunity structures

> While the extremist parties pick up the good vocabulary from the main-
> stream parties and keep the old bad grammar, the mainstream parties
> do just the opposite, keeping the good grammar but picking up the bad
> vocabulary in an attempt to be more successful. But such tactics will
> only create more confusion. (PER 2002: 30)

10.1 Introduction

The last few years have seen a growing number of studies showing the
importance of supply-side factors in the success and failure of populist
radical right parties (e.g. Carter 2005; Givens 2005; Norris 2005; Van der
Brug *et al.* 2005; Betz 2004; Decker 2004). Success will be interpreted
here primarily in electoral terms, in line with most of the academic literature on populist radical right parties. However, special attention will
be paid to the distinction between electoral *breakthrough* and *persistence*,
which are clearly related, but do not always have the same explanations
(Coffé 2004; Schain *et al.* 2002b). Moreover, electoral success does not
equal political success; in fact, it is a necessary, but not a sufficient condition (see further chapter 12).

The discussion of supply-side factors proceeds with the fairly straightforward distinction between internal and external factors. The next chapter will address the major internal factors, i.e. those directly related to the
populist radical right parties themselves. This chapter focuses on external factors, i.e. those not *inherent to* the populist radical right parties. In
aggregate external factors constitute the so-called political opportunity
structure, the overarching concept in this chapter.

The concept of the political opportunity structure (POS) derives from
the literature on new social movements and has only recently been
applied to the study of the populist radical right (e.g. Rydgren 2005b;
Decker 2004; Jungerstam-Mulders 2003; Minkenberg 1998; Kitschelt &
McGann 1995). Political opportunity structures are defined as "consistent, but not necessarily formal or permanent, dimensions of the political

environment that provide incentives for people to undertake collective action by affecting their expectations for success or failure" (Tarrow 1994: 85). As the meta-variable of political opportunity structure touches upon many different (sub)variables, the following discussion will be structured by distinguishing among three partly overlapping contexts: the institutional, the political, and the cultural. Since the media play an important and highly complex role in the success and failure of populist radical right parties, and influence each of these contexts, they will be discussed in a separate section.

10.2 The institutional context

A fertile breeding ground at the mass level is important to populist radical right parties, but it is only one factor in their success or the lack thereof. Indeed, "populist politics is defined not only by idiosyncratic issue orientations, but also by structural constraints, such as those of the electoral system and the partisan alternatives it affords" (Denemark and Bowler 2002: 64). In recent years a number of studies have focused on the effects of the institutional framework on the electoral success and failure of populist radical right parties (e.g. Arzheimer & Carter 2006; Carter 2005; Norris 2005; Lubbers 2001). The hypothesis is that "different political systems provide different opportunities and limitations for Far Right parties to succeed in the electoral arena" (Jungerstam-Mulders 2003: 29).

The *electoral system* has been identified as an important hindrance to populist radical right parties (and other new or small parties). This has been particularly strong in studies on countries that use some form of plurality system, most notably the first-past-the-post system of the United Kingdom (e.g. Eatwell 2000; Copsey 1996), However, as the NF demonstrated in the late 1970s and the BNP affirmed in recent local elections, (incidental) successes at the local level are definitely possible (Mudde 2002b) despite the tendency of the plurality system to conspire against these parties at the national level. Moreover, both the Greens and the UK Independence Party (UKIP) have proven that even in the nationwide European elections seats can be won by nationally irrelevant parties.[1]

The other major example of a plurality system, the two-tier majority system, has also been regarded as an important institutional hurdle for the populist radical right (on France, see Hainsworth 2004; Schmidt 2003).

---

[1] I'm using the term "relevant" in the Sartorian sense here, i.e. parliamentary political parties that have either coalition or blackmail potential (Sartori 1976).

These systems lead to run-offs between two candidates, which are most problematic for polarizing candidates, as has been clearly demonstrated in the run-offs in presidential elections in France (Le Pen in 2002), Romania (Tudor in 2000), and Slovakia (Mečiar in 2000 and 2004). However, these systems also produce bargaining opportunities for third parties, leading to significant electoral and political benefits, as the FN has experienced over the past decades.

Most European electoral systems, however, are proportional systems, or mixed systems with a dominant proportional character (e.g. Gallagher *et al.* 2005). Nonetheless, between these various proportional electoral systems there is a significant range of proportionality. As so often, empirical studies come to very different findings about the effects of these systems on the electoral support of populist radical right parties. Both univariate (e.g. Carter 2004, 2002) and multivariate (e.g. Carter 2005; Norris 2005; Van der Brug *et al.* 2005; Jesuit & Mahler 2004) analyses have found that the effect of the level of proportionality of the electoral system is not significant. But other multivariate analyses did find a significant effect of the disproportionality of the electoral system; however, some found a positive (Arzheimer & Carter 2006; Swank & Betz 2003), and others a negative effect on the electoral success of populist radical right parties (Veugelers & Magnan 2005; Golder 2003; Jackman & Volpert 1996). In short, the evidence indicates that electoral systems have some effect on the electoral opportunity structure of political parties, but help little in explaining the differences in electoral success between different countries, parties, periods, and regions.

Although the direct effect of the electoral system on the success of populist radical right parties is still an issue of academic debate, many key political actors have perceived it as being very important. Consequently, electoral successes are regularly followed by calls for changes in the electoral system. Russian President Boris Yeltsin, for example, reacted to the surprise victory of the LDPR in the 1993 parliamentary elections with an (unsuccessful) attempt to seriously reduce the number of party-list seats in favor of single-member districts (White 1997).[2] In other countries elites have called for the introduction of an electoral threshold (usually of 4–5 percent), pointing to the alleged success of such institutional hurdles in keeping populist radical right parties out of the federal and most regional parliaments in Germany (e.g. Van Donselaar 1995). In Germany, on the other hand, some mainstream politicians argued for

---

[2] In the 1995 parliamentary elections, the LDPR won 11.2 percent of the votes (and 50 seats) in the proportional election of the party lists, yet only 0.4 percent of the vote (and 1 seat) in the single member districts (White 1997: 112).

the adoption of the British first-past-the-post system after the electoral success of the REP in West Berlin in 1989. And in the UK, the Electoral Reform Society recommended a move to proportional representation in reaction to the local successes of the BNP in Burnley (Deacon et al. 2004).

In some countries anxious calls for reform are actually met by the political will to effect them. In a variety of cases the electoral system has been altered to weaken the populist radical right, with adjustments ranging from small detailed amendments to full-fledged system changes. In the Netherlands, for example, the number of signatories to contest districts was increased from 190 to 570 nationwide. This seemingly minor change limited the CD to contesting only seventeen of the nineteen electoral districts in the 1998 parliamentary elections, resulting in its failure to pass the very low threshold of 0.67 percent to maintain its presence in the Dutch parliament (Van Donselaar 2000: 37–9).

Obviously, the electoral system can also be changed to strengthen the populist radical right. In fact, when in power populist radical right parties have consistently attempted to manipulate the electoral system, most notably by gerrymandering, i.e. adjusting the district borders to create more favorable electoral results. In Croatia, for example, the HDZ redistricted the capital city, Zagreb, a stronghold of the opposition (Ottaway 2003). In Slovakia, on the other hand, the third Mečiar government was unsuccessful in its attempt to redraw the district boundaries to undermine the (particularly Hungarian-speaking) opposition. In this case the initiative came from the HZDS, but enjoyed the full support of the SNS.

France is a rare case in which a nonallied political party consciously changed the electoral system in favor of the populist radical right. In a modern version of Machiavellian politics, and in line with a long French tradition of using the electoral system for one's own party interests (Knapp 1987), socialist President François Mitterrand replaced the plurality system with a proportional one for the 1986 parliamentary elections, in an (only partly successful) effort to bolster the FN and thereby weaken the mainstream right (i.e. RPR and UDF). The RPR and UDF were similarly instrumental in their decision to change the regional electoral system in 1998 in an effort to weaken the FN.

In addition to the electoral system, other aspects of the *political system* have been considered relevant for the success of populist radical right parties as well. Frank Decker (2004) argues that federalism protects the federal level from "right-wing populist" success. His argument implicitly affirms the second-order election thesis (Reif & Schmitt 1980); people vote for radical parties in secondary elections, in this case regional elections. In a similar indirect way, Michael Minkenberg argues that the

French FN profited from the centralist French political system, which supports the "construction of an effective organization" (1998: 308) that again leads to electoral success. In sharp contrast, others have argued that federalism actually benefits radical parties, including populist radical right parties and Greens, as it provides them with the opportunity to start small and work their way up (e.g. Jungerstam-Mulders 2003; Müller-Rommel 1998).

Some scholars have linked electoral success to the structure of political cooperation in a country. For example, Decker (2000: 238) argues that corporatist structures have supported rather than hindered the rise of right-wing populist parties, because of the exclusion of new political actors at the expense of the privileged partners (i.e. the established parties). Similarly, various authors have argued that consociational political systems have facilitated populist radical right parties, because of their lack of transparency and party political alternation, leading to dissatisfaction and protest voting (e.g. Dehousse 2002; Kitschelt 2002; Andeweg 2001).

On the basis of an (admittedly provisional) empirical comparative analysis, the data do not provide clear answers (see also 9.2.2; Papadopoulos 2002). While there are federal systems with unsuccessful right-wing populist parties (including those termed populist radical right here), such as Germany and (with some stretching) Spain, there are others with some of the most successful parties, notably Austria, Belgium, and Switzerland. And while there are unitary states with successful populist radical right parties, including France and Romania, there are many more with unsuccessful parties, notably most postcommunist states and the United Kingdom (at least until devolution). Similarly, there are corporatist and consensual political systems that have seen substantial electoral successes of the populist radical right (e.g. Austria, Belgium, Denmark), and those that have not (e.g. the Netherlands, Sweden). If anything, these political systems seem to facilitate antiestablishment parties in general, rather than the populist radical right in particular.

A case can be made for the argument that (all) populist parties profit from the inherent tension of liberal democracy (e.g. Mény & Surel 2002b; Canovan 1999). Liberal democracy is based upon different, in part contradictory logics: democratic majoritarian rule versus liberal protection of minorities, rule of the people versus constitutional limitation. Populism provides a simple and attractive alternative to the complexities and contradictions of liberal democracies by choosing unequivocally for unmitigated majority rule. While this argument makes sense, it contributes little to understanding why certain types of populist parties are successful (e.g. neoliberal, radical right, social), or why populist radical right parties are more successful in certain countries and periods despite shared liberal democratic features.[3]

In conclusion, the institutional framework of a country is "rather a symptom than the true reason for [strengths and] weaknesses in mobilization" (Decker 2003a: 226). Political and electoral systems do not so much determine whether political parties have electoral success; they provide them with electoral and political opportunities. As such, they are important building blocks of the larger political opportunity structures within which populist radical right parties function. Whether or not these parties successfully exploit the potential of the institutional framework in which they operate depends to a large extent upon what other political actors do.

10.3   The political context

As populist radical right parties are first and foremost political parties, their key context is the competitive political arena of party politics. Like all other parties, they function within one or more party systems. The interaction between a populist radical right party and other political parties, especially the established ones, as well as the dynamics among parties within the system, to a large extent create or foreclose opportunities for populist radical right parties. The impact of the structured interaction of parties within the electoral arena has been referred to as the "electoral opportunity structure" (Van der Brug et al. 2005: 546ff.), which is shaped by various factors.

First of all, for populist radical right parties to gain electoral success there has to be space for new parties in the party system (e.g. Rydgren 2005b; Veugelers 1997; Linz 1976). If voters are fully loyal to their party, new parties will only appeal to new voters, i.e. people who for reason of status or inclination did not vote in the last elections. Even though most populist radical right parties do particularly well among first-time voters, as well as among previous nonvoters (e.g. Kreidl & Vlachová 1999; Ignazi 1996; Betz 1993a), they represent only a small subset of the electorate. Still, the statement that "loyalty to a political party makes citizens less susceptible to being swayed by demagogic leaders and extremist movements" (Dalton & Wattenberg 2002: 6) does not explain much, and is even tautological if the "political party" is defined as mainstream (i.e. nonextremist).

---

[3] The same holds for the highly plausible argument that the complex and opaque system of representative democracy of the EU increases the support for populists (e.g. Taggart 2004).

There is clear evidence that electoral volatility has increased significantly in Western Europe, particularly since the 1990s. One of the results of this development has been the rise of various new parties, including spectacular electoral successes by "flash parties" like the FPd and LPF (Gallagher *et al.* 2005; Mair 1997). In postcommunist countries electoral volatility has been extremely high from the beginning due to lack of party identification and indistinct party profiles along with a host of other reasons (e.g. Sikk 2005; Tóka 1997). This has led to landslide victories and earthquake losses. Importantly, quite often volatility is nearly as attributable to the behavior of political parties as it is to that of voters (e.g. Shabad & Slomczynski 2004; Mudde 2002c). For example, in the 2001 parliamentary elections in Poland, only 16 percent of the people who voted for the Polish right-wing AWS in 1997 remained loyal to the party. However, many of the other 84 percent voted for former AWS MPs contesting under new parties, notably PiS and LPR (Millard 2003: 80–2).

Over the past decades European parties have been confronted with various new developments (e.g. postindustrialism, mass immigration) and issues (e.g. environment, multicultural society). It has been argued that new parties could largely emerge because the old parties did not take up some of these new issues that parts of the electorate considered important; i.e. the environment in the case of the Green parties and immigration in the case of the populist radical right (e.g. Kriesi 1995; Betz 1994). This led to voters supporting the programs of new political parties out of anger and frustration with the established parties ignoring these new issues (see 9.6).

The positioning of the main established parties on key old issues (i.e. left–right divide) is also said to have a significant effect on the electoral opportunities of other parties, i.e. creating or closing political space for new competitors, including those of the populist radical right. However, how this plays out exactly has led to some controversy, which is summarized here as the Ignazi–Kitschelt–Ignazi debate. On one hand, the view that ideological convergence between the main (center-)right and (center-)left parties favors populist radical right parties garners broad support within the literature. This thesis, most elegantly presented by Kitschelt and McGann (1995), dates back to studies of the German NPD in the 1960s, when that party was believed to have profited heavily from the *Große Koalition* (Great Coalition) that governed Germany between 1966 and 1969 (cf. Stöss 2000; Backes & Jesse 1993).

One of the few dissenting voices is Piero Ignazi (1992), who argued in his seminal *EJPR* article that polarization was one of the key reasons for the "silent counter-revolution" of the 1990s. In his view, the populist radical right profited from the success of neoconservatives.[4] In his later work Ignazi responded to the challenge of Kitschelt and others by elaborating the relationship between polarization and convergence as a two-step process: first, some mainstream right-wing parties in Western Europe moved to the right in the late 1970s and early 1980s (polarization) and then they regained a more centrist position after the mid 1980s (convergence) (Ignazi 2003: ch. 12). According to the new Ignazi, populist radical right parties have benefited from convergence only when it has come *after* polarization.

Most empirical evidence seems to support the simple convergence thesis (e.g. Carter 2005; Abedi 2004; Kitschelt & McGann 1995), although there have been countervailing findings (e.g. Norris 2005). Kitschelt and McGann's analysis has been seriously criticized by John Veugelers (2001), however, who demonstrates that "a more appropriate, dynamic measure of convergence" yields far less convincing support for the convergence thesis (see also Veugelers & Magnan 2005). And Michael Minkenberg (2001) has argued that convergence is more relevant for electoral breakthrough than for the persistence of populist radical right parties.

While most authors agree with the convergence thesis, particularly with regard to Western Europe, they disagree somewhat on *which* party (or parties) favors the electoral success of populist radical right parties as they converge. Some argue that it is not so much the convergence of all mainstream parties, but rather the centrist position of the largest mainstream right-wing competitor that is crucial (Van der Brug *et al.* 2005; for critique, Norris 2005). Elisabeth Carter (2005) presents evidence that, ideally, it is a combination of the two. Other commentators focus primarily on the role of the main left-wing party in the system, i.e. the social democratic party, arguing that populist radical right parties have occupied "the terrain evacuated by the Left" (e.g. Žižek 2000: 38; also Van den Brink 2005; Betz 2003a; Cuperus 2003; Thompson 2000).

The situation in Eastern Europe is far less researched, and remains difficult to fit into either of the two theories, as postcommunist politics has been characterized by polarization rather than convergence. Even where coalition governments are well established, most party systems have been stable only with respect to a sharp division between two blocks of major parties, despite changing party formations. This dynamic was strongest in the early postcommunist years, when electoral competition was almost exclusively structured on the basis of an anticommunist vs. communist divide, in which only few populist radical right parties gained

---

[4] Ignazi's argument is similar to Lipset's (1955: 185) analysis of the situation in the US in the 1950s.

parliamentary representation in the region. Indeed, in various East European countries the polarization kept populist radical right individuals and organizations from contesting elections independently for many years (e.g. Mudde 2005b). To a certain extent this can be seen as inverse support for the convergence thesis, in the sense that it shows that polarization is bad for the populist radical right.

The Hungarian parliamentary elections of 2002 are a more recent example of the negative effect of polarization on the populist radical right. The intense struggle between the socialist-liberal block (MSzDP/SzDSz) and the national-conservative camp (FIDESz-MPS/MDF) left little space for the populist radical right MIÉP. Not only did the nationalist and populist campaign of Victor Orbán and his FIDESz-MPS prevent MIÉP from picking up disappointed nationalist voters,[5] the polarization lifted the turnout to a postcommunist high. Consequently, the 245,326 votes that MIÉP gained in the first round of the 2002 elections amounted to just 4.4 percent, while its 248,901 votes of 1998 had been the equivalent of 5.5 percent (e.g. Fowler 2003).

Surely, if the new Ignazi is right, there is still hope for MIÉP. After all, he hypothesizes that populist radical right parties will win once the polarization decreases. The 2001 parliamentary elections in Poland might provide some hope for the Hungarian populist radical right too. For over a decade Polish postcommunist politics had been dominated by the anti-communist vs. communist division between the various post-Solidarity formations, on the one hand, and the various communist successor formations, on the other. The 2001 parliamentary elections were heralded as the first postcommunist electoral contest not dominated by this polarization and among the winners were various populist parties, including Samoobrona and the LPR. This trend continued in the 2005 parliamentary election, in which both parties largely consolidated their positions.

Clearly, Ignazi's polarization–convergence thesis needs more robust empirical testing, for which the postcommunist countries might provide fertile ground in the coming years. That convergence between the main (center-)right and (center-)left parties favors the populist radical right seems fairly convincing. However, at least two important qualifications need to be made.

Firstly, convergence favors radical parties more generally, rather than only the populist radical right. True, communist parties in the 1960s and Greens in the (early) 1980s may have profited disproportionately from the convergence of the main center-left party, i.e. the socialist or social democratic party in their party system. But currently neoliberal

---

[5] One commentator even argued that Orban had "'out-Csurkaed' Csurka" (Shafir 2002a).

and, possibly to a slightly lesser extent, social populist parties also profit from both sides of the convergence. Consequently, this thesis can also be substantiated on the basis of research on parties like the Dutch LPF or the Scandinavian Progress Parties (e.g. Pennings & Keman 2003; Kitschelt & McGann 1995).

Secondly, under certain conditions populist radical right parties can also profit from polarization. This holds true, most notably, when they are part of one of the (two) main blocks of competition. This was the case for the LN, in the 1994 Italian parliamentary elections, and the SNS in the 1994 and 1998 Slovak parliamentary elections. Notably, in the highly polarized elections of 1998, the SNS was the only party of the third Mečiar government actually to gain votes. Interestingly, in run-offs for presidential elections the positive effect of polarlization seems very limited, as populist radical right candidates gain only marginally more votes in the second-round run-off than in the multicandidate first round (see also 10.2).

The issue that has raised most debate within the literature is the effect of "copying" by mainstream parties (e.g. Schain *et al.* 2002b; Minkenberg 1998). One could dub this the Chirac–Thatcher debate. Many commentators have accused particularly mainstream right-wing parties of copying the policies and rhetoric of populist radical right parties in an effort to limit electoral losses or even gain electoral successes. However, the effects of this strategy are variable and in some cases copy-catting may favor the populist radical right. Some authors contend that the copy-cat actions of the mainstream (right-wing) parties have "legitimized" (the themes of) the populist radical right and thereby increased their electoral success (e.g. Arzheimer & Carter 2006). This is argued most forcefully with regard to the French case (and Chirac), and has led to Le Pen's famous dictum that the voters prefer the original over the copy (e.g. Hainsworth 2000b). However, where the populist radical right has remained unsuccessful, commentators attribute their failure to the "successful" copy-cat actions of the mainstream parties. The most mentioned case of the latter is Margaret Thatcher and the British NF at the end of the 1970s (e.g. Kitschelt & McGann 1995; Elbers & Fennema 1993), but the VVD and CD in the Netherlands (e.g. Bale 2003; Husbands 1996; Fennema 1995) and the FIDESz-MPS and MIÉP in Hungary (e.g. Shafir 2002b) are also well-cited examples.

At first sight, there seems to be a contradiction; it is either the one or the other. However, both could be true, if an essential intervening variable is included: *issue ownership* (Petrocik 1996: 826; also Budge & Farlie 1983). When a populist radical right party is able to persuade voters that it is better suited to "handle" an issue than the other parties, the increased salience of that issue will profit the populist radical right party (Bélanger & Meguid 2005; Meguid 2005; Mudde 1999). For example, as early as 1986 half of the Viennese believed that the FPÖ was the most competent party on the immigration issue. Consequently, the ÖVP campaign around the slogan "Vienna to the Viennese" mainly strengthened the party that was considered to be the most competent in this field, i.e. the FPÖ (Ahlemeyer 2006; Müller 2002). Where one party has not established ownership with respect to an issue, other parties can run away with the topic.

Issue ownership is also one of the main reasons for the striking weakness of populist radical right parties in most postcommunist countries (e.g. Mudde 2002a). In this region, all political parties are still very young and volatile, and few have been able to establish ownership over any issue. Consequently, while in Eastern Europe, in the words of Michael Shafir, "the vocabulary of extreme nationalism has been made acceptable after having been absorbed by mainstream parties" (in Naegele 2002), populist radical right parties have hardly been able to profit.

It is important to note that these parties have not only been marginalized by the copy-cat actions of *right-wing* competitors. Different studies have pointed to the role of the communist PCF and the socialist PS in France or of the (local) Labour Party in the United Kingdom (e.g. Rydgren 2004a; Eatwell 2000). In the Czech Republic, the left wing has been the main competitor for the populist radical right. In the 1998 parliamentary elections, the social democratic ČSSD managed "to attract former republican supporters by radicalizing its appeal and alleging that liberal-conservative rule has ruined the country" (Marada 1998: 58). Empirical research showed that 41.4 percent of people intending to vote SPR-RSČ in 1996 had a (radical) left-wing party as their second choice (Vlachová 2001: 491), while this group had grown to 65.5 percent in 1998 (Kreidl & Vlachová 1999: 19).

More generally, the populist radical right in Eastern Europe has serious competition in the struggle for the alleged "modernization losers" from social populists, mostly little- or unreformed communist parties that have transformed themselves from the voice of the working class into the *vox populi* (e.g. March & Mudde 2005; Mudde 2002a). Viola Neu has captured this process in the Eastern part of Germany very perceptively: "The PDS tries to present itself as the voice of all those who feel second class people, who have lost orientation because of the enormous changes, and look back nostalgically at the secure relations in the former GDR" (2003: 268). Various electoral studies have shown that populist radical right parties and social populist parties have fairly similar electorates, both in terms of attitudinal and sociodemographic characteristics (e.g. Shafir 2001; Clark 1995).

To conclude the discussion of issue positioning of party competitors of populist radical right parties, the most important effect of the behavior of the mainstream parties is often on the *salience* of the issue: increasing confrontation over an issue, without finding a solution, augments the salience of an issue (Ahlemeyer 2006; Bélanger & Meguid 2005). This can profit *either* a populist radical right party, if it has established ownership of that issue, *or* another (radical or mainstream) party, if it has not. Given the many examples of successful adoption of "populist radical right" themes by mainstream parties (e.g. Estonia, Germany, Hungary, Netherlands), the conclusion that "the populist accentuating of so-called right-wing [sic!] themes by established parties so far has almost always benefited the right-wing extremists" (Eith 2003: 261) seems a politicized misrepresentation of recent political developments within European party politics.

In addition to the positioning of the other parties on certain issues, their behavior towards the populist radical right parties may also play an important role in explaining the (lack of) success of the populist radical right. Terri Givens has argued that a populist radical right party "will have difficulty attracting voters and winning seats in electoral systems that encourage strategic voting and/or strategic coordination by the mainstream parties" (Givens & Luedtke 2005: 150). While not completely convinced by her institutionalist argumentation, I agree that electoral systems provide political actors with opportunities to open or close the party system to new contenders. However, Givens' theoretical assertion that this elite behavior also significantly influences mass behavior, by increasing the number of strategic voters, is based on some highly questionable rational choice assumptions, most notably that of the "game of complete information" (Givens 2005: 92, 96).

Empirical research into the electoral effects of mainstream party strategies towards populist radical right parties is still in its infancy. Givens' analysis has the disadvantage that the hypotheses put forward are all highly specific to the cases selected. A very preliminary cross-national study of seven West European countries, based on a fairly rough expert study, found that whether or not a populist radical right party is ostracized by mainstream parties, through a so-called *cordon sanitaire*, seems to have little effect on its electoral support (Van der Brug & Van Spanje 2004). However, it does also suggest that if there is an effect, it will probably be limited to the electoral breakthrough stage.

10.4   Cultural context

The third and last context of the political opportunity structure of populist radical right parties is the cultural. While the concept of "political culture" is notoriously difficult to use in empirical research (cf. Welch 1993), there is little doubt that countries differ with respect to national and political mores and values. Consequently, some cultures may be more conducive to the populist radical right than others (e.g. Art 2006; Minkenberg 2001; Helms 1997). The question, however, is what makes one culture "damp" populist radical right party success, and others "aggravate" it (Wendt 2003).

In this respect, much has been written about the alleged importance of *nouvelle droite* (new right) intellectuals in the rise of populist radical right parties (e.g. Spektorowski 2000; Minkenberg 1998). These self-proclaimed "neo-Gramscians of the Right" believe that a political victory can only come *after* a cultural victory, and therefore aim to establish a new right cultural hegemony (see De Benoist 1985). The influence of these groups is sometimes made out to be of stunning proportions, as authors will claim that populist radical right parties merely pick the fruits of the "cultural revolution" instigated by the new right. Obviously, this claim is hugely overstated, if only because few European countries have a functioning *nouvelle droite* subculture. Moreover, much of the new right ideology, with the notable exception of the features of "ethnopluralism" and "national preference" within the FN and those it influenced, remains marginal within both the general public and most populist radical right parties.[6]

The case of a favorable intellectual environment seems more convincing in various Eastern European countries, such as Croatia, Romania, and Serbia, where public intellectuals espouse more or less openly nativist and revisionist theses that are largely similar to the views held by the local populist radical right. In this respect, "intellectuals" who were educated under and worked for the former communist regimes play a particularly dubious role (e.g. Shafir 2002a; Markotich 2000; Sekelj 1998). Not all of these intellectuals are close to populist radical right parties, however, and given the broader use of these theses in (some) East European countries, the populist radical right often cannot really profit from this ideologically favorable cultural environment.

However, as a favorable intellectual climate might help explain success in some countries, a hostile environment is an equally important factor in explaining the failure of populist radical right parties in others. In many European countries these parties have to operate in an environment

---

[6] Possibly the only somewhat relevant exception is the French MNR, the FN-split of Bruno Mégret, which is almost exclusively led by prominent members of the former *nouvelle droite* faction of the FN (see Adler 2001). Before the split, this group also played an important role within the FN (1989–1999), although without dominating it.

where "being tarred with the extremist brush" (Eatwell 2000: 364) means instant political death. In Western Europe, stigmatization is one of the main obstacles to the electoral and political success of populist radical right parties in countries like Germany and the Netherlands (see Klandermans & Mayer 2005; Decker 2003a; Van Donselaar 2003; Schikhof 1998), not surprisingly countries where the Second World War and the Holocaust have been the key point of reference for the distinction between good and evil in the postwar period (Van Donselaar 1991).

Nonna Mayer's observation that the populist radical right is particularly successful in West European countries and regions that had official administrative collaboration with Nazi Germany during the Second World War is particular interesting in this respect (Coffé 2004: 146–7). At first sight, the relationship between a fascist past and the electoral success of populist radical right parties seems quite convincing: eighteen of the thirty-two (56 percent) European countries included in table 10.1 fit the hypothesis.

But this leaves the question of how exactly the two relate theoretically. Given that populist radical right parties are not simply the successors to the historical fascist parties, the relationship can be at best indirect. David Art (2006) has argued that the way national elites deal with the Nazi past has a profound effect on the electoral success of the postwar (populist) radical right. I would suggest that this effect is, to a large extent, mediated through strong nativist subcultures – countries in which the elites take a revisionist approach to their Nazi past have provided a favorable environment for the development of a strong nativist subculture after the war, bridging the political extreme and mainstream. As will be argued below, these subcultures have a facilitating effect upon both the discursive and organizational opportunities of the populist radical right, sometimes giving way to a virtuous circle.

It is important to emphasize that by subcultures we do not so much refer to "crack-pot extremist groups" (Lipset 1955: 196), i.e. extreme right or neo-Nazi subcultures (e.g. Mudde 2005b; Minkenberg 2003), but rather to the broader nationalist ones. In countries and regions like Austria, Croatia, France, or Slovakia, large nationalist subcultures exist outside of the realm of the dominant populist radical right party, which directly feed important facilities and competent personnel into the local party (e.g. Hossay 2002; Mudde & Van Holsteyn 2000; Koopmans 1998).

An extreme example of crucial subcultural support for a (new) populist radical right party can be found in Poland. The LPR was founded only a few months before the 2001 parliamentary elections, as a hotchpotch of former members and delegates of mainstream and (populist) radical right

Table 10.1 *Fascist past and populist radical right electoral success (1990–2005) by country**

Country	Fascist past	Populist radical right success
Albania	no	low
Austria	yes	high
Belgium	no	high
Bulgaria	yes	low
Croatia	yes	high
Czech Republic	no	moderate
Denmark	no	high
Estonia	no	low
Finland	no	low
France	yes	high
Germany	yes	moderate
Greece	no	low
Hungary	yes	moderate
Ireland	no	low
Italy	yes	high
Latvia	no	low
Lithuania	no	low
Luxemburg	no	low
Netherlands	no	low
Norway	no	low
Poland	no	moderate
Portugal	yes	low
Romania	yes	high
Russia	no	high
Serbia	no	high
Slovakia	yes	high
Slovenia	no	moderate
Spain	yes	low
Sweden	no	low
Switzerland	no	high
Ukraine	no	low
United Kingdom	no	low

Note: *The variable "fascist past" indicates whether the country had an indigenous "fascist" regime that was either part of or aligned to the German–Italian Axis during the Second World War.

parties (see Millard 2003). Notwithstanding its novelty, the party gained over one million votes (7.9 percent) in the election. Rather than the result of a remarkable electoral campaign, or the attraction of a charismatic leader, the success was the result of the impressive mobilization potential of the orthodox Catholic-nationalist subculture around Radio Maria and its powerful director, Father Tadeusz Rydzyk. They command a vast network of local organizations, including the so-called *Rodina* (Family) of Radio Maria, the satellite television channel Trwam (I Insist), and various publications such as the daily *Nasz Dziennik* (Our Newspaper). It even runs its own college, the Wyższa Szkoła Kultury Społecznej i Medialnej (College for National and Media Culture) in Toruń, where journalists and political scientists are educated (see Kostrzębski 2005; Pankowski & Kornak 2005; Strobel 2001).

Some authors have argued that active antiracist movements have been instrumental in hindering the electoral success of populist radical right parties (e.g. Copsey 1996). Although empirical evidence is scarce, at best it provides only weak support for this thesis (e.g. Husbands 2001; C. Lloyd 1998).[7] In some cases antiracist mass demonstrations directly follow populist radical right electoral successes, but if a party does face electoral defeat in subsequent elections there are many other (more) plausible factors to consider before concluding that there is any relationship between the protests and the party's losses. There could also be a relationship between the level of stigmatization and the effectiveness of antiracist mobilization. In countries like the Czech Republic and the Netherlands relatively low levels of antiracist mobilization might be (somewhat) more effective than comparatively higher levels of similar mobilization in, say, France or Hungary (cf. Veugelers & Chiarini 2002; Szôcs 1998).

The detrimental effects of cultural stigmatization on the electoral success of populist radical right parties are both direct and indirect. Obviously, fewer people are inclined to vote for a stigmatized party; even if its pariah status increases the party's protest credentials among a small hardcore of antiestablishment voters. At least of equal importance, however, is the effect of stigmatization on the party organization, which is essential for the persistence of electoral success (see 11.4). Here the effect works in two ways, leading to a vicious circle: (1) an aspiring populist radical right party that does not have overt links to extreme right groups will nevertheless hardly attract mainstream or successful people, who have a lot to lose from the damning stigma; (2) at the same time, the party will be very attractive to right-wing extremists, who see an opportunity to lose their even greater stigma. Consequently, marginally successful parties like the CP and the REP were *unterwandert* (flooded) by activists from the extreme right NVU and NPD, respectively, during the 1980s (Mudde 2000a). In

[7] The most famous "success story" is the struggle of the Anti-Nazi League (ANL) against the NF in Great Britain. Even NF deputy leader Martin Webster claimed that the activities of the ANL played a key part in the party's demise at the end of the 1970s. However, the ANL collapsed in early 1979, a few months before the NF stood its largest number of candidates in any parliamentary election (en.wikipedia.org/wiki/British_National_Front).

fact, this migration from the extreme right has even been a problem for neoliberal populist parties like the German Schill-Partei and, to a lesser extent, the Dutch LPF (see Decker 2003a; Kreutzberger 2003).

In sharp contrast, a favorable political culture can have significant advantages for the development of the populist radical right. In countries where nativist issues are at the core of the political agenda, various subcultural organizations function as bridges between the political mainstream and the populist radical right (Mudde & Van Holsteyn 2000; De Witte 1998). These organizations will strengthen the populist radical right parties in a variety of ways. They will (1) heighten the salience of the nativist issue in domestic politics; (2) facilitate contacts between mainstream and populist radical right politicians, possibly leading to electoral and other cooperation; and (3) function as recruiting bases for competent new personnel for the parties. Altogether, they lead to a virtuous circle that promotes a positive image of the populist radical right and further decreases the already limited stigmatization of the populist radical right. These processes can be observed in almost every country and region where the populist radical right has been particularly successful over extended periods: Austria, Belgium, France, Romania, and Slovakia.

However, a favorable political culture also presents a danger to populist radical right parties: they risk redundancy. To a certain extent, this was the case in many Eastern European countries in the first years of postcommunism. Most of the populist radical right themes were taken up by mainstream parties, which implemented them in a more or less moderate form in their policies. Consequently, little electoral space was left for the "real" populist radical right. At the same time, in some cases there truly was little need for a separate populist radical right party, as the ruling party/parties executed most of their program. This was the case in Estonia and Latvia in the early 1990s (see 6.2.2), while in Croatia, in part as a consequence of the continuing war, the ruling HDZ became a populist radical right party (see 12.2.1).

10.5   The media: friend *and* foe

The role of the media in the success and failure of populist radical right parties has received little serious attention in social scientific studies (but see Walgrave & De Swert 2004; Mazzoleni *et al.* 2003; Goot 1999; Statham 1996). This is remarkable, given how much power is ascribed to the media in most discussions on politics in general, and on the populist radical right in particular. Many commentators have linked the success of these parties directly to the alleged nativist and populist campaigns of parts of the media, especially tabloids and commercial television (e.g.

Decker 2004; Bergsdorf 2000; Deutchman & Ellison 1999). In fact, some have suggested a relationship of mutual dependence: "Haider needed the media and they needed him" (Ritterband 2003: 28).

Interestingly, within the populist radical right the opposite view on the role of the media holds sway. Particularly within the smaller parties leaders and followers alike will blame the media for their lack of success. The late John Tyndall, leader of various populist radical right and extreme right organizations in the United Kingdom (including the BNP and NF), expressed the unequal struggle between his party press and the established media in the following terms: "In the propaganda war we were like an army equipped with bows and arrows facing an adversary using heavy artillery, bombers, missiles and all the other accoutrements of modern fire-power" (in Copsey 1996: 123).

There is little doubt that sections of the media, particularly tabloids and commercial television, discuss issues and use discourses very similar to those of the populist radical right (e.g. Norris 2000). Consequently, they are setting a public agenda highly favorable to populist radical right parties, which raise similar issues and present solutions in line with those offered or suggested in these media (e.g. Vliegenthart & Boomgaarden 2005; Walgrave & De Swert 2004). But the link between the agenda-setting of tabloids and commercial television and the electoral success of populist radical right parties is far from straightforward. There are many countries in Europe where the media express particularly populist radical right sentiments, yet these parties are quite marginal in electoral and political terms (e.g. the UK and much of Eastern Europe). There are two explanations, one external to the media and one internal to it.

The external explanation for the lack of a clear relationship between media agenda-setting and populist radical right party success is linked to the concept of issue ownership, as discussed above (see also Walgrave & De Swert 2004). As the media are at least as much a reflection of the public agenda as the setters of it, countries with highly nativist, authoritarian, and populist media will most probably have a relatively populist radical right mainstream. Consequently, it can be very difficult for populist radical right parties to differentiate themselves from the established parties and to profit fully from the media discourse.

The internal explanation has to do with the logic of most of these media: "while the media might at times pander to racial stereotyping, in general they are hostile to the extreme right" (Eatwell 2003: 60). This can best be illustrated by the case of Germany, home to the influential *Bild Zeitung*, the prototype of the (Continental) European tabloids. Many commentators in and outside of academia have pointed to the populist radical right discourse employed by this popular newspaper (e.g. Eatwell 2000; Jäger 1993; Quinkert & Jäger 1991). But the same *Bild Zeitung* has often been highly critical of the populist radical right parties in Germany (e.g. Art 2006: 165–6). The same is true for the commercial television channel RTL, which combines sensationalist reporting in line with populist radical right propaganda with explicit anti(populist) radical right campaigns.

There are important exceptions to this general rule, of course. One famous example of a tabloid that not only supported the issues of the populist radical right, but also its main political actor, was the Austrian *Neue Kronen Zeitung* during much of the 1990s. This tabloid, which reaches a daily audience of some 43 percent of the Austrian population, not only pushed the issues of the FPÖ, it also presented the party as the political voice of common sense on these issues (e.g. Ahlemeyer 2006; Art 2006; Plasser & Ulram 2003). The tabloid's broad coverage and positive profile of the FPÖ helped the party to establish ownership over issues like immigration and *Politikverdrossenheit* (political dissatisfaction), on the one hand, and raised the importance of those issues for the broader public, on the other. Not surprisingly the (huge) readership of *Die Krone* had a "stronger empathy" with the FPÖ than the rest of the Austrian population (Plasser & Ulram 2003: 35).

In Poland an even deeper symbiotic relationship used to exist between the populist radical right and the Catholic fundamentalist Radio Maryja (Maria) and its extensive media network.[8] As one commentator noted: "At least twenty parliamentarians in the previous Parliament [1997– 2001, CM] owed their seats to Radio Maria, which makes it the only radio station with parliamentary representation! In some cases, candidates endorsed by Radio Maria got more votes than those at the head of the party list" (PER 2002: 9; also Millard 1999: 120). This reference is to populist radical right candidates on mainstream lists, most notably the Akcja Wyborcza Solidarność (Solidarity Electoral Coalition, AWS), but in the 2001 parliamentary elections Radio Maria was also essential in getting the newly founded and until then largely inactive and unknown LPR elected to the Sejm.[9]

In some cases, populist radical right parties have benefited from media favoritism through their alliance with another political actor. This has been the case most notably with the AN and the LN and the Berlusconi

---

[8] An even more singular case is the German DVU, the "phantom party" that is built upon the readership of the nativist media empire of entrepreneur-politician Gerhard Frey (see Mudde 2000a: chapter 3).

[9] Electoral studies showed a large overlap between the electorate of the LPR and the heartland of the orthodox Catholic subculture (see Millard 2003).

media empire in Italy (Biorcio 2003; Statham 1996). Similar situations have occurred in Eastern Europe with regard to the SNS and Mečiar in Slovakia and during certain periods with the SRS and Milošević in Serbia (see Bieber 2005; Pribićević 1999). There is no doubt that positive media attention has created a favorable setting for these parties, but it has likely been of greater consequence to their electoral breakthrough than to their electoral persistence.

However, in many more cases significant parts of the media are *un*sympathetic to the populist radical right. This is the case particularly with the so-called "elite media" (e.g. Schellenberg 2005; Mazzoleni 2003; Stewart *et al.* 2003), which are also attacked by populist actors: either directly, as active agents of the establishment, or indirectly, as passive defenders of elite culture (see also 3.2.1). In many cases, the elite media is actually involved (actively or passively) in the struggle against populist radical right challengers, as more or less passive "transmission belts" of political elites and as active defenders of elite culture against the "populist menace." Obviously, this situation is very different in countries where populist radical right parties are part of the establishment in general and the government in particular.

Even if (parts of) the media are not openly sympathetic towards the populist radical right, they can still provide them with a highly favorable forum. This is particularly true when a populist radical right party has a mediagenic or charismatic leader (see 11.3.1) who can work the media better than her/his political rivals. Research on the 1993 parliamentary elections in Russia showed that supporters of the highly successful LDPR mentioned the impact of the coverage of the electoral campaign twice as often as the electorate as a whole (Tolz 2003: 264). In Romania, PRM leader Tudor performed the best of all candidates in the television debates before the first round of the presidential elections of 2000, shifting the opinions of a considerable portion of the electorate (Shafir 2001: 105). The media drew immediate lessons from this, however, and "exercised a virtual ban on Tudor" until the second round of the elections (Popescu 2003: 330). Jean-Marie Le Pen has met with a similar tactics by the media in France (e.g. Birenbaum & Villa 2003).

It is important to note that all kind of populists (or more broadly: political outsiders) can profit from (exaggerated) media attention. This is a consequence of the "media logic" that dominates most media in contemporary Europe, leading to a type of reporting that is sometimes termed "media populism" (e.g. Mazzoleni 2003). This logic, which is particularly dominant in (commercial) television and the tabloid media, shares at least three traits with party populism: personalization, emotionalization, and an antiestablishment attitude (e.g. Decker 2004; Plasser & Ulram

2003). Not surprisingly the most extreme cases of media–party fusion have involved owners of commercial television, i.e. the Italian neoliberal populist FI of Silvio Berlusconi (e.g. Grassi & Rensmann 2005; Statham 1996) and the Slovak "centrist-populist" ANO of Pavel Rusko, co-owner of the country's main commercial television channel Markíza Televizia (see Učeň 2004).

However, if media control is rarely as complete as it is in Berlusconi's Italy or, to a lesser extent, Tuđman's Croatia (see Basom 1996), politicians of all persuasions must remain vigilant with respect to the media: the media giveth, and the media taketh away. Hamburg's *Richter Gnadenlos* (Judge Merciless) Ronald B. Schill of the neoliberal populist PRO learnt this the hard way. While his meteoric rise was largely due to a favorable press, his equally sudden downfall was precipitated by the negative reporting of largely the same media (see Hartleb 2004; Klein & Ohr 2002).

Notwithstanding these examples, there is much debate about whether the normative bias of the coverage has much effect on the success of the populist radical right. While one could logically assert that *positive* media coverage favors the populist radical right, common political wisdom says that *any* publicity is good publicity. In fact, this position is particularly popular among populist radical right politicians (the late Hans Janmaat used it as a mantra). Given that potential voters of populist radical right parties tend to be most suspicious of elites, including the media, the argument that even (highly) negative coverage in the media will bring these parties electoral success, because of the rise in their profile and the salience of their issues (e.g. Wendt 2003), makes perfect sense. As one supporter of Australian populist rightist Pauline Hanson told a journalist, "[y]ou people in the media don't get it: the more you criticize her, the more we rally for her" (in Goot 1999: 217).

Unfortunately, it is very hard to test empirically the exact influence of "the media" on the electoral success of the populist radical right. First of all, there is virtually no country where populist radical right parties are truly ignored, i.e. where they are deprived of what Margaret Thatcher has called the "oxygen of publicity" (Goot 1999). This is even true for countries where the media claim to follow a strategy of "silencing to death" (*doodzwijgen*), like Belgium (Wallonia) and the Netherlands (e.g Coffé 2004; De Witte 1997). Similarly, there are few countries with unsuccessful populist radical right parties that receive a relatively high level of media attention.[10] In most cases high media attention goes hand in hand

---

[10] A notable exception is Germany, where in 2000–01 public television devoted an average of no less than thirty minutes a day to "the extreme right" (Schellenberg 2005: 41).

with strong populist radical right parties and is often at least as much the result of the parties' successes as (merely) the cause. After all, even if the media would like to downplay the importance of the parties, which might still be a possibility when they are electorally and politically insignificant, it becomes virtually impossible once they are the major opposition party or even a part of the (national) government. This also suggests that the effect of the media will be most pronounced in the phase of electoral breakthrough.

In short, it is a truism to state that "media action is ineluctably embroiled in the emergence of neopopulist movements" (Mazzoleni 2003: 6). In today's world, "the media" have an effect upon virtually everything public and political, although less than usually claimed (Newton 2006), and there is no reason to assume that the populist radical right would be an exception to this general rule. The real question is: *what* effect? Or, in moral terms, is the media a friend or foe of the populist radical right (e.g. Mazzoleni 2004)? A general answer would have to be that "the media," as a heterogeneous sphere of institutions, is *both* friend *and* foe of populist radical right parties. There are periods in which significant media actors are explicit or implicit friends, such as the *Neue Kronen Zeitung* in the 1990s, and there are others when they are explicit or implicit foes, like *De Morgen* in Belgium.[11] In most periods, however, they are both at the same time, pushing the (salience of) key issues of the populist radical right while simultaneously denouncing the parties themselves. Whether or not the parties benefit depends to a large extent on the interaction between the populist radical right and other political parties in the country; for example, can populist radical right parties establish issue ownership? Do they have media-genic leaders (and the others not or less)?, etc.

10.6 Conclusion

Political opportunity structures are facilitating rather than determining factors in the success and failure of populist radical right parties. They explain not so much why parties will gain support from voters, but rather why this support does or does not lead to electoral breakthrough and persistence. Overall, it seems fair to argue that the political opportunity structure plays a more important role in the electoral breakthrough stage; particularly with respect to political and cultural factors.

---

[11] Most longitudinal studies of the relationship between the media and populist radical right parties distinguish between various periods in which very different (dominant) relationships between the two exist (e.g. Mazzoleni *et al.* 2003).

In the electoral breakthrough phase the political opportunity structure entails a mix of institutional, political, and cultural factors. At the institutional level, the electoral system plays a limited role; plurality systems will hinder electoral breakthrough. However, very few European countries have (pure) plurality electoral systems, therefore this variable does not account for much variance. At the political level, convergence between the major established parties facilitates electoral breakthrough. Whether this convergence must follow a period of polarization remains to be answered in cross-national and cross-temporal empirical research. At the cultural level the detrimental effects of stigmatization (explaining failure) and the facilitating effects of a broad nativist subculture (explaining success) are particularly important. A fascist past might favor the development of linkages between nativist subcultures and mainstream politics. Finally, the media can encourage (or obstruct) electoral breakthrough by influencing which issues gain salience, and providing positive (including neutral) reporting on populist radical right actors can help them gain electoral breakthrough.

In the electoral persistence phase, some of these factors lose much of their importance (see Jungerstam-Mulders 2003). Moreover, although political opportunity structures are relatively stable, they can and do change over time: both in *content* and in *impact*. Most importantly, once a populist radical right party achieves electoral breakthrough, it can have a significant effect on the content of the political opportunity structure, changing it in a more favorable direction. The cultural level remains very important, because of its influence on the populist radical right party itself, which becomes one of the prime factors in its future success (or the lack thereof), as will be developed in the next chapter.

This is most important with respect to the role of the media. While positive media coverage is important to achieve electoral breakthrough, in the persistence phase the role of the media declines in two ways: (1) parties will be involved in creating their own image and will thus become less reliant upon positive coverage by the media, which will indeed lead to a situation in which any attention is good attention (particularly when they have established issue ownership); (2) the media will have less space to determine whether or not to report on these parties, as electoral breakthrough makes them newsworthy.

At the moment, the situation in Eastern Europe is still somewhat different from that in most West European countries. The differentiation between the mainstream and radical parties is less clear, partly because of the radical rhetoric of some mainstream parties, partly because of the high level of elite volatility, i.e. the still high number of "new" parties of "old" elites in each election. Consequently, it is more difficult for populist radical right parties to present themselves as the only alternative to the "antinational corrupt elite." In addition, many party systems are still polarized between two party blocks, thereby decreasing the chances for nonaligned populist radical right parties. This applies to a somewhat lesser extent to the Southern European countries of the second wave of democratization.

However, without wanting to argue that the East will necessarily become identical to the West, there are good reasons to suggest that the differences will continue to decrease. First, a higher level of stabilization of the various party systems is inevitable, as recent developments in various countries indicate (e.g. Bakke & Sitter 2005; Toole 2000).[12] This will lead to a clearer and more consistent identification of the "established parties" in the various countries. Second, party politics in Western Europe has become more fluid and less predictable since the end of the Cold War. Consequently, the two regions grow closer together, not just because the East replicates the "Western model," but also because the West increasingly shows some "Eastern" features.

It is important to note that many aspects of a favorable political opportunity structure are conducive to populist or outside parties more generally. Political opportunity structures alone cannot explain why the populist radical right rather than, for example, neoliberal or social populist parties profit from openings within it. Understanding its impact on the populist radical right in particular requires consideration of demand-side variables, on the one hand, and internal supply-side factors, i.e. the populist radical right party itself, on the other. It is to the latter that we now turn in our final explanatory chapter.

---

[12] It might be true that this stability shows itself differently outside of Western Europe, i.e. more at the mass than at the elite level (cf. Birch 2001), but the hypothesized results will be largely the same, if possibly a bit slower and more moderate.

11 Internal supply-side: the populist radical right party

> [S]uccessful parties recognize both the opportunities and constraints offered by the prevailing political environment and design their actions accordingly.
> (Berman 1997: 118)

11.1 Introduction

Irrespective of how favorable the breeding ground and the political opportunity structure might be to new political parties, they merely present political actors with a series of possibilities. In the end, it is still up to the populist radical right parties to profit from them. In line with scholarship on political parties in general, populist radical right parties should no longer be seen simply as "hapless victims of their economic or demographic environments, but as . . . the active shapers of their own fates" (Berman 1997: 102; also Sartori 1990). In other words, the party itself should be included as a major factor in explaining its electoral success and failure.

The strategies of contemporary populist radical right parties are part of almost every account of the party family. Nearly every scholar points to the importance of the "modern image" of populist radical right parties. Indeed, image production by these parties has generated some marvelously creative terminology, including "Haiderization" to designate the process (Marcus 2000: 36) and "designer fascism" in reference to the final product (Wolin 1998). This process of "restyling" is often believed to be only superficial, involving mainly the selection of physically attractive representatives, such as former beauty queens and (young) men in tailor-made suits, rather than a genuine transformation of the ideology and style of the parties.

However, in addition to the likely appeal of these purely decorative aspects, more fundamental elements (can) decide whether a populist radical right party will gain and sustain electoral support. Among the most important internal factors are party ideology, leadership, and organization. While these are occasionally mentioned in the literature, their conceptual and theoretical elaboration has remained meager.[1] In this chapter the literature on these three important aspects of populist radical right parties will be critically assessed with the aim of developing a clearer picture of the various factors that influence the electoral success and failure of populist radical right parties, and the theoretical linkages between them.

11.2   Ideology

Party ideology is the most frequently mentioned internal supply-side factor in the literature. Many authors attribute the success of populist radical right parties largely to their relatively moderate ideology, although there is debate about whether the moderation is real or strategic. Various scholars even see a dichotomy within the larger party family: on the one hand, the "old" or "extreme" parties are unsuccessful *because of* their ideological extremity or oldness, and, on the other hand, the "new" or "moderate" parties are successful *because of* the moderation or newness of their ideology (e.g. Cole 2005; Taggart 1995; Ignazi 1992). Paul Hainsworth has summarized this argument as follows: "Indeed, the contemporary extreme right has been more successful electorally in Western Europe when it has been able to mark its distance from past extremist forms, such as Nazism and fascism, and appear as a populist response to current anxieties" (2000b: 1).

A more elaborate framework has been provided by Kitschelt and McGann, who distinguish between four different ideological strands within the "radical right" political family: fascist, welfare chauvinist, new radical right, and populist antistatist (1995: 19ff.). Parties achieve different levels of electoral success in part due to demand-side and external supply-side factors, in part because of their ideological strand, with the "winning formula" of the new radical right being the most significant. In essence, their argument largely resembles that summarized by Hainsworth: ideological links to the historical extreme right lead to electoral failure.

Not surprisingly, there is no consensus on the exact content of the "winning formula." While Kitschelt and McGann define it as "extreme

---

[1] In one of the few and most comprehensive empirical cross-national studies of populist radical right party politics to include supply-side factors, internal party factors are not included in the model that is tested, although interesting suggestions are made in the final discussion of the article (see Van der Brug *et al.* 2005). The expert studies of Marcel Lubbers (2001; Lubbers *et al.* 2002; also Norris 2005) did include them, but both the conceptualization and the operationalization are highly questionable.

and economically rightists, free-marketeering as well as politically and culturally authoritarian positions" (1995: vii), Betz sees it rather as a combination of "differentialist nativism and comprehensive protectionism" (2003a: 207). Overall, most authors are a lot closer to the latter interpretation (e.g. Decker 2004; Taggart 1995). Yet, in empirical research this broadly accepted theory does not prove very robust.

Obviously, Kitschelt and McGann claim to have tested their theoretical model successfully on the basis of a wealth of empirical data. However, whereas their thesis might be correct for the new radical right, their winning formula more aptly defines neoconservatism than the populist radical right. The model might explain the successes of Margaret Thatcher and Ronald Reagan in the 1980s, or possibly even the Danish conservative liberal Venstre (which oddly enough means "Left") and the Dutch VVD in the 1990s, but it cannot explain the success of *most* populist radical right parties during these periods. In more recent work, the authors amended aspects of their theory, though leaving the main claims intact (McGann & Kitschelt 2005; Kitschelt 2004). Their new position is somewhat closer to the operationalizations of the populist radical right more commonly found in the literature, but it leaves many important aspects unspecified (most notably their antiestablishment position; see De Lange 2007a).

Less contentious definitions by other authors have been employed in various studies that claim to provide evidence in support of the thesis that "new" or "moderate" populist radical right parties are far more successful than their "old" or "extreme" sister parties (e.g. Cole 2005; Ignazi 2003, 1992). However, the established overlap between the success and ideology of populist radical right parties is not so much the result of the strength of the theory, as of the weakness of the party classifications. Few authors provide convincing arguments for why parties are put into particular categories. Indeed, when the ideologies of the parties in question are studied in more detail, some important miscategorizations appear (Mudde 2000a; also chapter 2), significantly weakening the strength and applicability of the theory.

First and foremost, most authors group together what in our terms should be distinguished as radical and extreme right parties. There is no doubt that extreme right parties, i.e. parties that are antidemocratic and nonegalitarian, are electorally and politically unsuccessful in contemporary Europe (see also Carter 2005). However, even within the group of political parties that are labeled populist radical right here, authors distinguish between different subgroups and include some important misclassifications. For example, the Belgian VB clearly fits the "old" or "extreme" subgroup, in the definitions of Ignazi (1992) or Taggart (1995), while it would fit the "welfare chauvinist" category in the scheme of Kitschelt and

McGann (1995). In any case, it should be unsuccessful according to all three authors (Mudde 2000a). A similar argument could be developed for the Italian MSI/AN, before its full transformation into a conservative party. Although Eastern Europe is not part of the analysis of these authors, the same would apply to at least the Croatian HSP, the Romanian PRM and the Slovak SNS (e.g. Mudde 2000b). At the same time, various parties that fit the "new" or "moderate" category have clearly not been successful in electoral terms – e.g. the Dutch CD, the French MNR, or the German REP.

Obviously, this is not to say that ideological extremity is irrelevant to electoral success. However, like all potential explanatory factors, it has to be considered within the broader political context. It would make sense to argue that ideological extremity (including links to the historical extreme right) is particularly damaging to the populist radical right in countries with an unreceptive political culture. In countries where the period of the Second World War is interpreted in less absolute terms (at least within certain subcultures) – like Austria, Belgium (Flanders), Croatia, Italy, Romania, or Slovakia – the stain of extremity is less damaging. Nonetheless, even in these cases a more modern and moderate ideology and image is advantageous to populist radical right parties. However, it is neither a necessary nor a sufficient condition for electoral success.

What might be more important than the ideology itself is the presentation of that ideology through party propaganda. While the party image is transmitted largely through the mainstream media, and therefore outside of the control of the party, extensive professional propaganda campaigns can be very effective in generating electoral success. Indeed, well-organized parties like the FN and VB are broadly perceived as highly effective in their propaganda campaigns. However, the most striking example of this is the German DVU, a "phantom party" that gained some impressive regional successes purely on the basis of mail order campaigns (e.g. Backes & Mudde 2000).

Interestingly, many populist radical right parties have some of the best party websites in their countries. While websites currently still mainly preach to the converted (e.g. Norris 2003), the growing popularity of the internet will inevitably increase their prominence in years to come (e.g. Römmele 2003). Websites are particularly important for new and so far unsuccessful parties that for a variety of reasons (e.g. lack of money and personnel, political opposition) are unable to engage in traditional propaganda campaigns. Because websites are inexpensive to construct and maintain as well as difficult to censor, less relevant and organized populist radical right parties are able to get their message across to at least some part of the population even under a boycott by the established media (see 10.5).

Overall, it seems plausible that the (independent) media are primarily important for new (populist radical right) parties in achieving electoral breakthrough, while party propaganda plays a role chiefly during the phase of electoral persistence. By achieving electoral breakthrough, the parties pass the threshold of recognition, which means that their propaganda will no longer only reach the converted. In this phase well-developed party propaganda does not only attract the attention of outsiders with similar attitudes, it can also help transform (first-time party) voters into loyal party supporters.

11.3   Leadership

Various authors have stressed the importance of leadership to the (lack of) electoral and political success of populist radical right parties (e.g. Husbands 1998; Minkenberg 1998). Increased centralization of power and personalization of leadership have been noted for contemporary political parties in general (e.g. Panebianco 1988; Kirchheimer 1966), yet these processes are believed to be even more extremely pronounced in the case of the populist radical right party family. Several authors refer to "charismatic leaders" (e.g. Carter 2005; Zaslove 2004b; Eatwell 2003) and the "leadership principle" (Gunther & Diamond 2003), or even "*Führer*" and "*Führerparteien*" (e.g. Decker 2004; Gunther & Diamond 2003; Scharsach & Kurt 2000; Rizman 1999; Pfahl-Traughber 1994), clearly linking the contemporary populist radical right parties to the extreme right parties of the prewar period.

However, at least two very different types of leadership are important within political parties; I'll refer to them here, somewhat simplistically, as external and internal. These two orientations of party leadership roughly correspond to two key functions of political parties, i.e. the electoral and the institutional. Some leaders might be successful externally, and bring electoral success to the party, but fail miserably internally, and harm the party institutionally (for example, by frustrating qualified members or the building of a strong organization). Most of the literature has focused on external leadership, typified by the prime leader, whose role has been at times grossly overstated. Internal or institutional leadership of (other) key figures within populist radical right parties has been largely ignored or underestimated.

11.3.1   *External leadership: the enigma of charisma*

If one follows the insights from electoral research, it would make sense to assume that leaders play a particularly important role within the (populist) radical right. Anthony King has hypothesized that "the impact of leaders' personalities and other personal characteristics will be greatest when voters' emotional ties to parties are at their weakest" and "when voters can discern few other grounds – whether grounds of performance or of policy" (2002: 41–2), both of which seem to be the case with regard to most populist radical right parties.

The literature on populism in general stresses the importance of charismatic leaders (e.g. Weyland 2001; Papadopoulos 2000; Taggart 2000). Similarly, in the works on the contemporary populist radical right, electoral success is very often related to the alleged charismatic qualities of the party leader (e.g. Probst 2003; Immerfall 1998). Consequently, the literature is filled with phrases such as "l'effet Le Pen" (Plenel & Rollat 1984), the "Haider Phenomenon" (Sully 1997), or the "Schirinowski-Effekt" (Eichwede 1994). Electoral studies do provide (some) support for the argument that leaders are *at certain times* very important to the electoral successes of populist radical right parties. For example, Ian McAllister and his collaborators have demonstrated that Vladimir Zhirinovsky was "a major factor in support for the Liberal Democrats" in the 1995 Duma elections (1997: 120).[2] Similar convincing evidence has been provided in support of the importance of Jean-Marie Le Pen or Jörg Haider (e.g. Mayer 2002; Plasser & Ulram 1995).

Still, the importance of charismatic party leaders should not be overstated. There are various (moderately) successful populist radical right parties that have not always been led by "charismatic" personalities: for example, István Cszurka (MIÉP), Daniel Féret (FNb), Roman Giertych (LPR), or Pia Kjærsgaard (DFP) can hardly be described as charismatic leaders according to any definition. In addition, there are unsuccessful parties with leaders who are broadly regarded as charismatic; the most prominent example was Franz Schönhuber (REP).

However, even leaders like Le Pen and Haider, whose charisma is not even contested by their opponents, seem to have been less important in the persistence of party support than is generally assumed. While they were crucial in getting many people *into* the party electorate in the late 1980s and early 1990s, their role declined in the following years (e.g. Ignazi 2003; Plasser & Ulram 1995). Nonna Mayer (1997) has described this process as a development "du vote Lepéniste au vote Frontiste" (from the Le Pen vote to the National Front vote). Thus, it seems that

---

[2] It should be noted, however, that party leaders play a more important role in the less institutionalized party politics of postcommunist Europe than in the fairly stable party politics of the Western world. For example, in the 1995 Duma elections "leader evaluation" (i.e. a positive evaluation of the party leader) was a major factor for all political parties (McAllister *et al.* 1997).

external (charismatic) leadership is more important in the breakthrough phase, while party organization is imperative in the phase of electoral persistence.

This could also point to a broader process of socialization that voters of successful populist radical right parties go through: while charismatic *leaders* are important in bringing in new voters, through what Eatwell (2006, 2005) refers to as "centripetal charisma," the (well-structured) *party* socializes them into true party supporters (see also below). This process seems reminiscent of what Weber (1987) has described as the routinization of charisma.

Another important qualification to be made is that charismatic leaders are almost always polarizing personalities, to a large extent "because the symbolic logic of charisma hangs upon binary coding and salvation narratives" (Smith 2000: 103). In other words, you either like them, or you hate them. While many commentators have focused exclusively on the former, the importance of the latter should not be underestimated. Le Pen has been an important reason for people to vote for the FN, but he also seems to have been a compelling reason not to do so. In various surveys large groups of the French electorate considered Le Pen "a handicap" for the development of the FN. In March 1998, not surprisingly around the time of growing opposition of the group-Mégret within the FN, no less than 59 percent of the French electorate considered Le Pen a handicap to the party while only 29 percent did not (Mayer 2002: 177; also Minkenberg & Schain 2003: 177).

The key problem with the variable "charismatic leader" is the vagueness of the term. Some authors even speak of "the inherent tautological nature of the concept of charisma" (Van der Brug *et al.* 2005: 542). However, operationalizing charisma as electoral success is not an inherent conceptual problem, but an extrinsic practical one. Moreover, it shows that many scholars in the field do not use the concept in the Weberian sense, which is relative, but in an absolute sense. Charisma does not refer to an essentialist set of personal characteristics of a leader. What makes a leader charismatic depends more on the followers than on the leader (e.g. Weber 1987 [1919]); i.e. the key is the "charismatic bond" between the two (Eatwell 2006: 142). Robert Tucker has summarized this position succinctly: "To *be* a charismatic leader is essentially to be *perceived* as such" (1968: 737). This does not render the concept useless in empirical research (cf. Smith 2000; Van Dooren 1994), but it necessarily invokes another notoriously hazardous concept in defining charisma, that of political culture (cf. Eatwell 2005).

Charismatic leadership is advantageous to political parties. But how advantageous it will be depends upon the political culture and the political system. For example, strong and dominant leaders, charismatic or not, will profit more from majoritarian and personalized institutional systems, most notably where presidents or prime ministers are directly elected by the people, than from political systems that are consensual and where the institution of the political party itself (still) plays an important role. A good example is France, where the institutional condition is strengthened by the political culture of personal leadership based on the towering symbol of the Fifth Republic, former president Charles de Gaulle (e.g. Schmidt 2003).

11.3.2 Internal (practical) leadership

External leadership, of which charismatic leadership is one (extreme) form, is just one side of the coin of successful leadership. Equally vital to the party, and its political success, is internal leadership. After all, political parties are not just electoral vehicles that contest elections, even though this is their most important feature (e.g. Sartori 1976), they are also organizations that recruit and socialize political personnel, design and run electoral campaigns, and ultimately (try to) influence public policy.

According to common wisdom in the literature on political parties, charismatic leadership and party institutionalization seldom go hand in hand (e.g. Harmel & Svåsand 1993; Panebianco 1988). Among the reasons mentioned for the improbability of charismatic parties becoming institutionalized, Angelo Panebianco mentions that the leader often deliberately tries to block the process, that charisma cannot be objectified, and that the organization is forced to fold at its leader's political eclipse (1988: 147). In other words, a successful external leader, who brings the party electoral victory, is normally a bad internal leader, who weakens the organization and thereby undermines the political success of the party (e.g. Probst 2003). This is clearly the message of this disgruntled ex-MP of the Italian LN: "Lega is Bossi and Bossi is Lega, the last Leninist-Stalinist party. To survive within Lega, if Bossi is in the tenth floor, you must stop at the fifth. If you arrive at the ninth floor, you will end up down in the cellar. He will never allow the growth of intermediate cadres and a ruling class" (in Gomez-Reino 2001: 15).

The process of party institutionalization is divided into three different phases, which each require a different form of leadership (Pedahzur & Brichta 2002; Harmel and Svåsand 1993). In the first phase, the prime objective of the party is *identification*, i.e. getting the party message across, which is best achieved by a charismatic leader, who is both a creator and a preacher. In the second phase, the emphasis is on *organization* of the party, which requires a more practical leader who can effectively build the party infrastructure. Finally, in the third stage, *stabilization*, the leader should be a stabilizer of both the organization and the electoral success of the party. While most authors would contend that charismatic leaders become a liability to the party after the first stage, recent research provides evidence that "charismatic parties" can become institutionalized (Pedahzur & Brichta 2002).

Although there is disagreement in the literature about the exact combination of features, and the likelihood of their occurrence, there is a general assumption that party leadership is the affair of one person, particularly in the case of charismatic leadership. However, as the cases of the FN and VB clearly demonstrate, charismatic leaders can combine different skills; Filip Dewinter is both a preacher and an organizer. Moreover, charismatic leaders can work with more practical leaders, even if this leads to tensions. The creator and preacher Jean-Marie Le Pen and the organizer Bruno Mégret, or preacher-organizer Dewinter with the stabilizers Gerolf Annemans and Frank Vanhecke are examples of such complementarity.

11.4   Organization

While it might be an overstatement to speak of a "general consensus" in the field (Carter 2005: 64), many recent studies note the crucial importance of party organization for the electoral success of populist radical right parties (e.g. Betz 1998). While agreeing with the general point that party organization is a key variable in explaining the highly diverse levels of electoral success of the populist radical right, I would argue that it is more important in explaining its *persistence* than its breakthrough (cf. Coffé 2004). A strong party organization enhances party cohesion and leadership stability, without which other parties will not take the populist radical right party seriously and voters will not continue to support it (Betz 2002b).

Much literature on the populist radical right links party organization to electoral success, arguing that a well-developed party infrastructure is critical to electoral successes. Empirical evidence for this thesis is often limited to anecdotal references to a handful of successful or unsuccessful parties. Unfortunately, the few authors who have used this variable in systematic empirical research remain vague about the operationalization of party institutionalization, relying either on "expert studies" (e.g. Norris 2005; Lubbers 2001) or on insights from case studies (e.g. Carter 2005) that are limited in their generalizability. Very little empirical information is available on the internal life and structure of populist radical right parties, thus it is highly problematic to speak of "experts" in this respect (with possibly a handful of notable exceptions).

11.4.1   Cause or consequence?

A variety of examples prove that incidental electoral success can be achieved without any organizational backup. In June 1993 the Russian LDPR was "little more than a group of fifty individuals with affiliates in only a few dozen cities," yet half a year later the party won 22.9 percent of the vote in the parliamentary elections (Clark 1995: 771). Slightly less dramatically, the DVU gained 12.9 percent in the 2002 regional elections in Saxony-Anhalt, a postwar record for the German (populist) radical right, despite counting hardly more than thirty members in that state (Backes & Mudde 2000). In the 2005 Bulgarian parliamentary elections, the electoral coalition Nacionalen sayuz Ataka (National Union Attack, NSA) gained almost 9 percent of the vote despite being a mere two months in existence;[3] the LPR had already established the potential of new contenders through its success in the Polish parliamentary elections of 2001.

However, electoral success can hardly be *sustained* without a functioning party organization. A well-functioning organization is essential to a party's translation of its electoral success into political influence, as incompetent personnel, disorganized behavior, and internal splits undermine its bargaining power. The examples of the effects of organizational pathology are manifold, including the Dutch CD in many local councils, the German DVU in virtually all regional parliaments, the Bulgarian Ataka in the national parliament, or the German REP in the European Parliament (e.g. Hoffmann & Lepszy 1998; Van Riel & Van Holsteyn 1998; Butterwege et al. 1997; Schmidt 1997).

The relationship between a dysfunctional party organization and political failure seems, at first sight, the chicken or egg question: does a bad party organization bring political failure or does political failure prevent a party from establishing a good organization? While continuing electoral defeat will definitely weaken the opportunities for building a well-organized political party, many populist radical right parties have imploded only *after* their electoral breakthrough. For example, the German REP got into a leadership battle after its biggest electoral successes in 1989, the Dutch CD always saw party splits following electoral success, and the Czech SPR-RSČ was doing fine in the polls before it

---

[3] The NSA is a coalition of five radical right groupuscules: the Protection Union of Patriotic Forces, the Warriors of the Reserve, the Fatherland National Movement for Salvation, the Bulgarian National Patriotic Party, and the Zora Political Circle (*Radio Bulgaria* 30/06/2005; on some of these groups, see Ivanov & Ilieva 2005). After various internal struggles, the bulk of the parliamentary faction went on as Partija Ataka (Party Attack, Ataka).

imploded in 1998. Even the most famous party split, i.e. that of the French FN in 1998–99, happened at the zenith of the party's success; in the words of one observer, "never had the FN been more influential than it was immediately prior to the crisis" (Adler 2001: 35).

To a large extent then, most badly organized populist radical right parties were the victim of their own success. They were unable to cope with the pressure conferred by their substantial electoral victory without a well-structured party organization. Lacking the capacity to fill positions on the basis of objective (or at least broadly accepted) criteria and with competent personnel, for example, most party leaders appointed personal cronies to lucrative positions, causing great frustration among rivals and long-standing party activists.

The organizational weakness of some parties can also be seen in their inability to contest the same districts over sustained periods of time. In one of the few comprehensive studies, Lisa Harrison concludes that "we rarely see the same *Gemeinden* and even Länder being contested in consecutive elections, primarily due to the organizational difficulties which have plagued far right parties in Germany" (1997: 147). Comparable situations have been noted with respect to unsuccessful populist radical right parties in other countries. For example, the British BNP contested only fourteen of the same districts in the 2001 and 1997 parliamentary elections, losing votes in all but one (Mudde 2002b). The Belgian FNb has shown a similar inability to build upon its success (Delwit 2007).

Finally, organizational weakness can have disastrous effects on governing parties. There is a growing debate in the literature on the alleged inability of the populist radical right to govern (e.g. Delwit & Poirier 2007; Fröhlich-Steffen & Rensmann 2005a). Pointing to various recent examples, including the Austrian FPÖ and the Italian LN, some authors go as far as arguing that populist (radical right) parties are intrinsically incapable of governing. The alleged incapacity is linked to their leadership structure, which supposedly prevents the construction of a strong party organization. Whether intrinsic or not, organizational weakness has caused most populist radical right parties problems in office, which were in turn punished by the voters in the following elections. Christopher T. Husbands has referred to this as the "'shooting-themselves-in-the-foot' theme" (2001: 24).[4]

---

[4] Populist radical right parties have not been the only parties to suffer from the combination of weak party organization and quick electoral success. Neoliberal populist parties like the Danish FPd, the Dutch LPF, and the German PRO or Schill Party (e.g. Decker 2003a) are extreme examples of this phenomenon – although in all cases events involving the charismatic leader also played a role (prison, murder and scandal, respectively).

Interestingly, in some cases party splits did not so much diminish the number of populist radical right votes, at least initially, but simply divided them among different parties. For example, both in France, in the 1999 European elections, and in Slovakia, in the 2002 parliamentary elections, the total vote for the original party and its split was not much less than that for the original party in the previous elections. The relatively constant level of support notwithstanding, in both cases the political influence of the populist radical right party family seriously decreased: in Slovakia neither of the two parties (PSNS and SNS) returned to parliament, whereas in France the populist radical right delegation in the European Parliament was more than halved, decreasing from eleven MEPs in 1994 to five in 1999 (all FN).

11.4.2 Internal organization

While the process of party failure is fairly easy to trace, if only because examples are abundant, party success is notably more difficult to study. First of all, electoral persistence is rare within Europe. Second, what constitutes a well-organized (populist radical right) political party? Various authors have linked populist radical right parties to a specific type of party organization; some have even defined these parties in part upon that basis (e.g. Fröhlich-Steffen & Rensmann 2005b; Decker 2004; Taggart 1995). Generally speaking, these scholars note that the parties have a minimalist organization, i.e. simple structures and few members, which is structured hierarchically and completely dominated by a charismatic leader. However, as they often link the populist radical right party's organizational model to their ideology, this would presuppose that all populist radical right parties have the same organizational structure. In this way, it cannot explain cross-national or cross-temporal variation.

The internal life of political parties is an endless frustration to party scholars; it is extremely difficult to study. Most organizations prefer to keep their important decision-making processes out of the public eye or else cloak them in official democratic procedures. Populist radical right parties, given their general suspicion of academics and journalists, are even more inclined toward circumspection, fearing that the information they provide will not only be used for strictly academic purposes (not always without reason). Consequently, it is frequently impossible to get reliable information on even the most basic characteristics of a party.

Take the issue of party membership. As far as numbers are available, they are either based on information provided by the parties themselves or on wild speculation. In the case of the (former) Czech SPR-RSČ, some authors just repeated the party's official number of 55,000 members (e.g. Jenne 1998; Turnovec 1997), which according to virtually all experts was highly inflated, whereas others took educated guesses of a few thousand (e.g. Segert 2005a; Havelková 2002). In the Netherlands, Hans Janmaat maintained for years that the membership of the CD was growing rapidly, at the same time claiming a consistent 3,000 members for several years in a row. However, according to various experts, even that number was highly inflated. The real number was estimated to be between 1,500 and 1,000, of whom at most some 100 were active (see in Mudde & Van Holsteyn 2000: 149). In a flagrant inflation of membership, the party paper of the Italian LN claimed 200,000 members in March 1992, 40,000 in June, and again 200,000 in November that year. However, even according to its own account the party had at best some 90,000 "members" in 1993 (Gomez-Reino 2001: 9–10).

It seems safe to assume that, on average, populist radical right parties have relatively few members and at best a moderately elaborated party organization, compared to the older, established parties. Indeed, this is true for most relatively new political parties (e.g. Tamas 2002; Mair & Van Biezen 2001). Some authors argue that populist radical rightists prefer to construct *Bewegungsparteien* (movement parties) around charismatic leaders (e.g. Gunther & Diamond 2003), which is said to be in line with their alleged antiparty ideology (e.g. Geden 2005; Mény & Surel 2002a). At the organization level, however, most parties remained at best very small movements. And despite their lack of elaborate organizational structures, they have strict internal hierarchies and demand a high level of internal discipline of their members (see also below).

The FN is one of the few contemporary examples of a populist radical right party that had some degree of success in following the old model of the mass party.[5] From the beginning, it has been a collection of different "tendencies" (Veugelers & Chiarini 2002: 99), ranging from *nouvelle droite* (new right) think tanks like the Club de l'Horloge to "national solidarists" of the Mouvement Solidariste, and orthodox Catholics of the Chrétienté-Solidarité (Christian Solidarity). While all factions have their own leaders and suborganizations, they are all integrated in the FN through the towering presence of party leader Jean-Marie Le Pen. Before the split in 1999, the FN had between 70,000 and 80,000 members, organized in 100 party federations throughout France and its overseas territories (Declair 1999: 159). The party still

---

[5] The FN was probably more influenced by the organization model of the Italian MSI than by the historical mass party models of the Catholic and socialist parties (Ignazi 1998). The Italian LN also tried to create a mass party, but failed (see Gomez-Reino 2001). For an overview of its many *associazioni* (associations), see www.leganord.org/c_1_associazioni_paginasezione.htm (read 25/07/2005).

consists of a wide range of sub- and front-organizations, the so-called "sous-société national-frontiste" (Birnbaum 1992: 219), including various interest groups, which provide it with roots into French society that stretch well beyond the party membership (e.g. Bastow 1998; Ivaldi 1998; Fromm & Kernbach 1994: 180–95).

The use of front-organizations, a strategy most associated with Trotskyist groups, is used more broadly within the populist radical right. Also in this respect the Belgian VB is the most loyal copy-cat of the FN. The party has founded various single-issue front-organizations in recent times, none officially part of the VB itself: these include the Actiecomité tegen het stemrecht voor vreemdelingen (Action Committee against the Right to Vote for Aliens), Leefbaar Antwerpen (Livable Antwerp), and the Comité "Nee tegen Turkije" (Committee "No to Turkey"). Christoph Blocher, the leader of the Swiss SVP, has founded the AUNS to mobilize for referendums, most notably on foreign policy issues (see Hennecke 2003).

Practically all successful populist radical right parties can count upon the support of a strong and successful youth organization, such as the French Front National de la Jeunesse (FNJ), the Austrian Ring Freiheitlicher Jugend (Circle of Freedomite Youth, RFJ), or the Belgian Vlaams Belang Jongeren (Flemish Interest Youth, VBJ). The Polish Mlodziez Wszechpolska (All-Polish Youth), the youth-wing of the LPR, is even the strongest youth organization of all political parties in Poland (Kostrzębski 2005). These youth organizations tend to be more radical than the mother party, which sometimes leads to embarrassing liaisons with extreme right groups or individuals, and they tend to be very active both nationally and internationally. More importantly, they bring new and young people into the broader movement, socialize them into its culture, educate them in both ideological and practical terms, and then promote them to the mother party. To a large extent, they are the lifeblood of the party, which ensures the organization's survival beyond its historic founding leaders.

While it is difficult to provide a concise description of a strong party organization, recent developments seem to indicate that two aspects increase the chance of electoral persistence and even political survival: a grass-roots basis and local *Hochbürge* (strongholds). Virtually all successful populist radical right parties have strong links to the grass-roots and have based their organizational elaboration and electoral success on one or more local and regional strongholds; for example, Antwerp for the VB, Carinthia for the FPÖ, Cluj for the PRM, the southern region of PACA for the FN, and cities like Žilina for the Slovak SNS. In the case of electoral defeats and even party splits, such local and regional strongholds provide much needed sources of finance and patronage as well as bases from which the party can start rebuilding its electorate and organization.

11.4.3   Internal democracy

According to some authors, populist radical right parties are organized upon the Marxist-Leninist principle of "democratic centralism" (e.g. Minkenberg 1998; Mudde 1995a). Unfortunately, very little empirical research is available, but the few studies that do exist mostly confirm a strong authoritarian and centralist party structure (e.g. Segert 2005a: 193–4; DeClair 1999), if with some qualifications (e.g. Deschouwer 2001; Gomez-Reino 2001). On the basis of the 1998 party statute of the Italian LN, Anna Cento Bull and Mark Gilbert (2001: 121–4) paint a picture of a highly centralized party under the strict leadership of Umberto Bossi, which structurally resembles the (former) communist PCI. With regard to the VB, different authors have shown that both formally and informally it is the least internally democratic of all major Flemish political parties (e.g. Jagers 2002; Deschouwer 2001).

Some populist radical right parties do not even try to create a democratic façade. Motivated by both practical and ideological considerations, they simply create a minimalist structure around the party leader(ship), limiting the lower echelons to an advisory capacity. For example, whereas the LDPR initially had some nominally democratic internal elections and procedures,[6] these were suspended in 1994, and all major party positions have since been filled through personal appointment by party leader Zhirinovsky (Shenfield 2001: 98–100). Tellingly, Evgenii Mikhailov, the former LDPR governor of the *oblast* (region) Pskov, said about the role of Zhirinovsky: "[He] does not interfere in operational questions. But I get his approval for any decision concerning the most important policy directions" (in Slider 1999: 756).[7]

Even where populist radical right parties do have relatively democratic statutes, which some countries require as a precondition for official registration (e.g. Germany; see Venice Commission 1999), the practice within the parties is not so democratic and transparent. While the populist radical right is certainly not unique in this respect (e.g. Michels 1925), their undemocratic tendencies stand out among party families, with the

---

[6] Both in terms of ideology and party organization, the program and statute of the initial party, then still named Liberal Democratic Party of the Soviet Union, were perfectly democratic (see LDPSU 1990).

[7] In 1993 the party also officially adopted the subtitle "The Party of Zhirinovsky," while its newspapers are known as "Zhirinovsky's Truth" and "Zhirinovsky's Falcon" (Service 1998: 182).

notable exception of Marxist-Leninist parties. There are at least two reasons for this: (1) the limited number of individuals active within the party (leadership), which creates significant personal overlap between functions and institutions; (2) the importance of patronage to the leader(ship), strengthened by the fact that many leading members either had mediocre careers before becoming professional politicians, or have no way back into their old careers because of stigmatization through their engagement within the populist radical right. This has led to a particularly high number of family relations between leading party members within populist radical right parties (e.g. Gomez-Reino 2001; DeClair 1999).

In some cases, party leaders run "their" political party as a small family business; or, according to their opponents, a political fiefdom. After having been kicked out of the CP, Janmaat made sure that this could not happen again in "his" new party. Together with his partner and later wife Wil Schuurman he dominated the CD at all levels. The only time the party had more than one MP, Janmaat was joined by Schuurman and Wim Elshout; the latter was jokingly described as the "adopted son" within the party. Additionally, the party office was housed in one of Janmaat's private properties, rented out according to competitive market prices, while Schuurman's son was the only official employee. The colonization of the Czech SPR-RSČ by party leader Sládek was even more extreme; his stepdaughter and mistress were MPs, while his wife worked for the party. According to some disgruntled former party members all state financing for the party went "exclusively to Sladek," who used the money, among other things, to build a very luxurious house in the country (*CTK* 21/06/1998; also Penc & Urban 1998).

Nonetheless, it would be incorrect to regard all populist radical right parties as *Führerparteien* or one-*man* parties. First of all, history shows that these alleged *Führer* are not always so crucial to or almighty within the party. For example, only two years after one scholar had proclaimed "[w]ithin the SNS, Slota's position as leader is unquestioned" (Fried 1997: 101), he was ousted as party leader. A similar fate befell Franz Schönhuber, often portrayed as the *Führer* of the German REP. Second, many populist radical right parties are far more than mere vehicles of the leader. In fact, among the more successful cases one finds some parties with several strong leadership figures (e.g. SRS and VB). And, third, some parties do not even have one strong leader.

11.4.4 Practical leadership

Why do some populist radical right parties have strong organizations while others do not? This is not an easy question to answer. Without any doubt, the person of the leader plays an important role. After having been thrown out of the CP, Janmaat frustrated all attempts of would-be leaders within his CD. Similarly, the erratic behavior and problematic personality of Sládek goes a long way toward explaining the organizational weakness of the Czech SPR-RSČ. In sharp contrast, the lack of personal ego of founding leader Karel Dillen enabled him to bring various ambitious young leaders into the party as part of the Operatie Verjonging (Operation Rejuvenation), which has been vital to the elaboration and professionalization of the party organization of the VB (Mudde 1995a; Dewinter & Van Overmeire 1993).

Obviously, organizational talent and practical leadership are also vital to this process. Filip Dewinter has an almost unique combination of external and internal leadership qualities: he is both a charismatic leader, ranking among the top Belgian politicians in terms of preferential votes, and a talented practical leader, as he demonstrated by founding the thriving VBJ and by building and elaborating the organization of the VB. In the shadow of Le Pen, Bruno Mégret's skillful internal leadership has been instrumental in developing the FN from a loose confederation of distinct groups into a well-organized political party.

In this respect, Eatwell's distinction between "centripetal charisma" and "coterie charisma" is important to note. Most studies focus exclusively on the former, i.e. "the ability of leaders to attract a broad swathe of support by becoming the personalization of politics" (2004: 2). However, charisma can also play a role internally, i.e. "the leader's appeal to an inner core" (Eatwell 2004: 2). This coterie charisma can keep a party with strong subdivisions together, as is the case with Le Pen in the FN. But it can also be crucial in activating and disciplining the membership. Importantly, while some leaders are charismatic both externally and internally (like Dewinter or Le Pen), others enjoy only coterie charisma (like Csurka and Dillen).

Well-developed sections within the party, particularly if headed by coterie charismatic leaders, can even instill some form of "subparty identification." Klandermans and Mayer found that "inside the larger organizations like the AN, the VB, or the FN there is [sic] a whole lot of subgroups that might be more important as a source of identification than the organization as a whole" (2005: 273). If managed well, the possibility of subparty identities allows for the accommodation of different subgroups within a party. However, it can also promote and strengthen internal struggles, thereby leading to weaker party loyalties than exist within smaller and more homogeneous parties.

11.4.5 Fractionalism

Finally, we could also ask the opposite question: why do populist radical right parties split? This is a question that only a few people have explicitly addressed. According to the former leader of the BNP and NF, the late John Tyndall, populist radical right parties split simply because it is "human nature" (in Holmes 2000: 152). In a more academic account, Michael Minkenberg (1998: 369) argued that the French FN split was the logical result of its electoral growth, i.e. of its success. A similar argument can be made regarding splits in the Dutch CP (and later CD) or the German REP. However, in the cases of the Czech SPR-RSČ and Slovak SNS personal differences seem more significant than organizational overload.

Jonathan Marcus has called factionalism "a perennial problem" for the populist radical right (2000: 35). Whether the populist radical right is indeed more prone to internal splits than other party families is debatable. Factionalism is not specific to populist radical right parties, or nonmainstream parties more generally: virtually all political parties experience factionalism and splits, particularly in the early stages of their institutionalization (cf. Pedersen 1982). Moreover, other nonmainstream party families have been at least as notorious for their infighting, most notably Trotskyists and Maoists (e.g. March & Mudde 2005; Alexander 2001; Newman 1994). One could argue that radical parties in general face internal pressures between *Fundis* (fundamentalists/ideologues) and *Realos* (realists/pragmatists).

Irrespective of whether factionalism is indeed more common among populist radical right parties than among established parties, there is no doubt that the effects have been particularly detrimental to populist radical right parties. The reasons are practical rather than ideological: populist radical right parties are usually younger organizations and (thus) less institutionalized than established parties, rendering them more dependent upon one or a few individuals (cf. Tamas 2002). The recent cases of the Austrian FPÖ-BZÖ and the French FN-MNR splits tend to support the institutionalization thesis: both relatively old and well-organized parties seem to (have) overcome their splits without disappearing into political oblivion.

11.5   Internationalization

Most electoral studies of party politics work with the implicit assumption that political parties compete in a more or less closed national political system. However, in these globalizing times no country is immune to developments outside of its borders. Consequently, developments with respect to a populist radical right party in one (European) country can have significant effects on the opportunities for populist radical right parties in other (European) countries.

Martin Schain and his collaborators (2002b: 16–17) have argued that the internationalization of populist radical right party success can occur in at least three ways: (1) assistance and support from populist right parties to like-minded parties across borders; (2) one (or more) populist radical right party providing a model for success to others; and (3) a successful party in country A can make the populist radical right program more acceptable in country B. So far, little research is available on any of these three points, so the following discussion should be regarded as highly provisional.[8]

The importance of foreign assistance and support for radical parties has been most significant with regard to the communist parties during the Cold War. In fact, it can be argued that many of these parties would have suffered a fate similar to most populist radical right parties, i.e. fractionalization and marginalization, had it not been for the substantial support of the Soviet Union. Similarly, many center-right and -left parties in Southern Europe and Latin America, and more recently in Eastern Europe, have profited greatly from the support of Western European parties, most notably the two main German party foundations, the Christian democratic Konrad-Adenauer-Stiftung and the social democratic Friedrich-Ebert-Stiftung.

While numerous stories are told about assistance and support from populist radical right parties to like-minded parties abroad, there is very little evidence to substantiate them (see also chapter 7). Moreover, various compelling arguments caution against ascribing much importance to this factor: (1) the absence of their own "Soviet Union," i.e. a (strong) state that considers itself the political center of the populist radical right ideology;[9] (2) the problematic relationship between many European populist radical right parties (see chapter 7); and (3) the generally poor

---

[8] In the only study (I know) to have empirically tested the internationalization thesis at the level of support for populist radical right parties in five West European countries (Austria, Belgium/Flanders, France, Germany, and the Netherlands), Husbands (1996: 107–8) finds some evidence of "mutual influence" between Flanders and the Netherlands and between East and West Germany.

[9] There is some evidence that Saddam Hussein's Iraq has provided financial support to European populist radical right parties, but in this case the contacts seem to have been only with already successful parties like the FN, FPÖ, and LDPR (e.g. Hunter 1998a, 1998b).

infrastructure of even the more successful populist radical right parties, particularly compared to the established parties in their own countries.

More convincing is the argument that successful populist radical right parties have provided models for new and unsuccessful parties. In this respect, the French FN does function as the prototype of part of the Western European party family (Rydgren 2005b, Kitschelt & McGann 1995); even though the FN itself took its inspiration initially from the Italian MSI (Ignazi 1992). However, while some populist radical right parties that were influenced by the FN have been successful (notably the VB in Belgium), others have not (see the various FN initiatives in Spain or the BNP in the United Kingdom). In Eastern Europe the German REP functioned initially as a role model for aspiring populist radical right parties, with equally mixed results; while the Czech SPR-RSČ made significant strides in the early 1990s, the Hungarian and Ukrainian "Republicans" never developed beyond embryo parties (*Der Republikaner* 12/1991).

Finally, the success of a populist radical right party in one country can lead to the acceptance of parts of the populist radical right program in other countries. This acceptability can be both at the mass and the elite level. It is highly plausible that the success of a party like the FN has increased the salience of populist radical right issues in other countries, most notably in Wallonia, the French-speaking part of Belgium (e.g. Coffé 2004). However, it can also weaken local parties, particularly when the link with successful populist radical right parties abroad increases the stigmatization at home; this might have been the case with relatively moderate parties like the Dutch CD and the German REP, which were often equated with more (openly) radical parties like the FN and VB.

11.6   Conclusion

Few theoretical frameworks include internal supply-side factors, i.e. aspects of the populist radical right itself. Like so much research on political parties, the success or failure of populist radical right parties is primarily explained by external factors and the parties themselves are regarded as "hapless victims" (Berman 1997: 102) of the demand-side and the external supply-side. While there might be some truth to this with regard to the first phase of electoral breakthrough, populist radical right parties play a crucial role in shaping their own fate at the stage of electoral persistence. The internal supply-side is even the most important variable in explaining the many examples of electoral failure *after* electoral breakthrough.

The literature highlights three factors: a "moderate" ideology, a "charismatic" leader, and a "well-structured" organization. While party ideology can explain some of the difference in electoral breakthrough between extreme and radical right parties, it cannot account for electoral persistence or for the divergent electoral successes within the populist radical right party family. Similarly, while charismatic leadership, leaving aside the problems of operationalization, plays a role in the breakthrough phase, its importance decreases significantly during the phase of electoral persistence. This leaves three key variables to explain the crucial process of electoral persistence: party organization (including local implantation), party propaganda, and internal (practical) leadership.

One way in which populist radical right parties can increase their chances of electoral persistence is by attractive and professional propaganda campaigns. As soon as the party has achieved electoral breakthrough, its propaganda will reach a far broader audience than before, in part through the independent media. This means that the party no longer only preaches to the converted, but can reach out to its potential electorate as well. Moreover, it can play an important role in creating a new support base. Still, the direct effect of party propaganda should not be overstated; while parties like the FN and VB clearly excel in their propaganda, as even many opponents will acknowledge, they will only reach a part of their (potential) supporters through it. Most effects will be indirect, mediated through the independent media.

Undoubtedly the most important factor to decide whether or not a party fails or succeeds in persisting electorally is party organization and local implantation. In this regard, leadership is crucial. The most successful populist radical right parties have both skillful external and internal leaders, working in unity towards the same goal. For a long time this has been the ultimate strength of the French FN, where "the charisma of Le Pen was combined with the administrative competence of Mégret" (Adler 2001: 48). A similar situation exists within the VB, where party chairman and practical leader Frank Vanhecke complements charismatic leader Filip Dewinter, while Gerolf Annemans performs both tasks for a smaller subset of members and voters.

12 Assessing impact: populist radical right parties vs. European democracies

> Minor parties that succeeded in passing the threshold of representation, even though they are electorally weak, function in various ways . . . They challenge either the ideological and symbolic aspects of the system or its rules of the game . . . Because of the ways they bypass obstacles, they are also initiators of new patterns of political competition. As such, they are relevant to the political system and to its understanding.
>
> (Herzog 1987: 326)

> On the surface nothing trembled, no walls collapsed, even the windows remained intact, but the earth moved in the depths.
>
> (Epstein 1996: 20)

12.1 Introduction

Both inside and outside of the academic community, scores of claims are made about the political impact of the populist radical right party family on European democracies. According to various commentators populist radical right parties "poison the political atmosphere" (PER 2002: 11). While much speculation abounds about the alleged impact of populist radical right parties on European democracies, few commentators have addressed the other side of the coin, i.e. the impact of European democracies on populist radical right parties.

This chapter discusses the crucial issue of political *impact*, largely on the basis of the insights of the few academic studies on the topic published so far. The focus is on the impact both *of* populist radical right parties on European democracies and of European democracies *on* populist radical right parties. Despite the increased political importance of populist radical right parties, if anything in terms of coalition potential, the study of its political impact is still in its infancy and much of the following will inevitably remain speculative.

12.2   From electoral to political relevance: the impact of

According to Jens Rydgren (2003: 60), "the presence of a xenophobic RRP [Radical Right Populist] party may cause an increase in racism and xenophobia because (1) it has an influence on people's frame of thought; and (2) because it has an influence on other political actors." Indeed, there seems to be a broad consensus on the significant impact of populist radical right parties on certain policy terrains, most notably immigration (e.g. Schain 2006; Tschiyembé 2001; Minkenberg & Schain 2003; Husbands 1996). Some authors have even argued that the parties are responsible for the outbursts of racist violence in their countries (e.g. Marcus 2000; Van Donselaar 1993).

One of the main reasons for these bold assertions is probably the almost complete lack of (comparative) research on the impact of populist radical right parties on contemporary European democracies (Goodwin 2005). Only very recently have scholars started to study the impact of the populist radical right on different policy areas (notably Schain *et al.* 2002a). This section can provide only a provisional discussion of the insights from these first few studies on the impact of populist radical right parties on European democracies. It will try to assess the existing empirical evidence for some of the key assertions regarding the impact of the populist radical right and set out some paths for further research in this highly important and topical field of study. To structure the discussion, the section is divided into three subsections: policy impact, party impact, and social impact. This division is mainly of heuristic value given that the various fields of impact influence each other.

12.2.1   Policy impact

Particularly since the 1990s it has become widely accepted that the populist radical right weighs heavily on certain policy fields in European countries. In fact, many commentators see the recent "*verrechtsing*" (right-wing turn), which they believe can be observed in European politics, as proof of the mainstream parties' attempts to compete with the populist radical right (e.g. Bale 2003; Heinisch 2003; Minkenberg 2001). But not only political opponents and scholars have argued this; various populist radical rightist leaders believe so as well. Quite bitterly, Miroslav Sládek, then leader of the SPR-RSČ, complained to a German journalist in 1997:

The big parties have plundered everything. The referendum on EU membership, which was proposed by us. Our answers to immigration and foreigners. The problem of the Sudeten Germans. When I demanded five years ago that the

Benes decrees should be anchored solidly into Czech law, people still wanted to imprison me. (*Die Zeit* 25/2002)

Here we will discuss only the direct policy impact of the populist radical right party family; the more tricky issue of indirect policy impact will be addressed in the section on party impact.

For many populist radical right parties the local level provides the first and only experience of government participation. Moreover, whereas national government is mostly coalition politics, in which the populist radical right is usually only a junior partner, at the local level they can be the dominant or even the only party in government. Consequently, many parties will try to use local government as a showcase for the nation. In the words of Vojislav Šešelj, leader of the Serbian SRS and then chairman of the municipality of Zemun, a suburb of Belgrade: "For us Radicals, Zemun is conceived as a demonstration. Through the example of Zemun, we shall show what Radical government in the whole of Serbia would be like" (in Čolović 2002: 237).

Overall, it is impossible to distinguish one particular form of populist radical right local rule in Europe. Even the FN ruled relatively differently in the four municipalities that it controlled in the late 1990s (e.g. Davies 1999: ch. 4). However, one of the few points standing out among virtually all cases of populist radical right rule at the local level is the emphasis on symbolic measures. As the parties rapidly notice that local power is highly limited, particularly with regard to the nativist policies at the core of their program, and that they get little support from higher levels, they refocus much of their efforts on cultural policies and symbolic politics. Among the most important are the renaming of streets, the increase of national symbols in the cities, and the redistribution of local subsidies. In all cases the change is away from "alien" and "antinational" (e.g. left-wing and minority) individuals and organizations and towards "national" or "patriotic" actors.

There have been only a few instances where a populist radical right party had a chance to really implement its policies (see table 12.1). In fact, the only pure example of populist radical right government at the national level has been the HDZ one-party government under the presidency of Franjo Tuđjman, which ruled Croatia in the 1990s. As such, it does not provide a particularly pretty picture: a fierce hegemonic nativist discourse, irredentist wars and ethnic cleansing campaigns, authoritarian rule (democratically legitimized in relatively free elections), populist attacks on opponents (including human rights NGOs), and perverse levels of corruption (e.g. Ottaway 2003: ch. 5; Malešević 2002: ch. 5; Pusić 1998). However, the Croatian case is highly specific, as the country was

Table 12.1 *Populist radical right parties in European national government since 1980*

Country	Party	Period(s)	Coalition partners (party ideology)
Austria	FPÖ	2000–02	ÖVP (Christian democratic)
		2002–05	ÖVP
	BZÖ	2005–	ÖVP
Croatia	HDZ	1990–2000	
Estonia	ERSP	1992–95	Isamaa (conservative)
Italy	LN	1994	FI (neoliberal populist) & AN (radical right)
		2001–05	FI & AN (conservative) & MDC (Christian democratic)
Poland	LPR	2006–	PiS (conservative) & Samoobrona (social populist)
Romania	PUNR	1994–96	PDSR (diffuse) & PSM (social populist)
	PRM	1995	
Serbia	SRS	1998–2000	SPS (social populist) & JUL (communist)
Slovakia	SNS	1994–98	HZDS (diffuse) & ZRS (communist)
		2006–	Smer (social populist) & HZDS

at war for most of that period, and many of the most negative aspects of the regime were at least in part a reaction to largely similar actions and attacks by Milošević's Yugoslavia/Serbia.

In most cases Eastern European populist radical right parties were junior partners in the national coalition government. The senior partner of the government would generally be large and ideologically diffuse movement parties of the transition phase, which tended to include strong nationalists and former communists (sometimes the same people). Given that the populist radical right parties were lacking both experience and power, their role in the governments was usually fairly limited. Moreover, the specific impact of the populist radical right party is not always easy to discern, if only because (more) influential populist radical rightists operated within the senior coalition party.

Generally speaking, populist radical right parties held weaker ministries and their leader would stay outside of the government altogether. Their wishes were often ignored by the leading party, and at times they were used as excuses for less popular policies (either in the country or abroad). Overall, it seems that their direct influence on government policies has remained fairly limited, which quite often also led to disappointment and withdrawal from the coalition. Their main "success" was the temporary delaying of pro-minority legislation and a pro-Western foreign policy, rather than fully defeating it, and even in these cases radical forces within the senior partner played at least an equally important role (e.g. Kelley 2004; Simon 2004; Melvin 2000).

In some cases the senior party forced its coalition partners to sign an agreement prior to entering the government in which the populist radical right parties by and large agreed not to try and implement certain aspects of their program. For example, upon entering the government in January 1995, the two populist radical right parties PRM and PUNR, together with their coalition partners PDSR and PSM, had to sign a protocol that "forbids any manifestation of racism, antisemitism, extremism and totalitarianism" (Shafir 1996: 91). Similarly, a precondition for the inclusion of the FPÖ into the Austrian government in 2000 was the signing of the declaration "Responsibility for Austria – A Future in the Heart of Europe," which started with the following statement: "The Federal Government reaffirms its unswerving adherence to the spiritual and moral values which are the common heritage of the peoples of Europe and the true source of individual freedom, political liberty and the rule of law, principles which form the basis of all genuine democracy" (Schüssel & Haider 2000).

In both cases, the senior partners bowed to substantial pressures from foreign countries, mainly the EU and US, but the effects were significant. In Romania, the PDSR used the alleged breach of the protocol as its official reason to oust the PRM from the government (Shafir 1996), whereas in Austria adherence to the coalition agreement became a main cause for the self-defeating struggle within the FPÖ leadership.

The few scholarly studies of populist radical right parties in government in Western Europe stress their impact on immigration policies. Andrej Zaslove (2004a), for example, has argued that the FPÖ and LN have been "instrumental" in introducing more restrictive immigration policy in Austria and Italy. Other authors have come to similar conclusions (e.g. Fallend 2004; Colombo & Sciortino 2003; Heinisch 2003; Minkenberg 2001). However, while there is little doubt that, when in power, populist radical right parties have played a crucial role in tightening the immigration policy, it can be debated whether the end result would have been much different if they had stayed in opposition. After all, various earlier amendments to the immigration policy, in the same direction, had been made under previous governments, such as the Austrian SPÖ–ÖVP coalition (e.g. Bale 2003).

Moreover, preliminary findings show that European immigration policies are increasingly converging, not least because of cooperation within the European Union (e.g. Givens & Luedtke 2005, 2004). One can seriously question the role of populist radical right parties in this whole process, given the weak position of the party family in European politics (see also chapter 7). Moreover, much of the pressure towards an EU-wide immigration policy has come from the Spanish former Prime Minister José María Aznar and his British colleague

Tony Blair, both from countries with no credible populist radical right contender.

A similar argument can be made with regard to the effect of populist radical right parties on law and order policies. There is no doubt that successful electoral campaigns of the populist radical right, in which law and order issues always feature prominently, have often been followed by a toughening of the positions and policies of the established parties (not only of the right-wing). The original "Black Sunday" of 1991, for example, was followed by the introduction of the so-called *Veiligheidscontracten* (safety contracts), which clearly were in line with the VB's tough discourse and policy demands on crime and security (De Decker *et al.* 2005). But a toughening of law and order policies could be observed in many European countries in the past two decades, including those without a strong populist radical right party (e.g. the Netherlands and the United Kingdom).

The (international) electoral successes of populist radical right parties have not always led to policy shifts in their preferred direction. In fact, in many cases at least some policies were introduced that went directly against their wishes. Good examples are progressive social policies (e.g. in housing and urban development) that explicitly included immigrants, the support for multicultural activities and organizations, and the toughening of antiracist and antirevisionist legislation. For instance, the same "Black Sunday" that brought the established parties to introduce the safety contracts also inspired them to install a Royal Commissioner on Immigration Policies, who became one of the most outspoken defenders of the multicultural society in Belgium and the fiercest opponent of the VB (De Decker *et al.* 2005).

In conclusion, it seems that Frank Decker's observations on right-wing populists in power are also valid for the subcategory of the populist radical right: they are in general more influential (a) at the subnational levels than at the national level and (b) with regard to cultural themes rather than social, economic, and foreign policies (Decker 2004: 269–70). Moreover, as Lothar Höbelt has argued with regard to Haider, the policy impact of the populist radical right in general has been "that of a catalyst rather than that of an original contribution" (2003: 220). In other words, they have not so much set a new agenda, but rather pushed through and radicalized an older (largely national conservative) agenda – in line with the pathological normalcy thesis.

12.2.2   Party impact

The importance of the populist radical right in contemporary European politics is probably through their impact on other parties (which includes indirect policy impact) far more than through direct policy impact. Populist radical right parties are said to have "contaminated" various aspects of the established parties in their party systems, such as their style of leadership, their type of political discourse, and the relationship between leaders and followers within established parties (Bale 2003; Mény & Surel 2002b: 19). Put shortly and simply, the other political parties are believed to have copied the charismatic style of leadership, the populist discourse, and the direct relation between leader and followers from the successful populist radical right parties in an attempt to keep or regain their electorate.

Studies point to contemporary developments in European party politics to substantiate their point. However, even if these different aspects can be found in most established parties in Europe, and this point itself is debatable, it does not directly follow that this is a *reaction* to the success of the populist radical right. In fact, both established and populist radical right parties are the product of earlier developments within party politics. To some extent, populist radical right parties are radical versions of the catch-all party type, defined by its small organization, central role of the leader(ship), and "catch-all" discourse (Krouwel 1999; Kirchheimer 1966). Additionally, they have reacted similarly to the rising influence of the mass media, and most notably (commercial) television, which has led to a more prominent role for party leaders and a more direct relationship between leaders and voters in all political parties (e.g. Katz & Mair 1995).

The strongest effect is claimed at the level of discourse (e.g. Decker 2003b; Bayer 2002), but even here the relationship is far from straightforward. We are currently experiencing a populist *Zeitgeist* in Europe (Mudde 2004), in which most political parties express some elements of populism in their discourse (e.g. Jagers 2006). However, this is true in countries with strong populist radical right parties, but also in those with no or weak parties. For example, within Europe populist discourse is particularly strong in Eastern Europe and the UK (e.g. Mair 2002; Mudde 2001), areas where populist radical right parties are not particularly successful in elections.

Somewhat related to the populism thesis is the argument that the populist radical right has repoliticized some countries, either by introducing new issues on the political agenda (e.g. immigration) or by breaking the party political consensus on old issues (e.g. crime). This process has also been observed with respect to the neoliberal populist LPF, which according to some authors transformed the Netherlands from a depoliticized into a centrifugal democracy (Pellikaan et al. 2003). Additional research will have to test whether this thesis holds true for other consociational democracies as well, notably Austria, Belgium and Switzerland, where the main populist challenge has come from the radical right.

Similarly, there is a widely held belief that populist radical right parties have had a significant impact on the policy positions of other parties (e.g. Schain 2006; Meguid 2005). So far, little empirical proof has been provided to substantiate this assertion. While a toughening of position in the fields of crime and immigration can be noted in many European countries, it is doubtful whether this is a direct effect of the competition of the populist radical right. In fact, both might react to the same cues from the media and society. Clearly, the situation in countries like Spain and the UK shows that the development is not limited to countries with successful populist radical right parties. Still, these countries might respond to the successes of populist radical right parties in other countries, notably the FN in France, by trying to pre-empt a similar development at home. At the same time, this could also be used as a convenient excuse to push through preferred policies which are known to be unpopular among the own support base.

Obviously, as elections are zero-sum games the rise of the populist radical right has also had electoral effects. This is not just the case with successful parties like the Belgian VB or the Romanian PRM, which have (at times) taken more than 20 percent of the electorate away from the other parties, but even with some fairly tiny parties. In the 2005 British parliamentary elections, for example, the populist radical right Veritas and the Euroreject UKIP are believed to have affected the outcome of twenty-seven seats (North 2005). The only victim of the participation of the two outsider parties was their most important right-wing rival, the Conservative Party, at least when one assumes that these voters were first and foremost inspired by Euroskepticism. Similarly, scholars have noted that the FN has played "an influential role in the left's return to power" (Hainsworth 2000b: 22).

While center-right parties will have suffered electorally from the rise of populist radical right parties, although not necessarily more than their left-wing rivals, some authors argue that they have profited politically (e.g. Bale 2003; Heinisch 2003). However, this is only the case where the center-right has accepted the populist radical right as a (potential) coalition partner, thereby squaring the competitive position *vis-à-vis* the center-left parties, which had their coalition options increased by the rise of the Greens in the 1980s. But in parties where a *cordon sanitaire* has survived, notably in Belgium, the rise of the populist radical right has mainly strengthened the coalition position of the left, notably social democrats and Greens, which are now needed in every coalition. More-over, the thesis mainly holds for Western Europe, as the postcommunist East tended towards so-called "red–brown" coalitions (Ishiyama 1998) between populist radical left and populist radical right parties.

Referring most notably to recent developments in Austria, Reinhard Heinisch (2003: 125) has argued that "conservative parties tend to be the main beneficiaries from the political fallout" following populist radical right government participation. This thesis seems to be supported also with regard to neoliberal populist parties like the Dutch LPF and the German Schill Party. However, current studies do not yet clarify whether conservative parties gain back the voters they lost earlier to the populist radical right (or neoliberal populists), or whether they actually gain new voters.

It might be the case that populist radical right parties (and neoliberal populist parties) function as halfway houses between the center-left and center-right. In other words, while voters might not change from a social democratic party to a conservative or Christian democratic party directly, they might do it indirectly, by voting once or twice for a populist party. Panel studies would be needed to research this complex process.

12.2.3 Social impact

Many scholars would agree with Seymour Martin Lipset's observation that "radical right agitation has facilitated the growth of practices which threaten to undermine the social fabric of democratic politics" (1955: 176). But while this statement makes both intuitive and theoretical sense, very little empirical evidence has been presented to substantiate it. In most cases the observations are presented as so self-evident that further proof is deemed superfluous.

One of the most heatedly contested issues has been the impact of the electoral success of the populist radical right on the level of nativist violence in a country. Many authors argue that "the xenophobic rhetoric [of populist radical right parties is] often spilling over into violence" (Marcus 2000: 40). One of the few studies providing some empirical support for this relationship is a pilot study of the situation in Switzerland in the period 1984–93 (in Altermatt & Kriesi 1995). In other parts of Europe there also seems to exist a very slight positive correlation (cf. Mudde 2005b; Eatwell 2000; Björgo & Witte 1993b), which is not the same as causation!

In contrast, some scholars believe that successful populist radical right parties actually channel the frustrations of would-be perpetrators of nativist violence (e.g. Minkenberg 2003; Wilensky 1998). In the most comprehensive study of racist and extreme right violence in Western Europe to date, Ruud Koopmans concludes that "[i]n general, strong extreme right parties serve to limit the potential for extreme right and racist violence" (1996: 211). Analysis of the comparative data of the

European Monitoring Centre on Racism and Xenophobia (EUMC 2005), particularly relating to the number of racially motivated murders and threats, confirms that the relationship between the levels of racist violence and populist radical right electoral success is inverse, if significant at all (see also in Backes 2003b: 364–5).

However, as all scholars in the field admit, serious comparative studies are at this stage impossible, given the huge inconsistencies in data collection between European countries. This problem is also acknowledged by the EUMC, which states in its annual report: "In general, the enormous difference across the 25 EU Member States in numbers of recorded incidents of racist violence and crime tells us as much about the inadequacy and inconsistency of data collection as it does about the actual extent of racist violence and crimes in the EU" (EUMC 2005: 15).

This problem can be somewhat undercut by using data from the same country but in different regions or at different times. However, these analyses seem to point in the same direction. For example, within Germany an inverse relationship between the levels of antiforeigner violence and populist radical right voting can be found at the state level (e.g. Karapin 2002). And in the seven EU member states that have reliable data on the numbers of racist crimes and incidents, though only over the short period of 2001–03, the only significant increase is reported in Ireland (+88.4 percent), a country which never had a significant populist radical right party (EUMC 2005). In contrast, the two countries with the strongest such parties, Austria and Denmark, belong to those with the largest *de*crease (−17.4 percent and −55.2 percent, respectively). Interestingly, in Austria the FPÖ was part of the coalition government during that period, while in Denmark the DFP was a vital supporter of the minority government.

In an overview article on antiforeigner violence, Peter Merkl concludes that "it would be difficult to overlook the vast preponderance of the unorganized, unpolitical, and less political outrages against asylum-seekers and other visible foreigners" (1995: 114). In fact, most national studies on nativist violence find that only a minority of (arrested) perpetrators are members of nativist organizations (e.g. Björgo & Witte 1993a). Moreover, the perpetrators who are organized tend to engage overwhelmingly in small neo-Nazi groups rather than populist radical right parties. And even when official members of these parties are involved, they are very often passive members rather than activists, let alone leaders. Obviously, there are individual exceptions (e.g. BNP and CD), but in general the *direct* involvement of populist radical right parties in nativist violence remains very limited.

It has also become widely accepted that electoral and political successes of populist radical right parties increase the tolerance for intolerance (e.g.

Schain *et al.* 2002b). Empirical evidence for this belief is hard to come by, although some studies do point in this direction (e.g. Westin 2003). A comparative study of seven West European countries found that electoral success of populist radical right parties does correlate with ethnic prejudice within countries, but has fairly limited "impact" on other authoritarian values (Andersen & Evans 2004). Other studies find an increase in tolerance towards immigrants (e.g. Bjørklund & Andersen 2002). However, it might be more logical to assume that populist radical right electoral success not so much changes the attitudes of people as increases the salience of that attitude. It also seems plausible to argue this with relation to the alleged "cueing effects" of populist radical right parties regarding (exclusive) national identity and European integration (e.g. Netjes & Edwards 2005).

Another effect of electoral success of the populist radical right might be the increased mobilization of its opponents. There seems to be a clear relationship between highly published radical right events and antiradical right mobilization. Most mass mobilizations are direct reactions to either extreme right violence or populist radical right electoral success. Some studies even suggest that electoral successes of populist radical right parties "provoke a backlash among those with liberal attitudes" (Andersen & Evans 2004: 24; also Kitschelt & McGann 1995). The question is then which will be larger and more long-lasting. That this is highly dependent upon the strength of the populist radical right party can be shown by two recent examples: while the mass mobilization after the BNP's election victory in Tower Hamlets largely ended the party's chances in the area, the impact of the "republican front" against Le Pen in the second round of the 2002 presidential elections seems to have been more modest and temporary.

12.3   Democracy strikes back: impact *on*

Obviously, the relationship between European democracies and populist radical right parties is not one-directional. European democracies also have an impact on radical right parties. This section will not discuss the various concepts of "defending democracy" in detail, nor the highly important and interesting work that has recently been conducted in this field (e.g. Capoccia 2005; Eatwell & Mudde 2004; Pedahzur 2003; Van Donselaar 2003, 1995). Instead, the emphasis is on the impact that democratic reactions have had on the populist radical right parties and on the internal changes this impact has given rise to.

We hereby start from the assumption that there is an inherent tension between the populist radical right and liberal democracy (see chapter 6), which will confront all populist radical right parties with an "adaptation dilemma" (Van Donselaar 1995); i.e. to function fully within a liberal democratic context the populist radical right party must moderate, but to keep its unique position and ensure the loyalty of its hardcore support it has to remain radical (also Dézé 2004; Heinisch 2003). However, different legal, political, and social contexts will lead to dissimilar impacts and dilemmas.

12.3.1   Coalition vs. cordon sanitaire

Given that European democracies are essentially party democracies, the most important responses are those by mainstream political parties. In fact, in his study of defending democracy in the interwar period, Giovanni Capoccia (2005) concludes that the behavior of party elites is the vital variable in explaining democratic survival. While the survival of the democratic system is no longer at stake, some of the key values underlying the system of liberal democracy are challenged. Consequently, much of the debate on how "the democratic parties" should respond to the populist radical right party challenge is still voiced in terms of defending democracy.

Until 1980 cooperation with radical right parties was almost universally rejected in Europe. There were few short-term exceptions, most notably with respect to the MSI in Italy (e.g. Dézé 2004). Particularly since the early 1990s the situation has changed significantly, leading to a wide diversity of approaches between and within European countries. At the two poles are coalition as the most accommodative, on the one hand, and a *cordon sanitaire* as the most adversarial, on the other (e.g. De Lange 2007b). Much more analysis is needed to be able to ascertain why some mainstream parties decide upon an accommodative approach and others on an adversarial one. Moreover, little is known about the impact of those strategies on the populist radical right parties (on the electoral effects, see Van der Brug & Van Spanje 2004).

As far as the issue is discussed, it is in terms of the best approach "to deal with" populist radical right parties, which has spurred debate inside and outside of academia. While many self-professed "democrats" tended to reject any cooperation ("collaboration") before, some have changed their opinion in the light of the dismal performance of populist parties in government (i.e. internal splits and subsequent electoral defeat) – though this applies mainly to neoliberal populist parties like the Schill Party and the LPF, it also pertains to the FPÖ and, to a lesser extent, the LN (cf. Delwit & Poirrier 2007; Fröhlich-Steffen & Rensmann 2005a). Moreover, they will point to parties like the FN and VB, which achieve long-term electoral successes despite a *cordon sanitaire*.

In fact, one could argue that populist radical right parties achieve these successes in part *because of* the cordon. The cordon not only helps these parties to keep the *Fundis* and *Realos* together, as the exclusion by the mainstream parties takes away the incentive to moderate, but it also helps the populist radical right parties to focus themselves fully on a vote-maximizing strategy. Unlike mainstream parties, which have to keep in mind possible coalition talks after the election campaign, pariah parties like the Belgian VB need not concern themselves with these kind of tactical considerations. Moreover, they can pursue the ideal vote-maximizing campaign of "overpromising" (Papadopoulos 2000: 6), uninhibited by concerns of how everything should be implemented. In other words, "[t]he extreme right can campaign continuously and does so. Meantime, the others govern or keep themselves ready to do so" (Deschouwer 2001: 84).

But political cooperation at the level of formal coalition addresses only one aspect of political relations between populist radical right and mainstream parties. Various authors have contended that most mainstream parties will exclude the populist radical right parties and include "their" issues and solutions in an attempt to defeat the outsiders.

The most effective strategy . . . appears to be a combination of cooptation, confrontation and marginalization. Established political parties seize on the themes of right-wing populist parties (cooptation) while simultaneously denouncing them as enemies of the system (confrontation) and refusing to cooperate with them, or even speak with them, at any political level (marginalization). (Art 2006: 8)

However, this is almost exactly what has been happening in Flanders since 1991, and in France since the late 1990s. Still, in both cases the populist radical right has not diminished in strength; in France not even despite the painful party split.

The problem is that this model (again) ignores the role of the populist radical right party itself. As argued in chapter 10, with regard to the Thatcher–Chirac debate, whether this strategy weakens or strengthens the populist radical right party depends to a large extent on the variable of issue ownership. Once a populist radical right party has established itself as a credible political actor that owns certain salient issues (e.g. crime and immigration), it is largely immune to counter-strategies of other political actors (including the media and social movements).

Similarly, the impact of the strategy of the established parties is largely mitigated by the populist radical right party itself. Both coalitions and cordons can lead to internal cohesion and strife. Much depends on the level of institutionalization of the populist radical right. Less institutionalized parties will falter under both a cordon (e.g. CD and REP) and a coalition (e.g. LPF and Schill Party). However, more institutionalized parties can thrive under both a cordon (e.g. VB) and a coalition (e.g. SNS), or at the very least survive the latter (e.g. FPÖ and LN). Like nearly all measures of defending democracy, these strategies are most successful, in terms of breaking or transforming the populist radical right party, when applied in the early phase of party institutionalization. Once a populist radical right party becomes institutionalized, its role in determining its own future increases.

12.3.2 Socialization into liberal democracy?

Based on the experiences with the socialist parties in the early twentieth century, and some communist parties in the postwar period, scholars have come to believe that "in the long run, revolutionary parties lose their original impetus and accommodate themselves to the regimes they have been unable to overthrow" (Sartori 1976: 140). Although populist radical right parties are not revolutionary in the true sense, i.e. changing the democratic system by violence, they do claim to want to overthrow "the regime," i.e. the dominant actors and values in their contemporary liberal democracies.

Husbands has argued that "[s]uccess tends to moderate," but also that "it is a historical fact that most examples of such metamorphoses [from antisystem party to system party, CM] are reactions to persistent failure, not to growth and success" (1996: 113). Systematic research into the development of political parties leads to the view that moderation "is not the automatic response to electoral defeat . . . Normally, when moderation is observed, it is due to the fact that the party tempers its ideological rigidity through organizational reforms or leadership renovation" (Sánchez-Cuenca 2004: 325).

However, while correlation is one thing, causality is another. Does success lead to moderation or moderation to success? The answer is probably both: there are examples of populist radical right parties that moderated after (initial) electoral success (e.g. VB) and of those that gained success after moderation (notably Tudor and Le Pen in the presidential elections of 2000 and 2002, respectively). However, there are at least as many examples of parties that did not moderate after (initial) electoral success (e.g. FN, recent NPD, SNS) – some even radicalized in certain respects (e.g. LN, PRM) – or that did not gain electoral victories

12.4   Conclusion

Despite more than twenty-five years of the third wave of populist radical right party politics, sporting unprecedented electoral and political successes (including several coalitions involving members of the party family), the academic study of the impact of populist radical right parties on European democracies and vice versa has hardly started. With a few notable exceptions (particularly Schain *et al.* 2002a), studies of populist radical right parties often claim significant impact upon policies (immigration) and society (violence), but provide very little empirical evidence for those claims.

Most such claims do not seem to hold up against serious empirical and theoretical scrutiny. While many of the noted changes in policies could be observed, particularly in the fields of immigration and law and order, the link to populist radical right influence seems weak at best. Most developments can be observed Europe-wide, not only in countries with a strong populist radical right party (whether in government or not). The same applies to the asserted changes in party behavior and organization; rather than the mainstream parties following the populist radical right, it seems more plausible that both are reacting to the same societal developments (notably the rise of (commercial) media power).

With regard to the alleged societal impact, the claim that electoral success of populist radical right parties leads to nativist violence cannot be substantiated. Indeed, an inverse relationship seems more plausible, although the lack of reliable cross-national data so far prevents any strong conclusion. What can be substantiated by empirical data, however, is that the direct involvement of populist radical right parties in nativist violence is very small. Finally, while more research is needed to assess whether electoral success of populist radical right parties has an impact on mass attitudes and, if so, what type of impact, it seems reasonable to assume that the effect will be more pronounced on the salience rather than the content of those attitudes.

The impact of European democracies on populist radical right parties has been even less addressed in the literature. Recent years have seen an increased academic and political debate on the effect of the behavior of the mainstream parties, i.e. coalition or cordon, in part resulting from some spectacular failures of populist parties in government. However, the impact of both coalition and cordon is strongly mediated through the populist radical right party itself, particularly through its level of party institutionalization. More institutionalized parties can be strengthened by both coalition and cordon, while less institutionalized parties can be weakened by both.

Finally, little is known about the impact of European democracies on the internal life of populist radical right parties. As we know from the socialist parties of the early and late twentieth century, as well as some contemporary former radical right parties (e.g. HDZ, MSI/AN, SPO), political parties can and do change their ideology. Under which conditions they moderate, rather than stabilize or radicalize, is a question still waiting for an answer. At first glance there doesn't seem to be a straightforward relationship with electoral or political success.

13 Conclusions

The enemy is the gramophone mind, whether or not one agrees with
the record that is being played at the moment.   (Orwell 1996: 63)

13.1 Introduction

Coming to the end of this book makes me realize primarily how many
important and interesting topics within the field of populist radical right
studies still need further exploration. This study can at best open consideration of a few issues and begin to answer some of the many questions
the subject provokes.

In this final chapter, I want to look both back and forward. This book
addresses three aspects of the study of populist radical right parties: iden-
tifications, issues, and explanations. On the basis of a pan-European
approach I have collected, integrated, and revised insights from existing studies and combined them with new findings from original research.
The next sections present some of the main findings of this study and
sketch posssible avenues for further research.

The key message of this book is reiterated throughout this concluding chapter: the populist radical right parties themselves must be put at
the center of research on the phenomenon. Populist radical right parties
are not just dependent variables, passively molded by structural factors,
but they also constitute independent variables, actively shaping part of
their own destiny. This point is too often ignored in the sociological and
economical deterministic studies in political science.

13.2 From conceptualization to classification

While many scholars still devote little or no attention to definitional matters, there is increasing debate about the best term and definition for
these parties. This study introduces the term populist radical right to
describe their core ideology: nativism, authoritarianism, and populism.

293

Obviously, neither the term nor the definition will convince many of my colleagues, who will adhere to the nomenclature of their earlier work. But this was not the objective of the first chapter. Rather, it sought to expose and overcome the key problems involved in defining the topic at hand: notably, circularity, the relationships with other political ideologies, and the semantics of terminology.

Classification, the topic of the second chapter, is even more critical to advancing scholarly understanding of this phenomenon. While various authors do devote some attention to the conceptualization of the populist radical right, very few give similar consideration to the classification of the parties. This study provides a first and provisional attempt at classifying the most relevant European populist radical right parties. It has already led to some highly remarkable results: various usual suspects were excluded from the populist radical right family (e.g. FRP, LPF, NPD, Samoobrona), while some unsuspected cases were included in the family (e.g. DUP, HDZ). It also showed that there are many problems involved in classifying political parties, populist radical right or otherwise: markedly, internal division and ideological change. This is not a sign of weakness of the conceptual categories, but a consequence of the complexity and dynamism of political phenomena.

Much more work will have to be done to come to a more accurate and comprehensive classification of all populist radical right parties. This can only be accomplished by original research, as so many European parties remain understudied (e.g. De Lange & Mudde 2005). In addition, classifications should be based upon systematic academic analyses of party literature. Too often (new) parties are simply classified on the basis of "common wisdom" supported by a smattering of highly selective quotes. It is also important to remember that not every new political actor that criticizes the political mainstream is populist and not every novel party that criticizes (past) immigration policies or that is Islamophobic is radical right.

This study has distinguished between different families of populist parties, of which the populist radical right and the neoliberal populist are the most notable. Together, they are part of the category of right-wing populism. However, given the different intellectual traditions underlying the ideologies of the two party families, it does not make much sense to use this overly broad category in the study of party families. Moreover, the distinction between the two groups, which makes sense in an ideological sense, probes the interesting question of the different electoral successes of the two party families. With the notable exception of Italy, no European party system has both successful populist radical right and neoliberal populist parties (Mudde 2006). Are the populist radical right and the neoliberal populist parties functional equivalents, similar to Christian democrats and conservatives? Which factors explain the ascendance of one party over the other? I suggest that the explanation is mainly to be found on the supply-side, particularly in political culture, i.e. the centrality of nativism and the (related) level of stigmatization of the populist radical right.

13.3 From received wisdom to original research

One of the key problems in the field of populist radical right studies is the lack of original research. Despite the plethora of publications that have appeared over the past twenty-five years, the field is still full of "received wisdom" that (so far) has not been tested scientifically. The reason is quite simple: only a very few researchers actually study populist radical right parties themselves. The vast majority of the literature is based almost exclusively upon secondary "analysis" of often highly debatable sources, be they nonacademic studies of populist radical right parties or large cross-national data sets with concomitant methodological and operationalizational problems.

This study has shown the limited accuracy of some commonly held "truths." On the basis of a cross-national analysis of the party literature we found no proof for the popular thesis that populist radical right parties are essentially neoliberal in ideology. Conversely, the party family has a nativist economic program, which is secondary to both the parties and its voters. Similarly, the belief that the populist radical right party family consists only of *Männerparteien* (male parties) was seriously revised. While the thesis is supported for the electorates of most parties, particularly at the leadership level the party family compares favorably with mainstream parties in terms of female representation. Moreover, the feminist bias in much research overstates the significance of the underrepresentation of women within populist radical right parties by comparing it only to the percentages in the population or in left-wing parties. It also provided incorrect and highly normative explanations. Rather than resulting from some innate positive characteristics of women, or (by negation) negative features of men, the disproportionately low level of support for populist radical right parties among women is best explained by their lower level of political efficacy. Finally, contrary to the received wisdom that nativists are isolationists uninterested in international cooperation, the study demonstrated that the populist radical right does combine nativist ambitions with support for European cooperation. While faced with even larger obstacles than other party families, the absence of a populist radical right transnational federation has less to do with ideology (i.e. competing

nationalisms) than with practicalities (e.g. conflicting egos, lack of institutional stability, stigmatization).

This book has addressed only some of the issues that can help us to
better understand the populist radical right phenomenon, including its
electoral and political failures and successes. Moreover, the analysis has
necessarily been limited to only some of the party literature, given the lack
of substantive academic studies of the ideology of most populist radical
right parties.

Among the issues that remain to be addressed is the relationship
between religion and populist radical right parties, a topic that has
received only scant attention in the literature so far despite the importance ascribed to it in some explanations of success (e.g. Mayer 2002;
Billiet 1995; Falter 1994). While religion has always been important for
many parties in Eastern Europe, regional differences with respect to religion appear to be less salient in the wake of 9/11, which strengthened the
emphasis on Christianity within populist radical right parties in the West
(e.g. FN, FPÖ, VB).

13.4   From "normal pathology" to "pathological normalcy"

Like the research on nationalism and fascism, studies of the contemporary
populist radical right have been based upon the thesis of "normal pathology" (Scheuch & Klingemann 1967), in which the populist radical right
is seen as a pathology common to all (liberal) democracies. Under normal circumstances the level of support will be marginal (some 5 percent),
but in times of "crisis" – linked to socioeconomic and sociodemographic
developments like modernization, economic crisis, mass immigration –
it can increase significantly (e.g. Taggart 2002; Minkenberg 1998). This
means that the populist radical right is considered to be an anomaly of
(liberal) democracies and the key puzzle is at the demand-side, i.e. why
do people hold populist radical right attitudes?

The normal-pathology-thesis is not supported by empirical evidence.
First of all, surveys show large support for populist radical right attitudes,
extending well beyond the levels of a small pathological marginalized
minority. Second, "[m]uch of the discourse of radical right-wing parties
represents nothing more than a radicalized version of mainstream positions promoted and defended by the established parties" (Betz 2003b:
88; also Minkenberg 2001: 5). Nativism is a radical interpretation of the
idea of the nation-state, the founding principle of many Western countries and recognized as such by the United Nations. Authoritarianism is
a core feature of mainstream ideologies (e.g. conservatism) and religions
(notably Catholic and Orthodox Christianity), although not always to

the same degree. And populism builds to a large extent on the democratic promise so central to European politics (e.g. Mény & Surel 2002b; Canovan 1999).

Consequently, it makes much more sense to consider the populist radical right essentially as a "pathological normalcy," i.e. a radicalized version of mainstream ideas, and not as a "normal pathology," unconnected to the mainstream and requiring explanation from completely different (demand-side) theories. If the populist radical right is indeed understood as a pathological normalcy, it follows that (1) a relatively high level of demand for populist radical right politics is available in all (Western) liberal democracies,[1] and (2) the main puzzle is no longer why people hold populist radical right values, but why they are (not) voting for populist radical right parties. The answer is to be found mainly on the supply-side: shifting from the external supply-side during the phase of electoral breakthrough to the internal supply-side in the phase of electoral persistence.

13.5   From the demand-side to the supply-side

All politics is about the relationship between demand and supply, and the populist radical right is no exception to this general rule. Most research on the topic has focused almost exclusively on the demand-side, i.e. the search for and explanation of the most fertile breeding ground of the populist radical right. While in itself valuable, there are two empirical arguments against this approach: (1) the cross-national, cross-regional, and cross-temporal variations in breeding grounds can account for only a small degree of the substantial electoral differences between populist radical right parties (e.g. Carter 2005; Givens 2005; Norris 2005); (2) in all countries these parties mobilize only a (small) part of their potential supporters, i.e. the breeding ground is (more) fertile everywhere (e.g. Van der Brug *et al.* 2005).

Critical study of the literature in the field teaches us that the perfect breeding ground for populist radical right parties is one in which there are widespread insecurities and resentments related to the three core features of the populist radical right ideology: nativism, authoritarianism, and populism. Nativism feeds upon the feeling of endangered or threatened ethnic or national identity, linked most notably to (perceptions of) the process of European integration, mass immigration, and the mechanics of "multiculturalism." Authoritarianism attracts people who are worried

---

[1] The pathological normalcy thesis certainly holds true for the broader European and Western contexts. Given the hegemony of Western views on democracy and the nation-state, however, I would argue that the thesis has near-universal validity.

about crime and the wavering of traditional values, while populism speaks to dissatisfaction with political representation as well as the increased sense of individual's efficacy.

Obviously, these fears and insecurities are available at all times and in all societies, both inside and outside of Europe. However, most of the time only *some* fears are present within *certain* subgroups. In recent decades large groups of Europeans have come to share a *combination* of these frustrations and insecurities. The populist radical right parties are unique in their integration of all these sentiments. As a consequence they are more favourably positioned to capture this discontent among a growing number of Europeans than other nationalists (who deal primarily with national identity issues), populists (who mainly speak to political resentment), and conservatives (who primarily address authoritarianism).

To be sure, the breeding ground of the populist radical right is undoubtedly linked to processes like modernization in general and globalization in particular. However, these processes are so broad and vague that they are of little use in empirical research. Modernization, like globalization, is a continuous process, and as such is hard to measure in a given temporal context. Similarly, populist radical right parties probably profit from oppositions to multicultural and postindustrial societies, but what these terms mean exactly and how these variables relate causally remains vague.

Admittedly, the populist radical right is unlikely to find fertile breeding ground in countries that are (perceived as) monocultural, crimeless, and without political problems, but neither do such places exist. This is not to say that there is no relationship between objective facts (e.g. numbers of immigrants) and subjective feelings (e.g. xenophobia), but rather to problematize their relevance for the electoral success of populist radical right parties. Simply said, every European country has a (relatively) fertile breeding ground for the populist radical right, yet only in some countries do these parties also flourish in elections. The answer to that puzzle is not to be found in the demand-side, but in the supply-side.

Few authors have provided a theoretical model of electoral success of populist radical right parties that includes both demand-side and (internal and external) supply-side factors. Most theories are either monocausal, often referring to very broad and vague macro-level processes such as globalization or postindustrialization, or multicausal, but still exclusively based upon macro- and micro-level demand-side variables. Then there are some shopping list theories, which simply present a staggering number of demand- and supply-side variables without clearly indicating how they influence the success of populist radical right parties or each other.

Two relatively parsimonious integrated theories deserve more detailed attention. The first was developed by Herbert Kitschelt and further elaborated upon in his work with Anthony McGann (Kischelt & McGann 1995). One of its key strengths is that the theory tries to address both the successes and failures of different subtypes of "new radical right" parties. In short, it combines demand- (postindustrial society), external supply- (mainstream party convergence), and internal supply-side variables (ideological offer of the radical right) to account for the differences in electoral success of the new radical right in Western Europe. Despite the major importance of this theory, it has several major drawbacks. Most notably, the theory is relatively vague (Veugelers 2001), misclassifies the major parties (e.g. De Lange 2007a), is mostly applicable to only a small subset of European democracies (excluding the East and South), and has questionable underlying assumptions (essentially class voting; see Knutsen 2005).

Less well-known, but possibly even more promising, is the "legitimacy, efficacy and trust (LET) hypothesis" of Roger Eatwell (2003, 2000, 1998). According to this hypothesis, "extreme right voting is likely to stem from a combination of three (partly related) perceptions. These are growing extremist *Legitimacy* + rising personal *Efficacy* + declining system *Trust*" (Eatwell 2003: 68). Obviously, there are some problematic sides to this theory too, most notably the dynamic terminology, which explains the *act* of voting by three (aggregate and individual) *processes*. In addition, one can question why the variable of "system trust" is operationalized at the aggregate rather than the individual level. Still, the theory has the advantage of combining the macro-, meso-, and micro-levels as well as the demand and (external and internal) supply-sides.

Both theories still basically work from the normal-pathology assumption. Here, the populist radical right is seen as a pathological normalcy, and their parties as *purifiers*, referring to "an ideology that has been betrayed or diluted by established parties," rather than *prophets*, "which articulate a new ideology" (Lucardie 2000: 175). For purifiers, the supply-side of politics is far more important than the demand-side, as they essentially refer to mainstream values, although in a radicalized manner. Whereas prophetic parties have to articulate or construct new political divisions, purifiers have to establish themselves on either old issues or new issues related to old political divisions. While this also means that the issues of purifiers have potential salience, it is important for populist radical right parties to ensure that "their" issues gain or hold a high salience.

Various factors can influence the increase in issue salience. Obviously, objective facts are in some way related to the politicization of issues. For example, the attacks of 9/11 pushed terrorism to the top of the public agenda. However, the way the issue enters public discourse is not an objective given, but is influenced by a variety of political and social actors, most notably political parties and the media. Parties and the media largely, though not solely, decide how an issue is framed and thus to which attitudes and values an issue is related. It is through the process of "framing" and "selecting" of issues that certain policies become salient, and others do not (e.g. Schain *et al.* 2002b; Minkenberg 2001).

Certain issues are clearly favorable to populist radical right parties as they are easily linked to their core features: e.g. corruption and political failure (populism), crime and terrorism (authoritarianism), multicultural society and immigration (nativism). When these issues gain salience, populist radical right parties stand a chance of increasing their electoral relevance, in contrast to situations in which socioeconomic issues dominate the electoral campaign. The main variable that decides whether populist radical right or other parties will profit from the salience of issues like crime or corruption is *issue ownership*. If one of the other parties has already established ownership over these issues, that party will benefit from their increased salience. However, if the issue is perceived as being ignored or ineptly handled by the established parties, at least in the eyes of voters who consider the issue important, there is an opportunity for the populist radical right to gain support.

In this respect, the theories of convergence (e.g. Kitschelt & McGann 1995) and cartelization (Katz & Mair 1995) are of particular importance. A combination of both can possibly explain why the new democracies of both the second (Greece, Portugal, and Spain) and third wave (postcommunist countries) do have relatively unsuccessful populist radical right parties at this moment. Most democratizing countries have polarized party systems in the first decades; during transition between the old and new elites, and during consolidation between different new elites. In this period the population will perceive party competition as a fairly radical choice between very different options, with clear winners and losers. Moreover, particularly in the postcommunist world, parties were initially mere vehicles of small groups of elites, which changed allegiances and names regularly (e.g. Lewis 2000; Kopecký 1995), providing the impression of a continuous offer of new alternatives.

In time, the polarization of the new democracies will slowly but steadily develop into "normal" opposition, probably developing into ideological converging between the two parties (blocs) later on, while strict alternation of power is increasingly softened by power-sharing agreements and mild forms of cartelization. Consequently, chances for the nonaligned populist radical right will increase significantly (e.g. Von Beyme 1996).

Interestingly, polarization seems to have very different effects on the electoral and political success of populist radical right parties. While the electoral position of populist radical right parties is weakened by polarization, their political position can be strengthened. If the two center (or main) parties are polarized, they will have fewer coalition options. In most cases this leads to blocks of parties in which the populist radical right can play a role. In Western Europe these blocks have normally followed the usual left–right divide, while in Eastern Europe the division seems more related to a relatively vague antipro-Western division.

During the phase of *electoral breakthrough*, the populist radical right party does not play a particularly important role as an independent variable. Having a charismatic leader, professional propaganda, and a strong party organization will all help, but are not necessary to achieve electoral breakthrough. Similarly, (positive) media attention will be a plus, but does not have to be excessive. As long as the right group of people know that the party exists, which can be achieved largely by the party's own propaganda, it can mobilize enough voters to gain initial electoral success, normally measured in terms of gaining enough support to enter parliament. The populist radical right party does not even have to establish issue ownership yet. It can garner support simply by being seen as a party that acknowledges the importance of the issue, or that holds a certain underrepresented view on the issue.

There are a few intervening variables that influence the significance of the impact of initial electoral success. A favorable institutional framework, for example, will mean that a relatively small degree of electoral support can already lead to electoral breakthrough. A highly proportional electoral system ensures that even small parties can achieve parliamentary representation, while a federal system helps parties with a highly localized support basis. Moreover, generous and egalitarian state financing rules create opportunities for all new parties, whereas strict and tough legal requirements for electoral participation provide extra hurdles (e.g. Norris 2005). It should be remembered, however, that these factors do not so much influence the electoral support, but rather determine how this support is translated into parliamentary representation and political impact.

Once a populist radical right party has achieved electoral breakthrough, a largely different set of factors decides upon the question of *electoral persistence*. The focus shifts from the external to the internal supply-side: in other words, the importance of the political opportunity structure decreases, while the populist radical right party itself becomes the crucial independent variable. The party now becomes *a* major factor in its own success and often *the* major factor in its own failure.

It has to be able to break out of the ghetto of its hardcore support and speak to new voters who are less convinced of the party's message. But it has to do this without losing its old hardcore voters (and members). Once new soft supporters are brought into the party electorate, partly as protest voters, they must be transformed into loyal party supporters. To achieve this, the populist radical right has to become a legitimate political actor (Eatwell 1998) that establishes ownership over "its" issues, at least in the eyes of a sizeable part of the country's electorate.

In this process, three internal supply-side variables are vital: organization, personnel, and propaganda. A party has to be well organized to build upon its breakthrough. It has to be able to extend its coverage in terms of both electoral districts contested and subgroups of the electorate addressed. To do this, the party needs at least some competent personnel, and particularly a practical leader with organizational skills. Also, to attract larger groups of the electorate, a charismatic or at least media-genic leader is important as he or she can make use of the increased media attention that inevitably follows electoral breakthrough. Similarly, with more external focus, the party no longer mainly addresses the converted, who were looking for the party themselves, but has to convince a wider audience that it has an important role to play in the political arena; either directly, through its own policies, or indirectly, by pushing the other parties in the desired direction. For this, professional propaganda is of crucial importance.

Again, certain intervening variables exist during the phase of electoral persistence that influence the party's ability to establish itself as a credible political actor. Most important in this respect is the political culture of a country, most notably the role of nationalism within it. In countries where nationalism is regarded with great suspicion and easily linked to the period of the Second World War, populist radical right parties run the risk of "being tarred by the extremist brush" (Eatwell 2000: 364; Art 2006). As a consequence of this stigmatization, the party will have great difficulties finding competent people to become active in the party, yet attract many true extremists, further strengthening the stigmatization. In sharp contrast, in countries where nationalism is part of mainstream political culture, and a thriving nationalist subculture exists, populist radical right parties will find it much easier to attract competent people and to build bridges to the mainstream.

While campaigns by the media and political opponents can surely have an effect on the electoral success of populist radical right parties, their impact will be strongly mediated by the political culture. In other words, where stigmatization is strong, they will be influential and will further reduce the chances for the populist radical right to establish itself. However, in countries with a favorable political culture, antiracist and media campaigns will be far less effective, given that part of the establishment (including the media) defends similar policies and values. Here, the main problem of the populist radical right is finding the political space to establish itself as a distinct and independent actor; a problem more generally faced in the new democracies of the East than in the established democracies in the West.

This highly complex interaction of internal and external supply-side factors should be studied largely through the application of completely different research designs than those used in most current explanatory studies of populist radical right electoral success. Cross-national studies based upon secondary data sets, either at the aggregate or individual level, can catch only part of the demand-side of the equation. While expert studies seem to provide a reliable source of data for cross-national studies of the supply-side, we should be extremely careful about accepting the validity of these data sets. Most importantly, does it really make sense to ask five or more "experts" about a highly complex topic that we have virtually no publications on? If we want to use expert studies, they should be more than mere peer surveys – not every political scientist from country x is also an expert on specific aspects of populist radical right politics in that country.

In addition to gathering new data and using innovative methodologies, future research will also have to focus more attention on the meso-level. It is particularly at this level that the relationship between macro-level theories and micro-level attitudes can be studied. It is here that the role of the supply-side, and particularly the connections between the various supply-side factors, can be researched in all their complexities. Studies at the meso-level also have the advantage of generating far more cases, enhancing the possibilities for advanced statistical analysis and for controlling for various variables (primarily institutional).

13.6   Last words

Over the past decades the field of populist radical right parties has proved particularly popular and productive. Within the ECPR Standing Group on Extremism & Democracy currently some one-third of the over six hundred members are working primarily or secondarily on the topic. And unlike so many other fields of the social sciences, the study of the populist radical right is not dominated by one academic or national tradition. In fact, English, French, and German (language) publications very much compete at the same high level, with the Germans producing almost half of all publications in the field (cf. De Lange & Mudde 2005).

Despite the huge intellectual capital and the deeply felt commitment of the many scholars in the field, academic research on populist radical right parties has largely stabilized since influential scholars like Hans-Georg Betz, Piero Ignazi, and Herbert Kitschelt integrated insights from classic party politics into the field in the early 1990s. One of the main hindrances towards further progress is the lack of originality in terms of approaches, cases, data, and methods. If this book has at least triggered some interest in exploring new venues and breaking out of the more comfortable studies of the usual suspects on the basis of the usual data sets, it has achieved its main aim.

Appendix A   Populist radical right parties

Table 1. *Populist radical right parties in contemporary Europe (1980–2005).*

Country	– Populist radical right parties	Period
Albania	– Balli Kombëtar (BK)	Since 1991
	– Partia Demokratike e Djahte (PDD)	Since 1994
	– Partia e Unitetit Kombëtar (PUK)	Since 1991
Austria	– Bündnis Zukunft Österreich (BZÖ)	Since 2005
	– Freiheitliche Partei Österreichs (FPÖ)	Since 1986
Belarus	– Belarusskaya partiya svobody (BPS)	
	– Liberalno-demokraticheskaya partiya Belarusa (LDPB)	
Belgium	– Agir	1989–1994
	– Front National (Belge) (FNb)	Since 1985
	– Front Nouveau de Belgique (FNB)	Since 1995
	– Vlaams Blok (VB)	1979–2004
	– Vlaams Belang (VB)	Since 2004
Bosnia & Herzegovina	– Hrvatska demokratska zajednica Bosne i Hercegovine (HDZBiH)	Since 1990
	– Srpska demokratska stranka (SDS)	1990–1998
	– Srpska radikalna stranka Republike Srpske (SRS RS)	Since 1991
	– Stranka demokratska akcije (SDA)	1990–?
Bulgaria	– Bălgarska Christijandemokratičeska partija (Centăr) (BChP)	Since 1990
	– Bălgarska nacionalna radikalna partija (BNRP)	Since 1989
	– Nacionalen sayuz Ataka (NSA)	Since 2005
	– Partiya Ataka (Ataka)	Since 2005
	– Vătrešna makedonska revoljucionna organizacija–Săjuz na makedonskite družestva (VMRO-SMD)	Since 1990
Croatia	– Hrvatski blok (HB)	Since 2000
	– Hrvatska demokratska zajednica (HDZ)	1989–2000
	– Hrvatski istinski preporod (HIP)	Since 2001
	– Hrvatska stranka prava (HSP)	Since 1990
	– Hrvatska stranka prava-1861 (HSP 1861)	Since 1995
Cyprus	– Yeni Doğuş Partisi (YDP)	Since 1984

(Cont.)

Table 1. (*Cont.*)

Country	– Populist radical right parties	Period
Czech Republic	– Národní strana (NS)	Since 1998
	– Republikáni Miroslava Sládka (RMS)	Since 2001
	– Sdruženi pro republiku–Republikánská strana Československa (SPR-RSČ)	1989–2001
Denmark	– Dansk Folkeparti (DFP)	Since 1995
Estonia	– Eesti Iseseisvuspartei (EIP)	Since 1999
	– Eesti Kodanik (EK)	1992–1995
	– Eesti Rahvuslik Eduerakond (ERE)	1993–?
	– Eesti Rahvusliku Sõltumatuse Partei (ERSP)	1988–1995
	– Eesti Rahvuslaste Keskliit (ERKL)	1994–1996
	– Parem Eesti (PE)	1994–1995
Finland	– *Isänmaallinen kansanliike-Liitto (IKL)*	Since 1993
France	– Alsace d'abord	Since 1989
	– Front national (FN)	Since 1972
	– *Mouvement Corse pour l'Autodétermination (MCA)*	*1984–?*
	– Mouvement national républicaine (MNR)	Since 1999
Germany	– Deutsche Liga für Volk und Heimat (DLVH)	Since 1991
	– Deutsche Volksunion (DVU)	Since 1987
	– Republikaner (REP)	Since 1983
Greece	– Eoniko Komma (EK)	Since 1989
	– Front Line (FL)	*Since 1999*
	– Elliniko Metopo (EM)	Since 1994
	– ΚΟΜΜΑ ΕΛΛΗΝΙΣΜΟΥ (KE)	*Since 1996*
	– Laikos Orthodoxos Synagermos (LAOS)	Since 2000
Hungary	– Magyar Igazság és Élet Pártja (MIÉP)	Since 1993
Iceland		
Ireland	– Immigration Control Platform (ICP)	Since 1997
Italy	– Die Freiheitlichen (F)	*Since 1998*
	– Lega Lombarda (LL)	1984–1991
	– Lega Nord (LN)	Since 1991
	– Lega Veneto (LV)	1982–1991
	– Movimento Sociale–Fiamma Tricolore (MS-FT)	Since 1994
Latvia	– Tēvzeme un Brīvībai (TB)	1993–1995
Lithuania		
Luxemburg	– *Aktiounskomitee fir Demokratie a Rentegerechtegkeet*	Since ?
	– Lëtzebuerger Partei	1989–?
	– Nationalbewegong (NB)	1987–1995
Macedonia	– Dviženje za Semakedonska Akcija (MAAK)	Since 1990
	– Partia Demokratika Shqiptare	Since 1997
	– Vnatreška Makedonska Revolucionerna Organizacija – Demokratska Partija (VMRO-DP)	Since 1991

Table 1. (*Cont.*)

Country	– Populist radical right parties	Period
	– Vnatreška Makedonska Revolucionerna Organizacija– Demokratska Partija za Makedonsko Nacionalno Edinstvo (VMRO-DPMNE) *– Vnatreška Makedonska Revolucionerna Organizacija– Makedonska (VMRO-Makedonska)*	1990–1998
Netherlands	– Centrumpartij (CP)	1980–1986
	– Centrumdemocraten (CD)	1984–2002
	– Centrumpartij '86/Nationale Volkspartij (CP'86)	1986–1998
	– Nederlandse Volksunie (NVU)	1971–1996
	– Nieuw Rechts	Since 2003
Norway		
Poland	– Alternatywa Partia Pracy (APP)	Since 2001
	– Konfederacja Polski Niepodległej–Ojczyzna (KPN-O)	Since 1999
	– Liga Polskich Rodzin (LPR)	Since 2001
	– Party X	1990–1991
	– Ruch Odbudowy Polski (ROP)	*Since 1995*
	– Ruch Społeczny Alternatywa (RSA)	*1998–2001*
	– Stronnictwo Narodowe (SR)	Since 1989
Portugal	– Aliança Nacional *– Partido Renovador Nacional (PRN)*	
Romania	– Partidul (Popular) România Mare (PRM)	Since 1991
	– Partidul Unității Naționale a Românilor (PUNR)	Since 1990
Russia	– Liberal'no-demokraticheskoi partii Rossii (LDPR)	Since 1989
Serbia &	– Lëvizja Kombëtare për Çlirimin e Kosovës (LKÇK)	Since 1993
Montenegro	– Srpski pokret obnove (SPO)	1990–1996
	– Srpska radikalna stranka (SRS)	Since 1991
	– Stranka srpskog jedinstva (SSJ)	Since 1990
Slovakia	– Prava Slovenská národná strana (PSNS)	2001–2003
	– Slovenská národná strana (SNS)	Since 1993
Slovenia	– Republikanci Slovenije (RS)	Since 1992
	– Slovenska nacionalna desnica (SND)	1993-*1996*
	– Slovenska nacionalna stranka (SNS)	1990-*2000*
	– Stranka slovenskega naroda (SSN)	Since *1996*
Spain	– Alternativa Española	Since 2005
	– Democracia nacional (DN)	Since 1994
	– España 2000	*Since 2002*
	– Frente Nacional	Since 1986
Sweden	– Nationaldemokraterna (ND)	Since 2001
	– Skånes Väl (SV)	Since 1997
	– Sverigedemokraterna (SD)	Since 1988

(*Cont.*)

Table 1. (*Cont.*)

Country	– Populist radical right parties	Period
Switzerland	– Freiheits-Partei der Schweiz (FPS)	Since 1994
	– Nationale Aktion für Volk und Heimat (NA)	1961–1990
	– Schweizer Demokraten/Démocrates suisses (SD)	Since 1990
	– Schweizer Republikaner Bewegung/Mouvement républicaine Suisse (SRB)	1971–1989
	– Vigilance	1964–*1993*
Ukraine	– *All-Ukrainian Union "Svoboda"*	Since 2004
	– Kongres Ukraiins'kikh Natsionalistiv (KUN)	Since 1992
United Kingdom	– British National Party (BNP)	*Since 1980*
	– Freedom Party	Since 2004
	– National Front (NF)	*Since 1967*
	– Veritas	Since 2005

Source: The information is taken from a broad range of books, articles and websites.
Note: Whenever there exists doubt about the populist radical right status of the party in question, of the period, or of the date of foundation, the information is indicated in italics.

Appendix B   Questionnaire

1   Self-definition

– What is the self-definition of the party?
   (e.g. the Vlaams Blok defines itself as "right-wing nationalist")
– Does the party see itself as '**right**,' '**left**,' '**centre**,' or does it reject these categories for itself?

2   Ideology

2a   *Globalization*

– How does the party value the process of globalization *(i.e. positive, neutral, negative)*? Is it a prominent theme in the party propaganda?
– Does the party distinguish between **cultural, economic and political** (effects of) globalization? If so, which effects does the party see and how does it speak about them?
   (e.g. does it speak of the New World Order, of McDonaldization, etc.?)

2b   *Economy*

– Which term(s) does the party use for its preferred (socio)economic policy?
   (e.g. 'social market economy,' 'fair market economy')
– What are the important features of the economic policy for the party?
   (e.g. ethnic or national preference; protection of certain national or social groups, state vs. market, etc.)
– Is the economic policy a primary or secondary issue for the party?
– And for its voters?
   (please substantiate with references to empirical data, if available)

309

2c   Democracy

- How does the party value 'democracy' as an ideology? How does it value the state of democracy in the country?
- What does the party say about central elements of *liberal* democracy? *(e.g. constitutional limitations to the rule of the majority, minority rights)*
- How does it define a 'real' democracy?
- Does it define 'the people' as a homogeneous or heterogeneous entity? And 'the elite'?

2d   Enemies

- Which groups does the party see as enemies within the state, but outside of the nation? *(e.g. Muslims, Roma, Jews, Hungarians, Germans)*
- Which groups (if any) does the party see as enemies within the own nation? *(e.g. pro-Western elites, homosexuals, nonbelievers)*
- Which groups (if any) does the party see as enemies outside of the state and of the nation? *(e.g. International Jewry, 'the West,' 'Islam,' the US)*

3   Leaders, Members, Voters

- Are there prominent women in the party? *(e.g. the leader, in the leadership, in localities)*
- Are there any data available on the party membership? *(if so, please stress most important characteristics)*
- Are there any (reliable) data available on the electorate of the party? *(if so, please stress most important characteristics; particularly the representation of women and the most important reasons to vote for the party)*

4   Supply-Side

- What are the characteristics of the party organization? *(e.g. well-structured and -organized; auxiliary or front-organizations)*
- Is the party embedded in a larger subculture? *(e.g. a nationalist or religious movement)*
- Does the party have various leaders, performing different tasks and attracting different electorates?

- What is the importance of the party leader? Is she or he considered to be 'charismatic'?
  (are data available on the attractiveness of the leader to the electorate?)

5 International Contacts

- Is the party a member of any transnational party grouping?
  (e.g. party group in European Parliament or pan-Slavic group)
- Are there official contacts with and visits to and from foreign parties?
- Which foreign parties does the party consider to be similar or ideologically related?

6 Various

- How is the party generally perceived in your country – i.e. both by the elites (e.g. academics, journalists, other parties) and by the masses (e.g. voters)?
  (e.g. as extreme right, as part of the mainstream, as different from all others)
- Are there any important characteristics or points about the party that have not been addressed by these questions?
  (feel free to add whatever you find important to note!)

Thanks a lot for your help!!!

Bibliography

Abedi, Amir (2002) "Challenges to established parties: the effects of party system features on the electoral fortunes of anti-political-establishment parties," *European Journal of Political Research* 41(4): 551–83.

— (2004) *Anti-Political Establishment Parties: A Comparative Analysis*. London: Routledge.

Abizadeh, Arash (2004) "Liberal nationalist versus postnational social integration: on the nation's ethno-cultural particularity and 'concreteness'," *Nations and Nationalism* 10(3): 231–50.

Abts, Koen and Stefan Rummens (2005) "Populistische democratie: een contradictie?!," paper presented at the Politicologenetmaal, Antwerp, May 19–20.

Adler, Frank (2001) "Immigration, insecurity and the French far right," *Telos*, 120: 31–48.

Adorno, T. W., Else Frenkel-Brunswik, Daniel J. Levinson and R. Nevitt Sanford (1969) *The Authoritarian Personality*. New York: W.W. Norton.

Agir (n.d.) *AGIR. Un programme. Une action . . .*

Ahlemeyer, Volker (2006) "The coalition potential of extreme right parties in Western Europe." Cambridge University: unpublished Ph.D thesis.

Akgun, Birol (2002) "Twins or enemies: comparing nationalist and Islamist traditions in Turkish politics", *Middle East Review of International Affairs* 6(1): 17–35.

Akkerman, Tjitske (2005) "Anti-immigration parties and the defence of liberal values: the exceptional case of the List Pim Fortuyn", paper presented at the Politicologenetmaal, Antwerp, May 19–20.

Alaluf, Mateo (1998) "L'émergence du Front national en Belgique est plus redevable aux circonstances qu'à son programme", in Pascal Delwit, Jean-Michel De Waele, and Andrea Rea (eds.), *L'extrême droite en France et en Belgique*. Brussels: Éditions Complexe, 101–18.

Albertazzi, Daniele (2006) "The Lega dei Ticinesi: the embodiment of populism", *Politics* 26(2): 133–9.

Alexander, Robert J. (2001) *Maoism in the Developed World*. Westport: Praeger.

Allwood, Gill and Khursheed Wadia (2000) *Women and Politics in France 1958–2000*. London: Routledge.

Almond, Gabriel A. (1956) "Comparative political systems", *Journal of Politics* 18(3): 391–409.

Altemeyer, Bob (1981) *Right-Wing Authoritarianism*. Winnipeg: The University of Manitoba Press.

Alter, Peter (1989) *Nationalism*. London: Arnold, 2nd edn.

Altermatt, Urs and Markus Furrer (1994) "Die Autopartei: Protest für Freiheit, Wohlstand und das Auto", in Urs Altermatt *et al.* (eds.), *Rechte und linke Fundamentalopposition. Studien zur Schweizer Politik 1965–1990*. Basel: Helbing & Lichtenhahn, 135–53.

Altermatt, Urs and Hanspeter Kriesi (1995) *Rechtsextremismus in der Schweiz: Organisationen und Radikalisierung in den 1980er und 1990er Jahren*. Zurich: Verlag Neue Zürcher Zeitung.

Altermatt, Urs and Damir Skenderovic (1999) "Die rechtsextreme Landschaft in der Schweiz: Typologie und aktuelle Entwicklungen", *Österreichische Zeitschrift für Politikwissenschaft* 28(1): 101–9.

Amesberger, Helga and Brigitte Halbmayr (eds.) (2002a) *Rechtsextreme Parteien – eine mögliche Heimat für Frauen?* Opladen: Leske + Budrich.

— (2002b) "Einleitung", in Helga Amesberger and Brigitte Halbmayr (eds.), *Rechtsextreme Parteien – eine mögliche Heimat für Frauen?* Opladen: Leske + Budrich, 17–26.

— (in collaboration with Claudia Lohinger) (2002c) "Österreich: Die Freiheitliche Partei Österreichs", in Helga Amesberger and Brigitte Halbmayr (eds.), *Rechtsextreme Parteien – eine mögliche Heimat für Frauen?* Opladen: Leske + Budrich, 251–405.

Amin, Samir (1997) *Capitalism in the Age of Globalization*. London: Zed.

Anastasakis, Othon (2000) "Extreme right in Europe: a comparative study of recent trends", *Discussion Paper Series* 3, from: www.lse.ac.uk/Depts/European/hellenic/Anastasakis_Discussion_Paper3.PDF (accessed 12/02/2003).

— (2002) "Political extremism in Eastern Europe: a reaction to transition", *Papeles del Este; Transiciones poscomunistas* 3, from: www.ucm.es/BUCM/cee/papeles/03/02.PDF (accessed 12/02/2003).

Andersen, Jørgen Goul (2002) "Denmark: a landslide to the right by trustful voters", in *Europe and the Crisis of Democracy: Elections in Europe: 1999–2002*. Paris: Notre Europe, 13–15.

Andersen, Robert and Jocelyn A.J. Evans (2004) *Social-Political Context and Authoritarian Attitudes: Evidence from Seven European Countries*. Glasgow: CREST Working Paper (No. 104).

Andersen, Walter K. (1998) "Bharatiya Janata Party: searching for the Hindu nationalist face," in Hans-George Betz and Stefan Immerfall (eds.), *The New Politics of the Right: Neo-Populist Parties and Movements in Established Democracies*. New York: St. Martin's, 219–32.

Anderson, Benedict (1983) *Imagined Communities: Reflections on the Origin and Spread of Nationalism*. New York: Verso.

Andeweg, Rudy B. (1995) "The reshaping of national party systems", *West European Politics* 18(3): 58–78.

— (2001) "Lijphart versus Lijphart: the cons of consensus democracy in homogeneous societies", *Acta Politica* 36: 117–28.

Andreescu, Gabriel (2005) "Romania", in Cas Mudde (ed.), *Racist Extremism in Central and Eastern Europe*. London: Routledge, 184–209.

Antić Gaber, Milica (1999) "Slovene political parties and their influence on the electoral prospects of women", in Chris Corrin (ed.), *Gender and Identity in Central and Eastern Europe*. London: Frank Cass, 7–29.

— (2003) "Factors influencing women's presence in Slovene parliament", in Richard E. Matland and Kathleen A. Montgomery (eds.), *Women's Access to Political Power in Post-Communist Europe*. Oxford: Oxford University Press, 267–84.

Antić Gaber, Milica and Gabrielle Ilonszki (2003) *Women in Parliamentary Politics: Hungarian and Slovene Cases Compared*. Ljubljana: Mirovni Inštitut.

Antonio, Robert J. (2000) "After postmodernism: reactionary tribalism", *American Journal of Sociology* 106(2): 40–87.

Aras, Bülent and Gökhan Bacik (2000) "The rise of Nationalist Action Party and Turkish politics", *Nationalism & Ethnic Politics* 6(4): 48–64.

Art, David (2006) *The Politics of the Nazi Past in Germany and Austria*. New York: Cambridge University Press.

Arzheimer, Kai and Elisabeth Carter (2006) "Political opportunity structures and right-wing extremist party success", *European Journal of Political Research* 45(3): 419–44.

AS (2005) *Programma POLITICO*, from: www.aseuropa.it/progpol1.htm (accessed 25/05/2005).

Ataka (2005) *Programna Shema na Partiya ATAKA*, from: www.ataka.bg/index.php?option=com_content&task=view&id=124&Itemid=32 (accessed 24/01/2006).

Backes, Uwe (1991) "Nationalpopulistische Protestparteien in Europa: Vergleichende Betrachtung zur phänomologischen und demokratietheoretischen Einordnung", *Österreichische Zeitschrift für Politikwissenschaft* 20(1): 7–17.

— (1996) "Ideologie und Programmatik rechtsextremer Parteien – Unterschiede und Gemeinsamkeiten", in Jürgen W. Falter, Hans-Gerd Jaschke, and Jürgen R. Winkler (eds.), *Rechtsextremismus: Ergebnisse und Perspektiven der Forschung*. Opladen: Westdeutscher, 376–87.

— (2003a) "Rechtsextremismus – Konzeptionen und Kontroversen", in Uwe Backes (ed.), *Rechtsextreme Ideologien in Geschichte und Gegenwart*. Cologne: Böhlau, 15–52.

— (2003b) "Extremismus und politisch motivierte Gewalt", in Eckhard Jesse and Roland Sturm (eds.), *Demokratien des 21. Jahrhunderts im Vergleich: Historische Zugänge, Gegenwartsprobleme, Reformperspektiven*. Opladen: Leske + Budrich, 341–67.

Backes, Uwe and Eckhard Jesse (1993) *Politischer Extremismus in der Bundesrepublik Deutschland*. Berlin: Propyläen.

Backes, Uwe and Cas Mudde (2000) "Germany: extremism without successful parties", *Parliamentary Affairs* 53(3): 457–68.

Bakke, Elisabeth and Nick Sitter (2005) "Patterns of stability: party competition and strategy in Central Europe since 1989", *Party Politics* 11(3): 243–63.

Bale, Tim (2003) "Cinderella and her ugly sisters: the mainstream and extreme right in Europe's bipolarising party systems", *West European Politics* 26(3): 67–90.

Ball, Terence (1999) "From 'core' to 'sore' concepts: ideological innovation and conceptual change", *Journal of Political Ideologies* 4(3): 391–6.

Barany, Zoltan (2002) *The East European Gypsies: Regime Change, Marginality, and Ethnopolitics.* Cambridge: Cambridge University Press.

Barber, Benjamin (1995) *Jihad vs. McWorld.* New York: Times Books.

Bardi, Luciano (1994) "Transnational party federations, European Parliamentary Groups, and the building of Europarties", in Richard S. Katz and Peter Mair (eds.), *How Parties Organize: Change and Adaptation in Party Organizations in Western Democracies.* London: Sage, 357–72.

Barney, Darin David and David Laycock (1999) "Right-populists and plebiscitary politics in Canada", *Party Politics* 5(3): 317–39.

Basom, Kenneth E. (1996) "Prospects for democracy in Serbia and Croatia", *East European Qaurterly* 29(4): 509–28.

Bastow, Steve (1997) "Front National economic policy: from neo-liberalism to protectionism", *Modern & Contemporary France* 5(1): 61–72.

— (1998) "The radicalization of the Front national discourse: a politics of the 'third way'?", *Patterns of Prejudice* 32(3): 55–68.

— (2000) "Le Mouvement national républicain: moderate right-wing party or party of the extreme right?," *Patterns of Prejudice* 34(2): 3–18.

— (2002) "A neo-fascist third way: the discourse of ethno-differentialist revolutionary nationalism", *Journal of Political Ideologies* 7(3): 351–68.

Batory, Agnes (2002) "Attitudes to Europe: ideology, strategy, and the question of EU membership in Hungarian party politics", *Party Politics* 8(5): 525–39.

Bauer, Petra and Oskar Niedermayer (1990) "Extrem rechtes Potential in den Ländern der Europäischen Gemeinschaft", *Aus Politik und Zeitgeschichte* 43(46–47): 15–26.

Bayer, Josef (2002) "Rechtspopulismus und Rechtsextremismus in Ostmitteleuropa", *Österreichische Zeitschrift für Politikwissenschaft* 31(3): 265–80.

— (2005) "Die Fidesz im Wechsel zwischen Oppositions- und Regierungspartei: Populistische Politik in der ungarischen Demokratie", in Susanne Frölich-Steffen and Lars Rensmann (eds.), *Populisten an der Macht: Populistische Regierungsparteien in West- und Osteuropa.* Vienna: Braumüller, 173–89.

Beck, Ulrich (1992) *Risk Society: Towards a New Modernity.* London: Sage.

Beichelt, Timm (2004) "Euro-skepticism in the EU accession countries", *Comparative European Politics* 2(1): 29–50.

Beichelt, Timm and Michael Minkenberg (2002) "Rechtsradikalismus in Transformationsgesellschaften: Entstehungsbedingungen und Erklärungs modell", *Osteuropa* 52(2): 247–62.

Beissinger, Mark (2002) *Nationalist Mobilization and the Collapse of the Soviet State.* Cambridge: Cambridge University Press.

Bélanger, Éric (2004) "Antipartyism and third-party vote choice: a comparison of Canada, Britain, and Australia", *Party Politics* 37(9): 1054–78.

Bélanger, Éric and Bonnie M. Meguid (2005) "Issue salience, issue ownership and issue-based vote choice: evidence from Canada", paper presented at the Canadian Political Science Association, London, Ontario, June 2–4.

Bell, Daniel (1960) *The End of Ideology: On the Exhaustion of Political Ideas in the Fifties.* Glencoe: Free Press.

Bell, David S. (2000) *Parties and Democracy in France: Parties under Presidentialism.* Aldershot: Ashgate.

Bell, John D. (1999) "The radical right in Bulgaria", in Sabrina P. Ramet (ed.), *The Radical Right in Central and Eastern Europe since 1989.* University Park: Pennsylvania State University Press, 233–54.

Bennett, David H. (1990) *The Party of Fear: From Nativist Movements to the New Right in American History.* New York: Vintage.

Benton, Sarah (1998) "Founding fathers and earth mothers: women's place at the 'birth' of nations", in Nickie Charles and Helen Hintjes (eds.), *Gender, Ethnicity and Political Ideologies.* London: Routledge, 27–45.

Berger, Peter B. and Samuel P. Huntington (eds.) (2002) *Many Globalizations: Cultural Diversity in the Contemporary World.* Oxford: Oxford University Press.

Bergh, Johannes (2004) "Protest voting in Austria, Denmark, and Norway", *Scandinavian Political Studies* 27(4): 367–89.

Bergsdorf, Harald (2000) "Rhetorik des Populismus am Beispiel rechtsextremer und rechtspopulistischer Parteien wie der 'Republikaner', der FPÖ und des 'Front National'", *Zeitschrift für Parlamentsfragen* 31(3): 620–6.

Berman, Sheri (1997) "The life of the party", *Comparative Politics* 30(1): 101–22.

Bernáth, Gábor, Gábor Milkósi and Cas Mudde (2005) "Hungary", in Cas Mudde (ed.), *Racist Extremism in Central and Eastern Europe.* London: Routledge, 80–100.

Bernstein, Herman (1935) *The Truth about "The Protocols of Zion."* New York: Covici and Friede.

Betz, Hans-Georg (1993a) "The two faces of radical right-wing populism in Western Europe", *Review of Politics* 55(4): 663–85.

— (1993b) "The new politics of resentment: radical right-wing populist parties in Western Europe", *Comparative Politics* 25(4): 413–27.

— (1994) *Radical Right-Wing Populism in Western Europe.* Basingstoke: Macmillan.

— (1998) "Against Rome: the Lega Nord", in Hans-Georg Betz and Stefan Immerfall (eds.), *The New Politics of the Right: Neo-Populist Parties and Movements in Established Democracies.* New York: St. Martin's, 45–57.

— (1999) "Contemporary right-wing radicalism in Europe", *Contemporary European History* 8(2): 299–316.

— (2001) "Exclusionary populism in Austria, Italy, and Switzerland", *International Journal* 56(3): 393–420.

— (2002a) "The divergent paths of the FPÖ and the Lega Nord", in Martin Schain, Aristide Zolberg and Patrick Hossay (eds.), *Shadows over Europe: The Development and Impact of the Extreme Right in Western Europe.* New York: Palgrave, 61–81.

— (2002b) "Conditions favouring the success and failure of radical right-wing populist parties in contemporary democracies", in Yves Mény and Yves Surel (eds.), *Democracies and the Populist Challenge.* Basingstoke: Palgrave, 197–213.

— (2003a) "Xenophobia, identity politics and exclusionary populism in Western Europe", in Leo Panitch and Colin Leys (eds.), *Fighting Identities: Race, Religion and Ethno-Nationalism*. London: Merlin, 193–210.

— (2003b) "The growing threat of the radical right", in Peter H. Merkl and Leonard Weinberg (eds.), *Right-Wing Extremism in the Twenty-First Century*. London: Frank Cass, 74–93.

— (2004) *La droite populiste en Europe: Extrême et démocrate?* Paris: CEVIPOF/Autrement.

Betz, Hans-Georg and Stefan Immerfall (eds.) (1998) *The New Politics of the Right: Neo-Populist Parties and Movements in Established Democracies*. New York: St. Martin's.

Betz, Hans-Georg and Carol Johnson (2004) "Against the current – stemming the tide: the nostalgic ideology of the contemporary radical populist right", *Journal of Political Ideologies* 9(3): 311–27.

Bieber, Florian (2005) *Nationalismus in Serbien vom Tode Titos bis zum Ende der Ära Milosevic*. Münster: LIT.

Billiet, Jaak (1995) "Church involvement, ethnocentrism, and voting for a radical right-wing party: diverging behavioral outcomes of equal attitudinal dispositions", *Sociology of Religion* 56(3): 303–26.

Billiet, Jaak and Hans De Witte (1995) "Attitudinal disposition to vote for an extreme right-wing party: the case of 'Vlaams Blok'", *European Journal of Political Research* 27(2): 181–202.

Billig, Michael (1995) *Banal Nationalism*. London: Sage.

Binder, Tanja (2003) "Heirat und Familie: Das Frauenbild in postsozialistischen Parteiprogrammen", *Osteuropa* 53(5): 675–88.

Biorcio, Roberto (2003) "The *Lega Nord* and the Italian media system", in Gianpietro Mazzoleni *et al.* (eds.), *The Media and Neo-Populism: A Contemporary Analysis*. Westport: Praeger, 71–94.

Birch, Sarah (2001) "Electoral systems and party system stability in post-communist Europe", paper presented at the 97th annual APSA meeting, San Francisco, August 30 – September 2.

Birenbaum, Guy and Marina Villa (2003) "The media and neo-populism in France", in Gianpietro Mazzoleni *et al.* (eds.), *The Media and Neo-Populism: A Contemporary Analysis*. Westport: Praeger, 45–70.

Birnbaum, Pierre (1992) *Anti-Semitism in France: A Political History from Léon Blum to the Present*. Oxford: Blackwell.

Birsl, Ursula (1994) *Rechtsextremismus: weiblich – männlich? Eine Fallstudie zu geschlechtsspezifischen Lebensverläufen, Handlungsspielräumen und Orientierungsweisen*. Opladen: Leske + Budrich.

— (1996) "Rechtsextremismus und Fremdenfeindlichkeit. Reagieren Frauen anders? Zur theoretischen Verortung der Kategorie Geschlecht in der feministischen Rechtsextremismus-Forschung", *Politische Vierteljahresschrift Sonderheft* 27: 48–65.

Björgo, Tore and Rob Witte (eds.) (1993a) *Racist Violence in Europe*. New York: St. Martin's.

— (1993b) "Introduction", in Tore Björgo and Rob Witte (eds.), *Racist Violence in Europe*. New York: St. Martin's, 1–16.

Bjørklund, Tor and Jørgen Goul Andersen (2002) "Anti-immigration parties in Denmark and Norway: the Progress Parties and the Danish People's Party", in Martin Schain, Aristide Zolberg, and Patrick Hossay (eds.), *Shadows over Europe: The Development and Impact of the Extreme Right in Western Europe.* New York: Palgrave, 107–36.

Blaise, Pierre and Patrick Moreau (eds.) (2004) *Extrême droite et national-populisme en Europe de l'Ouest.* Brussels: CRISP.

Blee, Kathleen (2002) *Inside Organized Racism: Women in the Hate Movement.* Berkeley: University of California Press.

Blokker, Paul (2005) "Populist nationalism, anti-Europeanism, post-nationalism, and the East–West distinction", *German Law Journal* 6(2): 371–89.

Blyth, Mark (2003) "Globalization and the limits of democratic choice: social democracy and the rise of political cartelization", *Internationale Politik und Gesellschaft* 3: 60–82.

Blyth, Mark and Richard S. Katz (2005) "From catch-all politics to cartelisation: the political economy of the cartel party", *West European Politics* 28(1): 33–60.

BNP (1994) *British Nationalist: For Race and Nation*, Number 143.

— (2004) *London Needs the BNP: British National Party London Mayoral & Greater London Assembly Manifesto 2004.* Waltham Cross, Herts: BNP.

— (2005) *Rebuilding British Democracy: British National Party General Election Manifesto 2005*, from www.bnp.org.uk/candidates2005/man_menu.htm (accessed 04/02/2006).

— (n.d.) "What we stand for", from: www.bnp.org.uk/policies.html (accessed 20/05/2003).

Bobbio, Norberto (1994) "Rechts und Links: Zum Sinn einer politischen Unterscheidung", *Blätter für deutsche und internationale Politik* 39(5): 543–9.

Bock, Andreas (2002) "Ungarn: die 'Wahrheits- und Lebenspartei' zwischen Ethnozentrismus und Rassismus", *Osteuropa* 52(3): 280–92.

Bogdanor, Vernon (1995) "Overcoming the twentieth century: democracy and nationalism in Central and Eastern Europe", *The Political Quarterly* 66(1): 84–97.

Bohlen, Celestine (2002) "Hungary's odd affair with the right", *New York Times*, 12 May.

Bohrer II, Robert E., Alexander C. Pacek, and Benjamin Radcliff (2000) "Electoral participation, ideology, and party politics in post-communist Europe", *Journal of Politics* 62(4): 1161–72.

Boisserie, Etienne (1998) "Slovakia", in Jean-Yves Camus (ed.), *Extremism in Europe: 1998 Survey.* Paris: CERA/l'aube essay, 291–303.

Bottom, Karen (2004) *The Changing Fortunes of Parties without Establishment Status: New Populism in the Cartel?* Manchester: European Policy and Research Unit Working Paper (No.8/2004).

Bowen, John R. (1996) "The myth of global ethnic conflict", *Journal of Democracy* 7(4): 3–14.

Braun, Aurel (1997) "The incomplete revolutions: the rise of extremism in East-Central Europe and the Former Soviet Union", in Aurel Braun and Stephen

Scheinberg (eds.), *The Extreme Right: Freedom and Security at Risk*. Boulder: Westview, 138–60.

Brauner-Orthen, Alice (2001) *Die neue Rechte in Deutschland: Antidemokratische und rassistische Tendenzen*. Opladen: Leske + Budrich.

Brewer, Marilynn B. (1999) "The psychology of prejudice: ingroup love or outgroup hate?", *Journal of Social Issues* 55(3): 429–44.

Brubaker, Roger (1992) *Citizenship and Nationhood in France and Germany*. Cambridge, MA: Harvard University Press.

Brück, Brigitte (2005) *Frauen und Rechtsradikalismus in Europa. Eine Studie zu Frauen in Führungspositionen rechtsradikaler Parteien in Deutschland, Frankreich und Italien*. Wiesbaden: VS Verlag für Sozialwissenschaften.

Brune, Nancy and Geoffrey Garrett (2005) "The globalization Rorschach test: international economic integration, inequality, and the role of government," *Annual Review of Political Science* 8: 399–423.

Buchanan, Patrick J. (2000) "A den of thieves", speech delivered to Boston University, Boston, MA, 31 March, from: www.buchanan.org/pa-00-331-opecspeech.html (accessed 22/05/2003).

Buchowski, Michał (2004) "European integration and the question of national identity: fear and its consequence", *The Polish Review* 49(3): 891–901.

Büchsenschütz, Ulrich and Ivo Georgiev (2001) "Nationalismus, nationalistische Parteien und Demokratie in Bulgarien seit 1989", *Südosteuropa* 50(3–4): 233–62.

Budge, Ian and Dennis J. Farlie (1983) *Explaining and Predicting Elections: Issue Effects and Party Strategies in Twenty-Three Democracies*. London: Allen & Unwin.

Budge, Ian, David Robertson, and Derek Hearl (eds.) (1987) *Ideology, Strategy and Party Change: Spatial Analysis of Post-War Election Programmes in 19 Democracies*. Cambridge: Cambridge University Press.

Buelens, Jo and Kris Deschouwer (2003) *De verboden vleespotten: De partijorganisatie van het Vlaams Blok tussen oppositie en machtsdeelname*. Brussels: VUB – Vakgroep Politieke Wetenschappen.

Bugajski, Janusz (1994) *Ethnic Politics in Eastern Europe: A Guide to Nationality Policies, Organizations, and Parties*. Armonk: M.E. Sharpe.

Buric, Christian (2002) "Kroatiens Innenpolitik und seine euro-atlantischen Integrationsbestrebungen", *Südosteuropa* 51(4–6): 250–65.

Butenschøn, Nils (1993) *The Politics of Ethnocracies: Principles and Dilemmas of Ethnic Domination*. Oslo: Department of Political Science Working Paper (No. 01/03).

Butterwege, Christoph (2002) "Traditioneller Rechtsextremismus im Osten – modernisierter Rechtsextremismus im Westen: Ideologische Ausdifferenzierung durch neoliberale Globalisierung", *Osteuropa* 52(7): 914–20.

Butterwege, Christoph et al. (1997) *Rechtsextremisten in Parlamenten. Forschungsstand, Fallstudien, Gegenstrategien*. Opladen: Leske + Budrich.

BZÖ (2005) *Bündnispositionen*, from: www.bzoe.at (accessed 25/05/2005).

Camus, Jean-Yves (2003) "Strömungen der europäischen extremen Rechten – Populisten, Integristen, Nationalrevolutionäre, Neue Rechte", in Uwe

Backes (ed.), *Rechtsextreme Ideologien in Geschichte und Gegenwart*. Cologne: Böhlau, 235–59.

Canovan, Margaret (1999) "Trust the people! Populism and the two faces of democracy", *Political Studies*, 47(1): 2–16.

Capitan, Colette and Colette Guillaumin (1997) "L'ordre et le sexe. Discours de gauche, discours de droite", in Claudie Lesselier and Fiametta Venner (eds.), *L'extrême droite et les femmes. Enjeux & actualité*. Villeurbanne: Golias, 17–24.

Capoccia, Giovanni (2005) *Defending Democracy: Reactions to Extremism in Interwar Europe*. Baltimore: Johns Hopkins University Press.

Carter, Elisabeth L. (2002) "Proportional representation and the fortunes of right-wing extremist parties", *West European Politics* 25(3): 125–46.

— (2004) "Does PR promote political extremism? Evidence from the West European parties of the extreme right", *Representation* 40(2): 82–100.

— (2005) *The Extreme Right in Western Europe: Success or Failure?* Manchester: Manchester University Press.

Caul, Miki (1999) "Women's representation in parliament: the role of parties", *Party Politics* 5(1): 79–98.

CD (1998) *Trouw aan Rood Wit Blauw!* The Hague: Centrumdemocraten.

CDC (2003) *Reproductive, Maternal and Child Health in Eastern Europe and Russia: A Comparative Report*. Atlanta: Centers for Disease Control and Prevention.

Cento Bull, Anna and Mark Gilbert (2001) *The Lega Nord and the Northern Question in Italian Politics*. Basingstoke: Palgrave.

Centrumnieuws (party paper CP'86).

Chapin, Wesley D. (1997) "Explaining the electoral success of the new right: the German case", *West European Politics* 20(2): 53–72.

Chari, Raj S., Suvi Iltanen, and Sylvia Kritzinger (2004) "Examining and explaining the Northern League's 'u-turn' from Europe", *Government & Opposition* 39(3): 423–50.

Charitos, Christos (2001) "Euro comes, Greece goes", from: www.e-grammes.gr/2001/12/erhetai_euro_en.htm (accessed 14/07/2005).

Cheles, L., R. Ferguson, and M. Vaughan (eds.) (1991) *Neo-Fascism in Europe*. London: Longman.

— (eds.) (1995) *The Far Right in Western and Eastern Europe*. London: Longman.

Chianterra-Stutte, Patricia and Andrea Pető (2003) "Cultures of populism and the political right in Central Europe", *CLCWeb: Comparative Literature and Culture: A WWWeb Journal* 5(4), from: http://clcwebjournal.lib.purdue.edu/clcweb03-4/chiantera&peto03.html (accessed 02/04/2005).

Christiansen, Thomas (1998) "*Plaid Cymru*: dilemmas and ambiguities of Welsh regional nationalism", in Lieven De Winter and Huri Türsan (eds.), *Regionalist Parties in Western Europe*. London: Routledge, 125–42.

Christie, Richard and Marie Jahoda (eds.) (1954) *Studies in the Scope and Method of "The Authoritarian Personality."* Westport: Greenwood.

Christofferson, Thomas R. (2003) "The French elections of 2002: the issue of insecurity and the Le Pen effect", *Acta Politica* 38(1): 109–23.

Cibulka, Frank (1999) "The radical right in Slovakia", in Sabrina P. Ramet (ed.), *The Radical Right in Central and Eastern Europe since 1989*. University Park: Pennsylvania State University Press, 109–31.

Clark, Terry D. (1995) "The Zhirinovsky electoral victory: antecedence and aftermath", *Nationalities Papers* 34(4): 767–78.

— (2002) *Beyond Post-Communist Studies: Political Science and the New Democracies*. Armonk: M.E. Sharpe.

Clift, Ben (2002) "Social democracy and globalization: the cases of France and the UK", *Government & Opposition* 37(4): 466–500.

CLW (1999) "Current United Nations peace operations and U.S. troops level", from: www.clw.org/pub/clw/un/troops0499.html (accessed 23/05/2003).

CoE (2002) *Women in Politics in the Council of Europe Member States*. Strasbourg: Council of Europe.

Coenders, Marcel, Mérove Gijsberts and Peer Scheepers (2004) "Resistance to the presence of immigrants and refugees in 22 countries", in Mérove Gijsberts, Louk Hagendoorn, and Peer Scheepers (eds.), *Nationalism and Exclusion of Migrants: Cross-National Comparisons*. Aldershot: Ashgate, 97–120.

Coffé, Hilde (2004) "Groot in Vlaanderen, klein(er) in Wallonië: Een analyse van het electorale succes van de extreem-rechtse partijen." Brussels: unpublished Ph.D thesis (VUB).

— (2005) *Extreem-rechts in Vlaanderen en Wallonië: het verschil*. Roeselare: Roulerta.

Coffé, Hilde, Bruno Heyndel, and Jan Vermeir (2007) "Fertile grounds for extreme right-wing parties: explaining the Vlaams Blok's electoral success", *Electoral Studies*, 26(7): 142–55.

Cohn, Norman (1971) "Introduction", in Herman Bernstein, *The Truth about "The Protocols of Zion": A Complete Exposure*. New York: Ktav, ix–xxviii.

Cole, Alexandra (2005) "Old right or new right? The ideological positioning of parties of the far right", *European Journal of Political Research* 44(1): 203–30.

Collier, David and James E. Mahon Jr. (1993) "Conceptual 'stretching' revisited: adapting categories in comparative analysis", *American Political Science Review* 87(4): 845–55.

Colombo, Asher and Giuseppe Sciortino (2003) "The Bossi–Fini law: explicit fanaticism, implicit moderation, and poisoned fruits", in Jean Blondel and Paolo Segatti (eds.), *Italian Politics: The Second Berlusconi Government*. New York: Berghahn, 162–79.

Čolović, Ivan (2002) *Politics of Identity in Serbia: Essays in Political Anthropology*. New York: New York University Press.

Comité Nationalisten tegen Globalisering (n.d.) "Nationalisten tegen globalisering", from: www.strijd.be/platform.htm (accessed 02/06/2003).

Conway, M. Margaret, Gertrude A. Steuernagel and David W. Ahern (1997) *Women and Political Participation: Cultural Change in the Political Arena*. Washington, DC: Congressional Quarterly.

Copsey, Nigel (1996) "Contemporary fascism in the local arena: the British National Party and 'Rights for Whites'", in Mike Cronin (ed.), *The Failure of British Fascism: The Far Right and the Fight for Political Recognition.* Basingstoke: Macmillan, 118–40.

CP (1980) untitled campaign pamphlet.

CP'86 (1989) *Nationaaldemocratische gedachten voor een menswaardige toekomst.*
— (1990) *Voor een veilig en leefbaar Nederland!*

Csergő, Zsuzsa and James M. Goldgeier (2004) "Nationalist strategies and European integration", *Perspectives on Politics* 2(7): 21–37.

Csurka, István (1997) "Istvan Csurka, Vorsitzender der Magyar Ignzsag Ez Elet Part (MIEP) in Ungarn", in Rolf-Josef Eibicht (ed.), *Jörg Haider. Patriot im Zwielicht?* Stuttgart: DS, 259–63.

— (2000) "Mit ungarischen Augen", *Magyar Fórum*, 10 February, from: www.miep.hu/hirek/other/augen.htm (accessed 01/02/2001).

— (2004) *Magyar Szemmel IV.* Budapest: Magyar Fórum Könyvek.

Cuperus, René (2003) "The populist deficiency of European social democracy", *Internationale Politik und Gesellschaft* 3: 83–109.

Daalder, Hans (1992) "A crisis of party?", *Scandinavian Political Studies* 15(4): 269–87.

Dahl, Robert A. (2000) "A democratic paradox?", *Political Science Quarterly* 115(1): 35–40.

Dalton, Russell J. and Martin P. Wattenberg (2002) "Unthinkable democracy: political change in advanced industrial democracies", in Russell J. Dalton and Martin P. Wattenberg (eds.), *Parties without Partisans: Political Change in Advanced Industrial Democracies.* Oxford: Oxford University Press, 3–16.

Davies, Peter (1999) *The National Front in France: Ideology, Discourse and Power.* London: Routledge.

Davis, James W. (1998) *Leadership Selection in Six Western Democracies.* Westport: Greenwood.

Deacon, Greg, Ahmed Keita, and Ken Ritchie (2004) *Burnley and the BNP and the Case for Electoral Reform.* London: Electoral Reform Society.

DeAngelis, Richard A. (2003) "A rising tide for Jean-Marie, Jörg, & Pauline? Xenophobic populism in comparative perspective", *Australian Journal of Politics & History* 49(1): 75–92.

De Benoist, Alain (1985) *Kulturrevolution von rechts.* Krefeld: Sinus.

Dechezelles, Stéphanie (2004) "The right/extreme-right and the No-Global movement in Italy", paper presented at the 54th annual PSA meeting, Lincoln (UK), April 5–8.

Decker, Frank (2000) *Parteien unter Druck: Der neue Rechtspopulismus in den westlichen Demokratien.* Opladen: Leske + Budrich.

— (2003) "Rechtspopulismus in der Bundesrepublik Deutschland: Die Schill-Partei", in Nikolaus Werz (ed.), *Populismus: Populisten in Übersee und Europa.* Opladen: Leske + Budrich, 223–42.

— (2004) *Der neue Rechtspopulismus.* Opladen: Leske + Budrich.

DeClair, Edward G. (1999) *Politics on the Fringe: The People, Policies and Organization of the French Front National.* Durham, NC: Duke University Press.

De Decker, Pascal, Christian Kesteloot, Filip De Maesschalck, and Jan Vranken (2005) "Revitalizing the city in an anti-urban context: extreme right and the rise of urban policies in Flanders, Belgium", *International Journal of Urban and Regional Research* 29(1): 152–71.

De Felice, Renzo (1977) *Interpretations of Fascism*. Cambridge, MA: Harvard University Press.

Dehousse, Renaud (2002) "Introduction", in *Europe and the Crisis of Democracy: Elections in Europe: 1999–2002*. Paris: Notre Europe, 1–6.

De Lange, Sarah L. (2007a) "A new winning formula? The programmatic appeal of the radical right", *Party Politics*, forthcoming.

— (2007b) "From pariah to power broker. The radical right and government in Western Europe", in Pascal Delwit and Philippe Poirier (eds.), *The Extreme Right Parties and Power in Europe*. Brussels: Éditions de l'Université de Bruxelles, forthcoming.

De Lange, Sarah L. and Cas Mudde (2005) "Political extremism in Europe", *European Political Science* 4(4): 476–88.

Delwit, Pascal (2001) "La notion de 'parti alternatif': une comparaison France, Allemagne, Belgique", in Dominique Andolfatto, Fabienna Greffet, and Laurent Olivier (eds.), *Les parties politiques: Quelles perspectives?* Paris: L'Harmattan, 115–34.

— (ed.) (2003) *Démocraties chrétiennes et conservatismes en Europe: Une nouvelle convergence?* Brussels: Editions de l'Université de Bruxelles.

— (2007) "The Belgian National Front and power: an unthought relationship", in Pascal Delwit and Philippe Poirier (eds.), *The Extreme Right Parties and Power in Europe*. Brussels: Éditions de l'Université de Bruxelles.

Delwit, Pascal and Philippe Poirier (eds.) (2007) *The Extreme Right Parties and Power in Europe*. Brussels: Éditions de l'Université de Bruxelles.

Denemark, David and Shaun Bowler (2002) "Minor parties and protest votes in Australia and New Zealand: locating populist politics", *Electoral Studies* 21(1): 47–67.

De Neve, Dorothée (2001) "Wahlen in Rumänien – eine ganz normale Katastrophe?" *Osteuropa* 51(3): 281–98.

De Raad, Leonie (2005) "Nieuw rechts: Extreem-rechts?" Leiden: unpublished MA thesis.

Derks, Anton (2005) "Populisme en de ambivalentie van het egalitarisme: hoe rijmen sociaal wakkeren een rechtse partijvoorkeur met hun sociaal-economische attitudes?", paper presented at the Politicologenetmaal, Antwerp, May 19–20.

Deschouwer, Kris (2001) "De zorgeloze consensus: De statuten van het Vlaams Blok en de partijentheorie", *Tijdschrift voor Sociologie* 22(1): 63–87.

Detterbeck, Klaus (2005) "Cartel parties in Western Europe?", *Party Politics* 11(2): 173–91.

Deutchman, Iva Ellen and Anne Ellison (1999) "A star is born: the roller coaster ride of Pauline Hanson in the news", *Media, Culture & Society* 21(2): 33–50.

Deutsch, Karl W. (1953) *Nationalism and Social Communication: An Enquiry into the Foundations of Nationality*. Cambridge, MA: MIT Press.

De Weerdt, Yves, Hans De Witte, Patrizia Catellani, and Patrizia Milesi (2004) *Turning Right? Socio-Economic Change and the Receptiveness of European Workers to the Extreme Right: Report on the Survey Analysis and Results*. Leuven: HIVA.

Dewinter, Filip (1992) *Immigratie: de oplossingen. 70 voorstellen ter oplossing van het vreemdelingenprobleem.* Brussels: Nationalistisch Vormingsinstituut.

Dewinter, Filip and Karim Van Overmeire (1993) *Eén tegen allen: Opkomst van het Vlaams Blok.* Antwerp: Tyr.

De Winter, Lieven (1998) "The Volksunie and the dilemma between policy success and electoral survival in Flanders", in Lieven De Winter and Huri Türsan (eds.), *Regionalist Parties in Western Europe.* London: Routledge, 28–50.

De Winter, Lieven and Huri Türsan (eds.) (1998) *Regionalist Parties in Western Europe.* London: Routledge.

De Witte, Hans (1997) "Een overzicht en evaluatie van strategieën ter bestrijding van extreem-rechtse partijen", in Hans De Witte (ed.), *Bestrijding van racisme en rechts-extremisme: Wetenschappelijke bijdragen aan het maatschappelijk debat.* Leuven: Acco, 171–87.

— (1998) "Torenhoge verschillen in de lage landen: over het verschil in succes tussen de Centrumdemocraten en het Vlaams Blok", in Joop Van Holsteyn and Cas Mudde (eds.), *Extreem-rechts in Nederland.* The Hague: Sdu, 157–73.

De Witte, Hans, Jaak Billiet, and Peer Scheepers (1994) "Hoe zwart is Vlaanderen? Een exploratief onderzoek naar uiterst-rechtse denkbeelden in Vlaanderen in 1991", *Res Publica* 36(1): 85–102.

Dézé, Alexandre (2004) "Between adaptation, differentation and distinction: extreme right-wing parties within democratic political systems", in Roger Eatwell and Cas Mudde (eds.), *Western Democracies and the New Extreme Right Challenge.* London: Routledge, 19–40.

DFP (n.d.) "The Danish People's Party", from: www.danskfolkeparti.dk/sw/frontend/show.asp?parent=3293&menu_parent=&layout=0 (accessed 13/07/2005).

Dinan, Desmond (1994) *An Ever Closer Union? Introduction to the European Community.* Basingstoke: Macmillan.

DN (2002) *Documentos ideológicos y programáticos de Democracia Nacional.*

— (n.d.) "Twelve fundamental principles", from: www.democracianacional.org/index_old.htm (accessed 23/02/2005).

Downs, Anthony (1957) *An Economic Theory of Democracy.* New York: Harper.

DPNI (2004) "How many Russians are there left in Moscow?" from: www.dpni.org/eng.htm (accessed 01/05/2004).

Drakulic, Slobodan (2002) "Revising Franjo Tudjman's revisionism? A response to Ivo and Slavko Goldstein", *East European Jewish Affairs* 32(2): 61–9.

Dülmer, Hermann and Markus Klein (2005) "Extreme right-wing voting in Germany in a multilevel perspective: a rejoinder to Lubbers and Scheepers", *European Journal of Political Research* 44(2): 243–63.

Durham, Martin (1991) "Women and the National Front", in Luciano Cheles, Ronnie Ferguson, and Michalina Vaughan (eds.), *Neo-Fascism in Europe.* London: Longman, 264–83.

— (1998) *Women and Fascism.* London: Routledge.

Duverger, Maurice (1954) *Political Parties: Their Organization and Activity in the Modern State*. London: Methuen.

Dvořáková, Vladimíra and Jan Rataj (2006) "Historical roots of current Czech radical right wing movements", paper presented at the 20th IPSA World Congress, July 9–13, Fukuoka, Japan.

DVU (n.d.) *Partei-Programm*. Munich: Deutsche Volksunion.

Dymerskaya-Tsigelman, Liudmila and Leonid Finberg (1999) *Antisemitism of the Ukrainian Radical Nationalists: Ideology and Policy*. Jerusalem: The Vidal Sassoon International Center for the Study of Antisemitism (ACTA 14).

Eatwell, Roger (1989) "The nature of the right: the right as a variety of styles of thought", in Roger Eatwell and Noel O'Sullivan (eds.) *The Nature of the Right: European and American Political Thought since 1789*. London: Pinter, 62–76.

— (1996) "On defining the 'fascist minimum': the centrality of ideology", *Journal of Political Ideologies* 1(3): 303–19.

— (1998) "The dynamics of right-wing electoral breakthrough", *Patterns of Prejudice* 32(3): 3–31.

— (2000) "The extreme right and British exceptionalism: the primacy of politics", in Paul Hainsworth (ed.), *The Politics of the Extreme Right: From the Margins to the Mainstream*. London: Pinter, 172–92.

— (2003) "Ten theories of the extreme right", in Peter H. Merkl and Leonard Weinberg (eds.), *Right-Wing Extremism in the Twenty-First Century*. London: Frank Cass, 47–73.

— (2004) "The concept and theory of charismatic leadership", unpublished manuscript.

— (2005) "Charisma and the revival of the European extreme right", in Jens Rydgren (ed.), *Movements of Exclusion: Radical Right-Wing Populism in the West*. Hauppage: Nova Science, 101–20.

— (2006) "The concept and theory of charismatic leadership", *Totalitarian Movements and Political Religions* 7(2): 141–56.

Eatwell, Roger and Cas Mudde (eds.) (2004) *Democracy and the New Extreme Right Challenge*. London: Routledge.

EF (n.d.) "England First", from: www.englandfirst.net (accessed 23/05/2003).

Eichwede, Wolfgang (ed.) (1994) *Der Schirinowski-Effekt: Wohin treibt Rußland?* Reinbeck bei Hamburg: Rowohlt.

Eismann, Wolfgang (ed.) (2002) *Rechtspopulismus: Österreichische Krankheit oder europäische Normalität*. Vienna: Czernin.

Eith, Ulrich (2003) "Die Republikaner in Baden-Württemberg: Mehr als nur populistischer Protest", in Nikolaus Werz (ed.), *Populismus: Populisten in Übersee und Europa*. Opladen: Leske + Budrich, 243–61.

Elbers, Frank and Meindert Fennema (1993) *Racistische partijen in West-Europa. Tussen nationale traditie en Europese samenwerking*. Leiden: Stichting Burgerschapskunde.

Eminov, Ali (1997) *Turkish and Other Muslim Minorities in Bulgaria*. London: Hurst.

Enyedi, Zsolt (2005) "The role of agency in cleavage formation", *European Journal of Political Research* 44(5): 697–720.

Epstein, Simon (1996) *Extreme Right Electoral Upsurges in Western Europe: The 1984–1995 Wave as Compared with the Previous Ones.* Jerusalem: The Vidal Sassoon International Center for the Study of Antisemitism (ACTA 8).

Erk, Jan (2005) "From Vlaams Blok to Vlaams Belang: Belgian far-right renames itself", *West European Politics* 28(3): 493–502.

Esser, Marco and Joop van Holsteyn (1998) "Kleur bekennen. Over leden van de Centrumdemocraten", in Joop van Holsteyn and Cas Mudde (eds.), *Extreemrechts in Nederland.* The Hague: Sdu, 75–92.

EUMC (2005) *Racism and Xenophobia in the EU Member States: Trends, Developments and Good Practice. Annual Report 2005 – Part 2.* Vienna: European Monitoring Centre on Racism and Xenophobia.

Evans, Geoffrey and Ariana Need (2002) "Explaining ethnic polarization over attitudes towards minority rights in Eastern Europe: a multilevel analysis", *Social Science Research* 31(4): 653–80.

Evans, Jocelyn A.J. (2005) "The dynamics of social change in radical right-wing populist party support", *Comparative European Politics* 3(1): 76–101.

Evans, Jocelyn A.J. and Gilles Ivaldi (2002) "Les dynamiques électorales de l'extrême droite européenne", *Revue politique et parlementaire* 104(1019): 67–83.

— (2005) "An extremist autarky: the systematic separation of the French extreme right", *South European Society & Politics* 10(2): 351–66.

Evans, Jocelyn A.J., K. Arzheimer, G. Baldini, T. Bjørkland, *et al.* (2001) "Comparative mapping of extreme right electoral dynamics: an overview of EREPS ('Extreme Right Electorates and Party Success')", *European Political Science* 1(1).

F (n.d.) "Politik mit Herz und Verstand für Südtirol!", from: www.die-freiheitlichen.com/index.php?id=15 (accessed 31/12/2005).

FA (2005) "Wiener Erklärung des Kontaktforums der europäische patriotischen und nationalen Parteien und Bewegungen", November 14.

Fabbrini, Sergio (2002) "The domestic sources of European anti-Americanism", *Government & Opposition* 37(1): 3–14.

Fallend, Franz (2004) "Are right-wing populism and government participation incompatible? The case of the Freedom Party of Austria", *Representation* 40(2): 115–30.

Falter, Jürgen W. (1994) *Wer wählt rechts? Die Wähler und Anhänger rechtsextremistischer Parteien im vereinigten Deutschland.* München: CH Beck.

Feeney, Brian (2002) *Sinn Féin: A Hundred Turbulent Years.* Dublin: O'Brien.

Fennema, Meindert (1995) "Some theoretical problems and issues in the comparison of racist parties in Europe", paper presented at the ECPR Joint Sessions of Workshops, Bordeaux, April 27–May 2.

— (1997) "Some conceptual issues and problems in the comparison of anti-immigrant parties in Western Europe", *Party Politics* 3(4): 473–92.

Fennema, Meindert and Christopher Pollmann (1998) "Ideology of anti-immigrant parties in the European Parliament", *Acta Politica* 33(2): 111–38.

Fenner, Angelica and Eric D. Weitz (eds.) (2004) *Fascism and Neofascism: Critical Writings on the Radical Right in Europe*. New York: Palgrave.

Fetzer, John (2000) "Economic self-interest or cultural marginality? Anti-immigration sentiment and nativist political movements in France, Germany and the USA", *Journal of Ethnic and Migration Studies* 26(1): 5–23.

Fieschi, Catherine and Paul Heywood (2004) "Trust, cynicism and populist anti-politics", *Journal of Political Ideologies* 9(3): 289–309.

Fieschi, Catherine, James Shields and Roger Woods (1996) "Extreme right-wing parties and the European Union: France, Germany and Italy", in John Gaffney (ed.), *Political Parties and the European Union*. London: Routledge, 235–53.

Filc, Dani and Uri Lebel (2005) "The post-Oslo Israeli populist radical right in comparative perspective: leadership, voter characteristics and political discourse", *Mediterranean Politics* 10(1): 85–97.

Fischer-Galati, Stephen (1993) "The political right in Eastern Europe in historical perspective", in Joseph Held (ed.), *Democracy and Right-Wing Politics in Eastern Europe in the 1990s*. Boulder: East European Monographs, 1–12.

Fisher, Sharon (2000) "Representations of the nation in Slovakia's 1998 parliamentary election campaign", in Kieran Williams (ed.), *Slovakia after Communism and Mečiarism*. London: School of Slavonic and East European Studies, 33–50.

Flemming, Lars (2004) "Die NPD nach dem Verbotsverfahren – Der Weg aus der Bedeutungslosigkeit in die Bedeutungslosigkeit?", in Uwe Backes and Eckhard Jesse (eds.), *Jahrbuch Extremismus & Demokratie* 16. Baden-Baden: Nomos, 144–54.

FN (1991) *Immigration: 50 mesures concrètes: Les Français ont la parole*. Paris: Front National.

Ford, Glyn (1992) *Fascist Europe: The Rise of Racism and Xenophobia*. London: Pluto.

Fowler, B. (2003) "The parliamentary elections in Hungary, April 2002", *Electoral Studies* 22(4): 799–807.

FP (2005) *Manifesto of The Freedom Party*, from: www.freedompartyuk.net/public/manifesto/index.html (accessed 15/01/2006).

FPd (1998) "The Progress Party & the Treaty of Maastricht", from: www.frp.dk/foreign/engelsk2.htm (accessed 21/05/2003).

FPÖ (1997) *Program of the Austrian Freedom Party*. Vienna: FPÖ Die Freiheitlichen.

— (2005) *Das Parteiprogramm der Freiheitlichen Partei Österreichs: Mit Berücksichtigung der beschlossenen Änderungen vom 27. Ordentlichen Bundesparteitag der FPÖ am 23. April 2005 in Salzburg*, from: www.fpoe.at/fileadmin/Contentpool/Portal/PDFs/Parteiprogramm_Neu.pdf (accessed 02/08/2005).

FPS (1999) *Parteiprogramm der Freiheits-Partei der Schweiz FPS*, from: www.freiheits-partei.ch/article-369-parteiprogramm-fps.html (accessed 05/02/2006).

— (2003) "Neues Waffengesetz: Bedenkliches Waffengesetz", from: www.freiheits-partei.ch/article-entry-209.html (accessed 05/02/2006).

Freeden, Michael (1996) *Ideologies and Political Theory: A Conceptual Approach.* Oxford: Clarendon.

— (1997) "Editorial: ideologies and conceptual history", *Journal of Political Ideologies* 2(1): 3–12.

— (1999) "The ideology of New Labour", *The Political Quarterly* 70(1): 42–51.

Fried, Susannah (1997) "Ultra-nationalism in Slovak life: an assessment", *East European Jewish Affairs* 27(2): 93–107

Friedman, Norman L. (1967) "Nativism", *Phylon* 28(4): 408–15.

Frölich-Steffen, Susanne and Lars Rensmann (2005a) *Populisten an der Macht: Populistische Regierungsparteien in West- und Osteuropa.* Vienna: Braumüller.

— (2005b) "Populistische Regierungsparteien in Ost- und Westeuropa: Vergleichende Perspektiven der politikwissenschaftlichen Forschung", in Susanne Frölich-Steffen and Lars Rensmann (eds.), *Populisten an der Macht: Populistische Regierungsparteien in West- und Osteuropa.* Vienna: Braumüller, 3–34.

Fromm, Rainer and Barbara Kernbach (1994) *... und morgen die ganze Welt? Rechtsextreme Publizistik in Westeuropa.* Marburg: Schüren.

— (2001) *Rechtsextremismus im Internet: Die neue Gefahr.* Munich: Olzog.

— (n.d.) "Rechtsextremismus – ein Männerphänomen? Frauen im organisierten Rechtsextremismus", from: www.mediageneration.net/jugendszene/buch6.pdf (accessed 03/02/2006).

Fuchs, Dieter and Hans-Dieter Klingemann (1990) "The left–right schema", in M. Kent Jennings *et al.*, *Continuities in Political Action: A Longitudinal Study of Political Orientations in Three Western Democracies.* Berlin: De Gruyter, 203–34.

Furedi, Frank (2005) *Politics of Fear: Beyond Left and Right.* London: Continuum.

Gallagher, Michael, Michael Laver and Peter Mair (1995) *Representative Government in Modern Europe.* New York: McGraw-Hill, 2nd edn.

— (2001) *Representative Government in Modern Europe: Institutions, Parties, and Governments.* Boston: McGraw-Hill, 3rd edn.

— (2005) *Representative Government in Modern Europe: Institutions, Parties, and Governments.* Boston: McGraw-Hill, 4th edn.

Gallagher, Tom (1997) "Nationalism and post-communist politics: the Party of Romanian National Unity, 1990–1996", in Lavinia Stan (ed.), *Romania in Transition.* Aldershot: Dartmouth, 25–47.

Gardberg, Annvi (1993) *Against the Stranger, the Gangster and the Establishment: A Comparative Study of the Ideologies of the Swedish Ny Demokrati, the German Republikaner, the French Front National and the Belgian Vlaams Block.* Helsinki: Universitetstryckeriet.

Geden, Oliver (2004) "Männerparteien: Geschlechterpolitische Strategien im österreichischen und schweizerischen Rechtspopulismus", *Aus Politik und Zeitgeschichte* 46: 24–30.

— (2005) "Identitätsdiskurs und politische Macht: Die rechtspopulistische Mobilisierung von Ethnozentrismus im Spannungsfeld von Oppositionspolitik und Regierung am Beispiel von FPÖ und SVP", in Susanne Frölich-Steffen and Lars Rensmann (eds.), *Populisten an der Macht: Populistische Regierungsparteien in West- und Osteuropa.* Vienna: Braumuller, 69–84.

Gellner, Ernest (1983) *Nations and Nationalism*. Oxford: Blackwell.
— (1995) "Nationalism and xenophobia", in Bernd Baumgartl and Adrian Favell (eds.), *New Xenophobia in Europe*. London: Kluwer, 6–9.
— (1997) *Nationalism*. London: Weidenfeld & Nicolson.
Gerring, John and Paul A. Barresi (2003) "Putting ordinary language to work: a min-max strategy of concept formation in the social sciences", *Journal of Theoretical Politics* 15(2): 201–32.
Gerrits, André (1995) "Antisemitism and anti-communism: the myth of 'Judeo-Communism' in Eastern Europe", *East European Jewish Affairs* 25(1): 49–72.
Gerrits, André W. M. (1993) "Paradox of freedom: the 'Jewish question' in post-communist East Central Europe", in Ian M. Cuthbertson and Jane Leibowitz (eds.), *Minorities: The New Europe's Old Issue*. Prague: Institute for East West Studies, 99–121.
Gessenharter, Wolfgang (1991) "Die Parteiprogramme der Rechtsparteien. Zur Kontinuität ihres ideologischen Kernbestandes", *Sowi* 20(4): 227–33.
Gibson, Rachel (2002) *The Growth of Anti-Immigrant Parties in Western Europe*. Ceredigion: Edwin Mellen.
Gibson, Rachel, Ian McAllister, and Tami Swenson (2002) "The politics of race and immigration in Australia: One Nation voting in the 1998 election", *Ethnic and Racial Studies* 25(5): 823–44.
Gidengil, Elisabeth, Andre Blais, Neil Nevitte, and Richard Nadeau (2001) "The correlates and consequences of anti-partyism in the 1997 Canadian election", *Party Politics* 7(4): 491–513.
Gidengil, Elisabeth and Matthew Hennigar (2000) "The gender gap in support for the radical right in Western Europe", paper presented at the 96th annual APSA meeting, Washington, DC, August 31 – September 3.
Gidengil, Elisabeth, Matthew Hennigar, Andre Blais, and Neil Nevitte (2005) "Explaining the gender gap in support for the new right: the case of Canada", *Comparative Political Studies* 38(10): 1171–95.
Girvin, Brian (1988) *The Transformation of Contemporary Conservatism*. London: Sage.
Givens, Terri (2002) "The role of socioeconomic variables in the success of radical right parties", in Martin Schain, Aristide Zolberg, and Patrick Hossay (eds.), *Shadows over Europe: The Development and Impact of the Extreme Right in Western Europe*. New York: Palgrave, 137–58.
— (2004) "The radical right gender gap", *Comparative Political Studies* 37(1): 30–54.
— (2005) *Voting Radical Right in Western Europe*. New York: Cambridge University Press.
Givens, Terri and Adam Luedtke (2004) "The politics of European Union immigration policy: institutions, salience, and harmonization", *The Policy Studies Journal* 32(1): 145–65.
— (2005) "European immigration policies in comparative perspective: issue salience, partisanship and immigrant rights", *Comparative European Politics* 3(1): 1–22.
Golder, Matt (2003) "Explaining variation in the success of extreme right parties in Western Europe", *Comparative Political Studies* 36(4): 432–66.

Goldstein, Ivo and Slavko Goldstein (2002) "Revisionism in Croatia: the case of Franjo Tuđjman", *East European Jewish Affairs* 32(1): 52–64.

Gomez-Reino, Marga (2001) "Do new party organizations matter? Party dynamics and the new radical right wing family", paper presented at the ECPR Joint Sessions of Workshops, Grenoble, April 6–11.

Gomez-Reino Cachafeiro, Margarita (2002) *Ethnicity and Nationalism in Italian Politics*. Aldershot: Ashgate.

Goodwin, Matthew J. (2005) "Beyond the war of words? The extreme right paradigm in the twenty-first century", *Political Perspectives* 2: 1–11.

Gooskens, M. P. J. (1994) "The budget approach: political distance measured in *Kroner*", *Acta Politica* 29(4): 377–407.

Goot, Murray (1999) "Pauline Hanson and the power of the media", in Ghussan Hage and Rowanne Couch (eds.), *The Future of Australian Multiculturalism*. Sydney: Research Institute for Humanities & Social Sciences, 205–28.

— (2006) "The Australian party system, Pauline Hanson's One Nation, and the party cartelisation thesis", in Ian Marsh (ed.), *Australian Parties in Transition? The Australian Party System in an Era of Globalisation*. Annandale: Federation Press, 181–217.

Goot, Murray and Ian Watson (2001) "One Nation's electoral support: where does it come from, what makes it different and how does it fit?", *Australian Journal of Politics and History* 47(2): 159–91.

Govaert, Serge (1998) "Le programme économique du Vlaams Blok", in Pascal Delwit, Jean-Michel De Waele, and Andrea Rea (eds.), *L'extrême droite en France et en Belgique*. Brussels: Éditions Complexe, 119–31.

Grassi, Mauro and Lars Rensmann (2005) "Die Forza Italia: Erfolgsmodell einer populistischen Regierungspartei oder temporäres Phänomen des italienischen Parteiensystems?", in Susanne Frölich-Steffen and Lars Rensmann (eds.), *Populisten an der Macht: Populistische Regierungsparteien in West- und Osteuropa*, Vienna: Braumüller, 121–46.

Grdešić, Ivan (1999) "The radical right in Croatia and its constituency", in Sabrina P. Ramet (ed.), *The Radical Right in Central and Eastern Europe since 1989*. University Park: Pennsylvania State University Press, 171–89.

Greenfeld, Liah (2001) "Etymology, definitions, types", in Alexander J. Motyl (ed.), *Encyclopedia of Nationalism. Volume I: Fundamental Themes*. San Diego: Academic Press, 251–65.

Gregor, A. James (1974) *The Fascist Persuasion in Radical Politics*. Princeton: Princeton University Press.

Gregor, Neil (2000) *Nazism*. Oxford: Oxford University Press.

Greskovits, Béla (1995) "Demagogic populism in Eastern Europe", *Telos* 102: 91–106.

— (1998) *The Political Economy of Protest and Patience: East European and Latin American Transformations Compared*. Budapest: Central European University Press.

Griffin, Roger (1991) *The Nature of Fascism*. London: Pinter.

— (1994) *Europe for the Europeans: Fascist Myths of the European New Order 1922–1992*. Oxford: Humanities Research Centre Occasional Paper (No. 1).

— (1996) "'The post-fascism of the Alleanza nazionale: a case-study in ideological morphology", *Journal of Political Ideologies* 1(2): 123–46.

— (1999a) "Afterword: last rights?", in Sabrina P. Ramet (ed.), *The Radical Right in Central and Eastern Europe since 1989*. University Park: Pennsylvania State University Press, 297–319.

— (1999b) "Net gains and GUD reactions: patterns of prejudice in a neo-fascist groupuscule", *Patterns of Prejudice* 33(2): 31–50.

— (2000) "Interregnum or endgame? The radical right in the 'post-fascist' era", *Journal of Political Ideologies* 5(2): 163–78.

Grillo, Ralph (2005) "'Saltdean can't cope': protests against asylum-seekers in an English seaside suburb", *Ethnic and Racial Studies* 28(2): 235–60.

Gunther, Richard and Larry Diamond (2003) "Species of political parties: a new typology", *Party Politics* 9(2): 167–99.

Gyárfášová, Ol'ga (2002) "Slovakia: The Slovak National Party", in Helga Amesberger and Brigitte Halbmayr (eds.), *Rechtsextreme Parteien – eine mögliche Heimat für Frauen?* Opladen: Leske + Budrich, 161–210.

Haerpfer, Christian W. (2002) *Democracy and Enlargement in Post-Communist Europe: The Democratisation of the General Public in Fifteen Central and Eastern European Countries, 1991–1998*. London: Routledge.

Hafeneger, Bruno (1994) "Rechtsextreme Europabilder", in Wolfgang Kowalsky and Wolfgang Schroeder (eds.), *Rechtsextremismus: Einführung und Forschungsbilanz*. Opladen: Westdeutscher, 212–27.

Hagen, William W. (1999) "The Balkans' lethal nationalisms", *Foreign Affairs* 78(4): 52–64.

Haider, Jörg (1993) *Die Freiheit, die ich meine*. Frankfurt am Main: Ullstein.

Haider, Jörg (1997) *Befreite Zukunft jenseits von links und rechts: Menschliche Alternativen für eine Brücke ins neue Jahrtausend*. Vienna: Ibera & Molden.

Hainsworth, Paul (ed.) (2000a) *The Politics of the Extreme Right: From the Margins to the Mainstream*. London: Pinter.

— (2000b) "Introduction: the extreme right", in Paul Hainsworth (ed.), *The Politics of the Extreme Right: From the Margins to the Mainstream*. London: Pinter, 1–17.

— (2004) "The extreme right in France: the rise and rise of Jean-Marie Le Pen's *Front National*", *Representation* 40(2): 101–14.

Hall, Ian and Magali Perrault (2000) "The re-Austrianisation of Central Europe?", *Central Europe Review*, from: www.ce-review.org/00/15/essay15.html (accessed 11/05/2005).

Hammann, Kerstin (2002) *Frauen im rechtsextremen Spektrum: Analysen und Prävention*. Frankfurt am Main: VAS.

Hanley, Séan (2004) "From neo-liberalism to national interests: ideology, strategy, and party development in the Euroscepticism of the Czech right", *East European Politics and Societies* 18(3): 513–48.

Hari, Johann (2003) "Porous borders", *Chartist*, from: www.chartist.org.uk/articles/intpol/jan03_hari.htm (accessed 21/05/2003).

Harmel, Robert and Lars Svåsand (1993) "Party leadership and party institutionalization: three phases of development", *West European Politics* 16(2): 67–88.

Harrison, Lisa (1997) "Maximising small party potential: the effects of electoral system rules on the far right in German sub-national elections", *German Politics* 6(3): 132–51.

Harrop, Martin and William L. Miller (1987) *Elections and Voters: A Comparative Introduction*. Basingstoke: Macmillan.

Hartleb, Florian (2004) *Rechts- und Linkspopulismus: Eine Fallstudie anhand von Schill-Partei und PDS*. Wiesbaden: VS Verlag für Sozialwissenschaften.

Hasselbach, Sven (2002) "Pia Kjærsgaard: Es gibt nur eine Zivilisation", in Michael Jungwirth (ed.), *Haider, Le Pen & Co: Europas Rechtspopulisten*. Graz: Styria, 152–63.

Haubrich, Dirk (2003) "Anti-terror laws and civil liberties: Britain, France and Germany compared", *Government & Opposition* 38(1): 3–28.

Haughton, Tim (2001) "HZDS: the ideology, organisation and support base of Slovakia's most successful party", *Europe-Asia Studies* 53(5): 745–69.

Havelková, Hana (2002) "Tschechien: Die Republikanische Partei der Tschechoslowakei", in Helga Amesberger and Brigitte Halbmayr (eds.), *Rechtsextreme Parteien – eine mögliche Heimat für Frauen?* Opladen: Leske + Budrich, 211–50.

Hayes, Carleton B. (1931) *The Historical Evolution of Modern Nationalism*. New York: R.R. Smith.

Heinisch, Reinhard (2003) "Success in opposition – failure in government: explaining the performance of right-wing populist parties in public office", *West European Politics* 26(3): 91–130.

Held, David (1999) *Models of Democracy*. Cambridge: Polity, 2nd edn.

Held, David and Anthony McGrew (2000) *The Global Transformations Reader: An Introduction to the Globalization Debate*. Cambridge: Polity.

Helms, Ludger (1997) "Right-wing populist parties in Austria and Switzerland: a comparative analysis of electoral support and conditions of success", *West European Politics* 20(2): 37–52.

— (2001) "Die 'Kartellparteien': These und ihre Kritiker", *Politische Vierteljahresschrift* 42(4): 698–708.

Henig, Ruth and Simon Henig (2001) *Women and Political Power: Europe since 1945*. London: Routledge.

Henley, Jon (2005) "Le Pen rules out daughter as National Front leader", *The Guardian*, 2 March.

Hennecke, Hans Jörg (2003) "Das Salz in den Wunden der Konkordanz: Christoph Blocher und die Schweizer Politik", in Nikolaus Werz (ed.), *Populismus: Populisten in Übersee und Europa*. Opladen: Leske + Budrich, 145–62.

Herman, Didi (2001) "Globalism's 'siren song': the United Nations and international law in Christian Right thought and prophecy", *The Sociological Review* 49(1): 56–77.

Herzog, Hanna (1987) "Minor parties: the relevancy perspective", *Comparative Politics* 19(3): 317–29.

HF (2001) "The Islamic infiltration in Greece and Europe", from: www.e-grammes.gr/2001/09/islamists_en.htm (accessed 14/07/2005).

Higham, John (1955) *Strangers in the Land: Patterns of American Nativism, 1860–1925*. New Brunswick: Rutgers University Press.

Hix, Simon and Christopher Lord (1997) *Political Parties in the European Union*. Basingstoke: Macmillan.

Höbelt, Lothar (2003) *Defiant Populist: Jörg Haider and the Politics of Austria*. West Lafayette: Purdue University Press.

Hobsbawm, Eric J. (1990) *Nations and Nationalism since 1780*. Cambridge: Cambridge University Press.

Hockenos, Paul (1993) *Free to Hate: The Rise of the Right in Post-Communist Eastern Europe*. London: Routledge.

Hoffmann, Jürgen and Norbert Lepszy (1998) *Die DVU in den Landesparlamenten: Inkompetent, zerstritten, politikunfähig. Eine Bilanz rechtsextremer Politik nach zehn Jahren*. Sankt Augustin: Konrad-Adenauer-Stiftung (Interne Studie No. 163).

Hofinger, Christoph and Günther Ogris (1996) "Achtung: *gender gap*! Geschlecht und Wahlverhalten, 1979–1995", in Fritz Plasser, Peter A. Ulram and Günther Ogris (eds.), *Wahlkampf und Wählerentscheidung: Analysen zur Nationalratswahl 1995*. Wien: Signum, 211–32.

Hofmann-Göttig, Joachim (1989) "Die neue Rechte: Die Männerparteien", *Aus Politik und Zeitgeschichte* B41–42: 21–31.

Holmes, Douglas R. (2000) *Integral Europe: Fast-Capitalism, Multiculturalism, Neo-Fascism*. Princeton: Princeton University Press.

Holmes, Leslie (1997) "Corruption and the crisis of the post-communist state," *Crime, Law and Social Change* 27(3–4): 275–97.

Hossay, Patrick (2002) "Why Flanders?", in Martin Schain, Aristide Zolberg and Patrick Hossay (eds.), *Shadows over Europe: The Development and Impact of the Extreme Right in Western Europe*. New York: Palgrave, 159–85.

HSP (2004) "Kroatien in Europa", from: www.hsp.hr/deu/strana3.htm (accessed 13/07/2005).

— (n.d.a) "Geschichte der Kroatischen Partei des Staatsrechts", from: www.hsp.hr/deu/strana2.htm (accessed 11/02/2005).

— (n.d.b) "Auszüge aus den 'Grundsätzen der Kroatischen Partei des Staatsrechts'", from: www.hsp.hr/deu/strana1.htm (accessed 17/02/2006).

HSP-1861 (1997a) "Croatians Wake Up – Unprivileged Fight For Your Rights – With Croatian Party of Rights 1861", from: www.hsp1861.hr/english/national.html (accessed 10/05/2005).

— (1997b) *Election Programme of Croatian Party of Rights-1861 for City of Zagreb*, from: www.hsp1861.hr/english/zagreb.html (accessed 10/05/2005).

— (n.d.) *Basic Principles Croatian Party of Rights 1861*, from: www.hsp1861.hr/english/basicpr.html (accessed 10/05/2005).

Hunter, Mark (1998a) "Nationalism unleashed: Jean-Marie Le Pen, head of France's National Front, moves east", *Transitions* 5(7): 18–28.

— (1998b) "Oil, guns, and money: The National Front goes to Chechnya", *Transitions* 5(7): 29–32.

Huntington, Nicholas and Tim Bale (2002) "New Labour: New Christian Democracy?", *The Political Quarterly* 73(1): 44–50.

Huntington, Samuel P. (1993) "The Clash of Civilizations", *Foreign Affairs* 72(3): 22–49.

Husbands, Christopher T. (1988) "The dynamics of racial exclusion and expulsion: racist politics in Western Europe", *European Journal of Political Research* 16(6): 701–20.

— (1996) "Racism, xenophobia and the extreme right: a five-country assessment", in Simon Bekker and David Carlton (eds.), *Racism, Xenophobia and Ethnic Conflict*. Durban: Indicator, 97–118.

— (1998) "De Centrumstroming in perspectief: hoe verschillend is Nederland?", in Joop van Holsteyn and Cas Mudde (eds.), *Extreem-rechts in Nederland*. The Hague: Sdu, 175–91.

— (2000) "Switzerland: right-wing and xenophobic parties, from margin to mainstream?", *Parliamentary Affairs* 53(3): 501–16.

— (2001) "Combating the extreme right with the instruments of the constitutional state: lessons from experiences in western Europe", paper presented at the 96th annual ASA meeting, Anaheim, August 18–21.

— (2002) "How to tame the dragon, or what goes around comes around: a critical review of some major contemporary attempts to account for extreme-right racist politics in Western Europe" in Martin Schain, Aristide Zolberg, and Patrick Hossay (eds.), *Shadows over Europe: The Development and Impact of the Extreme Right in Western Europe*. New York: Palgrave, 39–59.

Huysmans, Jef (2004) "Minding exceptions: the politics of insecurity and liberal democracy", *Contemporary Political Theory* 3(3): 321–41.

Hynynen, Pertti (1999) "The Patriotic National Alliance: between a brotherhood and a party", in Kyösti Pekonen (ed.), *The New Radical Right in Finland*. Helsinki: Finnish Political Science Association, 137–43.

Ignazi, Piero (1992) "The silent counter-revolution: hypotheses on the emergence of extreme-right wing parties in Europe", *European Journal of Political Research* 22(1–2): 3–34.

— (1994) *L'estrema destra in Europa*. Bologna: Il Mulino.

— (1996) "The crisis of parties and the rise of new political parties", *Party Politics* 2(4): 549–66.

— (1997) "The extreme right in Europe: a survey", in Peter H. Merkl and Leonard Weinberg (eds.), *The Revival of Right-Wing Extremism in the Nineties*. London: Frank Cass, 47–64.

— (1998) "MSI/AN: a mass party with the temptation of the Führer-Prinzip", in Piero Ignazi and Colette Ysmal (eds.), *The Organization of Political Parties in Southern Europe*. Westport: Praeger, 157–77.

— (2003) *Extreme Right Parties in Western Europe*. Oxford: Oxford University Press.

— (2005) "Legitimation and evolution on the Italian right wing: social and ideological repositioning of *Alleanza Nazionale* and the *Lega Nord*", *South European Society & Politics* 10(2): 333–49.

IHF (2000) *Women 2000: An Investigation into the Status of Women's Rights in Central and South-Eastern Europe and the Newly Independent States*. Vienna: International Helsinki Federation for Human Rights.

IKL (n.d.) *The Political Program of IKL*, from: kauhajoki.fi/~ikl/ulkomaat/englanti.html (accessed 20/05/2003).

Immerfall, Stefan (1998) "The neo-populist agenda", in Hans-Georg Betz and Stefan Immerfall (eds.), *The New Politics of the Right: Neo-Populist Parties and Movements in Established Democracies*. New York: St. Martin's, 249–61.

Inglehart, Ronald (1977) *The Silent Revolution: Changing Values and Political Styles among Western Publics*. Princeton: Princeton University Press.

IPU (2005) "Women in national parliaments (situation as of 30 April 2005)", from: www.ipu.org/wmn-e/world.htm (accessed 01/08/2005).

Irvine, Jill A. (1995) "Nationalism and the extreme right in the former Yugoslavia", in Luciano Cheles, Ronnie Ferguson, and Michalina Vaughan, (eds.), *The Far Right in Western and Eastern Europe*. London: Longman, 2nd edn, 145–73.

— (1997) "Ultranationalist ideology and state-building in Croatia, 1990–1996", *Problems of Post-Communism* 44(4): 30–43.

— (1998) "Public opinion and the political position of women in Croatia", in Marilyn Rueschemeyer (ed.), *Women in the Politics of Postcommunist Eastern Europe*. Armonk: M.E. Sharpe, rev. and exp. edn, 215–34.

Irvine, Jill A. and Ivan Grdešić (1998) "Extreme right opinion and the transition to democracy: the Croatian case", paper presented at the 94th annual APSA conference, Boston, August 2–6.

Ishiyama, John T. (1998) "Strange bedfellows: explaining political cooperation between communist-successor parties and nationalists in Eastern Europe", *Nations and Nationalism* 4(1): 61–85.

Ivaldi, Gilles (1996) "Conservation, revolution, and protest: a case study in the political cultures of the French National Front's members and sympathizers", *Electoral Studies* 15(3): 339–62.

Ivaldi, Gilles (1998) "The Front National: the making of an authoritarian party", in Piero Ignazi and Colette Ysmal (eds.), *The Organization of Political Parties in Southern Europe*. Westport: Praeger, 43–69.

Ivaldi, Gilles and Marc Swyngedouw (2001) "The extreme-right utopia in Belgium and France: the ideology of the Flemish Vlaams Blok and the French Front National," *West European Politics* 24(3): 1–22.

Ivanov, Christo and Margarita Ilieva (2005) "Bulgaria", in Cas Mudde (ed.), *Racist Extremism in Central and Eastern Europe*. London: Routledge, 1–29.

Ivarsflaten, Elisabeth (2002) "The populist centre-authoritarian challenge: a revised account of the radical right's success in Western Europe", from: www.nuffield.ox.ac.uk/Politics/papers/2002/w25/centre-populists.pdf (accessed 21/06/2006).

— (2005) "The vulnerable populist right parties: no economic realignment fuelling their electoral success", *European Journal of Political Research* 44(3): 465–92.

Jackman, Robert W. and Karin Volpert (1996) "Conditions favouring parties of the extreme right in Western Europe", *British Journal of Political Science* 26(4): 501–21.

Jäger, Margret (1993) "BrandSätze und SchlagZeilen: Rassismus in den Medien", in *Entstehung von Fremdenfeindlichkeit: Die Verantwortung von Politik und Medien*. Bonn: FES, 73–92.

Jagers, Jan (2002) "Eigen democratie eerst! Een comparatief onderzoek naar het intern democratische gehalte van de Vlaamse politieke partijen", *Res Publica* 44(1): 73–96.

— (2006) "Stem van het volk! Populisme als concept getest bij Vlaamse politieke partijen." University of Antwerp: unpublished Ph.D thesis.

Jalušič, Vlasta (2002) "Xenophobia or self-protection? On the establishing of the new Slovene civic/citizenship identity", in Mojca Pajnik (ed.), *Xenophobia and Post-Socialism*. Ljubljana: Mirovni Inštitut, 45–72.

Jalušič, Vlasta and Milica Antić Gaber (2001) *Women – Politics – Equal Opportunities: Prospects for Gender Equality Politics in Central and Eastern Europe*. Ljubljana: Mirovni Inštitut.

Jaschke, Hans-Gerd (1994) *Die "Republikaner." Profile einer Rechtsaußen-Partei*. Bonn: Dietz, 3rd edn.

Jenne, Erin Kristin (1998) "Czech Republic", in Jean-Yves Camus (ed.), *Extremism in Europe: 1998 Survey*. Paris: CERA/l'aube essay, 111–17.

Jesuit, David and Vincent Mahler (2004) "Immigration, economic well-being and support for extreme right parties in Western European regions", paper presented at the conference "Immigration in a Cross-National Context: What are the Implications for Europe?", Bourlingster (Luxembourg), June 20–22.

Johnson, M., W. Phillips Shively and R.M. Stein (2002) "Contextual data and the study of elections and voting behavior: connecting individuals and environments", *Electoral Studies* 21(2): 219–33.

Jungerstam, Susanne Elisabeth (1995) "Die Republikaner och het Vlaams Blok – en komparativ studie av två högerextremistiska partier." University of Helsinki: unpublished MA thesis.

Jungerstam-Mulders, Susanne (2003) *Uneven Odds: The Electoral Success of the Freiheitliche Partei Österreichs, the Vlaams Blok, the Republikaner and the Centrumdemocraten under the Conditions Provided by the Political System in Austria, Belgium, Germany and the Netherlands*. Helsinki: Helsinki University Press.

Jungwirth, Michael (ed.) (2002a) *Haider, Le Pen & Co: Europas Rechtspopulisten*. Graz: Styria.

— (2002b) "Rebellen und Rattenfänger", in Michael Jungwirth (ed.), *Haider, Le Pen & Co: Europas Rechtspopulisten*. Graz: Styria, 7–23.

Kaillitz, Steffen (2005) "Das ideologische Profil rechter (und linker) Flügelparteien in den westeuropäischen Demokratien – Eine Auseinandersetzung mit den Thesen Herbert Kitschelts", in Uwe Backes and Eckhard Jesse (eds.), *Gefährdungen der Freiheit: Extremistische Ideologien im Vergleich*. Göttingen: Vandenhoeck & Ruprecht, 283–320.

Kalliala, Mari (1998) "Finland", in Jean-Yves Camus (ed.), *Extremism in Europe: 1998 Survey*. Paris: CERA/l'aube essay, 125–9.

Kalnina, Liene (1998) "Nationalism and its Changes in the Course of Development of the Party Systems: the Case of Baltic States." Budapest, Central European University: unpublished MA thesis.

Kang, Won-Taek (2004) "Protest voting and abstention under plurality rule elections: an alternative public choice approach", *Journal of Theoretical Politics* 16(1): 79–102.

Kántor, Zoltán, B. Majtenyi, O. Ieda, B. Vizi, and I. Halász, (eds.) (2004) *The Hungarian Status Law: Nation Building and/or Minority Protection*. Sapporo: Slavic Research Center, Hokkaido University.

Kaplan, Jeffrey and Leonard Weinberg (1999) *The Emergence of a Euro-American Radical Right*. New Brunswick: Rutgers University Press.

Karapin, Roger (1998) "Radical right and neo-fascist parties in Western Europe", *Comparative Politics* 30(2): 213–34.

— (2002) "Far-right parties and the construction of immigration issues in Germany", in Martin Schain, Aristide Zolberg, and Patrick Hossay (eds.), *Shadows over Europe: The Development and Impact of the Extreme Right in Western Europe*. New York: Palgrave, 187–219.

Karklins, Rasma (2005) *The System Made Me Do It: Corruption in Post-Communist Societies*. Armonk: M.E. Sharpe.

Karsai, László (1999) "The radical right in Hungary", in Sabrina P. Ramet (ed.), *The Radical Right in Central and Eastern Europe since 1989*. University Park: Pennsylvania State University Press, 133–46.

Kasch, Holger (2002) "Die HDZBiH und die Förderung nach kroatischer Souveränität in Bosnien-Herzegowina", *Südosteuropa* 51(7–9): 331–54.

Kasekamp, Andres (2003) "Extreme-right parties in contemporary Estonia", *Patterns of Prejudice* 37(4): 401–14.

Katz, Richard S. and Peter Mair (1995) "Changing models of party organization and party democracy: the emergence of the cartel party", *Party Politics* 1(1): 5–28.

Keating, Michael and John Loughlin (1997) "Introduction", in Michael Keating and John Loughlin (eds.), *The Political Economy of Regionalism*. London: Frank Cass, 1–13.

Kedar, Orit (2005) "When moderate voters prefer extreme parties: policy balancing in parliamentary elections", *American Political Science Review* 99(2): 185–99.

Kelley, Judith G. (2004) *Ethnic Politics in Europe: The Power of Norms and Incentives*. Princeton: Princeton University Press.

Keohane, Robert O. and Joseph S. Nye Jr. (2000) "Globalization: what's new? What's not? (and so what?)", *Foreign Policy* (Spring): 104–19.

Kernbach, Barbara and Rainer Fromm (1993) "Frauen- und Männerrolle bei den Rechten", in Rainer Fromm, *Am rechten Rand: Lexicon des Rechtsradikalismus*. Marburg: Schüren, 179–88.

Kiaulakis, Giedrius (2005) "Lithuania", in Cas Mudde (ed.), *Racist Extremism in Central and Eastern Europe*. London: Routledge, 129–55.

King, Anthony (2002) "Do leaders' personalities really matter?" in Anthony King (ed.), *Leaders' Personalities and the Outcomes of Democratic Elections*. Oxford: Oxford University Press, 1–43.

Kirchheimer, Otto (1966) "The transformation of West European party systems", in Joseph LaPalombara and Myron Weiner (eds.), *Political Parties and Political Development*. Princeton: Princeton University Press, 177–200.

Kirschbaum, Stanislav J. (1996) *A History of Slovakia: The Struggle for Survival*. New York: St. Martin's Griffin.

Kirscht, John P. and Ronald C. Dillehay (1967) *Dimenions of Authoritarianism: A Review of Research and Theory*. Lexington: University of Kentucky Press.

Kiss, Csilla (2002) "From liberalism to conservatism: the Federation of Young Democrats in post-communist Hungary", *East European Politics and Societies* 16(3): 739–63.

Kitschelt, Herbert (1989) "The internal politics of parties: the law of curvilinear disparity revisited", *Political Studies* 37(3): 400–21.

— (2002) "Popular dissatisfaction with democracy: populism and party systems", in Yves Mény and Yves Surel (eds.), *Democracies and the Populist Challenge*. Basingstoke: Palgrave, 179–96.

— (2004) *Diversification and Reconfiguration of Party Systems in Postindustrial Democracies*. Bonn: Friedrich Ebert Stiftung.

Kitschelt, Herbert and Anthony McGann (1995) *The Radical Right in Western Europe: A Comparative Analysis*. Ann Arbor: The University of Michigan Press.

Klandermans, Bert and Nonna Mayer (eds.) (2005) *Extreme Right Activists in Europe: Through the Magnifying Glass*. London: Routledge.

Klein, Markus and Dieter Ohr (2002) "Der Richter und sein Wähler. Ronald B. Schills Wahlerfolg als Beispiel extremer Personalisierung der Politik", *Zeitschrift für Parlamentsfragen* 33(1): 64–79.

Klingemann, Hans-Dieter (1995) "Party positions and voter orientations", in Hans-Dieter Klingemann and Dieter Fuchs (eds.), *Citizens and the State*. Oxford: Oxford University Press, 183–205.

Knapp, Andrew (1987) "Proportional but bipolar: France's electoral system in 1986", *West European Politics* 10(1): 89–114.

Kneuer, Marianne (2005) "Die Stabilität populistischer Regierungen am Beispiel der slowakischen HZDS: Wechselwirkungen innen- und außenpolitischer Prozesse", in Susanne Frölich-Steffen and Lars Rensmann (eds.), *Populisten an der Macht: Populistische Regierungsparteien in West- und Osteuropa*. Vienna: Braumüller, 149–71.

Knigge, Pia (1998) "The electoral correlates of right-wing extremism in Western Europe", *European Journal of Political Research* 34(2): 249–79.

Knight, Alan (1998) "Populism and neo-populism in Latin America, especially Mexico", *Journal of Latin American Studies* 30(2): 223–48.

Knutsen, Oddbjørn (2005) "The impact of sector employment on party choice: a comparative study of eight West European countries", *European Journal of Political Research* 44(4): 593–621.

Koch, Koen (1991) "Back to Sarajevo or beyond Trianon? Some thoughts on the problem of nationalism in Eastern Europe", *Netherlands Journal of Social Sciences* 27(1): 29–42.

Kofman, Eleonore (1998) "When society was simple: gender and ethnic division and the far and new right in France", in Nickie Charles and Helen Hintjes (eds.), *Gender, Ethnicity and Political Ideologies*. London: Routledge, 91–106.

Kohn, Hans (1944) *The Idea of Nationalism: A Study in its Origin and Background.* New York: Macmillan.

Kolovos, Ioannis (2003) "The ideological evolution of the Greek extreme right from 1974 to 2003." University of Sheffield: unpublished MA thesis.

— (2005) *ΑΚΡΑ ΔΕΞΙΑ & ΡΙΖΟΣΠΑΣΤΙΚΗ ΔΕΞΙΑ: στην Ελλάδα και στην Δμτική Εμρώπη 1974–2005. Akra Dexia Ke Rizospastiki Dexia stin Ellada Ke stin Dittiki Evropi 1974–2004* [Extreme Right and Radical Right in Greece and in West Europe 1974–2004]. Athens: Pelasgos Publications.

Koopmans, Ruud (1996) "Explaining the rise of racist and extreme right violence in Western Europe: grievances or opportunities?", *European Journal of Political Research* 30(2): 185–216.

— (1998) "Die neue Rechte in den Niederlanden – Oder: Warum es sie nicht gibt", in Wolfgang Gessenharter and Helmut Fröchling (eds.), *Rechtsextremismus und neue Rechte in Deutschland: Neuvermessung eines politisch-ideologischen Raumes?* Opladen: Leske + Budrich, 241–52.

Kopecký, Petr (1995) "Developing party organizations in East-Central Europe: what type of party is likely to emerge?" *party Politics* 1(4): 515–34.

Kopecký, Petr and Cas Mudde (2000) "What has Eastern Europe taught us about the democratisation literature (and vice versa)?" *European Journal of Political Research* 37(4): 517–39.

— (2002) "The two sides of Euroscepticism: party positions on European integration in East Central Europe", *European Union Politics* 3(3): 297–326

Kostrzębski, Karol (2005) "Die Mobilisierung von Euroskepsis: Populismus in Ostmitteleuropa am Beispiel Polens", in Susanne Frölich-Steffen and Lars Rensmann (eds.), *Populisten an der Macht: Populistische Regierungsparteien in West- und Osteuropa.* Vienna: Braumüller, 209–26.

Kovács, András (1999) *Antisemitic Prejudices in Contemporary Hungary.* Jerusalem: The Vidal Sassoon International Center for the Study of Antisemitism (ACTA 16).

Kreidl, Martin and Klára Vlachová (1999) *Rise and Decline of Right-Wing Extremism in the Czech Republic in the 1990s.* Prague: Academy of Sciences WP 99:10.

Kreutzberger, Wolfgang (2003) "Schill in Niedersachsen: Character und Chancen einer städtischen Protestpartei von rechts im Flächenstaat", in Joachim Perels (ed.), *Der Rechtsradikalismus – ein Randphänomen? Kritische Analysen.* Hannover: Offizin, 67–131.

Kriesi, Hanspeter (1995) "Bewegungen auf der Linken, Bewegungen auf der Rechten: Die Mobilisierung von zwei neuen Typen von sozialen Bewegungen in ihrem politischen Kontext", *Swiss Political Science Review* 1(1): 9–52.

— (1998) "The transformation of cleavage politics: the 1997 Stein Rokkan lecture", *European Journal of Political Research* 33(2): 165–85.

— (1999) "Movements of the left, movements of the right: putting the mobilization of two new types of social movements into political context", in Herbert Kitschelt *et al.* (eds.), *Continuity and Change in Contemporary Capitalism.* Cambridge: Cambridge University Press, 398–423.

Kriesi, Hanspeter *et al.* (2005a) *Der Aufstieg der SVP: Acht Kantone im Vergleich.* Zurich: Neue Zürcher Zeitung.

— (2005b) "Globalization and the transformation of the national political space: six European countries compared", unpublished paper.

Kriza, Borbala (2004) "Anti-Americanism and right-wing populism in Eastern Europe: the case of Hungary", paper presented at the 6th annual Kokkalis graduate student workshop, Cambridge (MA), 6 February.

Krok-Paszkowska, Ania (2003) "Samoobrona: the Polish self-defence movement", in Petr Kopecký and Cas Mudde (eds.), *Uncivil Society? Contentious Politics in Post-Communist Europe.* London: Routledge, 114–33.

Krouwel, André (1999) "The catch-all party in Western Europe 1945–1990: a study in arrested development." Amsterdam, Free University: unpublished Ph.D thesis.

Kuechler, Manfred and Russell Dalton (eds.) (1990) *Challenging the Political Order: New Social and Political Movements in Western Democracies.* New York: Oxford University Press.

Kühnen, Michael (n.d.) "Nationalsozialismus und homosexualität." Unpublished manuscript.

Kürti, László (1998) "Racism, the extreme right and anti-Gypsy sentiments in East-Central Europe", in Jean-Yves Camus (ed.), *Extremism in Europe: 1998 Survey.* Paris: CERA/l'aube essay, 421–44.

Kuzmanić, Tonči A. (1999) *Hate-Speech in Slovenia: Slovenian Racism, Sexism and Chauvinism.* Ljubljana: Open Society Institute-Slovenia.

Ladner, Andreas and Michael Braendle (1999) "Does direct democracy matter for political parties? An empirical test in the Swiss cantons", *Party Politics* 5(3): 283–302.

Ladrech, Robert (2002) "Europeanization and political parties: towards a framework for analysis", *Party Politics* 8(4): 89–103.

Lane, Jan-Erik and Svante Ersson (1999) *Politics and Societies in Western Europe.* London: Sage, 4th edn.

Lang, Kai-Olaf (2001) "Das slowakische Parteiensystem im Wandel", *Südosteuropa* 50(1–3): 85–122.

LAOS (n.d.) *The Ideological Platform of the First Congress.* Athens: LAOS.

LaPalombara, Joseph (1966) "Decline of ideology: a dissent and an interpretation", *American Political Science Review* 60(1): 5–16.

Laqueur, Walter (1996) *Fascism: Past, Present, Future.* Oxford: Oxford University Press.

Lasek, Wilhelm (1993) "Internationale Verbindungen und Zusammenhänge", in Stiftung Dokumentationsarchiv des österreichischen Widerstandes (ed.), *Handbuch des österreichischen Rechtsextremismus.* Vienna: Deuticke, 429–43.

Layton-Henry, Zig (ed.) (1982a) *Conservative Politics in Western Europe.* New York: St. Martin's.

— (1982b) "Introduction: conservatism and conservative politics", in Zig Layton-Henry (ed.), *Conservative Politics in Western Europe.* New York: St. Martin's, 1–20.

LDPR (1995) "Die Liberaldemokratische Partei Rußlands – Programm", in Galina Luchterhandt (ed.) (2000), *Politischen Parteien in Rußland: Dokumente und Kommentare*. Bremen: Temmen, 126–42. (excerpted and translated version of the original program)

— (n.d.a) "Zhenshchiny", from: www.ldpr.ru/azbuka_women.html (accessed 13/07/2004).

— (n.d.b) "Globalizatsiya", from: www.ldpr.ru/azbuka_globalizacia.html (accessed 13/07/2004).

LDPSU (1990) "Das Programm der Liberal-Demokratischen Partei der UdSSR," in Galina Luchterhandt (ed.), *Die politischen Parteien im neuen Rußland: Dokumente und Kommentare*. Bremen: Temmen, 210–12 (excerpted and translated version of the original program).

Lebioda, Tadeusz (2000) "Poland, *die Vertriebenen*, and the road to integration with the European Union", in Karl Cordell (ed.), *Poland and the European Union*. London: Routledge, 165–81.

Lee, Martin A. (2000) *The Beast Reawakens: Fascism's Resurgence from Hitler's Spymasters to Today's Neo-Nazi Groups and Right-Wing Extremists*. London: Routledge.

Leggewie, Claus (2003) "Rechts gegen Globalisierung", *Internationale Politik* 10(4): 33–40.

Lendvai, Paul (1972) *Anti-Semitism without Jews*. London: Macdonald.

Le Pen, Jean-Marie (ed.) (1992) "Die Front National: Selbtdarstellung einer modernen, national-populistischen Volkspartei", in *Jean-Marie Le Pen und die Front National: Hoffnung – für Frankreich? Vorbild – für Deutschland?* Weinheim: Germania/DAGD, 201–50.

Lesselier, Claudie (1988) "The women's movement and the extreme right in France", in Gill Seidel (ed.), *The Nature of the Right: A Feminist Analysis of Order Patterns*. Amsterdam: John Benjamins, 173–85.

— (2002) "Far-right women in France: the case of the National Front", in Paola Bacchetta and Margaret Power (eds.), *Right-Wing Women: From Conservatives to Extremists around the World*. London: Routledge, 127–40.

Lesselier, Claudie and Fiametta Venner (eds.) (1997) *L'extrême droite et les femmes: Enjeux & actualité*. Villeurbanne: Golias.

Lewis, Paul (2000) *Political Parties in Post-Communist Eastern Europe*. London: Routledge.

Lijphart, Arend (1984) *Democracies: Patterns of Majoritarian and Consensus Government in Twenty-One Countries*. New Haven: Yale University Press.

— (2001) "The pros and cons – but mainly pros – of consensus democracy", *Acta Politica* 36: 129–39.

Linz, Juan J. (1976) "Some notes toward a comparative study of fascism in sociological historical perspective", in Walter Laqueur (ed.), *Fascism: A Reader's Guide*. Berkeley: University of California Press, 3–121.

— (1993) "Authoritarianism", in Joel Krieger (ed.), *The Oxford Companion to Politics of the World*. Oxford: Oxford University Press, 60–4.

Linz, Juan J. and Alfred Stepan (1996) *Problems of Democratic Transition and Consolidation: Southern Europe, South America, and Post-Communist Europe*. Baltimore: Johns Hopkins University Press.

Lipset, Seymour Martin (1955) "The radical right: a problem for American democracy", *British Journal of Sociology* 6(2): 176–209.

— (1969) *Political Man*. London: Heinemann.

Lipset, Seymour Martin and Stein Rokkan (1967) *Party Systems and Voter Alignments: Cross-National Perspectives*. New York: The Free Press.

— (1990) "Cleavage structures, party systems, and voter alignments", in Peter Mair (ed.), *The West European Party System*. Oxford: Oxford University Press, 91–138.

Lloyd, Cathie (1998) "Antiracist mobilization in France and Britain in the 1970s and 1980s", in Danièle Joly (ed.), *Scapegoats and Social Actors: The Exclusion and Integration of Minorities in Western and Eastern Europe*. Basingstoke: Macmillan, 155–72.

Lloyd, John (2003) "The closing of the European gates? The new populist parties of Europe", *Political Quarterly* 74(10): 88–99.

Loch, Dietmar and Wilhelm Heitmeyer (2001) *Schattenseiten der Globalisierung: Rechtsradikalismus, Rechtspopulismus und Regionalismus in Westeuropa*. Frankfurt am Main: Suhrkamp.

Lord, Christopher (1998) "The untidy right in the European Parliament", in David S. Bell and Christopher Lord (eds.), *Transnational Parties in the European Union*. Aldershot: Ashgate, 117–38.

Lorenz, Einhart (2003) "Rechtspopulismus in Norwegen: Carl Ivar Hagen und die Fortschrittspartei", in Nikolaus Werz (ed.), *Populismus: Populisten in Übersee und Europa*. Opladen: Leske + Budrich, 195–207.

Lovenduski, Joni (1986) *Women and European Politics: Contemporary Feminism and Public Policy*. Amherst: University of Massachusetts Press.

Lovenduski, Joni and Pippa Norris (eds.) (1993) *Gender and Party Politics*. London: Sage.

LPF (2003) *Politiek is passie*. Rotterdam: LPF.

LPR (2002) "Program (platform)", from: pruszkow.lpr.pl/program_eng.html (accessed 24/07/2006).

— (2003) *Program Ligi Polskich Rodzin*, from: www.lpr.pl/?sr=!czytaj&id=1045 &dz=teksty_programowe&x=2&pocz=0&gr= (accessed 04/02/2006).

Lubbers, Marcel (2001) "Exclusionistic Electorates: Extreme Right-wing Voting in Western Europe." Radbout University, Nijmegen: unpublished PhD thesis.

Lubbers, Marcel, Mérove Gijberts and Peer Scheepers (2002) "Extreme right-wing voting in Western Europe", *European Journal of Political Research* 41(3): 345–78.

Lucardie, Paul (2000) "Prophets, purifiers and prolocutors: towards a theory on the emergence of new parties", *Party Politics* 6(2): 175–85.

Lucardie, Paul and Gerrit Voerman (2002) "Het gedachtegoed van Fortuyn: liberaal patriot of nationaal populist?" *Samenleving en Politiek* 9(6): 53–62.

Ludlam, Steve (2000) "New Labour: what's published is what counts", *British Journal of Politics and International Relations* 2(2): 264–76.

Luther, Kurt Richard (1991) "Die Freiheitliche Partei Österreichs", in Herbert Dachs *et al.* (eds.), *Handbuch des politischen Systems Österreichs*. Vienna: Manz, 247–62.

— (2003) "The FPÖ: from populist protest to incumbency", in Peter H. Merkl and Leonard Weinberg (eds.), *Right-Wing Extremism in the Twenty-First Century*. London: Frank Cass, 191–219.

Lynch, Peter (2002) *SNP: The History of the Scottish National Party*. Cardiff: Welsh Academic Press.

McAllister, Ian, Stephen White and Olga Kryshtanovskaya (1997) "Voting and party support in the December 1995 Duma elections", *Journal of Communist Studies and Transition Politics* 13(1): 115–22.

McAllister, Laura (1998) "The perils of community as a construct for the political ideology of Welsh nationalism", *Government & Opposition* 33(4): 447–517.

MacMaster, Neil (2001) *Racism in Europe*. Basingstoke: Palgrave.

Maddens, Bart and Kristine Vanden Berghe (2003) "The identity politics of multicultural nationalism: a comparison between the regular public addresses of the Belgian and the Spanish monarchs (1990–2000)", *European Journal of Political Research* 42(5): 601–27.

Madeley, John (2006) "The state and religion", in Paul M. Heywood, Erik Jones, Martin Rhodes, and Ulrich Sedelmeier (eds), *Developments in European Politics*. London: Palgrave.

Mahoney, James (2004) "Comparative-historical methodology", *Annual Review of Sociology* 30: 81–110.

Maillot, Agnes (2004) *New Sinn Féin: Irish Republicanism in the 21st Century*. London: Routledge.

Mair, Peter (1997) *Party System Change: Approaches and Interpretations*. Oxford: Clarendon.

— (2002) "Populist democracy vs party democracy", in Yves Mény and Yves Surel (eds.), *Democracies and the Populist Challenge*. Basingstoke: Palgrave, 81–98.

Mair, Peter and Cas Mudde (1998) "The party family and its study", *Annual Review of Political Science* 1: 211–29.

Mair, Peter and Ingrid Van Biezen (2001) "Party membership in twenty European democracies, 1980–2000", *Party Politics* 7(1): 5–21.

Malešević, Siniša (2002) *Ideology, Legitimacy and the New State: Yugoslavia, Serbia and Croatia*. London: Frank Cass.

Mallok, Katarína and Anne Tahirović (2003) "Der lange Weg zur Gleichberechtigung: Partizipation von Frauen in der Slowakei und Bosnien-Herzegowina", *Osteuropa* 53(5): 689–703.

Marada, Radim (1998) "The 1998 Czech elections", *East European Constitutional Review* 7(4): 51–8.

March, Luke and Cas Mudde (2005) "What's left of the radical left? The European radical left since 1989: decline *and* mutation", *Comparative European Politics* 3(1): 23–49.

Marcus, Jonathan (2000) "Exorcising Europe's demons: a far-right resurgence?" *The Washington Quarterly* 23(4): 31–40.

Markotich, Stan (2000) "Serbia: extremism from the top and a blurring of right into left", in Paul Hainsworth (ed.), *The Politics of the Extreme Right: From the Margins to the Mainstream*. London: Pinter, 268–86.

Markowski, Radoslaw (2002) "Disillusionment with democracy and populism in Poland", in *Europe and the Crisis of Democracy: Elections in Europe: 1999–2002*. Paris: Notre Europe, 28–31.

Martin, John Levi (2001) "*The Authoritarian Personality*, 50 years later: what questions are there for political psychology?", *Political Psychology* 22(1): 1–26.

Maryniak, Irena (2002) "Goodbye Solidarity . . .", *Index on Censorship* 31(1): 100–7.

Matland, Richard E. (2003) "Women's representation in post-communist Europe", in Richard E. Matland and Kathleen A. Montgomery (eds.), *Women's Access to Political Power in Post-Communist Europe*. Oxford: Oxford University Press, 321–42.

Matland, Richard E. and Kathleen A. Montgomery (eds.) (2003) *Women's Access to Political Power in Post-Communist Europe*. Oxford: Oxford University Press.

May, John D. (1973) "Opinion structure of political parties: the special law of curvilinear disparity", *Political Studies* 21(2): 135–51.

Mayer, Nonna (1997) "Du vote Lepéniste au vote Frontiste", *Revue Française de Science Politique* 47(3–4): 438–53.

— (1998) "The Front National vote in the plural", *Patterns of Prejudice* 32(1): 3–24.

— (2002) *Ces Français qui votent Le Pen*. Paris: Flammarion.

— (2005) "Radical right populism in France: how much of the 2002 Le Pen votes does populism explain?", paper presented at the symposium "Globalization and Radical Right Populism", Beer-Sheva, April 11–12.

Mayer, Nonna and Mariette Sineau (2002) "France: the Front National", in Helga Amesberger and Brigitte Halbmayr (eds.), *Rechtsextreme Parteien – eine mögliche Heimat für Frauen?* Opladen: Leske + Budrich, 61–112.

Mazzoleni, Gianpietro (2003) "The media and the growth of neo-populism in contemporary democracies", in Gianpietro Mazzoleni *et al.* (eds.), *The Media and Neo-Populism: A Contemporary Analysis*. Westport: Praeger, 1–20.

— (2004) *Media e populismo: Alleati o nemici?* Milan: Working Papers del Dipartimento di studi sociali e politici 4/2004.

Mazzoleni, Gianpietro, Julianne Stewart, and Bruce Horsfield (eds.) (2003) *The Media and Neo-Populism: A Contemporary Analysis*. Westport: Praeger.

McCauley, Martin and Domitilla Sagramoso (1994) "Russian Federation", in Bogdan Szajkowski (ed.), *Political Parties of Eastern Europe, Russia and the Successor States*. Harlow: Longman, 407–523.

McGann, Anthony J. and Herbert Kitschelt (2005) "The radical right in the Alps: the evolution of support for the Swiss SVP and the Austrian FPÖ", *Party Politics* 11(2): 147–71.

Meguid, Bonnie M. (2005) "Competition between unequals: the role of mainstream party strategy in niche party success", *American Political Science Review* 99(3): 347–59.

Meijerink, Frits, Cas Mudde and Joop van Holsteyn (1998) "Right-wing extremism", *Acta Politica* 33(2): 165–78.

Mellón, Joan Antón (ed.) (2002) *Orden, Jerarquía y Comunidad: Fascismos, Dictaduras y Postfascismos en la Europa Contemporánea*. Madrid: Tecnos.

Melvin, Neil J. (2000) "Post-imperial ethnocracy and the Russophone minorities of Estonia and Latvia", in Jonathan Stein (ed.), *The Politics of National Minority Participation in Post-Communist Europe: State-Building, Democracy, and Ethnic Mobilization.* Armonk: M.E. Sharpe, 129–66.

Mény, Yves and Yves Surel (eds.) (2002a) *Democracies and the Populist Challenge.* Basingstoke: Palgrave.

— (2002b) "The constitutive ambiguity of populism", in Yves Mény and Yves Surel (eds.), *Democracies and the Populist Challenge.* Basingstoke: Palgrave, 1–21.

Merkl, Peter H. (1995) "Radical right parties in Europe and anti-foreign violence: a comparative essay", *Terrorism & Political Violence* 7(1): 96–118.

— (2003a) "Introduction", in Peter H. Merkl and Leonard Weinberg (eds.), *Right-Wing Extremism in the Twenty-First Century.* London: Frank Cass, 1–19.

— (2003b) "Stronger than ever", in Peter H. Merkl and Leonard Weinberg (eds.), *Right-Wing Extremism in the Twenty-First Century.* London: Frank Cass, 23–46.

Merkl, Peter H. and Leonard Weinberg (eds.) (1993) *Encounters with the Contemporary Radical Right.* Boulder: Westview.

Meuhier, Sophie (2002) "Managing globalization the French way", from: www.princeton.edu/pr/news/02/q2/0501-meunier_qa.htm (accessed 21/05/2003).

Michaels, Walter Benn (1995) *Our America: Nativism, Modernism, and Pluralism.* Durham, NC: Duke University Press.

Michels, Robert (1925) [1911] *Zur Soziologie des Parteiwesens in der modernen Demokratie: Untersuchungen über die oligarchischen Tendenzen des Gruppenlebens.* Stuttgart: Alfred Kröner.

Michnik, Adam (1991) "Nationalism", *Social Research* 58(4): 757–64.

Mihancsik, Zsófia (2001) "Revealing quotes: Magyar Fórum, Magyar Demokrata, Vasárnapi újság", in András Gerő, László Varga, and Mátyás Vince (eds.), *Antiszemita Közbedséd Magyarországon 2000-ben/Anti-Semitic Discourse in Hungary in 2000.* Budapest: B'nai B'rith Első Budapesti Kösösség, 155–72.

Milentijevic, Radmila (1994) "Anti-semitism and the treatment of the Holocaust in postcommunist Yugoslavia", in Randolph L. Braham (ed.), *Anti-Semitism and the Treatment of the Holocaust in Postcommunist Eastern Europe.* Boulder: Social Science Monographs, 225–49.

Millard, Frances (1999) *Polish Politics and Society.* London: Routledge.

— (2003) "Elections in Poland 2001: electoral manipulation and party upheaval", *Communist and Post-Communist Studies* 36(1): 69–86.

Minkenberg, Michael (1998) *Die neue radikale Rechte im Vergleich: USA, Frankreich, Deutschland.* Opladen: Westdeutscher.

— (2000) "The renewal of the radical right: between modernity and anti-modernity", *Government & Opposition* 35(2): 170–88.

— (2001) "The radical right in public office: agenda-setting and policy effects", *West European Politics* 24(4): 1–21.

— (2002a) "Staat und Kirche in westlichen Demokratien", in Michael Minkenberg and Ulrich Willems (eds.), *Politik und Region*. Opladen: Westdeutscher, 115–38.

— (2002b) "The radical right in postsocialist Central and Eastern Europe: comparative observations and interpretations", *East European Politics and Societies* 16(2): 335–62.

— (2003) "The West European radical right as a collective actor: modeling the impact of cultural and structural variables on party formation and movement mobilization", *Comparative European Politics* 1(2): 149–70.

Minkenberg, Michael and Martin Schain (2003) "The Front National in context: French and European dimensions", in Peter H. Merkl and Leonard Weinberg (eds.), *Right-Wing Extremism in the Twenty-First Century*. London: Frank Cass, 161–90.

Mitev, Petar-Emil (1997) "The party manifestos for the Bulgarian 1994 elections", *Journal of Communist Studies and Transition Politics* 13(1): 64–90.

Mitra, Subrata (1988) "The National Front in France – a single-issue movement?", *West European Politics* 11(2): 47–64.

MNR (2002) "Journée des femmes: la femme française doit retrouver sa dignité et sa liberté", press communiqué on 7 March, from: www.m-n-r.net/news347.htm (accessed 02/08/2005).

— (n.d.) "La mondialisation économique: l'inadaptation de la France socialisée", from: 216.71.173.124/M-N-R/www.m-n-r.com/idees/pointsur/mondialisation_eco.htm (accessed 22/05/2003).

Mölzer, Andreas (2005a) "Rechter Aufbruch in Wien", report from the Freiheitlicher EU-Pressedienst Andreas Mölzer, 14 November.

— (2005b) "Mölzer: Rechtsdemokratische Fraktion in EU-Parlament vor der Schaffung!", report from the Freiheitlicher EU-Pressedienst Andreas Mölzer, 14 November.

Montgomery, Kathleen A. and Gabrielle Ilonszki (2003) "Weak mobilization, hidden majoritarianism, and resurgence of the right: a recipe for female under-representation in Hungary", in Richard E. Matland and Kathleen A. Montgomery (eds.), *Women's Access to Political Power in Post-Communist Europe*. Oxford: Oxford University Press, 105–29.

Morgan, Roger and Stefano Silvestri (eds.) (1982) *Moderates and Conservatives in Western Europe: Political Parties, the European Community and the Atlantic Alliance*. Aldershot: Ashgate.

Mostov, Julie (1999) "Women and the radical right: ethnocracy and body politics", in Sabrina P. Ramet (ed.), *The Radical Right in Central and Eastern Europe since 1989*. University Park: Pennsylvania State University Press, 49–63.

Mouffe, Chantal (1995) "The end of politics and the rise of the radical right", *Dissent* 42(4): 498–502.

Mudde, Cas (1995a) "One against all, all against one!: a portrait of the Vlaams Blok", *Patterns of Prejudice* 29(1): 5–28.

— (1995b) "Right-wing extremism analyzed: a comparative analysis of the ideologies of three alleged right-wing extremist parties (NPD, NDP, CP'86)", *European Journal of Political Research* 27(2): 203–24.

— (1999) "The single-issue party thesis: extreme right parties and the immigration issue", *West European Politics* 22(3): 182–97.

— (2000a) *The Ideology of the Extreme Right*. Manchester: Manchester University Press.

— (2000b) "Extreme right parties in Eastern Europe", *Patterns of Prejudice* 34(1): 5–27.

— (2001) "In the name of the peasantry, the proletariat, and the people: populisms in Eastern Europe", *East European Politics and Societies* 15(1): 33–53.

— (2002a) "Warum ist der Rechtsradikalismus im Osten so *schwach*?", *Osteuropa* 52(5): 626–30.

— (2002b) "'England belongs to me': the extreme right in the UK parliamentary election of 2001", *Representation* 39(1): 37–43.

— (2002c) "Slovak elections: go west!" *East European Perspectives* 4(21).

— (2004) "The populist *Zeitgeist*", *Government & Opposition* 39(3): 541–63.

— (ed.) (2005a) *Racist Extremism in Central and Eastern Europe*. London: Routledge.

— (2005b) "Racist extremism in Central and Eastern Europe", *East European Politics and Societies* 19(2): 161–84.

— (2005c) "Politischer Extremismus und Radikalismus in Westeuropa: Typologie und Bestandaufnahme", in Uwe Backes and Eckhard Jesse (eds.), *Gefährdungen der Freiheit: Extremistische Ideologien im Vergleich*. Göttingen: Vandenhoeck & Ruprecht, 87–104.

— (2006) "Anti-system politics", in Paul Heywood, Erik Jones, Martin Rhodes, and Ulrich Sedelmeier (eds.), *Developments in European Politics*. London: Palgrave, 178–95.

— (2007) "A Fortynist foreign policy", in Phillipe Burrin and Christina Schori Liang (eds.), *Europe for the Europeans: The Foreign and Security Policy of the Populist Radical Right*. Aldershot: Ashgate.

Mudde, Cas and Joop Van Holsteyn (2000) "The Netherlands: explaining the limited success of the extreme right", in Paul Hainsworth (ed.), *The Politics of the Extreme Right: From the Margins to the Mainstream*. London: Pinter, 144–71.

Müller, Wolfgang C. (1999) "Plebiscitary agenda-setting and party strategies: theoretical considerations and evidence from Austria", *Party Politics* 5(3): 303–15.

— (2002) "Evil or the 'engine of democracy'? Populism and party competition in Austria", in Yves Mény and Yves Surel (eds.), *Democracies and the Populist Challenge*. Basingstoke: Palgrave, 155–75.

Müller-Rommel, Ferdinand (1993) *Grüne Parteien in Westeuropa: Entwicklungsphasen und Erfolgsbedingungen*. Opladen: Westdeutscher.

— (1998) "Explaining the electoral success of Green parties: a cross-national analysis", *Environmental Politics* 7(4): 145–54.

Mungiu-Pippidi, Alina (2004) "Milosevic's voters: explaining grassroots nationalism in postcommunist Europe", in Alina Mungiu-Pippidi and Ivan Krastev (eds.), *Nationalism after Communism: Lessons Learned*. Budapest: Central European University Press, 43–80.

Mushaben, Joyce Marie (1996) "The rise of Femi-Nazis? Female participation in right-extremist movements in unified Germany", *German Politics* 5(2): 240–61.

Naegele, Jolyon (2002) "Political extremism in Eastern Europe – on the wane or going mainstream?", *RFE/RL (Un)Civil Societies* 3(20), May 15.

Nagel, Joane (1998) "Masculinity and nationalism: gender and sexuality in the making of nations", *Ethnic and Racial Studies* 21(2): 242–69.

Nairn, Tom (1995) "Breakwaters of 2000: from ethnic to civic nationalism", *New Left Review* 214: 91–103.

Narud, Hanne Marthe and Audun Skare (1999) "Are party activists the party extremists? The structure of opinion in political parties", *Scandinavian Political Studies* 22(1): 45–65.

Netjes, Catherine E. and Erica Edwards (2005) *Taking Europe to its Extremes: Examining Cueing Effects of Right-Wing Populist Parties on Public Opinion Regarding European Integration.* Berlin: WZB (Discussion Paper SP IV 2005–202).

Neu, Viola (2003) "Die PDS: eine populistische Partei?" in Nikolaus Werz (ed.), *Populismus: Populisten in Übersee und Europa.* Opladen: Leske + Budrich, 263–77.

Newman, Saul (1994) "Ethnoregional parties: a comparative perspective", *Regional Politics & Policy* 4(2): 28–66.

Newton, Kenneth (2006) "May the weak force be with you: the power of the mass media in modern politics", *European Journal of Political Research* 45(2): 209–34.

NF (1999) *The Flame: The Newspaper of the National Front*, Number 2.

Nimni, Ephraim (1999) "Nationalist multiculturalism in late imperial Austria as a critique of contemporary liberalism: the case of Bauer and Renner", *Journal of Political Ideologies* 4(3): 289–314.

Nolte, Ernst (1965) *Three Faces of Fascism.* London: Weidenfeld & Nicolson.

Nordberg, Camilla (2004) "Legitimising immigration control: Romani asylum-seekers in the Finnish debate", *Journal of Ethnic and Migration Studies* 30(4): 717–35.

Norris, Pippa (1993) "Conclusions: comparing legislative recruitment", in Joni Lovenduski and Pippa Norris (eds.), *Gender and Party Politics.* London: Sage, 309–30.

— (1997) "Conclusions: comparing passages to power", in Pippa Norris (ed.), *Passages to Power: Legislative Recruitment in Advanced Democracies.* Cambridge: Cambridge University Press, 209–31.

— (2000) *A Virtuous Circle? Political Communications in Post-Industrial Democracies.* Cambridge: Cambridge University Press.

— (2002) *Democratic Phoenix: Reinventing Political Activism.* New York: Cambridge University Press.

— (2003) "Preaching to the converted?: pluralism, participation and party websites", *Party Politics* 9(1): 21–45.

— (2005) *Radical Right: Voters and Parties in the Electoral Market.* New York: Cambridge University Press.

North, Richard (2005) "Election analysis: the effect of UKIP/Veritas", from: www.brugesgroup.com/mediacentre/releases.live?article=7629 (accessed 13/07/2005).

NPD (2002) *Zukunft und Arbeit für ein besseres Deutschland*. Berlin: NPD-Vorstand.

NS (2003) "Memorandum", admitted by participants of the Eurocritical Congress on February 8.

Nugent, Neil (1980) "Post-war fascism?", in Kenneth Lunn and Richard C. Thurlow (eds.), *British Fascism: Essays on the Radical Right in Inter-War Britain*. New York: St. Martin's, 205–23.

Olson, Jonathan (2000) "The rise of right-wing environmentalism", *Earth Island Journal* 15(2): 32–3.

Oltay, Edith (2003) "Hungary's largest right-wing party transforms into an alliance", *Südosteuropa* 52(4): 229–51.

Orfali, Birgitta (1997) "Right-wing extremists or fascists? From the French Front national to the Italian Alleanza nazionale through the Movimiento sociale italiano", in Göran Rystad (ed.), *Encountering Strangers – Responses and Consequences*. Lund: Lund University Press, 133–50.

Orwell, George (1996) "Telling people what they don't want to hear: the original preface to Animal Farm," *Dissent* 43: 59–64.

OSCE/ODIHR (2004) *Russian Federation: Elections to the State Duma 7 December 2003: OSCE/ODIHR Election Observation Mission Report*. Warsaw: OSCE/ODIHR.

OTS (2005) "Haider begrüßt Kooperation mit Rechtsparteien wie dem Vlaams Blok", November 14.

Ottaway, Marina (2003) *Democracy Challenged: The Rise of Semi-Authoritarianism*. Washington, DC: Carnegie Endowment for International Peace.

Ottens, Svenja (1997) "Ausmaß und Formen rechtsextremer Einstellungen bei Frauen: Ein Vergleich verschiedener Repräsentativ-Befragungen", in Renate Bitzan (ed.), *Rechte Frauen: Skingirls, Walküren und feine Damen*. Berlin: Elefanten, 178–90.

Panebianco, Angelo (1988) *Political Parties: Organization and Power*. Cambridge: Cambridge University Press.

Pankowski, Rafal and Marcin Kornak (2005) "Poland", in Cas Mudde (ed.), *Racist Extremism in Central and Eastern Europe*. London: Routledge, 156–83.

Papadopoulos, Yannis (2000) "National-populism in Western Europe: an ambivalent phenomenon", from: www.unil.ch:880/iepi/pdfs/papadopoulos.pdf (accessed 12/09/2003).

— (2002) "Populism, the democratic question, and contemporary governance", in Yves Mény and Yves Surel (eds.), *Democracies and the Populist Challenge*. Basingstoke: Palgrave, 45–61.

— (2005) "Populism as the other side of consociational multi-level democracies", in Daniele Caramani and Yves Mény (eds.), *Challenges to Consensual Politics: Democracy, Identity, and Populist Protest in the Alpine Region*. Brussels: PIE-Peter Lang, 71–81.

Pappas, Takis S. (2005) "Shared culture, individual strategy and collective action: explaining Slobodan Miloščvić's charismatic rise to power", *Southeast European and Black Sea Studies* 5(2): 191–211.

Parfenov, Victor and Marina Sergeeva (1998) "Russia: sowing nationalist grapes of wrath", *Transitions* 5(7): 34–5.

Pataki, Judith (1992) "Istvan Csurka's tract: summary and reactions", *RFE/RL Report*, October 9.

Payne, Stanley (1995) *A History of Fascism, 1914–1945*. Madison: University of Wisconsin Press.

Pedahzur, Ami (2003) *The Israeli Response to Jewish Extremism and Violence: Defending Democracy*. Manchester: Manchester University Press.

Pedahzur, Ami and Avarham Brichta (2002) "The institutionalization of extreme right-wing charismatic parties: a paradox?", *Party Politics* 8(1): 31–49.

Pedersen, Karen, L. Bille, R. Buch, J. Elklit, B. Hansen, and H. J. Nielsen, (2004) "Sleeping or active partners? Danish party members at the turn of the millennium", *Party Politics* 10(4): 367–83.

Pedersen, Mogens (1982) "Towards a new typology of party lifespans and minor parties", *Scandinavian Political Studies* 5(1): 1–16.

Pehe, Jiri (1991) "The emergence of right-wing extremism", *Report on Eastern Europe* 2(26): 1–6.

Pelinka, Anton (2002) "Vorwort", in Helga Amesberger and Brigitte Halbmayr (eds.), *Rechtsextreme Parteien – eine mögliche Heimat für Frauen?* Opladen: Leske + Budrich, 15–16.

— (2005) "Die FPÖ: Eine rechtspopulistische Regierungspartei zwischen Adaption und Opposition", in Susanne Frölich-Steffen and Lars Rensmann (eds.), *Populisten an der Macht: Populistische Regierungsparteien in West- und Osteuropa*. Vienna: Braumüller, 87–104.

Pellikaan, Huib, Tom van der Meer and Sarah de Lange (2003) "The road from a depoliticized to a centrifugal democracy", *Acta Politica* 38(1): 23–49.

Penc, Stanislav and Jan Urban (1998) "Czech Republic: extremist acts galvanize Roma population", *Transitions* 5(7): 39–40.

Pennings, Paul and Hans Keman (2003) "The Dutch parliamentary elections in 2002 and 2003: the rise and decline of the Fortuyn movement", *Acta Politica* 38(1): 51–68.

PER (2002) *Political Extremism and Interethnic Relations in the New Millennium*. Princeton: Project on Ethnic Relations.

Peri, Anat (2001) *Jörg Haider's Antisemitism*. Jerusalem: The Vidal Sassoon International Center for the Study of Antisemitism (ACTA 18).

Perner, Markus and Wolfgang Purtscheller (1994) "Die nationale Internationale", in Wolfgang Purtscheller (ed.), *Die Ordnung, die sie meinen*. Vienna: Picus, 72–99.

Perrineau, Pascal (ed.) (2001) *Les croisés de la société fremée: L'Europe des extrêmes droites*. Paris: l'aube essai.

— (2002) "Le vote d'extrême droite en France: adhésion ou protestation?", *Futuribles* 276: 5–20.

Perry, Duncan M. (1991) "Ethnic Turks face Bulgarian nationalism", *Report on Eastern Europe* 2(11): 5–8.

Pető, Andrea (2002) "Right wing political extremism and gender", paper presented at the EUI Gender Studies Program Open Seminar, Florence, February 20.

— (2005) "Populist use of memory and constitutionalism: two comments – II", *German Law Journal* 6(2): 399–405.

Petrocik, John R. (1996) "Issue ownership in presidential elections, with a 1980 case study", *American Journal of Political Science* 40(3): 825–50.

Pfahl-Traughber, Armin (1993) *Rechtsextremismus*. Bonn: Bouvier.

— (1994) *Volkes Stimme? Rechtspopulismus in Europa*. Bonn: Dietz.

Pharr, Susan J. and Robert D. Putnam (eds.) (2000) *Disaffected Democracies: What's Troubling the Trilateral Countries?* Princeton: Princeton University Press.

Pickel, Gert and Jörg Jacobs (2001) *Einstellungen zur Demokratie und zur Gewährleistung von Rechten und Freitheiten in den jungen Demokratien Mittel- und Osteuropas*. Frankfurt (Oder): Frankfurter Institut für Transformationsstudien (No.9/01).

Pissowotzki, Jörn (2003) "Der Populist Silvio Berlusconi", in Nikolaus Werz (ed.), *Populismus: Populisten in Übersee und Europa*. Opladen: Leske + Budrich, 127–43.

Plasser, Fritz and Peter A. Ulram (1995) "Wandel der politischen Konfliktdynamik: Radikaler Rechtspopulismus in Österreich", in Wolfgang Müller, Fritz Plasser, and Peter A. Ulram (eds.), *Wählerverhalten und Parteienwettbewerb: Analysen zur Nationalratswahl 1994*. Vienna: Signum, 471–503.

— (2003) "Striking a responsive chord: mass media and right-wing populism in Austria", in Gianpietro Mazzoleni *et al.* (eds.), *The Media and Neo-Populism: A Contemporary Analysis*. Westport: Praeger, 21–43.

— (n.d.) "Parteien ohne Stammwähler? Zerfall der Parteibindungen und Neuausrichtung des österreichischen Wahlverhaltens", from: www.demokratiezentrum.org/pdfs/plasserulram.pdf (accessed 18/02/2006).

Plasser, Fritz, Peter A. Ulram, and Harald Waldrauch (1998) *Democratic Consolidation in East-Central Europe*. Basingstoke: Macmillan.

Plenel, E. and A. Rollat (1984) *L'effet Le Pen*. Paris: La Découverte.

Poguntke, Thomas (2002) "Zur empirischen Evidenz der Kartellparteien-These", *Zeitschrift für Parlamentsfragen* 33(4): 790–806.

Poleshchuk, Vadim (2005) "Estonia", in Cas Mudde (ed.), *Racist Extremism in Central and Eastern Europe*. London: Routledge, 58–79.

Pollack, Detlef, Jörg Jacobs, Olaf Müller, and Gert Pickel (eds.) (2003) *Political Culture in Post-Communist Europe: Attitudes in New Democracies*. Aldershot: Ashgate.

Pop (2002) "The 'groupuscular Right': a neglected political genius", special issue of *Patterns of Prejudice* 36(3).

Pop-Elechus, Grigore (2001) "Romania's politics of dejection", *Journal of Democracy* 12(3): 156–69.

— (2003) "Radicalization or protest vote? Explaining the electoral success of unorthodox parties in Eastern Europe", paper presented at the 2002 annual AAASS meeting, Pittsburgh, November 21–24.

Popescu, Marina (2003) "The parliamentary and presidential elections in Romania, November 2000", *Electoral Studies* 22(2): 325–95.

Pribićević, Ognjen (1999) "Changing fortunes of the Serbian radical right", in Sabrina P. Ramet (ed.), *The Radical Right in Central and Eastern Europe since 1989*. University Park: Pennsylvania State University Press, 193–211.

Probst, Lothar (2003) "Jörg Haider und die FPÖ: Anmerkungen zum Rechtspopulismus in Österreich", in Nikolaus Werz (ed.), *Populismus: Populisten in Übersee und Europa*. Opladen: Leske + Budrich, 113–25.

Przeworski, Adam and Henry Teune (1970) *The Logic of Comparative Social Inquiry*. New York: Wiley.

PSNS (n.d.) "About us", from: www.prava-sns.sk/english/o_nas/privitanie.html (accessed 26/08/2004).

Ptak, Ralf (1999) "Die soziale Frage als Politikfeld der extremen Rechten. Zwischen marktwirtschaftlichen Grundsätzen, vormodernem Antikapitalismus und Sozialismus-Demagogie", in Jens Mecklenburg (ed.), *Braune Gefahr. DVU, NPD, REP: Geschichte und Zukunft*. Berlin: Elefanten, 97–145.

Puhle, Hans-Jürgen (2003) "Zwischen Protest und Politikstil: Populismus, Neo-Populismus und Demokratie", in Nikolaus Werz (ed.), *Populismus: Populisten in Übersee und Europa*. Opladen: Leske + Budrich, 15–43.

Pusić, Vesna (1998) "Croatia at the crossroads", *Journal of Democracy* 9(1): 111–24.

Quaglia, Lucia (2005) "The right and Europe in Italy: an ambivalent relationship", *South European Society & Politics* 10(2): 281–95.

Quinkert, Andreas and Siegfried Jäger (1991) *Warum dieser Haß in Hoyerswerda? Die rassistische Hetze von BILD gegen Flüchtlinge im Herbst 1991*. Duisburg: DISS.

Ramet, Sabrina P. (ed.) (1999a) *The Radical Right in Central and Eastern Europe since 1989*. University Park: Pennsylvania State University Press.

— (1999b) "Defining the radical right: values and behaviors of organized intolerance in post-communist Central and Eastern Europe", in Sabrina P. Ramet (ed.), *The Radical Right in Central and Eastern Europe since 1989*. University Park: Pennsylvania State University Press, 3–27.

— (2005) "Sliding backwards: the fate of women in post-1989 East-Central Europe", *Kakanien Revisited*, from: www.kakanien.ac.at/beitr/fallstudie/SRamet1.pdf (accessed 01/07/2005).

Randall, Vicky (1987) *Women and Politics: An International Perspective*. Chicago: University of Chicago Press, 2nd edn.

Raniolo, Francesco (2000) *Il partiti conservatori in Europa occidentale*. Bologna: Il Mulino.

Reich, Wilhelm (1970) *The Mass Psychology of Fascism*. Harmondsworth: Penguin.

Reif, Karlheinz and Hermann Schmitt (1980) "Nine second-order elections: a conceptual framework for analysis of the European election results", *European Journal of Political Research* 8: 3–44.

Rensmann, Lars (2003) "The new politics of prejudice: comparative perspectives on extreme right parties in European democracies", *German Politics and Society* 21(4): 93–123.

REP (1983) *Grundsatzprogramm*. Bonn: Bundesgeschäftsstelle der Republikaner.
— (1990) *Parteiprogramm*. Bonn: Die Republikaner.
— (2002) *Programm: Politik für Deutsche*. Berlin: Die Republikaner.
— (2003) *Wahlprogramm der Partei DIE REPUBLIKANER für die Europawahl 2003*, from: www.rep-bremen.de/Europawahlprogramm.html (accessed 15/02/2006).
— (n.d.) *Unser Programm für Landwirtschaft und Forsten*. Pamphlet.
Report (2000) *Report on the Issue of Extremism in the Czech Republic in 2000*, from: www.mvcr.cz/extremis/2000/angl/3.html (accessed 19/01/2006).
— (2002) *Report on the Issue of Extremism in the Czech Republic in 2002*, from: www.mvcr.cz/extremis/2002/angl/extrem.pdf (accessed 19/01/2006).
Riccio, Sandra (2002) "Italien: Die Alleanza Nazionale", in Helga Amesberger and Brigitte Halbmayr (eds.), *Rechtsextreme Parteien – eine mögliche Heimat für Frauen?* Opladen: Leske + Budrich, 113–59.
Riedlsperger, Max (1998) "The Freedom Party of Austria: from protest to radical right populism", in Hans-Georg Betz and Stefan Immerfall (eds.), *The New Politics of the Right: Neo-Populist Parties and Movements in Established Democracies*. New York: St. Martin's, 27–43.
Ritterband, Charles E. (2003) "Kärntner Chamäleon: Jörg Haiders Auf- und Abstieg in Österreich", *Internationale Politik* 58(4): 23–8.
Ritzer, George (2004) *The McDonaldization of Society*. London: Sage.
Rizman, Rudolf M. (1999) "Radical right politics in Slovenia", in Sabrina P. Ramet (ed.), *The Radical Right in Central and Eastern Europe since 1989*. University Park: Pennsylvania State University Press, 147–70.
Robotin, Monica-Emilia (2002) "The electorate of the extreme right: the case of Greater Romania Party". Budapest, Central European University: unpublished MA thesis.
Rogge, Joachim (2005) "Marine Le Pen (Front National)", *Das Parlament*, 7 November.
Römmele, Andrea (2003) "Political parties, party communication and new information and communication technologies", *Party Politics* 9(1): 7–20.
Rommelspacher, Birgit (2001) "Das Geschlechterverhältnis im Rechtsextremismus", in Wilfried Schubarth and Richard Stöss (eds.), *Rechtsextremismus in der Bundesrepublik Deutschland: Eine Bilanz*. Oploden: Leske + Budrich, 199–219.
Ronson, Jon (2002) *Them: Adventures with Extremists*. New York: Simon & Schuster.
Rosamond, Ben (2002) *Globalization and the European Union*. Canberra: National Europe Centre Paper (No. 12).
Rösel, Jakob (2003) "Populistische Politik in Indien", in Nikolaus Werz (ed.), *Populismus: Populisten in Übersee und Europa*. Opladen: Leske + Budrich, 65–87.
Rösslhumer, Maria (1999) "Politikerinnen in der Freiheitlichen Partei Österreichs (FPÖ)", in Andrea Pető and Béla Rásky (eds.), *Construction. Reconstruction: Women, Family and Politics in Central Europe, 1945–1998*. Budapest: CEU Progam on Gender and Culture, 71–92.

Roth, Dieter (1989) "Sind die Republikaner die fünfte Partei?", *Aus Politik und Zeitgeschichte* 41–42: 10–20.

— (1990) "Die Republikaner: Schneller Aufstieg und tiefer Fall einer Protestpartei am rechten Rand", *Aus Politik und Zeitgeschichte* 37–38: 27–39.

Roxburgh, Angus (2002) *Preachers of Hate: The Rise of the Far Right.* London: Gibson Square.

Roy, Jean-Philippe (1998) "Le programme économique et social du Front national en France", in Pascal Delwit, Jean-Michel De Waele, and Andrea Rea (eds.), *L'extrême droite en France et en Belgique.* Brussels: Éditions Complexe, 85–100.

Rudnicki, Szymon (2000) "Nationalismus und Extremismus im Polen von heute und ihre historischen Wurzeln," *Transodra* 21: 8–23.

Rueschemeyer, Marilyn (1998) "Difficulties and opportunities in the transition period: concluding observations", in Marilyn Rueschemeyer (ed.), *Women in the Politics of Postcommunist Eastern Europe.* Armonk: M. E. Sharpe, rev. and exp. edn, 285–97.

Rupert, Mark (2000) *Ideologies of Globalization: Contending Visions of a New World Order.* London: Routledge.

Rupnik, Jacques (2002) "Das andere Mitteleuropa: Die neuen Populismen und die Politik mit der Vergangenheit", *Transit* 23: 117–27.

Ruscino, Gian Enrico (2002) "Berlusconismo: Neuer Faschismus oder demokratischer Populismus?", *Blätter für deutsche und internationale Politik* 8: 973–80.

Rydgren, Jens (2003) "Meso-level reasons for racism and xenophobia: some converging and diverging effects of radical right populism in France and Sweden", *European Journal of Social Theory* 6(1): 45–68.

— (2004a) *The Populist Challenge: Political Protest and Ethno-Nationalist Mobilization in France.* New York: Berghahn.

— (2004b) "Explaining the emergence of radical right-wing populism: the case of Denmark", *West European Politics* 27(3): 474–502.

— (ed.) (2005a) *Movements of Exclusion: Radical Right-Wing Populism in the West.* Hauppage: Nova Science.

— (2005b) "Is extreme right-wing populism contagious? Explaining the emergence of a new party family", *European Journal of Political Research* 44(3): 413–37.

Salzborn, Samuel and Heribert Schiedel (2003) "'Nation Europa': Ethnoföderale Konzepte und kontinentale Vernetzung der extremen Rechten", *Blätter für deutsche und internationale Politik* 10: 1209–17.

Sánchez-Cuenca, Ignacio (2004) "Party moderation and politicians' ideological rigidity", *Party Politics* 10(3): 325–42.

Sapiro, Virginia (1983) *The Political Integration of Women: Roles, Socialization, and Politics.* Urbana: University of Illinois Press.

Sartori, Giovanni (1970) "Concept misformation in comparative politics", *American Political Science Review* 64(4): 1033–53.

— (1976) *Parties and Party Systems: A Framework for Analysis.* Cambridge: Cambridge University Press.

— (1990) [1968] "The sociology of parties: a critical review", in Peter Mair (ed.), *The West European Party System*. Oxford: Oxford University Press, 150–82.

— (2004) "Where is political science going?", *PS: Political Science & Politics* 37(4): 785–6.

Saxonberg, Steven (2003) *The Czech Republic before the New Millennium: Politics, Parties and Gender*. Boulder: East European Monographs.

Schain, Martin A. (2006) "The extreme-right and immigration policy-making: measuring direct and indirect effects", *West European Politics* 29(2): 270–89.

Schain, Martin, Aristide Zolberg, and Patrick Hossay (eds.) (2002a) *Shadows over Europe: The Development and Impact of the Extreme Right in Western Europe*. New York: Palgrave.

— (2002b) "The development of radical right parties in Western Europe", in Martin Schain, Aristide Zolberg, and Patrick Hossay (eds.), *Shadows over Europe: The Development and Impact of the Extreme Right in Western Europe*. New York: Palgrave, 3–17.

Scharsach, Hans-Hennig and Kurt Kuch (2000) *Haider: Schatten über Europa*. Cologne: Kiepenheuer & Witsch.

Schedler, Andreas (1996) "Anti-political-establishment parties", *Party Politics* 2(3): 291–312.

— (1997) "Introduction: antipolitics – closing and colonizing the public sphere", in Andreas Schedler (ed.), *The End of Politics? Explorations into Modern Antipolitics*. Basingstoke: Macmillan, 1–20.

Schellenberg, Britta (2005) "Rechtsextremismus und Medien", *Aus Politik und Zeitgeschichte* 42: 39–45.

Scheuch, Erwin K. and Hans Dieter Klingemann (1967) "Theorie des Rechtsradikalismus in westlichen Industriegesellschaften", *Hamburger Jahrbuch für Wirtschafts- und Sozialpolitik* 12: 11–19.

Schikhof, Marco (1998) "Strategieën tegen extreem-rechts en hun gevolgen", in Joop van Holsteyn and Cas Mudde (eds.), *Extreem-rechts in Nederland*. The Hague: Sdu, 143–56.

Schmid, Bernhard (2005) "Jeanne sagt Nein", *Blick nach Rechts* 22(10): 8.

Schmidt, Jochen (2003) "Der Front national und Jean-Marie Le Pen", in Nikolaus Werz (ed.), *Populismus: Populisten in Übersee und Europa*. Opladen: Leske + Budrich, 89–111.

Schmidt, Matthias (1997) *Die Parlamentsarbeit rechtsextremer Parteien und mögliche Gegenstrategien: Eine Untersuchung am Beispiel der 'Deutschen Volksunion' im Schleswig-Holsteinischen Landtag*. Münster: agenda.

Schmitter, Philippe C. and Terry L. Karl (1994) "The conceptual travels of transitologists and consolidologists: how far to the East should they go?", *Slavic Review* 53(1): 173–85.

Schönhuber, Franz (2000) "Eurorechte", *Nation [und] Europa* 50(6): 56.

Schulze, Joerg (1998) "The far right: a nationalist International?", from: www.bbc.co.uk/worldservice/theneweurope/wk19.htm (accessed 17/02/2006).

Schuman, Howard and Stanley Presser (1981) *Questions and Answers in Attitude Surveys: Experiments on Question Form, Wording, and Context*. San Diego: Academic.

Schumann, Siegfried (2001) "Die Wahl der Republikaner: Ideologisches Bekenntnis oder Ausdruck von Protest? Fortführung einer Debatte unter theoretischen und methodischen Gesichtspunkten", in Hans-Dieter Klingemann and Max Kaase (eds.), *Wahlen und Wähler*. Opladen: Westdeutscher, 717–38.

Schumann, Siegfried and Jürgen Falter (1988) "Affinity towards right-wing extremism in Western Europe", *West European Politics* 11(2): 96–110.

Schüssel, Wolfgang and Jörg Haider (2000) "Responsibility for Austria – A Future in the Heart of Europe", from: www.oe-journal.at/0300/06_030300_e.htm (accessed 20/02/2006).

Schuster, Anke Gerlinde (2005) "'Populist Watch' until Convergence and Beyond: Populist Parties in Poland and Romania, Legacies of Transition and Adaptation to EU-accession." European Centre Natolin: unpublished MA thesis.

Schwartz, Joseph M. (1993) "Left", in Joel Krieger (ed.), *The Oxford Companion to Politics of the World*. Oxford: Oxford University Press, 531–2.

Schwarzmantel, John (1998) *The Age of Ideology*. Basingstoke: Macmillan.

SD (2005) "Presentation", from www.sverigedemokraterna.se (accessed 25/01/2006).

Segert, Dieter (2005a) "Der tschechische Allparteienpopulismus: postsozialistische Instabilität als Grundlage für eine populistische Versuchung in Parlament und Regierung", in Susanne Frölich-Steffen and Lars Rensmann (eds.), *Populisten an der Macht: Populistische Regierungsparteien in West- und Osteuropa*. Vienna: Braumüller, 191–208.

— (2005b) "Der Gefahr des Allparteienpopulismus", *Das Parlament*, November 7.

Seidel, Gill (ed.) (1988a) *The Nature of the Right: A Feminist Analysis of Order Patterns*. Amsterdam: John Benjamins.

— (1988b) "Right-wing discourse and power: exclusions and resistance", in Gill Seidel (ed.), *The Nature of the Right: A Feminist Analysis of Order Patterns*. Amsterdam: John Benjamins, 7–19.

Sekelj, Laslo (1998) *Antisemitism and Jewish Identity in Serbia after the Collapse of the Yugoslav State*. Jerusalem: The Vidal Sassoon International Center for the Study of Antisemitism (ACTA 12).

Service, Robert (1998) "Zhirinovskii: ideas in search of an audience", in Geoffrey Hosking and Robert Service (eds.), *Russian Nationalism: Past and Present*. Basingstoke: Macmillan, 179–97.

Settembri, Pierpaolo (2004) "When is a group not a political group? The dissolution of the TDI Group in the European Parliament", *Journal of Legislative Studies* 10(1): 150–74.

SF (2001) *Many Voices One Country: Cherishing All the Children of the Nation Equally: Towards an Anti-Racist Ireland*. Dublin: Sinn Féin.

Shabad, Goldie and Kazimierz M. Slomczynski (2004) "Inter-party mobility among parliamentary candidates in post-communist East Central Europe", *Party Politics* 10(2): 151–76.

Shafir, Michael (1996) "Antisemitic candidates in Romania's 1996 presidential elections", *East European Jewish Affairs* 26(1): 89–105.

— (1997) "Marshal Antonescu's postcommunist rehabilitation: *cui bono?*", in Randolph L. Braham (ed.), *The Destruction of Romanian and Ukrainian Jews during the Antonescu Era*. New York: Columbia University Press, 349–410.

— (2000) "Marginalization or mainstream? The extreme right in post-communist Romania", in Paul Hainsworth (ed.), *The Politics of the Extreme Right: From the Margins to the Mainstream*. London: Pinter, 247–67.

— (2001) "The Greater Romania Party and the 2000 elections in Romania: how obvious is the obvious?", *Romanian Journal of Society and Politics* 1(2): 91–126.

— (2002a) *Between Denial and "Comparative Trivialization": Holocaust Negationism in Post-Communist East Central Europe*. Jerusalem: The Vidal Sassoon International Center for the Study of Antisemitism (ACTA 19).

— (2002b) "Six shots, six questions, one answer", *RFE/RL Newsline*, 13 May.

Shenfield, Stephen (2001) *Russian Fascism: Traditions, Tendencies, Movements*. Armonk: M.E. Sharpe.

Siderov, Volen (2002) "Globalization: the last stage of the colonization of the Orthodox East", excerpt from speech at the International Conference on Global Problems of World History, Moscow, January 26–27; from: www.radioislam.org/conferences (accessed 27/06/2005).

Siemieńska, Renata (2003) "Women in the Polish Sejm: political culture and party politics versus electoral rules", in Richard E. Matland and Kathleen A. Montgomery (eds.), *Women's Access to Political Power in Post-Communist Europe*. Oxford: Oxford University Press, 217–44.

Sigona, Nando (2005) "Locating 'the Gypsy problem': the Roma in Italy: stereotyping, labelling and 'Nomad camps'", *Journal of Ethnic and Migration Studies* 31(4): 741–56.

Sikk, Allan (2005) "How unstable? Volatility and the genuinely new parties in Eastern Europe", *European Journal of Political Research* 44(3): 391–412.

Siller, Gertrude (1997) *Rechtsextremismus bei Frauen: Zusammenhänge zwischen geschlechtsspezifischen Erfahrungen und politischen Orientierungen*. Opladen: Westdeutscher.

Simmons, Harvey G. (1996) *The French National Front: The Extremist Challenge to Democracy*. Boulder: Westview.

— (2003) "The French and European extreme right and globalization", paper presented at the international seminar "Challenges to the New World Order: Anti-Globalism and Counter-Globalism," Amsterdam, May 30–31.

Simon, Jeffrey (2004) *NATO and the Czech and Slovak Republics: A Comparative Study in Civil–Military Relations*. Lanham: Rowman & Littlefield.

Skenderovic, Damir (2005) *The Radical Right in Switzerland: Postwar Continuity and Recent Transformations: A Study of Politics, Ideology, and Organizations*. Fribourg: Cric Print.

Skrzydlo, Anette, Barbara Thiele and Nikola Wohllaib (1997) "Les femmes dans le Parti des Republikaner: Sur les rapports entre les femmes et l'extrême droite", in Claudie Lesselier and Fiametta Venner (eds.), *L'extrême droite et les femmes: Enjeux & actualité*. Villeurbanne: Golias, 229–48.

Slider, Darrell (1999) "Pskov under the LDPR: elections and dysfunctional federalism in one region", *Europe-Asia Studies* 51(5), 755–67.

Smart, Barry (ed.) (1999) *Resisting McDonaldization*. London: Sage.

Smith, David (1999) "The restoration principle in post communist Estonia", in Christopher Williams and Thanasis Sfikas (eds.), *Ethnicity and Nationalism in Russia, CIS and the Baltic States*. Aldershot: Ashgate, 287–323.

Smith, Graham, Aadne Aasland, and Richard Mole (1994) "Statehood, ethnic relations and citizenship", in Graham Smith (ed.), *The Baltic States: The National Self-Determination of Estonia, Latvia and Lithuania*. Basingstoke: Macmillan, 181–205.

Smith, M. Brewster (1967) "Foreword", in John P. Kirscht and Ronald C. Dillehay, *Dimenions of Authoritarianism: A Review of Research and Theory*. Lexington: University of Kentucky Press, v–ix.

Smith, Philip (2000) "Culture and charisma: outline of a theory", *Acta Sociologica* 43(2): 101–13.

SNS (2002) *Program národnej obnovy: Pre volobné obdobie 2002–2006*. Bratislava: SNS.

— (n.d.) *Programové východiská SNS*, from www.sns.sk/program.php (accessed 04/02/2006).

Sobotka, Eva (2003) "Roma in politics in the Czech Republic, Slovakia and Poland", *Roma Rights Quaterly* 4: 17–33.

Solchanyk, Roman (1999) "The radical right in Ukraine," in Sabrina P. Ramet (ed.), *The Radical Right in Central and Eastern Europe since 1989*. University Park: Pennsylvania State University Press, 279–96.

Sotiropoulos, Dimitri A. (1996) *Populism and Bureaucracy: The Case of Greece under PASOK, 1981–1989*. Notre Dame: University of Notre Dame Press.

Spannbauer, Andreas (1998) "Dr. Gerhard Frey: 500 Millionen stehen hinter ihm", in Jürgen Elsässer (ed.), *Braunbuch DVU: Eine deutsche Arbeiterpartei und ihre Freunde*. Hamburg: Konkret, 31–42.

Spektorowski, Alberto (2000) "The French New Right: differentialism and the idea of ethnophilian exclusionism", *Polity* 33(2): 283–303.

Spencer, Philip and Howard Wollman (1998) "Good and bad nationalisms: a critique of dualism", *Journal of Political Ideologies* 3(3): 255–74.

Spicker, Paul (2000) "A *Third* Way?", *The European Legacy* 5(2): 229–39.

Spourdalakis, Michalis (1988) *The Rise of the Greek Socialist Party*. London: Routledge.

SPR-RSČ (1999) *Návrh nového programu SPR-RSC*. Prague: SPR-RSČ.

Spruyt, Marc (1995) *Grove borstels: Stel dat het Vlaams Blok morgen zijn programma realiseert, hoe zou Vlaanderen er dan uitzien?* Leuven: Van Halewyck.

Stadtmüller, Elzbieta (2000) "Polish perceptions of the European Union in the 1990s", in Karl Cordell (ed.), *Poland and the European Union*. London: Routledge, 24–44.

Stankiewicz, Katharina (2002) "Die 'neuen Dmowskis' – eine alte Ideologie im neuen Gewand? Der Nationalismus der Zwischenkriegszeit als ideologische Leitlinie der radikalen Rechten in Polen", *Osteuropa* 52(3): 263–79.

Starr, Amy (2000) *Naming the Enemy: Anti-Corporate Movements Confront Globalization*. London: Zed.

Statham, Paul (1996) "Berlusconi, the media, and the new right in Italy", *Press/Politics* 1(1): 87–105.

Stern, Jessica (2004) *Terreur in de naam van God: Waarom religieuze extremisten doden.* Utrecht: Het Spectrum.

Sternhell, Zeev (1978) *Les origines françaises du fascisme.* Paris: Seuil.

— (1996) *Neither Right nor Left: Fascist Ideology in France.* Princeton: Princeton University Press.

Stewart, Julianne, Gianpietro Mazzoleni, and Bruce Horsfield (2003) "Conclusion: power to the media managers", in Gianpietro Mazzoleni *et al.* (eds.), *The Media and Neo-Populism: A Contemporary Analysis.* Westport: Praeger, 217–37.

Stojanović, Svetozar (2003) *Serbia: The Democratic Revolution.* New York: Humanity.

Stone, William F., Gerda Lederer and Richard Christie (eds.) (1993) *Strength and Weakness: The Authoritarian Personality Today.* New York: Springer.

Stöss, Richard (1991) *Politics against Democracy: Right-Wing Extremism in West Germany.* Oxford: Berg.

— (2000) *Rechtsextremismus im vereinten Deutschland.* Berlin: Friedrich-Ebert-Stiftung.

— (2001) *Zur Vernetzung der extremen Rechten in Europa.* Berlin: Otto-Stammer-Zentrum Working Paper (No. 5).

— (2005) *Rechtsextremismus im Wandel.* Berlin: Friedrich-Ebert-Stiftung.

Stouthuysen, Patrick (1993) *Extreem-rechts in na-oorlogs Europa.* Brussel: VUB-PRESS.

Strahan, Milan and Daniel P. Daniel (eds.) (1994) *Slovakia and the Slovaks: A Concise Encyclopedia.* Bratislava: Encyclopedical Institute of the Slovak Academy of Sciences.

Strobel, Georg W. (2001) "Das andere Polen: Struktur und Selbstverständnis der rechten und rechtsextremen Kräfte in der polnische Politik", *Osteuropa*, 51(3): 259–80.

Sturhan, Katrin (1997) "Zwischen Rechtskonservatismus und Neonazismus – Frauen in rechtsextremen Parteien und Organisationen", in Renate Bitzan (ed.), *Rechte Frauen: Skingirls, Walküren und feine Damen.* Berlin: Elefanten, 104–30.

Sully, Melanie A. (1997) *The Haider Phenomenon.* Boulder: East European Monographs.

Svoray, Yoran and Nick Taylor (1994) *In Hitler's Shadow: An Israeli's Amazing Journey inside Germany's Neo-Nazi Movement.* New York: Doubleday.

SVP (2003) *Schweizer Qualität.* Bern: Generalsekretariat SVP.

Swank, Duane and Hans-Georg Betz (2003) "Globalization, the welfare state and right-wing populism in Western Europe", *Socio-Economic Review* 1(2): 215–45.

Swyngedouw, Marc (1992) "Het Vlaams Blok 1980–1991: opkomst, groei en doorbraak", in Rudi Van Doorslaer *et al.*, *Herfsttij van de 20ste eeuw: Extreem-rechts in Vlaanderen 1920–1990.* Leuven: Kritak, 83–104.

— (2001) "The subjective cognitive and affective map of extreme right voters: using open-ended questions in exit polls", *Electoral Studies*, 20(2): 217–41.

Szelenyi, Ivan (2006) "Poverty and varieties of post-communist capitalism", paper presented at the SSRC workshop "Justice, Hegemony and Social Movements", New Brunswick (NJ), May 24–25.

Szôcs, László (1998) "A tale of the unexpected: the extreme right *vis-à-vis* democracy in post-communist Hungary", *Ethnic and Racial Studies* 21(6): 1096–115.

Taggart, Paul (1995) "New populist parties in Western Europe", *West European Politics* 18(1): 34–51.

— (1996) *The New Populism and the New Politics: New Protest Parties in Sweden in a Comparative Perspective*. Basingstoke: Macmillan.

— (2000) *Populism*. Buckingham: Open University Press.

— (2002) "Populism and the pathology of representative politics", in Yves Mény and Yves Surel (eds.), *Democracies and the Populist Challenge*. Basingstoke: Palgrave, 62–80.

— (2004) "Populism and representative politics in contemporary Europe", *Journal of Political Ideologies* 9(3): 269–88.

Taggart, Paul and Aleks Szczerbiak (2002) *The Party Politics of Euroscepticism in EU Member and Candidate States*. Farmer: SEI Working Paper (No. 51).

Taguieff, Pierre-André (1984), "La rhétorique du national-populisme", *Mots* 9.

— (2004) *Rising from the Muck: The New Anti-Semitism in Europe*. Chicago: Ivan R. Dee.

Tajfel, Henri (1982) "Social psychology of intergroup relations", *Annual Review of Psychology* 33: 1–39.

Tamas, Bernard (2002) "The self-destructive tendencies of minor parties: the implosion of the Reform Party", paper presented at the 98th annual APSA meeting, Boston (MA), August 29–31.

Tamir, Yael (1983) *Liberal Nationalism*. Princeton: Princeton University Press.

Taras, Ray (2003) "Poland's accession into the European Union: parties, policies and paradoxes", *The Polish Review* 48(1): 3–19.

Tarchi, Marco (2002) "Populism Italian style", in Yves Mény and Yves Surel (eds.), *Democracies and the Populist Challenge*. Basingstoke: Palgrave, 120–38.

— (2003) "The political culture of the Alleanza nazionale: an analysis of the party's programmatic documents (1995–2002)", *Journal of Modern Italian Studies* 8(2): 135–81.

Tarrow, Sydney (1994) *Power in Movement*. Cambridge: Cambridge University Press.

Ter Wal, Jessika (2000) "The discourse of the extreme right and its ideological implications: the case of the Alleanza nazionale on immigration", *Patterns of Prejudice* 34(3): 37–51.

Thanei, Christoph (2002) "Vladimír Mečiar: ein Mythos polarisiert", in Michael Jungwirth (ed.), *Haider, Le Pen & Co. Europas Rechtspopulisten*. Graz: Styria, 218–37.

Thieme, Tom (2005) "Politische Extremismus in Ostmitteleuropa – Entstehungsbedingungen und Erscheinungsformen", in Uwe Backes and Eckhard Jesse (eds.), *Gefährdungen der Freiheit: Extremistische Ideologien im Vergleich*. Göttingen: Vandenhoeck & Ruprecht, 321–58.

Thijssen, Peter (2001) "Extreem-rechts en politieke aliënatie: een causaal mysterie? Case-study: het Vlaams Blok", *Tijdschrift voor Sociologie* 22(3): 243–72.

Thijssen, Peter and Sarah De Lange (2005) "Explaining the varying electoral appeal of the Vlaams Blok in the districts of Antwerp", *Ethical Perspectives* 12(2): 231–58.

Thompson, Peter (2000) "Jörg Haider, Tony Blair und der Wirtschaftsliberalismus", *Berliner Debatte INITIAL* 11(4): 93–100.

Tiersky, Ronald (ed.) (2001) *Euro-skepticism: A Reader*. Lanham: Rowman & Littlefield.

Tismaneanu, Vladimir (1996) "The Leninist debris or waiting for Peron", *East European Politics and Societies* 10(3): 504–35.

— (1998) *Fantasies of Salvation: Democracy, Nationalism and Myth in Post-Communist Europe*. Princeton: Princeton University Press.

Tóka, Gábor (1997) *Political Parties and Democratic Consolidation in East Central Europe*. Glasgow: Centre for the Study of Public Policy (Studies in Public Policy 279).

Tolz, Vera (2003) "Right-wing extremism in Russia: the dynamics of the 1990s", in Peter H. Merkl and Leonard Weinberg (eds.), *Right-Wing Extremism in the Twenty-First Century*. London: Frank Cass, 251–71.

Toole, James (2000) "Government formation and party system stabilization in East Central Europe", *Party Politics* 6(4): 441–61.

Tschiyembé, Mwayila (2001) "Le discourse des parties ultra-nationalistes et l'évolution des parties de gouvernement en Europe", in Dominique Andolfatto, Fabienna Greffet, and Laurent Olivier (eds.), *Les parties politiques: Quelles perspectives?* Paris: L'Harmattan, 217–24.

Tucker, Robert C. (1968) "The theory of charismatic leadership", *Daedalus* 97(3): 731–56.

Tuominen, Kaius (2002) "New World Order: The American Right and Conspiracy Theories of International Politics." University of Edinburgh: unpublished M.Sc. thesis.

Turner, Derek (2003) "The state of the European 'right': a wide variety of fortunes for a wide variety of parties", *The Occidental Quarterly* 3(4), from: theoccidentalquarterly.com/vol3no4/dt-euroright.html (accessed 21/12/2005).

Turnovec, František (1997) "Votes, seats and power: 1996 parliamentary election in the Czech Republic", *Communist and Post-Communist Studies* 30(3): 289–305.

Učeň, Peter (2002) "Democratic disillusion in Slovakia," in *Europe and the Crisis of Democracy: Elections in Europe: 1999–2002*. Paris: Notre Europe, 35–40.

— (2004) "Centrist populism as a new competitive and mobilization strategy in Slovak politics", in Ol'ga Gyárfášová and Grigorij Mesežnikov (eds.), *Party Government in Slovakia: Experience and Perspectives*. Bratislava: Institute for Public Affairs, 45–73.

Umland, Andreas (1997a) "The post-Soviet Russian extreme right", *Problems of Post-Communism* 44(4): 53–61.

— (1997b) "Vladimir Zhirinovskii in Russian Politics: Three Approaches to the Emergence of the Liberal-Democratic Party of Russia 1990–1993." Berlin, Free University: unpublished Ph.D dissertation.

— (2005) "Neue ideologische Fusionen im russischen Antidemokratismus: West-liche Konzepte, antiwestliche Doktrinen und das postsowjetische politis-che Spektrum", in Uwe Backes and Eckhard Jesse (eds.), *Gefährdungen der Freiheit: Extremistische Ideologien im Vergleich*. Göttingen: Vandenhoeck & Ruprecht, 371–406.

UNCHR *Statistical Yearbook 2003*, from: www.unchr.org/cgi-bin/texis/vtx/statistics/opendoc.htm?tbl=STATISTICS&id=42aff7e84 (accessed 02/04/2005).

UNHCR (1998) *Refugees and Others of Concern to UNHCR – 1998 Statistical Overview*, from: www.unhcr.ch/cgi-bin/texis/vtx/statistics/opendoc.pdf?tbl=STATISTICS&id-3bfa31ac1#zoom-100   (accessed   15/01/2006).

Uzelak, Gordana (1998) "Franjo Tudjman's nationalist ideology", *East European Quarterly* 31(4): 449–72.

Van den Brink, Rinke (2005) *In de greep van de angst: De Europese sociaal-democratie en het rechtspopulisme*. Antwerp: Houtekiet.

Van der Brug, Wouter (2003) "How the LPF fuelled discontent: empirical tests of explanations of LPF support", *Acta Politica* 38(1): 89–106.

Van der Brug, Wouter and Meindert Fennema (2003) "Protest or mainstream? How the European anti-immigrant parties have developed into two sep-arate groups by 1999", *European Journal of Political Research* 42(1): 55–76.

Van der Brug, Wouter, Meindert Fennema, and Jean Tillie (2000) "Anti-immigrant parties in Europe: ideological or protest vote", *European Journal of Political Research* 37: 77–102.

— (2005) "Why some anti-immigrant parties fail and others succeed: a two-step model of aggregate electoral support", *Comparative Political Studies* 38(5): 537–73.

Van der Brug, Wouter and Joost Van Spanje (2004) "Consequences of the strategy of a 'cordon sanitaire' against anti-immigrant parties", paper presented at the ECPR Joint Sessions of Workshops, Uppsala, April 13–18.

Van dermeersch, Anke (2002) "Speech at the congress 'Zwartboek Verhofstadt'", December 8.

Van Donselaar, Jaap (1991) *Fout na de oorlog: Fascistische en racistische organisaties in Nederland 1950–1990*. Amsterdam: Bert Bakker.

— (1993) "The extreme right and racist violence in the Netherlands," in Tore Bjørgo and Rob Witte (eds.), *Racist Violence in Europe*. Basingstoke: Macmil-lan, 46–61.

— (1995) *De staat paraat? De bestrijding van extreem-rechts in West-Europa*. Amsterdam: Babylon-De Geus.

— (2000) *Monitor racisme en extreem-rechts: Derde rapportage*. Leiden: Universiteit Leiden.

— (2003) "Patterns of response to the extreme right in Western Europe", in Peter H. Merkl and Leonard Weinberg (eds.), *Right-Wing Extremism in the Twenty-First Century*. London: Frank Cass, 272–92.

Van Donselaar, Jaap and Carlo Van Praag (1983) *Stemmen op de Centrumpartij: De opkomst van anti-vreemdelingen partijen in Nederland*. Leiden: Centrum voor Onderzoek naar Maatschappelijke Tegenstellingen.

Van Dooren, Ron (1994) *Messengers from the Promised Land: An Interactive Theory of Political Charisma*. Leiden: DSWO.

Van Holsteyn, Joop (1990) "En wij dan? De kiezers van de Centrumdemocraten", *Socialisme & Democratie* 47(6): 158–61.

Van Riel, Carlo and Joop Van Holsteyn (1998) "In de raad: Over het functioneren van gemeenteraadsleden van extreem-rechts", in Joop van Holsteyn and Cas Mudde (eds.), *Extreem-rechts in Nederland*. The Hague: Sdu, 61–74.

Varga, László (2001) "A change in the course of discourse", in András Gerő, László Varga, and Mátyás Vince (eds.), *Antiszemita Közbedséd Magyarországon 2000-ben/Anti-Semitic Discourse in Hungary in 2000*. Budapest: B'nai B'rith Első Budapesti Kösösség, 137–45.

VB (1996) *Congres Vlaanderen Werkt!* Brussels: Vlaams Blok.

— (2004a) *Vlaamse staat, Europese natie: Verkiezingsprogramma 2004 Europees Parlement*. Brussels: Vlaams Blok.

— (2004b) *Beginselverklaring*. Brussels: Vlaams Belang.

— (2005a) *Sythesetekst – t.b.v. het economisch congres van het Vlaams Belang – 'Ondernemend Vlaanderen: Welvaart voor iedereen!'*. Brussels: Vlaams Belang.

— (2005b) "Waarom Vlaams Belang?", from: www.vlaamsbelang.org/index.php?p=16 (accessed 16/02/2006).

Veen, Hans-Joachim (1997) "Rechtsextremistische und rechtspopulistische Parteien in Europa (EU) und im Europarlament", in *Texte zur Inneren Sicherheit Band I/97*. Bonn: Der Bundesminister des Innern, 63–79.

— (ed.) (1983) *Christlich-demokratische und konservative Parteien in Westeuropa*, 4 volumes. Paderborn: Ferdinand Schöningh.

Venice Commission (1999) "Venice Commission: guidelines on prohibition and dissolution of political parties and analogous measures," adopted by the Venice Commission at its 41st plenary session, Venice, December 10–11.

Veritas (2005a) "Key points from the VERITAS General Election Manifesto", from: www.veritasparty.com/index.php?page=manifesto.htm (accessed 14/02/2005).

— (2005b) *Full Manifesto*, from: www.veritasparty.com/html/full_manifesto.HTM (accessed 15/02/2006).

Verkhovsky, Alexander and Galina Kozhevnikova (2005) "Main trends of radical nationalist movement and the government's response to it 2004 – early 2005", from: xeno.sova-center.ru/29481C8/62B93A6?print=on (accessed 30/10/2005).

Veugelers, John (1997) "Social cleavage and the revival of far right parties: the case of France's National Front", *Acta Sociologica* 40(1): 31–49.

— (2001) "Structural conditions of far-right emergence in contemporary Western Europe: a comparative analysis of Kitschelt's theory", paper presented at the ECPR Joint Sessions of Workshops, Grenoble, April 6–11.

Veugelers, John W. and Roberto Chiarini (2002) "The far right in France and Italy: nativist politics and anti-fascism", in Martin Schain, Aristide Zolberg, and Patrick Hossay (eds.), *Shadows over Europe: The Development and Impact of the Extreme Right in Western Europe*. New York: Palgrave, 83–103.

Veugelers, John and André Magnan (2005) "Conditions of far-right strength in contemporary Western Europe: an application of Kitschelt's theory", *European Journal of Political Research* 44(6): 837–60.

Visentini, Toni (1993) *Die Lega: Italien in Scherben*. Bolzano: Edition Rætia.

Vlachová, Klára (2001) "Party identification in the Czech Republic: inter-party hostility and party preference", *Communist and Post-Communist Studies* 34(4): 479–99.

Vliegenthart, Rens and Hajo Boomgaarden (2005) "Berichtgeving over immigratie en integratie en electorale steun voor anti-immigratiepartijen in Nederland", *Migrantenstudies* 21(3): 120–34.

Von Beyme, Klaus (1985) *Political Parties in Western Democracies*. Aldershot: Gower, 1–10.

— (1988) "Right-wing extremism in post-war Europe", *West European Politics* 11(2): 1–18.

— (1996) "Rechtsextremismus in Osteuropa", in Jürgen W. Falter, Hans-Gerd Jaschke, and Jürgen R. Winkler (eds.), *Rechtsextremismus: Ergebnisse und Perspektiven der Forschung*. Opladen: Westdeutscher, 423–42.

— (1999) "Zur Diskussion gestellt – Osteuropaforschung im Umbruch", *Osteuropa* 49(3): 285–304.

Voridis, Makis (2002) "Illegal immigration and the racism of 'antiracism'", from: www.e-grammes.gr/2002/02/voridis_en.htm (accessed 14/07/2005).

— (2003) "Address at the French Front National 12th Convention", from: www.e-grammes.gr/2003/04/nicaea_fn_en.htm (accessed 15/07/2005).

Walgrave, Stefaan and Knut De Swert (2004) "The making of the (issues of) Vlaams Blok", *Political Communication* 21(4): 479–500.

Wallace, Anthony F.C. (1969) *The Death and Rebirth of the Seneca*. New York: Vintage.

Wallerstein, Immanuel (2004) *World-Systems Analysis: An Introduction*. Durham, NC: Duke University Press.

Ware, Alan (1996) *Political Parties and Party Systems*. Oxford: Oxford University Press.

Weakliem, David L. (2001) "A new populism? The case of Patrick Buchanan", *Electoral Studies* 20(3): 447–61.

Weaver, Eric Beckett (2006) *National Narcissism: The Cult of Nation and Gender in Hungary*. Oxford: Peter Lang.

Weber, Max (1987) [1919] *Politik als Beruf*. Berlin: Duncker & Humblot, 8th edn.

Weichsel, Volker (2002) "Rechtsradikalismus in Osteuropa – ein Phänomen *sui generis*?", *Osteuropa* 52(5): 612–20.

Weinberg, Leonard (2003) "Conclusion", in Peter H. Merkl and Leonard Weinberg (eds.), *Right-Wing Extremism in the Twenty-First Century*. London: Frank Cass, 293–301.

Welch, Stephen (1993) *The Concept of Political Culture*. New York: St. Martin's.

Wendt, Christopher (2003) "Toward a majoritarian model for Western Europe", paper presented at the 99th annual APSA meeting, Philadelphia, August 28–31.

Werz, Nikolaus (ed.) (2003a) *Populismus: Populisten in Übersee und Europa*. Opladen: Leske + Budrich.

— (2003b) "Alte und neue Populisten in Lateinamerika", in Nikolaus Werz (ed.), *Populismus: Populisten in Übersee und Europa*. Opladen: Leske + Budrich, 45–64.

Westin, Charles (2003) "Racism and the political right: European perspectives", in Peter H. Merkl and Leonard Weinberg (eds.), *Right-Wing Extremism in the Twenty-First Century*. London: Frank Cass, 97–125.

Westlind, Dennis (1996) *The Politics of Popular Identity: Understanding Recent Populist Movements in Sweden and the United States*. Lund: Lund University Press.

Weyland, Kurt (1999) "Neoliberal populism in Latin America and Eastern Europe", *Comparative Politics* 31(4): 379–401.

— (2001) "Clarifying a contested concept: populism in the study of Latin American politics", *Comparative Politics* 34(1): 1–22.

Widfeldt, Anders (2000) "Scandinavia: mixed success for the populist right", *Parliamentary Affairs* 53(3): 486–500.

White, Stephen (1997) "The 1995 elections to the Russian State Duma", *Journal of Communist Studies and Transition Politics* 13(1): 107–14.

Wiegandt, Manfred H. (1995) "The 'Konservative Revolution' – then and now", *Telos* 105: 175–91.

Wilcox, Allen, Leonard Weinberg, and William Eubank (2003a) "Explaining national variations in support for far right political parties in Western Europe, 1990–2000", in Peter H. Merkl and Leonard Weinberg (eds.), *Right-Wing Extremism in the Twenty-First Century*. London: Frank Cass, 126–58.

Wilcox, Clyde, Beth Stark, and Sue Thomas (2003b) "Popular support for electing women in Eastern Europe", in Richard E. Matland and Kathleen A. Montgomery (eds.), *Women's Access to Political Power in Post-Communist Europe*. Oxford: Oxford University Press, 43–62.

Wilensky, Harold L. (1998) *Migration and Politics: Explaining Variation among Rich Democracies in Recent Nativist Protest*. Berkeley, CA: Institute of Industrial Relations Working Paper Series (No. 87).

Wilkiewicz, Zbigniew (2003), "Populismus in Polen: Das Beispiel der Samoobrona unter Andrzej Lepper", in Nikolaus Werz (ed.), *Populismus: Populisten in Übersee und Europa*. Opladen: Leske + Budrich, 163–75.

Williams, Christopher (1999) "Problems of transition and the rise of the radical right", in Sabrina P. Ramet (ed.), *The Radical Right in Central and Eastern Europe since 1989*. University Park: Pennsylvania State University Press, 29–47.

Williams, Christopher and Stephen Hanson (1999) "The 'radical right' in Russia", in Sabrina P. Ramet (ed.), *The Radical Right in Central and Eastern Europe since 1989*. University Park: Pennsylvania State University Press, 257–77.

Williams, Christopher and Thanasis Sfikas (eds.) (1999) *Ethnicity and Nationalism in Russia, CIS and the Baltic States*. Aldershot: Ashgate.

Wilson, Frank L. (ed.) (1998) *The European Center-Right at the End of the Twentieth Century*. New York: St. Martin's.

Wimmer, Andreas (2002) *Nationalist Exclusion and Ethnic Conflict: Shadows of Modernity*. Cambridge: Cambridge University Press.

Winkler, Jürgen R. (2003) "Ursachen fremdenfeindlicher Einstellungen in Westeuropa. Befunde einer international vergleichenden Studie", *Aus Politik und Zeitgeschichte* 26: 33–8.

Winter, Bronwyn (2002) "Pauline and other perils: women in Australian rightwing politics", in Paola Bacchetta and Margaret Power (eds.), *Right-Wing Women: From Conservatives to Extremists around the World*. London: Routledge, 197–210.

Wistrich, Robert S. (2003) "The old-new anti-Semitism", *The National Interest* 72: 59–70.

Witte, R.B.J. (1991) "De onbegrepen verkiezingsuitslag voor extreem-rechts", *Acta Politica* 26(4): 449–70.

Wodak, Ruth (2002) "Friend or foe: the defamation or legitimate and necessary criticism? Reflections on recent political discourse in Austria", *Language & Communication* 22(4): 495–517.

Wolin, Richard (1998) "Designer fascism", in Richard J. Golsan (ed.), *Fascism's Return: Scandal, Revision, and Ideology since 1980*. Lincoln: University of Nebraska Press, 48–62.

Worm, Alfred (2005) *Ein Streitgespräch mit Jörg Haider*. Wien: Carl Ueberreuter.

Yavuz, M. Hakan (2002) "The politics of fear: the rise of the Nationalist Action Party (MHP) in Turkey", *Middle East Journal* 56(2): 200–21.

Yiftachel, Oren (1998) "Ethnocracy or democracy? Israeli territorial politics", *Middle East Report* 207: 8–14

— (2000) "Ethnocracy and its discontents: minority protest in Israel", *Critical Inquiry* 26(4): 725–56

Yuval-Davis, Nira (1997) *Gender and Nation*. London: Sage.

Žagar, Igor Ž. (2002) "Xenophobia and Slovenia media? How the image of the other is constructed (and what it looks like)", in Mojca Pajnik (ed.), *Xenophobia and Post-Socialism*. Ljubljana: Mirovni Inštitut, 37–44.

Zakošek, Nenad (1994) "In gefährliche Nähe der Macht", *Ost-West Gegeninformationen* 6(2): 8–11.

Zaslove, Andrej (2004a) "Closing the door? The ideology and impact of radical right populism on immigration policy in Austria and Italy", *Journal of Political Ideologies* 9(1): 99–118.

— (2004b) "The dark side of European politics: unmasking the radical right", *Journal of European Integration* 26(1): 61–81.

Zhirinovsky, Vladimir (1992) "Kampf für das weiße Europa", *Nation und Europa* 42(7–8): 27–32.

Zimmermann, Ekkart (2003) "Right-wing extremism and xenophobia in Germany: escalation, exaggeration, or what?", in Peter H. Merkl and Leonard Weinberg (eds.), *Right-Wing Extremism in the Twenty-First Century*. London: Frank Cass, 220–50.

Zimmermann, Ekkart and Thomas Saalfeld (1993) "The three waves of West German right-wing extremism", in Peter H. Merkl and Leonard Weinberg (eds.), *Encounters with the Contemporary Radical Right*. Boulder: Westview, 50–75.

Zitny, Milan (1998) "Slovakia: party of 'pure Slovak blood'", *Transitions* 5(7): 37–8.

Zivkovic, Marko (2000) "The wish to be a Jew: the power of the Jewish trope in the Yugoslav conflict", *Cahiers de l'URMIS* 6: 69–84.

Žižek, Slavoj (2000) "Why we all love to hate Haider", *New Left Review* 2: 37–45.

Index

Note: Abbreviations of party names are as in the list in the front of the book.